YO-BNO-429

CALVINUS REFORMATOR
His contribution to
Theology, Church and Society

Potchefstroom University for Christian
Higher Education
1982

COVER DESIGN

* *Front:* Calvin's Academy in Geneva
* *Back:* Calvin's crest
Artist: Hans Schmitz, PU for CHE

South African Congress for Calvin Research

BX
9418
.S687
1980

WETENSKAPLIKE BYDRAES of the PU for CHE
Series F: Institute for Reformational Studies
F3 Collections
Number 17

CALVINUS REFORMATOR
His contribution to
Theology, Church and Society

**Potchefstroom University for Christian
Higher Education
1982**

100204

HIEBERT LIBRARY
Fresno P... ...nary
WITHDRAWN
Fresno, Calif. 93702

The University does not hold itself responsible for the opinions expressed in this publication.

Inquiries in connection with the *Wetenskaplike Bydraes* must be addressed to: The Central Publication Department, Potchefstroom University for CHE, Potchefstroom, 2520, Transvaal, Republic of South Africa.

Die Universiteit hou hom nie verantwoordelik vir die menings in hierdie publikasie uitgespreek nie.

Navrae in verband met die *Wetenskaplike Bydraes* moet gerig word aan: Die Sentrale Publikasie-Afdeling, Potchefstroomse Universiteit vir CHO, Potchefstroom, 2520, Transvaal, Republiek van Suid-Afrika.

ISBN 0 86990 686 0

CONTENTS

Foreword — *Prof. B.J. van der Walt* i

Introduction — *Dr A.J. van Rooy* iii

Welcoming Address — *Dr Hilgard Muller* vii

1. International Calvin research — *Prof. W.H. Neuser* 1

2. Research on Calvin and its influence in the field of Afrikaans theology — *Dr D. Kempff* 7

3. Research on and influence of Calvin in the English-speaking ecclesiastical sphere — *Rev. Prof. J.A.B. Holland* 13

4. Calvin research at Calvin — *Prof. C.J. Vos* 22

5. The *Editio Princeps* of the *Institutio Christianae Religionis* 1536 by John Calvin — *Prof. H.W. Simpson* 26

6. A brief characteristic of Calvin's theology — *Prof. Emeritus F.J.M. Potgieter* 33

7. Calvin and the theological trends of his time — *Dr W. Balke* 48

8. Calvin, Augustine and Platonism. A few aspects of Calvin's philosophical background — *Prof. N.T. van der Merwe* 69

9. Renaissance and Reformation: Contemporaries but not allies —*Prof. B.J. van der Walt* 85

10. Jacques Lefèvre D'Etaples (c. 1455—1536). Calvin's forerunner in France — *Prof. P.E. Hughes* 93

11. John Knox and the Word of God: A comparison with John Calvin — *Prof. V.E. D'Assonville* 109

12. Calvin as Scriptural theologian — *Dr P.C. Potgieter* 127

13. Calvin's view of man in the light of Gen. 2:15 *or* Man: Earth's servant or lord — *Prof. C.J. Vos* 131

14. The shadow and the sketch — *Prof. T.H.L. Parker* 142

15. Calvin's hermeneutics of Holy Scripture — *Prof. H.W. Rossouw* 149

16. The hermeneutics of Calvin — *Prof. L. Floor* 181

17. Is Christ the scopus of the Scriptures? — *Prof. B. Engelbrecht* 192

18. The problem of the concept of the "Personality" of the Holy Spirit according to Calvin — *Prof. B.J. Engelbrecht* 201

19. John Calvin and the Protestant hymns — *Dr W.J.B. Serfontein* 217

20. Calvin's canon law and influence on churches in South Africa — *Prof. B. Spoelstra* 232

21. The doctrine of Calvin as transmitted in the South African context by among others the *Oude Schrijvers* — an introductory survey — *Dr J.W. Hofmeyr* 259

22. Calvin and Puritanism in England and Scotland — some basic concepts in the development of "Federal Theology" — *Rev. Prof. J.B. Torrance* 264

23. Calvin and art — *Prof. P.W. Buys* 287

24. Calvin on art: Calvin defended against (some of) his supporters — *Mr J.J. Snyman* 300

25. Calvin and art. Introduction to the discussion — *Prof. L.F. Schulze* 314

26. Calvinus reformator hodie — *Prof. J.A. Heyns* 317

Publications on Calvin and Calvinism by the IRS 322

FOREWORD

PROF. B.J. VAN DER WALT*

It is a privilege for the *Institute for Reformational Studies* to act as publisher of this volume, which contains the addresses delivered at the First South African Congress for Calvin Research.

The name of this Institute (until 1981) was the *Institute for the Advancement of Calvinism* and the study and introduction of Calvin is still one of the most important objectives of the IRS.

The reader is requested to keep the following in mind while reading this work:

* Most of the addresses delivered at the Congress were in Afrikaans. Keeping overseas distribution in mind, it was decided to translate the volume into English in its entirety. The addresses, originally delivered in English have been published as they were delivered. An attempt has not been made to change the two American lectures to *English* English!

* As is usually the case at a congress, almost every addressee has used his own method of numbering, bibliographical style et cetera. To obtain uniformity as far as this is concerned, would mean that all the addresses would have to be adapted and retyped. It was therefore decided to publish the addresses as they were received (except for absolutely necessary technical editing), with the responsibility resting on the author.

* The length of the various chapters in this work varies as a result of the fact that some of the addressees had three quarters of an hour (and longer) in which to deliver their lectures while others had a maximum of a quarter of an hour at their disposal. This fact is mentioned in all fairness to the authors who are responsible for the shorter chapters: it was not a question that they did not have or could not say more, but the Organizing Committee could not allow them more time because of the full programme!

We trust that this collective work, in spite of the mentioned shortcomings, will find a wide reading public locally and overseas amongst those who are interested in the thoughts of the Great Reformer of Geneva.

May it also be a stimulus in preparation for the Second South African Calvin Research Congress (as you can read in the *"Introduction"* by

---

* Prof. Van der Walt is Director of the *Institute for Reformational Studies,* PU for CHE, Potchefstroom 2520, RSA.

Dr A.J. van Rooy) which will be held here in Potchefstroom in July 1984 D.V.

(Inquiries in connection with the Congress may be addressed to the IRS, PU for CHE, Potchefstroom, 2520, RSA.)

INTRODUCTION

Dr. A.J. VAN ROOY*

The idea of having a congress for the advancement of research on Calvin was born at the International Congress on Calvin Research held in Amsterdam from 25 to 28 September 1978. Four South Africans attended the congress and were sponsored by various institutions: Professor A.D. Pont of the University of Pretoria, Professor L.F. Schulze, at that stage of the Theological School at Hammanskraal, Professor B.J. van der Walt of the Institute for The Advancement of Calvinism[1], PU vir CHE, Potchefstroom and Dr A.J. van Rooy, Vice-President of the Human Sciences Research Council, Pretoria.

They were very favourably impressed by the proceedings in Amsterdam, but they found it strange that nobody from South Africa had been invited to read a paper at the congress, especially as the Calviniana *Bibliography* of Dr D. Kempff was widely accepted and used by most speakers.

To remedy this it was, *inter alia,* decided that the possibility of organizing a regional congress of Calvin scholars in South Africa should be explored. Such a congress where prominent Calvin scholars from Europe, England and the USA would take part, would have the advantage of acquainting the overseas visitors with the work done in this field in South Africa. At the same time it would give the South African scholars and researchers the opportunity to meet one another and their overseas counterparts. Such a congress, it was felt, could only be of positive value to all concerned.

The initial efforts of Professors Pont and Schulze and Doctors Van der Walt and Van Rooy met with immediate response in South Africa. It was clear that a South African regional congress on Calvin and Calvin Research would provide an essential focal point to stimulate and co-ordinate this work in South Africa. A Plenary Committee was then convened to decide on the possibilities of organizing such a congress. The following persons accepted a general invitation and attended the first meeting:

Dr S.J. Botha of the Association for Ecclesiastical History

* Secretary of the Steering Committee. His address is: 22 Button Road, 0081 Lynnwood Glen, RSA.

[1] Now the *Institute for Reformational Studies,* PU for CHE, Potchefstroom.

Prof. E. Brown of the University of Stellenbosch

Prof. P.J. du Plessis of the Rand Afrikaans University

Dr A.N. Helberg of the Afrikaans Calvinistic Movement

Prof. J.A. Heyns and Prof. A.D. Pont of the University of Pretoria

Dr J.W. Hofmeyr and Professor Adrio König of the University of South Africa

Prof. J.C. Lombard of the University of the Orange Free State who also represents the Society for Christian Higher Education

Prof. H. W. Rossouw of the University of Stellenbosch

Prof. H. van der Merwe of the University of the North

Prof. B.J. van der Walt of the Institute for the Advancement of Calvinism, Potchefstroom, and

Dr A.J. van Rooy of the Human Sciences Research Council, Pretoria.

At this meeting the whole idea of convening a regional congress on Calvin research was enthusiastically endorsed. A Steering Committee consisting of Prof. A.D. Pont as chairman, Dr A.J. van Rooy as secretary and Prof. J.A. Heyns and Prof. B.J. van der Walt as members were appointed. The Steering Committee succeeded in finding the necessary funds, and as 1980 was a Jubilee Year for the University of Pretoria, the regional congress was organized as a part of the University's academic and cultural activities for the festive year.

The Steering Committee would once again like to mention that it received financial contributions from:

Gereformeerde Kerk Totiusdal, Olifantshoek, Pretoria-Wes, Pretoria Wonderboom-Suid, Andeon, Bergsig and Linden.

Nederduitse Gereformeerde Kerk Onderstepoort, Pierneef, Pretoria-Oosterlig, Eloffsdal, Groenkloof and Pierneefrant.

Nederduitsch Hervormde Kerk Pretoria Tuine, Pretoria-Noord and Pretoria-Suid.

HAUM and N.G. Kerk-Uitgewers.

Afrikaanse Calvinistiese Beweging and Vereniging vir Christelike Hoër Onderwys, Potchefstroom University for Christian Higher Education.

Various individuals.

Valuable services were also rendered by the Department of Foreign Affairs and Information, Volkskas Insurance Brokers, Trust Bank of Africa, the Southern African Forum, the University of Pretoria and the Human Sciences Research Council.

The chairman of the Steering Committee, Prof. A.D. Pont said in his opening address:

> "It is an honour and a pleasure to welcome you all to the University of Pretoria and in particular to this regional, South African congress on Calvin and Calvin research. Your attendance in such great numbers proves that the interest in the life and work of the great church father, John Calvin of Geneva, is still a factor of importance in South Africa and in our theological and academic work.
>
> "We hope that you will find this congress of some value and that it will, at the same time, co-ordinate and stimulate Calvin studies in South Africa.
>
> "We are also most grateful that we may welcome some eminent Calvin researchers from abroad. I want to extend a special word of welcome to Prof. W.H. Neuser from Münster and also the secretary of the International Congress on Calvin Research, Prof. James Torrance from Aberdeen, Prof. Philip Hughes from Philadelphia, USA, Prof. Clarence Vos from Calvin College USA en Dr W. Balke from the Netherlands.
>
> "I wish to conclude my word of welcome by saying that we have been brought together by our mutual interest in the life and work of John Calvin. I hope that through this congress and all the work that will be done here we will all be stimulated anew to pursue our study and work in this field with renewed energy".

At the conclusion of the congress, which can be described as a great success, it was formally decided that a regional congress on Calvin and Calvin research would be organized and held every fourth year. This means that the next congress will be held at the Potchefstroom University for Christian Higher Education in the year 1984.

With this publication the Steering Committee is honoured to present the papers read at the first South African regional Congress on Calvin and Calvin research held at the University of Pretoria in the year 1980.

WELCOMING ADDRESS

DR HILGARD MULLER*

Ladies and Gentlemen,

The theological and ecclesiastical doctrines of John Calvin have left an indelible imprint on all the Afrikaans chuches, a number of English churches and several other churches in South Africa.

It is fitting, therefore, that constant and thorough attention be given to and research be done on the life, work and theology of this great church reformer.

The congress is not connected to a single church or organization, but has been organized by a plenary South African committee.

Although this congress is a regional one in which visitors from abroad are participating, it ties in with the work and aims of the organizers of the International Congress on Calvin Research which, if I remember correctly, last gathered in 1978 in Amsterdam. In addition to the ecclesiastical and theological value and significance of this congress and everything it entails, it can also have much advantage for our country. Do I need to remind you of South Africa's problems with the international community?

One of the most effective ways of improving the image of our country and its people is personal contact, discussions between South Africans and foreigners.

The interest in and research on Calvin create opportunities for personal contact and exchange of views with foreigners pursuing the same aims. They follow a scientific and objective approach free from the prejudices of the majority of our critics.

The University of Pretoria, with its two faculties of theology, is grateful that the Calvin congress for Southern Africa could form part of the festival programme for its fiftieth anniversary as an autonomous university.

1980 is indeed a year of celebration for the U.P. because of the anniversary just referred to. Fifty years is not a very long period in the history of a university and we cannot blame visitors from the old

* His address is: 377 Victoria Street, Waterkloof, Pretoria, 0181. RSA.

world if they are not impressed by our youthfulness, but for us the passed half a century viewed in the context of our history, is something for which we are deeply thankful.

In South Africa, and in the existential and the intellectual sphere of the three Afrikaans churches and of various English and other churches, the great Genevan reformer, John Calvin, with his vast theological contribution, is not unknown. We can, in fact take much pride in our Calvinistic theological and ecclesiastical heritage. For this reason it is important that we pay attention to and conduct research on the theology, the life and work of John Calvin. So much of what Calvin interpreted and emphasised as the message of Holy Scripture, remains the foundation of our theological thinking to this very day.

Thus it is a good thing that people have taken the initiative to stimulate and co-ordinate Calvin research in this country by organizing the Calvin congress. It must have been a formidable task for the organizers to attract well-known and distinguished scholars from abroad to the congress and to assemble a select group of South African researchers for this purpose.

Because of the representative and qualitative character of the congress it is a privilege for the University of Pretoria to act as host for a few days.

Nicolas Cólladon, a contemporary and colleaque of John Calvin in 1565, after learning of the death of Calvin said:

"The purpose of all the labours of this exceptional servant of God, a purpose that he incessantly strove to achieve, was to forget himself and to serve God and his fellowmen in all his activities."

May the research on Calvin be conducted in the spirit of this illustrious example.

1. INTERNATIONAL CALVIN RESEARCH

PROF. DR W.H. NEUSER*

The word "International" in the title encourages me to give an introductory remark. The knowledge I have gained about international Calvin research does not extend in equal measure to every country and region. Gaps exist for me especially for your country. Naturally I know about and have read some of your major writings and research. I can mention as an example A.M. Hugo's edition of Calvin's Seneca Commentary, V.E. d'Assonville's book about Knox and Calvin, and D. Kempff's "Bibliography of Calviniana". I was pleased to accept your invitation because it gives me an opportunity to get to know Calvin researchers here, to find out about their opinions, and to gain a perspective about research in this country. Then especially I want to express my appreciation to the Steering Committee for the honour of presenting the Opening Address to this Congress. It pleases me to extend greetings from the Presidium of the International Congress to this Congress, and to express the hope that you will have a fruitful and satisfactory Congress.

The Situation of International Calvin Research

You will surely not expect a detailed account here. At this point, while we are trying to survey the whole field, no one can give precise details. However, I would like to share a few viewpoints which seem to me to be most important.

Increasing Interest in Calvin

More important than a listing of names and single facts is the recognition that Calvin and Luther research (internationally considered, only those), are currently experiencing astonishing momentum and enormous expansion.

Great interest in this research is being manifested today throughout the world by ecclesiastical and academic circles. For Calvin research this is especially encouraging, for in my opinion there is a greater

* His address is: 17 Lehmbrock, 4401 Ostbevern bei Münster, West Germany.

need to catch up in Calvin than in Luther research. In spite of the fact that there are good Calvin bibliographies which give a lot of material and detail, this does not mean that the whole field of Calvin research has been exhausted. It must be stated that there are still vital areas which are waiting for further research. It is not our task here to compare Calvin and Luther research. What I want to point out is the following. Well-grounded hope exists that in Calvin research many long overdue themes are being developed, and new, basic knowledge is being shaped.

Roman Catholic Calvin Researchers

They need to be mentioned separately, for not only are they numerous, but also they contribute remarkably toward Calvin research. A. Ganoczy asked critical questions at the 1974 Amsterdam Congress about Calvin's Paulinism, and W. Schützeichel at the 1978 Congress pointed out the remarkable notice paid to Calvin at the 1551 Council of Trent. If I am correct, Calvin's teaching about justification, as well as his ecclesiology, especially his views of church order and office, are receiving special attention from Catholic researchers. The longer this contribution continues, the greater the enrichment of Calvin research will be. I myself cannot see a better development toward ecumenical understanding than through this shared labour on our common heritage.

Centers of Calvin Research

Strictly speaking, they exist only in Strassburg, where the heritage of Francois Wendel is being carried on by R. Peter and H. Rott, and in Grand Rapids, where through the unfortunate early death of F.L. Battles, his promising research programme needs to be resumed. Surely there are other centers to be mentioned, such as Geneva and Princeton among others. Most publications derive in the meantime from individual scholars and their students. At time I am taken by surprise by the unusual places and scholars from whom outstanding doctoral theses about Calvin appear, for example, in Germany or in the Netherlands. This to me characterizes the situation: Calvin research is widespread and definitely needs co-ordination. There is still a lack of proper exchange by researchers of information about their projects, about their research desires, and about new research beginnings.

The International Congress and Regional Congresses

Both of these should take up the task just mentioned. In 1972 when I discussed with the well-known researchers — G.W. Locher in Bern, S. van der Linde in Utrecht, D. Nauta in Amsterdam and J.I. McCord in Princeton — the possibility of convening a Congress on Calvin Research, I received a surprisingly strong positive response. We ventured to hold a European Congress in 1974 and an International Congress in 1978 — both times at the Free University of Amsterdam. Both of them were a great success. At the last Calvin Research Congress, a delegation from South Africa also participated. The next Congress will take place in 1982 in Geneva. Already in 1974 plans emerged for regional Congresses, not so much stimulated by us as created by the fact that a start had been made to enliven Calvin research and to co-ordinate it. In 1976 a "Colloquium on Calvin and Calvin Studies" was held in Grand Rapids, followed by a second in 1978. This year "The African Congress on Calvin Research" begins, and the regional Congress for Middle East Europe undertakes its work. Probably a Calvin Research Congress will be set up in South Korea, with a regular schedule for meetings. I have high expectations for the work of these Congresses.

Now let me close the account of the current list of activities, and turn to the great and small tasks ahead for international Calvin research.

The Pressing Tasks of Calvin Research

The New Edition of the Complete Works of Calvin

The International Congress for Calvin Research has not yet undertaken this task. Now an edition of the works of Calvin according to present-day academic standards must earnestly be envisaged. I think that this task should be considered as a theme at Geneva in 1982. For how can the best research into the thought of Calvin be accomplished if all of his texts, exactly prepared, are not at hand? At the first Colloquium in Grand Rapids the need for preparation of an "Editio Secunda" was emphatically recommended. Surely, the publication of Calvin's Sermons must proceed further. A scientific edition of Calvin's Main Writings is present in the "Opera Selecta" (with the exception of volume one). T.H.L. Parker is presently publishing Calvin's Commentary on the Letter to the Romans. Also several other texts of Calvin are available with commentaries. F.L. Battles and others have commented upon and edited excellent English translations. It seems to me, however, that these English translations and editions are, valuable as they may be, more of a secondary nature. Our primary concern should be the editing of the original Calvin texts. Perhaps the organizational and financial means needed for an "Editio Secunda" in a chronological series done in an orderly fashion are too great and make that task impractical. At any rate, the scientific, critical edition of the individual writings of Calvin and of his correspondence needs to be undertaken. The editing of all of the works of Calvin in the form needed today appears to me to be more important than the particular form and the precise chronological appearance of its separate parts.

The Use of Available Publications

Permit me at this point to ask a critical question: What help is it to give advice about different materials which are desired, when presently available research tools are not being made use of? In my opinion, available publications are not being used sufficiently. I am not thinking so much about bibliographies. Their helpfulness is obvious. Perhaps book reviews of the before-mentioned volumes might be duplicated and made available more widely. I am thinking in addition of the work by R.J. Mooi entitled "Het Kerk- en Dogmahistorisch Element in de Werken van Johannes Calvijn" (Wageningen, 1965). This work pinpoints Calvin's allusions to the church fathers and other theologians, and gives general information concerning his inclusion of ecclesiastical writers. Furthermore, it appears to me that the Concordance by F.L. Battles ("A Concordance of Calvin: Institutes of the Christian Religion", Pittsburgh, 1972, cf. D. Kempff, Bibliography of Calviniana, page 83), is not being used sufficiently. This work enables one to analyse and evaluate fully Calvin's use of a concept in the Institutes. For example, during a study of Calvin's "Two Kingdoms" teaching I came upon the fact that he used the word "regimen" only in the discourse on this teaching in the Institutes III, 19, 15-16 and IV, 20. It doesn't appear anywhere else in his writings. In my opinion, doctoral theses should not be allowed to be completed if they do not make full use of the relevant materials pertaining to their theme, at least so far as the institutes are concerned. I have heard that the second edition of the Concordance is being prepared. Its price will be reasonable.

The Great Task: Research into the Distinctive Character of Calvin's Theology

Until today no satisfactory presentation of Calvin's theology exists. A perspective upon his great life work, the Institutes, is no solution for the task before us. For Calvin presented no information concerning his rational presuppositions, his logic, and his theological method. They also cannot be derived from the Institutes. The fact that Calvin changed the structure of his Institutes in each successive edition makes judgement in this matter more difficult. In spite of a series of helpful individual conclusions, one cannot as yet arrive at a definitive statement about the structure of Calvin's theology. J. Bohatec in using the term a "theology of the diagonal"(Calvin's "Vorsehungslehre", in: *Calvinstudien* (Leipzig, 1909, page 353 and elsewhere), means by that only Calvin's reception of contemporary and patristic theology. F.L. Battles discovered in Calvin a "Theory of Limits", that is, a true-false principle through which occurred successively a fractioning off of true and false statements.

He cited many impressive examples out of the Institutes in support of his theory. ("Calculus Fidei", in: *Calvinus Ecclesiae Doctor Kampen,* 1980). These two examples must suffice here. Further work must be undertaken in order to discover the structure of Calvin's theology. Much research and thought will be required in order to complete this task acceptably. R. Stauffer showed at Amsterdam in 1978 how much Calvin's sermons deviated from his Institutes. When in the future a Calvin theology is attempted then all the available research material will have to be incorporated but then also special attention will have to be given to Calvin's sermons.

Calvin and Calvinism

Calvin and Calvinism must be distinguished and considered separately. Calvin is not Calvinism, and Calvinism is not Calvin. When one seeks to understand the relation of each to the other, this cannot be uncritically undertaken. I would like to present several examples from different centuries, in order to shed light upon the problem.

Soon after Calvin's death and in the seventeenth century, he was understood through the thought-forms of Calvinistic Orthodoxy. O. Fatio at Amsterdam in 1978 considered this theme in an attention-getting lecture. He presented evidence that Orthodox Calvinists wished without question to hold fast to Calvin's own teaching and to pass it on intact. However, Calvin's Institutes no longer expressed the Orthodox view of scientific method. In order to satisfy the methodology of Orthodoxy, the Institutes now were summarized or presented by means of commentaries. Colladon, Piscator and many other significant

5

theologians were the authors of this method. In this manner, the logic which Protestant Orthodoxy made use of came to exercise greater influence than it possessed in the Reformation age itself. This development illustrates the significant distance between Calvin and Calvinism. One cannot deny that Calvinism also continued to expound Calvin's own teaching faithfully. But one must make this judgment carefully. A division within Calvinism had become evident. Calvinism now presented both Aristotelian and Ramist forms. It is an open question which of these was more faithful to Calvin's theology. J. Moltmann presents the thesis that Ramism was "a legitimate development of Calvin's theology" just as much as was "Beza's Orthodoxy". (Zur Bedeutung des Petrus Ramus für Philosophie und Theologie im Calvinismus, in: ZKG 68, 1957, page 318). This interesting matter needs further discussion.

In the seventeenth and eighteenth centuries Puritanism in England and in the New England states became established. Again Calvin was interpreted in a new and a different way. In the nineteenth century, A. Kuyper developed a most impressive programme of Neo-Calvinism. The twentieth century presented a Calvin interpretation which brought Calvin into relation with the theology of Karl Barth or with Marxism. All of these programmes are witnesses to the effort to make Calvin's thought fruitful for one's own time or to make use of Calvin's authority to justify the theology of later times. An exact Calvin research, which seeks to lift up his principles correctly, has its single source in Calvin's own work and tries to remain as historically true as is possible to his own thought. Calvinism, whatever its tendency or source, belongs to the history of Calvin's influence and dare not deviate from the teaching of the Reformer of Geneva.

2. RESEARCH ON CALVIN AND ITS INFLUENCE IN THE FIELD OF AFRIKAANS THEOLOGY

DR D. KEMPFF*

Calvin's life was determined by the desire that all glory should go to God and that the Spirit of God should rule the lives of men with guidance from the Word of God. For that reason it would essentially be in contrast to his intentions if one should talk of a Calvinist theology or church — it is the *Church of Christ* which may not be named for a man and a *Scriptural theology,* because after reading Calvin one always has to turn to the Scriptures again. *The use of the expression Calvinism is therefore merely an expressive convenience.*

Calvin research in South Africa should be practised very prolifically, and should by right have a central position in the world. The reason lies in the fact that this country is in the exceptional position that

* the foundations and the historical course of matters in the first century and a half of White society have been influenced very strongly by Calvinist spiritual trends, which have had a determining influence;[1] and

* it has often been claimed and the claim is still being made that this is a Christian country and that Calvinism is a very strong determining factor.[2]

* Dr Kempff is Editor of *Die Kerkblad,* P.O. Box 20004, Noordbrug, RSA 2522

[1] In this respect you are referred to Kempff, D. *Gewortel en gegroei: die inslag van die Calvinisme in SA: 1652-1806* (Potchefstroom, PU for CHE, IAC, 1981). *(Rooted and grown: the impact of Calvinism in SA: 1652-1806.)*

[2] The most striking statement is perhaps the one by J.F. van Oordt (or D'Arbez) in 1908: "Nowhere in the world does the influence of Calvinism reign more strongly than in South Africa ... Would John Calvin be able to rise these days from his neglected grave ... then South Africa of all countries would be the one where he would be able to find the principles for which he lived and strove living on in purity and strength. And, should

Availability of research material

The possibilities to do theological research on Calvin in this country are many. His *Opera Omnia* is available in at least three libraries; copies of a shorter version *(Digesta)* are available in three places, while the *Opera Selecta* can be found in two localities. The newer *Supplementa* is available in one place.

On a random sampling basis I checked in one library whether parts of the *Opera Omnia* have been borrowed from the library in the course of the past 15 years. It appeared that about 12 volumes (such as shorter writings, letters, some Commentaries and sermons) have not been out of the library at all, while 16 volumes have been stamped a total of 30 times for loan periods.

Translations of his works are available in many localities, whether in the older or the newer editions.

There are also quite a number of books dealing directly with Calvin (also as compared with other thinkers). Efforts have also been made to acquire (according to material available in bibliographies, such as Niesel) as many works as possible (including theses) and to keep on doing this. Collections of this nature compare quite favourably in any event with similar collections abroad in any one locality. At the PU for CHE and at the HSRC, on catalogue cards, there is information on the libraries where books and theses are available overseas, if they are not in South Africa. By means of inter-library loans or copies (such as photocopies and microfiche) these texts may be obtained.

The necessary research material is therefore readily available. Relaxed academic requirements for Latin (for theological students) and a quite general trepidation about French must be seen as obstacles. Motivated and properly documented applications for bursaries would well be successful, but perhaps specific institutions, such as universities and churches, should think about rendering aid where Calvin research is contemplated.

he be able to come to this country, he would find here the man to whom he would be bound to give the credit for working unfailingly to establish this remarkable fact, insofar as anything of this kind might be said to be the work of man. We mean here our patriarch and predecessor, Dr Andrew Murray ... since the days of John Knox perhaps no man has been so strongly drenched in the spirit of Calvin than this man ..." (1908, Preface).

Scientific Calvin studies

Should one look critically at completed Calvin research (by Afrikaners) it would seem that the harvest is quite small. For that reason I allowed the survey of the harvest to encompass a somewhat wider field than merely the theological (of research done in this country).

In order to have some basis for comparison, I placed the Afrikaans production (mentioned in the above paragraph) next to data regarding overseas publications and theses (as well as dissertations). I also narrowed down the field considerably (to Calvin — in general, theology (general) as well as topics with a smaller scope, art and views of the Bible[3] which come to about one-quarter of the data in the work in question). The period in time of the works completed covers about the same years, but overseas data have been limited even more.[4]

From this then it would appear that overseas there are about 35 academic studies, about 20 scientific publications and a number of studies of a more general nature through which information about the life and work of Calvin have been introduced in various countries, such as in Korea, Japan, Hungary and Italy.

The production in Afrikaans, on the other hand, is relatively feeble. No single work of native origin has been published on Calvin's life and work (biographically and theologically). (And this is a matter to which publishers ought to give serious attention, because a great deal has been done for other causes which did not have equal merit with this one.)

In Afrikaans, in total, there have so far been 14 completed dissertations,[5]

---

[3] For this material was found in Kempff, D. (1975), and then only pp. 33-56 (thus only a part of the material on Calvin and not at all about Calvinism).

[4] Added to this, no comparative study was made of data in Niesel (1961), and thus of overseas production.

[5] J.J.F. du Rand: *Wysgerige grondslae van die "Ius resistendi" by Calvin*, 1956. *(Philosophical bases of the "Ius resistendi" in Calvin)*
C.F.C. Coetzee: *Skopus van die Skrif by Calvyn*, 1972. *(Scopus of the Scriptures in Calvin)*

theses[6] and monographs.[7]

From data made available by the HSRC some more information comes to light — although it is not too clearly indicated whether all the study projects indicated have been completed. In any event, these would add to the existing total a number of additional items — dissertations (4)[8] or theses (3)[9].

[6] J.J. Strydom: Een studie over den samenhang en de betrekking van Barth tot Calvijn in den Philipperbrief, 1931.
(A study of the links and the relationship between Barth and Calvin with reference to the Epistle to the Philippians)
F.J.M. Potgieter: Verhouding van teologie en filosofie by Calvyn, 1939.
(The relationship between theology and philosophy in Calvin)
E.A. Venter: Die gesagsbeskouing by Calvyn, 1947.
(Calvin's vision of authority.)
E.A. Venter: Kritiese beoordeling van Calvyn se soewereiniteitsleer in die lig van die Thomistiese en Cartesiaanse teorieë, 1948.
(Critical analysis of Calvin's doctrine of sovereignty in the light of Thomist and Cartesian theories)
A.M. Hugo: Calvyn en Seneca, 1957.
V.E. D'Assonville: John Knox and the Institutes of Calvin, 1968.
L.F. Schulze: Calvin's reply to Pighius, 1977.

[7] L.J. du Plessis: Etiek van Calvyn (s.d.) (Calvin's ethics)
L.J. du Plessis: Die staatsteorie van J. Calvyn, 1932.
(Calvin's political theory)
L.M. du Plessis: Calvyn oor die staat en die reg, 1974.
(Calvin on state and law)
F.N. Lee: Calvin on the sciences, 1968.
E.A. Venter: Calvyn en Calvinisme, 1972.

[8] J.A. Kruger: Christendom en simbool; wysgerige en hermeneutiese studie van die Reformatoriese beskouing van Calvyn in sy Institusie, 1975-?
(Christendom and symbol: a philosophical and hermeneutic study of the Reformatory vision of Calvin in his Institutes, 1975-?)
J.H. Malan: Die genoegsaamheid van die Heilige Skrif by Calvyn, die Synopsis, Kuyper, Bavinck en Berkouwer, 1976.
(The sufficiency of the Holy Scriptures in Calvin, the Synopsis, Kuyper, Bavinck and Berkouwer)
N.J. van der Merwe: 'n Pedagogiese evaluering van die Calvinistiese opvoedingsdoel, 1973.
(A pedagogical evaluation of the Calvinist educational goal)

[9] P.G. Schoeman: 'n Krities-vergelykende studie van bepaalde grondtrekke van die Calvinisties-geïnspireerde en fenomenologies-georiënteerde wysgerige pedagogiek in SA, met spesiale verwysing na die versoenings-dilemma en C.F.C. Gunter, 1972.
(A critically comparative study of specific foundations of Calvinist inspired and phenomenologically oriented philosophical pedagogics in SA, with special reference to the reconciliation dilemma of C.F.C. Gunter)
J.J. van Rensburg: Reformasie of revolusie; 'n ondersoek na die beginsels van die Gereformeerde sosiale etiek, 1973-?.
(Reformation or revolution; a study of the principles of Reformed social ethics)
C.F.C. Coetzee: Woord en Gees by J. Calvyn en Andrew Murray, 1977-?
(Word and Spirit in Calvin and in Andrew Murray)

Scientific articles

It has to be mentioned that a number of articles[10] which might be regarded as being scientific or semi-scientific have been published. Many of these appeared in journals (ecclesiastical in general or more specifically theological in the academic sense, or as part of theses or in books) published locally or overseas. These vary in scope and in depth and are of more thoroughgoing or superficial quality. One could here mention something in the vicinity of 80.[11] It is at times a section from a local academic study or then a completely independent study.

The importance of these (and more popular articles) of course lies in the fact that completed scientific work is introduced into a wider circle in this way and so has a wider sphere of influence. But perhaps this possibility is not adequately noticed and implemented.

More popular articles

Of these one could mention that there are more than 200 of varying quality and length.[12] These have been instrumental in disseminating ideas about Calvin, as well as about his role and his significance in a wide circle. But — and this has been stated already — not a great deal of really scientific work has been produced. For this reason there is a very real danger that these articles will not have properly founded and documented study as their basis — so that they can be popular but at the same time unfortunately be superficial and even one-sided.

Concluding view

Perhaps it would be most accurate to regard this survey as a *testimonium paupertatis* and a cry for help. Things should look better from the side of Afrikaans.

For that reason it is perhaps best to conclude with an exhortation or some advice: Before someone strives in future to say or write

---

[10] Full details in D. Kempff (1973)

[11] Of these, 13 are in *NG Teologiese Tydskrif,* 14 in *Koers* (and *Wagtoring)* and 7 in *In die Skriflig.*

[12] See: D. Kempff (1973)

something about Calvin, he should at least

* have struggled through his *Institutes;*

* have gained some knowledge of his Commentaries and his sermons; and

* have read a number of his letters — and then have spent another month reading about it all.

This would enrich knowledge about Calvin and would serve to stimulate further depth studies. The influence of Calvin — or, even better, of the Scriptures — in the field of theology would definitely be elevating and enriching and beneficial for spiritual insight.

BIBLIOGRAPHY

CALVIN, J. 1864-1890. Opera quae supersunt omnia. Ed.: G. Baum, E. Cunitz, E. Reuss. Brunsvigae, Schwetschke.
KEMPFF, D. 1973. (Compilor): Bibliografie van Suid-Afrikaanse Calviniana, Potchefstroom, PU for CHE, 53 p. (Scientific contributions — PU for CHE, Series F, no. 2)
KEMPFF, D. 1975. A bibliography of Calviniana 1959-1974. Potchefstroom, PU for CHE — IAC, 249 p. (Scientific contributions, F 3, no. 3)
NIESEL, W. 1961. Calvin-Bibliographie, 1901-1959. München, Kaiser, 120 p.
VAN OORDT, J.F. 1908. Het leven van Johannes Calvijn voor het Zuid-Afrikaanse volk gesschetst. Kaapstad, HAUM, 113 p. (Zuid-Afrikaanse Volksbiblioteek, no. 2)

3. RESEARCH ON AND INFLUENCE OF CALVIN IN THE ENGLISH-SPEAKING ECCLESIASTICAL SPHERE

REV. PROF. J.A.B. HOLLAND*

My first duty, Mr Chairman, is to offer you my sincerest thanks in Christ for the privilege of presenting this paper. My second duty, of a different character, is to give you my humblest apologies for having accepted your request, since in many ways I am not the most suitable man for the task. This honour should surely have gone to my academic colleague and superior, Professor Calvin Cook, whose devotion to the historical, intellectual, ecclesiastical and spiritual tradition of John Calvin far exceeds my own, whose field of teaching has so largely concerned the Reformation and the ecclesiastical history of South Africa, as well as the intervening periods, and who, for a period of at least two decades during which I had no conception of myself as working in this country, himself *lived* the relationship implied by the whole controversial juxtaposition of tonight's two papers.

One of the things that I have had to learn or re-learn from him earlier this year was the truth that we cannot separate the history of the Church as such from that of the society in which it is called to work. This is true, though in very different ways, of both the English-speaking and Afrikaans-speaking churches; this is one great distinction in both cases, from the American neo-Calvinists, and may account for the surprisingly small influence of the last mentioned. The influence of Calvin and Calvinism on the Afrikaans-speaking churches and communities is strong and direct, not to say proverbial. In the other case, it is much more indirect and diffuse, and — most important —mostly follows the international English-speaking world generally. Although the famous ethical strictness is one sign, it is not the principal one, in spite of the popular stereotype to the contrary, as it is by no means peculiar to Calvinism. Other signs are: *an acceptance of Scriptural Authority, usually to the point of fundamentalism; orthodoxy*

---

* His address is: Dept of Systematic Theology, Rhodes University, P.O. Box 94, Grahamstad, RSA 6140

*concerning the Trinity and the Person of Christ (with a few exceptions[1]);
a characteristic combination of belief in the supremacy of "the
spiritual" and the Church with lively concern with this world's affairs;
a certain "tough-mindedness" in secular matters; that complex of
values involving discipline, industry, and systematisation[2]; a palpable,
if attenuated, feeling of election combined with a sense that what is
good for the elect will in fact be good for everybody else; a certain
impatience and even hostility towards other traditions with which
they co-exist, notoriously and supremely Roman Catholicism[3]; in
political and social attitudes, whiggery – either whig-progressive or
whig-conservative; Kuyperian conservatism is rare;   and an unosten-
tatious and placid but very deep piety, by no means incompatible with
the other characteristics mentioned above.*

In contrast to what was undoubtedly my Afrikaner colleague's
experience, I found a great dearth of direct material for my paper. On
the other hand, the small quantity of material left certain telltale
signs, which require explanation. These characteristics are three in
number:

The dearth of material itself. There are the incidental references
inevitable in any account of South Africa, many of which are
pejorative.[4] There are signs of interest in the Baptist Church[5] and the

[1] There has been a certain tendency to Unitarianism in what were formerly Calvinist
circles, probably on the ground that the Doctrine of the Trinity is not unambiguously in
Scripture. Also, Christology is not so Chalcedonian as it should be on the basis of Calvin
himself.

[2] This is not just Max Weber. Calvinism was the most systematic and unitary doctrine
before the great monistic systems of the 19th century.

[3] This is due not only to Calvin's frequent denunciations of Romanism, but also to the
fact that Calvin was specifically prescriptive in many places where other traditions
were adiaphorist.

[4] E.g. "The truth is that the Calvinistic doctrines upon which the faith of the Afrikaner
is nourished, contain within themselves — like all deviations from Catholic truth
—exaggerations so distorting and so powerful that it is very hard indeed to recognise
the Christian faith they are supposed to enshrine". Trevor Huddleston, "Naught for
your Comfort", p. 63. See also similar references in Alan Paton, "Apartheid and the
Archbishop", under the subject index.

[5] There is a recognised school of Calvinist Baptists. Rev. Rex Mathie at this conference
is a testimony to this.

Church of England in South Africa[6], but the surprising thing about the Presbyterian Church of Southern Africa is not that there is any interest at all, but how little there is. By far the most notable interest in Calvin, and the Reformation in general, among Presbyterian ministers, has been shown by Rev. Douglas Bax, both in his writings[7] and in his teaching as leave substitute at Rhodes University, and it is an impressive irony that he is the minister most openly opposed to the official policy of the Nationalist Party and to the Afrikaans Reformed Churches insofar as they passively or actively support it.

As far as research is concerned, I have been informed that the late Archbishop Clayton of Cape Town, Metropolitan of the C.P.S.A., instituted a prize essay at St Paul's Theological College for a number of years on Calvinism or Islam (as alternatives), but I have not been able to trace any essays. The most that I have traced in universities, the *Journal of Theology for Southern Africa,* or the recent Bibliography of the Institute for the Advancement of Calvinism, (i.e. such material as is from an unquestionably English-speaking provenance), is four B.D. theses at Rhodes University, Robert Orr (1953) and Michael Moore (1957) on his Sacramental Theology (and other related matters), André E. Kaltenrieder on Genevan liturgy from Calvin to the present day, and J.R. Elias on the Doctrine of Election.[8] The liturgical emphasis was undoubtedly due to the interest of my illustrious predecessor, Professor W.D. Maxwell, who was already a celebrated liturgiologist in Scotland when he came to Rhodes University.

However, there have come to my notice two tell-tale signs of lack of interest in Calvin in English-speaking Church circles. One is the recent decision at Rhodes University to replace the Reformation period by South African Church History as the second component of the Ecclesiastical History I course (along with the First Five Centuries).

---

[6] The small group corresponding to the Evangelical wing of the Anglican Communion. In the 16th century, Anglican theology as a whole was far more Calvinist than now.

[7] In his writings on social and political policy, of which the most recent is "No other Gospel", Mr Bax goes out of his way to show that official South African policy and attitudes are, in spite of appearances, the wrong deductions, not only from Christ but also from Calvin. Klaus Nürnberger, reviewing the abovementioned, J.Th. S.A. June 1980, feels that Bax is too committed to Barth to impress the N.G.K. In that case, to parody "Alice Through the Looking Glass", I can show you a Barthian compared with whom Mr Bax would be Cornelius van Tal.

[8] Rev. James Elias's thesis was the most careful and faithful to Calvin, and this by and large is true of his subsequent interests — except for his recent support of the Eucharist for children.

The other is the failure of "Encounter" to note the withdrawal of the Continuing Presbyterian Church of Australia from the W.C.C., for five months.[9]

The second feature of such Calvin research that I have noticed is its abstraction from the Afrikaans Reformed tradition, with the exception Rev. D.S. Bax, whose attitude is one of outright opposition on the most sensitive issues. What can we make of the off-hand statement by Orr, repeated by, of all people, Elias[10], that Calvin is best understood on the continent of Europe, not so well in Britain, and least of all in South Africa? English-speaking South Africans interest by and large follows the mainstream of the English-speaking world, with relatively little influence even from the American neo-Calvinists[11], and diminished rather than increased in reaction to the Calvinist Afrikaner.

The third feature is a pointed sense that something has gone wrong, either with Calvin himself or with the general interpretation of Calvin, or both. This is characteristic of the mainstream of overseas attitudes to Calvin. Among people who are basically sympathetic, this takes one of three forms: (a) an acceptance that Calvin was in error in the particular concern in some respect, although not as much as his successors, who exaggerated rather than corrected the error[12], (b) a diversion of interest away from the sensitive issue[13], or (c) the proposition that Calvin did not have after all, the objectionable views usually attributed to him. There are many fields in which this shows: (a) Predestination and Election, (b) the sort of conservative aristocratic

[9] This is a long story; but I shall enlarge on it if raquested. See *Encounter* Feb. 1980. The decision was made in mid-September, 1979.

[10] In their B.D. thesis.

[11] There is some influence, but it is significant that there is not more. I have seen an essay on the Sovereignity of God, by P.E. Hughes; a South African now teaching in USA, in an American neo-Calvinist publication. *Soli Deo Gloria,* (1976).

[12] As is shown supremely by Barth, on election and predestination, as well as Baptism, and to a less extent on politics — see below.

[13] Calvin *was* interested in Liturgy and Worship, and William Maxwell's great interest is within his rights, and in fact it was necessary. However, an extreme believer in "contextualisation" could raise a question here.

[14] A classical case is Professor T.F. Torrance's attempt to deny that Calvin taught Reprobation, or the common tendency to exaggerate the difference between Calvin's doctrine of Scripture and verbal inspiration.

politics found in Institutes IV:XX[15], (c) the typically Calvinist position on the "spiritual" in relation to the "material"[16] (d) Scriptural authority, (e) Presbyterianism, and "Protestantism" in general[17]. The sum total of these differences is more interesting than appears at first sight, and requires explanation.

I am now convinced that the explanation is in the historical experience of the English-speaking community, which is so different from that of the Afrikaner (although Western Europe is closer to Britain than to Afrikanerdom). There are four phases (which apply to the Lutheran world in a similar, but not identical way, to Calvinism):

* After the Reformers' generation (with Calvin rather than Luther predominating in the English-speaking world) Reformed orthodoxy hardened, and such developments as Covenantism occurred, partly to add to people's assurance of being elect[18].

* After this phase, there developed a synthesis which set the tone for the Western world till 1914. The most extreme elements in Calvinist orthodoxy, like double predestination, were regarded with disfavour, and even the basic Reformation principle of "Soli Deo Gloria" was seriously obscured, but in a diluted and diffused form Calvinism played an essential part.[19] This syntheses included a great range of views, from Capitalism to moderate Socialism, from orthodox

---

[15] See Bax, passim. Another big issue, which I am prepared to discuss if requested.

[16] E.g. R. Orr, op. cit., feels that, in the context of the Eucharist, Calvin would have been better with the views of F.D. Maurice or Archbishop Temple on spirit in relation to matter.

[17] E.g. once again T.F. Torrance's support of a constitutional but permanent episcopate. Again, I shall discuss if necessary.

[18] It is a moot point how significant was the change here. Barth and his school believe that it was considerable. It is possible to contend that he is exaggerating.

[19] Another very long story, and one on which Barth has a lot to say. I believe that Max Weber is essentially correct. It has recently been pointed out (Times H.E. Supplt. 17/6/77) that there has been a revival of support for his position, based on the realisation that his critics misunderstood the title of his book, "Die protestantische Ethik und der Geist des Capitalismus" (actually, the spiritual factor that made capitalism is not the only possibility. Calvinist logic, as has become clearer since he wrote, can also produce an intense nationalism. The three outstanding cases are Covenanting Scotland, Afrikaner South Africa, and the Christians in Indonesia. However, there is the diffused imperialism, "manifest destiny" etc. of the whole English-speaking world, which can be legitimately cited as a fourth instance.

Protestantism to French liberal rationalism (after the first shock of 1792-4). The most reactionary military autocracy was outside this synthesis (although it was amazing to what extent Prussia was within); so was the most extreme wing of the working class[20]; so were the worst "tycoons"; in religion, it was conservative Roman Catholicism that felt itself out.[21] Otherwise, there was the sense that Western civilisation, for all its diversity, was a unity, progressive, and with an assurance not untinted with racialism and exclusivism; and in the solidification of this mixture, diffused Calvinism played a key role. Such was the world of July 1914, strong in spite of many serious wars.

* This world was all but killed by no less than four ruinous shocks. The first was World War I itself, the effects of which cannot be overestimated, *especially* on the Church. Indeed why civilisation needed such a war, and fought it with such a Para-ecchatological fervour, is almost a theological problem. It was a Protestant and liberalrationalist war (apart from Russia); the synthesis had torn itself apart. It was fought with a sense of eschatological ultimacy on all sides, each regarding the other as the embodiment of evil, and these things fed back positively into each other to enable the belligerents to inflict on each other a degree of destruction otherwise inconceivable. The effects of the war were (with special relevance to protestantism): firstly that Protestant was set against Protestant, so that they regarded each other as devils from hell; secondly it made a mocker of the whole Victorian tradition of strenuous improvement — "Per Ardua ad Astra" — "Keep right on to the end of the road" — for all too often the end of the road was Delville Wood and Passchendaele; finally, the whole tradition such as remained was coarsened and dehumanised, and became hostage to its extremists on all sides, which confirmed the disintegrative effects of the War.[22]

---

[20] Not so much Marxism before 1914 as the Anarcho-syndicalists like the I.W.W.

[21] Most Protestants did prefer a 1789-style liberal rationalist to a Roman Catholic. Once the first reaction to 1792-4 was over, there was very little corresponding to Kuyper's Conservative social Calvinism in the English-speaking world.

[22] My own feeling, for what it is worth, is that the deteriorating relations between the English-speaking and Afrikaans-speaking whites in South Africa, culminating in the war of 1899-1902, functions in the mind of the English-speaking world as a whole, both as a forerunner of 1914-18 and a permanently irritating reminder of the latter war. I wonder how significant this factor has been in recent years.

The second shock[23] in the English-speaking world was Ireland. This had always been the Achilles heel of Anglo-Saxon Protestantism, but after 1918 people no longer felt that they could cope with it. I am sure that the feeling was strengthened in the highly centralised English cultural and governing élite by the idea that to support Protestantism in Ireland would be to support a class that may have represented them, but was really peripheral, as the Danubian legions were to Rome. Rome relished being ruled from the Danube as little as being proletarianised from the Orontes. Ditto, London and Belfast. The third shock was Prohibition in the USA and its spectacular failure. This dealt a catastrophic blow to the traditional ethic, especially its Methodist element. Henceforth, White Anglo-Saxon Protestant and its acronym became a term of opprobrium in American cultural circles, and the fact became manifest which had been incubating since the Civil War[24] — the U.S.A. was no longer a WASP society.

The fourth shock was the Depression. It was universal in its impact, but at its most disastrous in the traditionally Protestant societies of Germany and the USA; In some parts of Britain conditions were even worse, and more prolonged. Scotland, the traditional heartland of Calvinism, almost died on its feet, and similar conditions prevailed in some other parts of the United Kingdom — precisely those areas where there was a strong tradition of a Protestant working class. "The Protestant Ethic" (in its actual and popular Weberian sense) received a stunning blow. The capitalist element of the common tradition could at best promise a little less unemployment, and the socialist alternative proved impotent. It looked as if traditional civilisation was finished.[25] The most effective alternatives were Italian Fascism, which, whatever its virtues, was neither Protestant nor democratic; Soviet Communism, a captivating ideal but a rude anti-Christian despotism, and Nazi Germany, which was in many ways the most attractive, but a moral disaster the more dangerous because of its dynamism and the more menacing in proportion to its

---

[23] In Germany, the second and third shocks were replaced by the collapse of Imperial and princely rule in 1918, and inflation in 1923.

[24] It is not often understood outside the USA how devastating the Civil War was. In some ways it was very like 1914-18. But the spiritual bases of the U.S.A. were then so secure that it seemed to take the war in its stride.

[25] Of course, there were five neutrals in 1914-18 in Europe that were together a very significant part of Protestant Christendom, but they were so close to the centre of these disasters that the net effect was not very different.

apparent success.[26]

* It was against this background that the first signs of revival took place, and it began with a return to the Reformation. The basic principle, that we cannot save ourselves and that salvation is only of God in Christ, which had been almost forgotten after three centuries of rationalism and activism, was at the very heart of the revived theology. At the same time this revival of the roots was combined with a bitter sense that something had gone wrong. Not surprisingly, politics was usually involved, and as, by now, they were immediately presented with a derelict Right-wing tradition or its unacceptable alternatives further to the Right, these theologians normally accepted, and often led, the "swing to the Left". This combination is the common factor in Barth,[27] Niebuhr,[28] Hromadka, Visser t'Hooft, and George Macleod and the Iona Community in general. Rev. Douglas Bax is simply a particularly clear and striking case of this great international tradition, which has continued to this day.[29]

The new tradition in theology, for all its strength, had a number of weaknesses. Firstly, it may have been too dependent in its origin on special circumstances; what would have happened if the revival of Reformation theology had been deferred till the Cold War? Again, it is unfamiliar, and requires a great deal of theological sophistication to justify it. Finally, the theologians did not pay nearly enough attention to establishing the relation of their Left-tending politics to the basis of

---

[26] F.D. Roosevelt and the "New Deal" perhaps should have been mentioned as a democratic alternative. Against that, it might be said that it did not make the obvious difference that the other three made, and that in any case it represented no more than a development of state and community control to a point long familiar in the remainder of the Western world.

[27] In spite of its lack of prominence, I believe that Barth never changed his earliest interest in "religious socialism". Of course, he denounced any tendency to treat it as the be-all and end-all of the Christian faith. Again, I am prepared to enlarge if requested.

[28] Reinhold Niebuhr was Lutheran. The others were Reformed by tradition. However, the difference between Lutheran and Reformed theology is not significant here, similarly to other people who could well be mentioned.

[29] The outstanding contemporary case is Jürgen Moltmann. Although in many cases the picture is highly complex (especially with Bonhoeffer), and it applies in different ways, the same remarks can be made of almost all the theologians of the main stream of the Protestant theological revival since World War I.

Reformation theology.[30] This meant that to a certain extent they have been undercut internally, when at a later stage Reformation theology was revived in a more conservative way, especially with Calvinism. Even greater was the effect when the revival spread to other traditions, and even beyond the Church. Catholicism in its many ramifications was the first, then Pentecostalism, then all sorts of blatant Pelagianism. Above all, the Third World rose to challenge the old ethnocentrism, of which this paper is palpably as guilty as anything has ever been. Judaism revived, in a militantly Zionist and even isolationist way, and similarly with non-Christian religions. Communism became intolerable, but also intolerably persistent. In one sense the earlier revival of the Reformation had the wherewithal to deal with all these challenges, but in another sense it was vulnerable to them, and it cannot be denied that it is showing signs of strain.

There is one group of Calvinists who are outside all these considerations — the Afrikaners.[31] This is why there is such mutual incomprehension between them and the white English-speaking community, even those who are traditionally Calvinist. If there is anything in the above analysis, the basic reason is evident. Not only did the Afrikaner remain closer to the 17th century than Europe or America, but the fore-runners of todays's dominant tradition, almost alone, contracted spiritually out of World War I, and were able to avoid the long-term effects. It almost looks as if those traditions that are either stone dead or palpably sick are those which fell for the war, hook, line, and sinker: "All they that take the sword ..." Meanwhile, it is no accident, as well as no secret, that Rev. Douglas Bax is acutely concerned with this issue.

[30] It is true that by and large this change has not penetrated to the laity, (a sociologist might well ask, would it?) who have mostly operated on the residue of the earlier position, and that this disagreement is the major source of weakness in so many churches. It is important to bear in mind that the failure of the older outlook was not immediately obvious. Indeed, there was a long period when it appeared to survive very well. But I am convinced that it was only in the sense of the Church of Sardis.

[31] Of course, I am treading delicately on these matters, but should appreciate comment.

4. CALVIN RESEARCH AT CALVIN

PROF. C.J. VOS*

The first part of my report deals with research in a broader sense, while the second part deals with research in the more narrow sense of focussing on the writings and history of Calvin and Calvinism.

This broader sense of which I speak has in mind first of all the Calvin Center for Christian Research. The Center was organized in 1976 "to promote rigorous, creative, and articulately Christian scholarship which is addressed to the solution of important theoretical and practical issues".

The need for the center was recognized from various considerations:

* There are pressing issues in our modern society which deserve serious and undivided attention.

* For most of us the teaching load is so heavy that there is little time for intensive research and reflection. As a fellow in the center a faculty member is relieved of 2/3 of his teaching load.

* Modern problems require a multi-disciplinary approach and for that reason the fellows are chosen from a variety of disciplines.

* In addressing oneself to the problems of the day, parochialism must be avoided and for this reason representatives from other academic institutions are included in the team. And to assure ourselves that we are not neglecting the perspectives of the more youthful, two college students are also invited to join the team.

It must be emphasized that while there is no statement declaring that each member of a team must be a Calvinist. It is very clear that the research is conducted from a Calvinistic basis or perspective.

During the '77-'78 academic year the topic for research was

---

* His address is: Calvin College, Grand Rapids, Michigan 49506, USA.

"Christian Stewardship and Natural Resources". The result of this study is scheduled to appear in a paperback by October of this year.

In the '78-'79 year the topic was "Public Justice and Educational Equity". The interest of course was on the American problem that private schools receive little or no state support. The result of this study should appear within the next academic year. It, of course, may not have the same cosmic appeal the first topic had.

In the '79-'80 year the topic was "Toward a Reformed View of Faith and Reason". If one may draw any conclusions from looking at the names on this team we may expect a very heavy, but definitive tome to be the result. You may have observed that this title which includes the words "Toward a Reformed View ..." betrays a consciously Calvinistic slant. But I am confident that the same may be said for all the research done at the Center.

In the year '80-'81 the topic is "Christian Economic Theory and Activity". The members of this team were just "getting under way" as we left Grand Rapids. This team achieves an international character in that one of its members is from England.

Another project which has been operating for a year is the "Faculty Enrichment Seminar". Again the members of the team are relieved of part of their load to engage in research and interdisciplinary discussion. I was privileged to be part of this team of five this year and our topic was "Human Dignity from a Christian Perspective". Among other writings, Calvin was read and Calvinistic literature was carefully considered in the course of our studies.

It is anticipated that a monograph will be the result of this study, but one of the primary goals is that faculty seminars will be held in which faculty members of the different disciplines may respond to the statement(s) offered by the group. This is the reason why it is called the "Faculty Enrichment Seminar".

This part of my report deals with the research that focusses on the writing, the life, and times of Calvin and his early followers.

At Calvin our industrious and able curator, Mr Peter de Klerk, continues his aggressive search for ancient editions of Calvin's writings or of those of his contemporaries; the latest acquisitions are:

* Beza's *tractatione theologicae* (1582)

* *Biblia sacra* ex Sebastioni Castalonis Postrema Recognitione (1573)

* *Sermons by J. Calvin on the book of Job*
London, Thomas Woodcocke 1584.Translated by Arthur Golding

* *An Abridgement of the Institutes of Christian Religion*
Wm. Lawne, from the Latin, Edinburgh 1586

Another type of acquisition is that of dissertations which deal with Calvin or some aspect of Calvinism.

There is also the constant watch for out-of-print books related to Calvin studies.

The "Calvin Collection" now exceeds 2 800 volumes.

Then of course there is the "Calvin Article" file which now contains more than 10 000 entries pointing to reviews of books on Calvin or Calvinism and articles from Periodicals.

My last comments deal with Prof. F.L. Battles, whose presence graced our campus for two years before he died November 22, 1979. His well-known interest in Calvin was an inspiration to faculty and students alike. Although his interests were broader than Calvin studies in the narrower sense, he continued to produce helpful works that have opened up the writings of Calvin. I think of course of *Calculus Fidei,* (1979), his translation (versification) of the *Six Psalms of John Calvin* (1978), and a revised edition of an *Analysis of the Institutes of John Calvin* (1980).

Professor Battles' Concordance on *The Institutes* has undergone a revision to fit a more sophisticated computer system under the direction of Prof. Richard Weaver. The concordance is now available in microfiche.

One of Prof. Battles students, Maria Bulgarella, has just completed the translation of Calvin's 1545 Catechism. It is planned that it shall soon be published under the auspices of the Calvin Foundation.

She is also continuing Prof. Battles' translation of the 1539 edition of

The Institutes, and she is continuing his system of collating it with the 1559 edition.

One item of interest which might interest many of you is the recent study by the CRC on the Belgic Confession. Admittedly this is probably more confessional and ecclesiastical than academic, but since the academic is that more universal umbrella which includes the ecclesiastical I shall inform you of some research and discussion that is carried on in the ecclesiastical area which concerns the Belgic Confession. In 1977 the Synod appointed a committee to provide a modern translation of the Belgic Confession. This has opened up an interesting "can of worms" because now the church is being made aware of the fact that the text of the Belgic Confession commonly used (subscribed to) in the Reformed churches is the 1566 Geneva (Beza's Geneva?) version and not the earlier version of 1559/61. The committee argued that the 1559/61 version deserves preference because it is "the original" and the CRC has already rejected the "magisterial" tone in Art. 36 which was introduced by the 1566 "Geneva" version. The question is not settled, and I hope it will not be settled without an international consultation of several Reformed churches.

Another ecclesiastical matter is popularly known as the "Boer Gravamen" in which Dr Harry Boer, formerly missionary to Nigeria, registered his grievance with the Canons of Dordt. The Committee who studies the *gravamen* recognized that the manner in which the formulators of the Canons utilized proof texts for their position cannot be defended, they felt, that Boer misread the Canons and that it was not necessary to revise the Canons. The Synod adopted this report.

5. THE *EDITIO PRINCEPS* OF THE *INSTITUTIO CHRISTIANAE RELIGIONIS* 1536 BY JOHN CALVIN

PROF. H.W. SIMPSON*

The theme of discussion as outlined above allows me to bring a variety of subjects to your attention drawn from the 520 pages of the first edition of the *Institutes of Christian Religion* compiled by Calvin. It is inevitable, however, that I should confine myself to only two aspects, viz. one that refers to the translation in Afrikaans of the *Editio Princeps* and a second which touches on the nature and the essence of this firstling *Institutes*.

The translation of the *Editio Princeps* in Afrikaans

You would be well aware of the fact that the 1559 edition of Calvin's *magnum opus* has already been translated into various languages, among them Japanese and Korean. For some unaccountable reason there has not been the same enthusiasm for translations of the *Editio Princeps*. There are, in fact, only two Spanish translations (by Dryander of Burgos in 1540, and Terán in 1958) and one German translation (by Spiess in 1887), as well as an English one (Ford Lewis Battles in 1975). Calvin did translate the *Institutes* in French in 1541, but it is generally accepted that he based this on the Latin edition of 1539, because there were additions in that edition which do not occur in the 1536 edition. The Afrikaans translation of the first edition therefore is only the fourth language into which it has been translated, and it is with a measure of pride that we make it available to you at this conference. In the light of the outline which I intend giving in the ensuing paper, you would readily understand that we would welcome criticism of any kind — whether harsh and destructive or genial and constructive!

The translation of the *Editio Princeps* had its origin in the desire to make the writings of the Early Christian Latin and reformatory authors available to the general public and to Calvin researchers.

* His address is: Dept. of Latin, Potchefstroom University for Christian Higher Education, Potchefstroom, RSA 2520.

With a view to this aim, a committee was appointed at the PU for CHE to investigate various aspects of this ideal. This included issues touching on the practice of translation, the priorities to be observed and the availability of funds. The committee investigating the various issues recommended that the works of Calvin should be given priority treatment, and the work that is being submitted to you here is the result of that effort. Where would this lead us, then?

The next task that we have set ourselves is to translate the 1559 edition into Afrikaans.

It is of course true that the text the translator uses for his translation is of the greatest importance. For the translation of the *Editio Princeps* a photocopy of the original was used, which is lodged in the University Library of Strassbourg and which was, please note, made available to us free of charge by Professor Peter of Strassbourg. We would like to extend our heartfelt appreciation to him for this gesture. A photocopy of the original text in the Bibliothéque Nationale (Res D⁰ 6386) which Professor Battles included in his 1975 edition was also at our disposal. According to our information, it is possible that as many as twenty copies of the original may still be extant worldwide.

We could therefore continually compare this photocopy of the original with the second edition of the Baum Cunitz and Reuss *(Corpus Reformatorum, Joannis Calvini Opera quae supersunt omnia,* Vol. 1, Brunsvigae, 1863). On the basis of this comparison we have come to the conclusion that it is an edition which differs from the original in many respects. The publishers not only often altered the punctuation in a meaningless way, but also changed words, which had an effect on the meaning. To mention only two examples:

Editio Princeps	*Corpus Reformatorum*
1 p. 355: sunt enim sumpta a simili eius debitoris, cui remissa erant *quingenta*	*p. 174* sunt enim sumpta a simili eius debitoris, cui remissa erant *quinguaginta*
2 p. 324: Hac regula videmus compositam *publicani* confessionem	*p. 159:* Hac regula videmus compositam *publicam* confessionem

A *public* confession and a *publican's* confession, after all, are two very different things! Apart from these there are also careless mistakes — for example, on p. 165 of the CR: *furiosalas civia* instead of *furiosa lascivia;* p. 161: *infinitus hodie stupris* instead of *infinitis.*

The third edition of the 1536 *Institutes* was compiled by Barth and Niesel *(Joannis Calvini Opera Selecta,* Vol. 1, Munich, 1926, reprinted 1963). From the viewpoint of textual criticism this edition was based on the text of the *Corpus Reformatorum.* It follows this text consistently, as in the reference above to the *publicani confessionem* and *publicam confessionem.* Yet this edition offers valuable prolegomena and footnotes. It is clear, however, that none of these editions offer a useful reference text according to which international Calvin research can be standardized. We would therefore like to enter a plea for such an international reference text to be published in conjunction with the Afrikaans translation of the works of Calvin

The 1536 edition consists of 514 pages of 24 lines each and about ten words per line. The 1559 edition consists of practically five times as many! In the practically 23 years that it took Calvin to round off his work to his own satisfaction *(nunc demum suo titulo respondens)* no less than eight editions appeared. The 1536 and the 1559 editions stand independently as the *Editio Princeps* and the *Ultima.* The 1539, the 1543 and the 1545 editions form a separate unit because these editions all appeared in Strassbourg. The 1550, the 1553 and the 1554 editions again, all appeared in Genève and for that reason form a unity.

While these original texts are available, a translator cannot depend on the later editions. It is therefore our purpose to collect all the editions, from the 1536 to the 1559, at least in photocopied form before a start is made with the translation of the 1559 edition.

From the compilation of the text and the translation it is inevitable that there should also be an index and a concordance; these are at the same time aspects which might fill an internationally felt need, through the use of Latin, Afrikaans, English, German and French. There are therefore four stages linked to the planning of the introduction of Calvin's *Institutes,* viz. an international text, an Afrikaans translation, an index and a concordance.

Each of these might well take years to complete, and competent researchers and controllers are a prerequisite. The financing of each aspect is still a problem at present, but we are planning to apply to the

HSRC for a larger research grant.

In the meantime we would like to thank the Institute for the Advancement of Calvinism, and particularly the Director, Prof. B.J. van der Walt, and the Calvin Jubilee Book Fund, for the financing and the publication of the Afrikaans translation of the *Editio Princeps*.

The nature of the 1536 edition of the *Institutes*

A translator of necessity has to determine certain things about the work that has to be translated. Aspects to which he should pay particular attention include the style of the author, the milieu which gave rise to the existence of the work, and form or the essential nature of the work which has to be translated. As far as the first two aspects are concerned, a great deal of research has already been done regarding the 1559 edition of the *Institutes*. As far as the last aspect is concerned (the nature of the 1536 edition), I would like to leave you with a few suggestions derived from my translating experience.

The word *Institutio* is etymologically derived from a Latin word with the meaning "to give a footing to someone who does not have it, to educate, to teach". *Institutiones* therefore are "Einführungsschrifte" or textbooks. Such textbooks were fairly well-known in the classical world, but were, as was the case with the *Institutio Oratoria* of Quintilian, directed at the teaching of rhetoric. In the period after Christ classical Institutes developed in two directions, viz. the juridical *Institutiones* such as those of Justinian, Ulpian, Modestinus and a variety of other writers. In the narrower sense of a *compendium praeceptorum* — that is, an *eruditio* or a *doctrina*, a teaching — this became the means by which the first Christian Institute of Lactantius (from 303 to 312 AD) sought to offer an encompassing lifeview to the (Roman) pagans. In this milieu the pagan religion had no philosophical anchor, while pagan ethics had no anchors in religion. This is also a period during which Christendom suffered from perhaps the worst persecution of all times. Lactantius was a jurist and an excellent rhetorician. He set himself the goal not only of disseminating the *doctrina Christiana* to the pagans, but also to defend the Christians against the *iniquitas* of the Roman persecution. Lactantius therefore impressed two aspects on the early Christian Institute, viz. *an educational* and *an apologetic* content.

In his *Divinae Institutiones* Lactantius uses the *diatribe,* a form of mass propaganda which was developed 300 years prior to the birth of Christ by Bion of Borysthenes. A characteristic of Lactantius' *diatribe* is that he made use of the *disputatio* (debate), in which there is a "Gesprechspardner" in the background who regularly came with an objection or an interjection to create an opportunity for discussion of a new aspect and for the sustaining of the literary unity of the work.

A further characteristic of Lactantius' *Divinae Institutiones* is that it combats pagan philosophy and religion *suis armis*. He finds the examples for the manner in which he has to combat his opponents and to persuade them to come to the *vera religio* in Cicero and in Seneca.

Lactantius' *Divinae Institutiones* were the first books to appear in Italy in 1465 shortly after the invention of printing — a brief seventy years before the publication of Calvin's *Institutes*. Following this publication, it saw no less than 112 editions in the course of 200 years!

What does all this have to do with Calvin? The generally accepted thesis, after all, is that the examples of Erasmus and others constituted the impulse for the writing of the *Institutio Christian Religionis*. A comparison between the two *Institutiones* is not so far fetched if one accepts that both authors found themselves, within the context of ecclesiastical history, at a watershed. Lactantius undoubtedly made a contribution to the announcement of the Edict of Milan in 313 AD through his influence on Constantine, whose son Crispus he instructed in the art of rhetoric. According to this the "suffering church" became the triumphant church because the *tertium genus* — Christendom — had become a *religio licita*. It does not need any argument to regard Calvin's contribution to the Reformation on the same level as a watershed. Pope Leo X's bulletin of 9 November 1518 in which he strongly admonishes Luther for turning his back on the church as his mother — *Romanum ecclesiam quam reliquae tanquam matrem sequi tenentur* — if he should leave the Roman church, in actual fact points to the important step that Calvin took in his own *conversio*.

In the outline above one notices too many similarities, anyway, for them to be purely coincidental. Apart from the fact that Calvin was also a jurist — his use of legal terms like *postlimium, exceptio, adoptio* and *testamentum* reveals his legal background — the title page of the 1536 *Institutes* also gives the following information:

* that it is a *summa pietatis* — that is, a *compendium praeceptorum doctrinae Christianae;*

* that it transmits knowledge of the *doctrina salutis* — the doctrine of salvation;

* and that it is at the same time a *confessio fidei* — a confession of faith.

The first two aspects mentioned here represent the *educational,* and the last aspect *(ad regem Franciae)* represents the *apologetic* character of the *Institutes.* Lactantius' *Institutes* aim at a paganism which does not have a *vera religio* as a result of their misconceptions (this in the first and the second books of his Institutiones) Calvin directs his *Institutes* to the simple of mind *(simpliciores)* and to those who work to effect true godliness *(vera pietas).*

In the preface to King Francis of France Calvin outlines his objectives with the first *Institutes* in the following terms:

* He merely wanted to leave some basic principles to those people who still sought religion to direct them to the true state of godliness *(ad veram pietatem);*

* Persecution, however, caused him to effect a change in his original objective, because now not only does he want to teach people whose educational burden he had assumed *(institutionem iis darem quos erudiendos susceperam),* but he also wanted to offer the king a confession of faith to motivate his request that a new investigation should be launched into the persecution of the protestants *(ut integram causae istius cognitionem suscipias).*

Calvin's *Institutio* was therefore also directed at the dissemination of the *doctrina vera* and the *iniquitas* of the government.

Further, the word *disputatio* (debate) occurs quite frequently in the *Editio Princeps.* Chapter 2, for example, begins with *Iam satis ex proxima disputatione intellegi potest.* In this too Calvin's *Institutes* corresponds to the first Christian Institute. In the same way, too, there is a conversational partner in the background —mostly a second person, "you", who constitutes the binding element in the work.

It is also true that Calvin fights his enemies in no way other than *suis armis*. He uses, in fact, the arguments that his opponents draw from the patriarchs to oppose their viewpoints. A surprising fact is that Calvin quotes directly from Cicero on at least two occasions without acknowledging it, and he also refers to Seneca with regard to his view of *clementia*. If one keeps in mind that Calvin's commentary on Seneca had only appeared a few years previously (his commentary on the *De Clementia,* in 1532) then the influence of Seneca on his pattern of thinking and on his style is not at all surprising. Calvin is thus in this respect too exposed to the same influences as Lactantius.

Let us then in conclusion note that Joseph Scaliger's remark *"Solus inter theologos Calvinus"* is most certainly true also of the 1536 edition. But I am convinced that Calvin, in the light of the objectives mentioned above, was first of all a reformer of the general movement away from the true religion, and a defender of true godliness rather than a theologian. I would even dare to suggest that the 1536 edition conveys much more of a practical lifeview than a theological work such as the one that the 1559 edition had developed into. This points once more to Calvin's continuation of the practice of Institution. The fact that Calvin refers to Lactantius at least four times — and there is material in several chapters which gives the impression that Lactantius had an influence on Calvin as far as content went too — confirms the point of departure that Calvin initiated the Reformation in his *opus magnum* by having recourse to a centuries-old institution.

With regard to the outline given above the reader can turn to the following sources to check on certain aspects.

PAULYS R.E.W., Vol. IX, 2 Column, 1566-1587, under *Institutiones.*
RAC 3, column 990 ff, under *diatrible.*
PICHON, R. 1901. Lactance: Étude sur le mouvement philosophique et religieux sous le règne de Constantin, Paris, Librairie Hachette.
HARDS, W.G. 1958. A collation of the Latin texts of the first edition of Calvin's Institution, Baltimore.
BÖTTGER, P.C. 1963. Calvins Institutio als Ermanungsbuch; Versuch einer literarischen Analyse, Göttingen.
THUDICHUM, M. Ch. 1915. Calvin als Pädagoge, Genf.
TODD, W.N. 1964. The function of the Patristic writings in the thought of John Calvin, NY.

6. A BRIEF CHARACTERISTIC OF CALVIN'S THEOLOGY

PROF. EMERITUS F.J.M. POTGIETER*

Any attempt to characterise a particular theology, presupposes a definition of this field of learning. If science connotes systematic and formulated knowledge, theology is to be regarded as a science. This definition of science is valid as far as it goes; but it is incomplete in that it does not include the postulational basis of all science.

It cannot be denied that reason and research have not probed questions of an ultimate nature, such as those relating to the origin and essence of reality. This means that science rests on presuppositions which have not been verified and in some cases cannot be proved or demonstrated. It can for example not be established experimentally or logically that an eternal and infinite God exists. Neither can it be disproved. For by definition such a God belongs to an order of existence totally different from the three-dimensional finite order to which we belong. This being the case, our experimentation and logic are confined to its bounds and cannot apply to a radically different and higher order.

The nature of a science is primarily determined by its object of study. The nature of geology depends on its investigation of the earth's crust and strata, that of botany on its study of plants. The question arises as to what is to be considered the object of theology. The concept is derived from the Greek θεος and λόγος. But being the Creator and not being part of the whole of the created order, God can only be the object of study in so far as He reveals Himself to man.

The fundamental difference of its object of study from that of any other science renders it a unique science.

Furthermore, it derives its *a priori* truths from the revelation of the triune God in Holy Scripture, which is αὐτόπιστος [1]. The

---

* His address is: University of Stellenbosch, Stellenbosch, RSA 7600.

[1] H. Bavinck, *Gereformeerde Dogmatiek* [4]. Kampen, 1928. *Vide 1,* pp. 425-27.

subjectivism of Schleiermacher and indeed all "Erfahrungstheologie" must be avoided, for if depraved religious experience be regarded as the object of theology, the resulting science will of necessity be characterised by the same depravity as its defiled source.

The subject of theology will no doubt influence it to some extent, but it is his calling to take heed of the promised guidance of the Holy Spirit through the ages, and thus to eliminate biblicism.[2] He should continuously scrutinise his own religious stance, his entire philosophy of life and ever be prepared to reform even his creeds and confessions of faith to the Word of God, which alone is the *norma normans.* As subject he can never be neutral, but in this manner he can attain to the highest degree of objectivity, a distinctive feature of all truth.

The question now arises in how far Calvin's theological thought is in consonance or at variance with the above attempt to define theology. What are his views on Holy Scripture? Does he believe it to be the only authoritative and trustworthy revelation? Does he look upon it as the object of theology? Does he formulate the knowledge acquired systematically? Does he avoid the pitfalls of biblicism? How does he acquire his knowledge? Does he obtain the presuppositions which are fundamental to his theological thought from the written Word of God? To what extent was he influenced by contemporary trends of thought?

As to Holy Scripture the pronouncements of Calvin are clear and unequivocal: "For certainly the Scripture is the source of all wisdom".[3] Rejecting papal *theologia* he extols doctrine taken *"ex verbo"*[4]. Particularly instructive is the following passage from the *Institutes:* "It must therefore be held as immutable, that those who are inwardly taught by the Holy Spirit acquiesce fully in Scripture, and that Scripture is αὐτόπιστος . Nor may it be subjected to proofs and arguments. It yet receives the certainty which it ought to have amongst us by the testimony of the Spirit. For though Scripture of its own accord by its own majesty *(sua ... majestate)* commands

---

[2] This term is grossly being misunderstood. For a proper appraisal the dissertation of dr. B.J. de Klerk, *Vorme en karakter van die biblisisme,* Kampen, 1937, should be consulted.

[3] *Epist. Pauli ad Timotheum I,* cap. 4, 13. CR LII, col. 302 : "Nam certe fons omnis sapientiae est scriptura".

[4] *Epist. Pauli ad Timotheum II,* cap. 1, 13. CR, col. 356s.

reverence, nevertheless, it only then truly touches us, when it is sealed in our hearts by the Spirit. Enlightened by his power, we no longer believe in our own judgement or that of others that Scripture is from God; but in a manner superior to human judgement, we determine with indubitable certainty — as much so as if we beheld the divinity of God Himself there *(ipsius Dei numen illic intueremur)* — that it came to us, by the agency of men, from the very mouth of God *(hominum ministerio, ab ipsissimc Dei ore)*"[5].

There is another pericope which is equally informative. Commenting on 2 Tim. 3:16, he writes: *"All Scripture;* or, *the whole of Scripture,* though it is of no importance as to the meaning ... In order to uphold the authority of Scripture *(scripturae auctoritatem)* he teaches that it is divinely inspired *(divinitus esse inspiratam)* ... this is a principle which distinguished our religion from all others, that we know that God has spoken to us *(Deum nobis loquutum esse),* and are fully convinced that the prophets did not speak of their own accord, but that being organs of the Holy Spirit *(spiritus sancti organa),* they only uttered what they had been enjoined from heaven. Whoever then desires to become more proficient in the Scriptures, let him first of all, accept that the Law and the Prophets are not a doctrine delivered by the will of men, but dictated by the Holy Spirit *(a spiritu sancto dictatam)* ... The majesty of God is displayed in it (Scripture) *(illic Dei majestas se ostendat)* ... This is the first clause, that we owe to Scripture the same reverence which we offer to God *(eandem scripturae reverentiam deberi quam Deo deferimus),* because it has come from him alone, and has nothing belonging to man mixed with it"[6].

From the above it is evident that Calvin had the highest esteem and greatest reverence for Holy Scripture, the written Word of God: it is the fountain of all wisdom; all true doctrine is taken from it; it is αὐτόπιστος, has its credibility vested in itself; as revealed truth, which is the object of faith (the gift of God's special grace), it is not subject or amenable to human reason; it possesses its own majesty; it is such that the divinity of God Himself, as it were, is perceived in it.

These sublime dicta stand out in bold relief against Niesel's attempt to portray Calvin as degrading the written Word. Quoting Peter Brunner

[5] *Inst.* I, 7, 5. CR II, col. 61.

[6] *Epist. Pauli ad Timotheum II,* cap. 3, 16. CR LII, col. 382s.

he adduces "dass Calvin das Wort der Schrift gerne mit einem Spiegel vergleiche".[7] Scripture as "Spiegelbild ist nicht die Sache selbst".[8] But, what does Calvin say in his commentary on 2 Cor. 5:7, to which is specially referred? "He (Paul) states the reason why we are now 'absent from the Lord' — because we do not as yet see Him 'face to face' (1 Cor. 13:12). The manner of that absence is this — that God is not openly seen by us. The reason why He is not seen by us is, that we 'walk by faith' ... The apostle says, that we have not as yet the privilege of 'sight', so long as we 'walk by faith'. For we 'see', indeed, but it is 'through a mirror, enigmatically' (1 Cor. 13:13), that is, in place of the reality we rest upon the word *(in verbo acquiescimus)*".[9] If one thing is clear it is that Calvin intends anything but degrading Scripture.

On the contrary, where God has ordained that we as yet do not enjoy the blessing of seeing God "face to face", which he terms "the reality", we now "acquiesce in the word". And no wonder, for "in a manner superior to human judgement, we determine with indubitable certainty — as much so as if we beheld the divinity of God Himself there — that it came to us ... from the very mouth of God" and "the majesty of God is displayed in it" *(supra)*.

Calvin also states emphatically "that those who are inwardly taught by the Holy Spirit acquisce fully in Scripture, and that Scripture is αὐτόπιστος... For, though Scripture of its own accord *sua majestate* commands reverence, nevertheless, it only then truly touches us, when it is sealed in our hearts by the Spirit" *(supra)*. Taking the context in which the sealing function of the Spirit is mentioned into consideration, Calvin could hardly be misconstrued. Yet Niesel, reacting against D.J. de Groot's "Auffassung": "Calvin habe die graphische Inspiration der Heiligen Schrift gelehrt", holds "dass das Wort der Bibel für uns eine tote und kraftlose Sache sei, wenn es uns nicht lebendig gemacht werde. Aber das ist nicht so zu verstehen, als habe der heilige Geist nur an uns sein Werk zu tun, damit wir die Schrift recht erfassen. Nein, auch das geschriebene Wort selber muss lebendig werden. Wenn Calvin vom Gesetz spricht, so weist er daraufhin, dass Christus das Ziel des Gesetzes sei, ja

---

[7] Wilhelm Niesel, *Die Theologie Calvins*. München, 1938. *Vide* p. 29.

[8] Ibid.

[9] *Epist, Pauli ad Corinthios II*, cap, 5, 7. CR L, col. 63.

dessen Seele. Wenn man es von ihm trenne, sei es ein toter Buchstabenkörper ohne Seele'[10].

But Niesel does not take into account what Calvin explicitly wrote in this very connection. Refering to "those who hold Scripture in contempt" he says that they "deride the simplicity of those who still delight in the dead and deadly letter — as they term it. But I wish they would inform me what spirit it is whose inspiration raises them to such a sublime height that they dare dispise the doctrine of Scripture as childish and meaningless. If they answer that it is the Spirit of Christ, their confidence is exceedingly rediculous. They will, I presume, admit that the apostles of Christ and other believers in the early Church were not illuminated by any other Spirit. Yet none of them were taught by this Spirit to despise the Word of God ... The eulogy which he pronounces on Scripture well deserves to be remembered (2 Tim. 3:16)".[11] Calvin clearly explains what Paul really means when he says: "The letter kills" (2 Cor. 3:6): he argues "against the false prophets who, by recommending the law without Christ *(legem citra Christum)* deprived the people of the benifit of the *novum testamentum*,"[12] i.e., the Covenant of grace, as realised in Christ. The phrase in question has no bearing whatsoever on "die graphische Inspiration" of Holy Scripture and any appeal to it in an endeavour to disprove such inspiration is quite misplaced.[13]

No reformed theologian would propound the viewpoint that the written Word may or can be severed from the Word incarnate. That is not the point in question, but the position assumed by Niesel that the written Word is "eine tote und kraftlose Sache" *erga nos* and even *in se* ("selber"), unless it be quickened by the Holy Spirit, cannot be defended.

The written word is the Word of Christ. Apart from him, the second Person of Holy Trinity, there is no revelation at all, and to belittle his

---

[10] W. Niesel, *op cit.*, pp. 27-30.

[11] *Inst.* 1, 9, 1. CR. II, col. 69s.

[12] *Inst.* 1, 9, 3. CR II, col. 71.

[13] The lucid comment of the learned editors of *De Bijbel in Nieuwe Vertaling, Het Nieuwe Testament,* on 2 Cor. 3:6 is in full agreement with Calvin's exposition: "'Niet der letter': Paulus is dienaar van het nieuwe verbond ... Het nieuwe is niet naar de Wet van Mozes, die den zondaar doodelijk treft, omdat hij haar niet houden kan. Het nieuwe is nu het Evangelie der genade, waardoor de H. Geest levend maak".

written Word as being in itself dead and powerless, unless it is enlivened by the Spirit would be to subordinate the second to the third Person.

Calvin confirms that the Word has power in itself, where he speaks of the sacrament as seal. He writes: "Properly speaking, it (the sacrament) does not so much confirm his Word as establish us in the faith of it.

For the truth of God is in itself sufficiently stable and certain, and cannot receive a better confirmation from any other quarter than from itself *(a se ipsa)"*[14] Elsewhere he stresses the enlightening power of the Holy Spirit and then continues: "But in another passage (1 Cor. 3:6), when he would remind them what the power of the Word in itself is *(quid per se valeat Dei verbum),* when preached by man, he compares ministers to farmers, who having industriously cultivated the ground, have nothing more that they can do".[15]

in Calvin's comment on 2 Tim. 3:16 *(supra)* he mentions that Scripture was *"a spiritu sancto dictatam"*. In his *Institutes* he says that "the Spirit of Christ went before (the apostles) and in a manner dictated words (to them)"[16]. It is of pivotal importance in *what manner* the words were dictated. In the same passage he characterises the *auctores secundarii* as *"spiritus sancti organa"*, and in his comment on 2 Pet. 1:20 he informs us in detail as to what he actually means: "He (Peter) says that they were 'moved' — not that they were bereaved of mind (as the Gentiles imagined their prophets to have been), but because they dared not to announce anything of their own, and obediently followed the Spirit as their guide, who ruled in their mouth as in his own sanctuary".[17] He deliberately repudiates the idea of a trance, so typical of the mechanical theory of inspiration. His is the organic mode of theopneusty. And the object unmistakebly is the Word, whether spoken or written — appropriately expressed by the terms *graphic* and *verbal*. It is significant that even Prof. Ethelbert Stauffer admits that, "... θεόπνευστος im N.T. auf die γραφή

---

[14] *Inst.* IV, 14, 3. CR II, col. 943.

[15] *Inst.* IV, 14, 11. CR II, col. 949.

[16] *Inst.* IV, 8, 8. CR II, col. 851: "... *praeeunte et verba quodammodo dictante Christi spiritu.*" He also uses the word *dictare* in his comments on Mt. 22:43 and 1 Pet. 1:11.

[17] *Epist. Petri* II, cap. 1, 20. CR LV, col. 458.

(2 Tim. 3:16) bezogen (ist) ..."[18]

It was necessary to elaborate on the object of theology according to Calvin, because, as has been emphasised *(supra),* the nature of any science is primarily determined by its object of study.

Calvin regards Scripture as the source of all wisdom *(supra): But does* he expressly state that it is the only source? In his comment on 2 Tim. 4:1 he definitely states that "... all wisdom is contained *(inclusa est)* in the Scriptures, and neither ought we to learn ... from any other source *(aliunde)*"[19]. Thus, for him Scripture was the sole object of theology.

Whosoever is conversant with the literary legacy of Calvin will affirm his ability to formulate and systematise. No one will query the competency of the editors of the *opera omnia,* who state that all men of learning are fully agreed "as to his large volume of doctrine, and his subject matter excellently arranged, and as to the force of his arguments and his command of dogmatics"[20]. Warfield makes mention of "the cogency of his logical analysis" and his "systematizing genius".[21]

Could Calvin be accused of biblicism? One needs to do no more than to peruse the *Institutes* to be convinced of his astounding knowledge of the history of dogma and, in fact, of the entire past of the Church. Book I, chapter 13, e.g., deals with: "The unity of the divine essence in three Persons, taught, in Scripture, from the foundation of the world", and Book II, chapter 14 bears the heading: "How two natures constitute the Person of the Mediator". Both these chapters testify of his insight into the circumstances leading to the fixation of the Ecumenical Creeds in question, as well as of his intimate knowledge of the Creeds themselves. Furthermore, he cites Augustine more than 300 times in the *Institutes,* and often alludes to other Fathers

---

[18] Kittel, *Theologisches Wörterbuch zum neuen Testament,* III, 122, *in voce* θεοδιδακτος.

[19] *Epist. Pauli ad Timotheum II,* cap. 4, 1.

[20] CRI, p. ix: "De cuius copia doctrinae, rerumque dispositione aptissime concinnata, et argumentorum vi ac validitate in dogmaticis ... inter cmnes viros doctos ... abunde constat".

[21] B.B. Warfield, *Calvin as a Theologian and Calvinism To-day.* Edinburgh, 1909.

like Irenaeus, Tertullian, Jerome, Cyprian and Chrysostom. Hence it cannot be contradicted that, subsequent to his *conversio subita* at least, he was lead and instructed by the *Doctor ecclesiae* to proceed in the ways of truth, indicated in the Ecumenical Creeds and "chosen vessels" like Augustine.

Although epistemology, strictly speaking, is a philosophic and not a theological discipline it is imperative to ascertain how he obtained his knowledge.

Partee expresses the opinion that experience according to Calvin is "an important epistemological category which comprehends (Scripture and faith)".[22] One can agree with Partee when he says that Calvin "appeals his doctrines of faith, Scripture and the Holy Spirit *to experience*. In this sense experience is the arena of human life where events occur which properly understood show that man deals with God in everything".[23] One can agree, provided that experience here signifies an observational act of consciousness which bears out the truth of what is accepted in faith from Scripture. There can be no objection as long as the accent is not shifted from God, and in particular from his written Word and from faith as "the special gift of God",[24] to depraved and fallible man, and provided that experience is not regarded as being basic to Scripture and faith, but as the *consequence* of faith in the Word of God.

Having posed the question in his *Catechism of the Church of Geneva:* "Tell me what experience you are talking about?" the child answers: "Our mind is certainly too dull to be able to grasp the spiritual wisdom of God, which is revealed to us by faith *(quae nobis per fidem revelatur);* and our hearts are too prone either to distrust or to a perverse confidence in ourselves or creatures, to rest in God of their own accord. But the Holy Spirit by his illumination makes us capable of understanding those things which would otherwise far exceed our comprehension, and brings us to a sure persuasion by sealing the promises of salvation in our hearts".[25] Epistemologically speaking,

---

[22] C. Partee, *Calvin and Classical Philosophy,* Leiden, 1977. *Vide* p. 41.

[23] *Idem,* p. 38.

[24] *Catechismus Genevensis,* CR VI, col. 46.

[25] *Ibid.* Also the *Belgic Confession* (Art. V.) teaches that we believe "without any doubt, all things contained in (the Holy Scriptures) ... more especially because the Holy Spirit witnesses in our hearts that they are from God". *Cf. The Westminster Confession of Faith,* chapter I, 5.

this passage is of great moment, and confirms that it is the view of Calvin that faith is the special gift of God by means of which revealed truth is apprehended and that experiential knowledge is too sceptical and perverse to acquiesce in God. It is the Holy Spirit who by his *testimonium internum speciale* and sealing grace persuades the hearts of men. Having referred to Calvin's comment on Is. 14:1, Partee admits: "In this quotation the teaching of experience is corrigible and faith is preferred".[26]

The next question: did Calvin as co-subject of theology take his presuppositions basic to his theology from Scripture? As regards so weighty a matter as that of special revelation, it is indisputable that he accepted the apostle's pronouncement: πᾶσα γραφῆ θεόπνευστος unconditionally *(supra)*. With respect to his conception of deity, there can be no doubt that it was that of the triune God, which is basic to his *Institutes*. It would indeed be superfluous to expound this point at length.

As the next paper is to be devoted to: "Calvin and the theological trends of his day", I shall leave that aspect out of account.

One is, however, obliged to touch upon the cardinal question, whether he was influenced by classical philosophy. Partee is correct in saying that, "Calvin does not attempt to synthesize classical philosophy and Christian doctrine ..."[27] In his preface to the French edition of the *Institutes* of 1541 he uses the phrase: "... la Philosophie Chrestienne" in the sense of the doctrine of the Christian religion, [28] so that Gilson is right in stating that this expression does not connote philosophy at all, but theology.[29] He often does refer to the philosophers, and in so far as they adhere to the truth by virtue of *gratia communis* and *revelatio generalis* can accept their views.[30]

---

[26] Partee, *op. cit.*, p. 40.

[27] Partee, *op. cit.*, p. 27.

[28] CR III, XXIII.

[29] Partee, *op. cit.*, p.4, footnote 5.

[30] *Inst.* II, 2, 15-17. CR. II, col. 198s. Partee cites Calvin's comment on Tit. 1:12: "(I)t is superstitious to refuse to make any use of secular authors. For since all truth is of God, if any ungodly man has said anything true, we should not reject it, for it also has come from God", *op. cit.*, p. 147.

However, since Calvin knows only one acid test for the truth, and since the Scripture is in the last resort his only source for all wisdom *(supra),* great care should be exercised not to categorise him as a Platonist.[31] It would, e.g., be quite unfounded to assert that, when Calvin writes: "Moreover, it is beyond controversy that man consists of a body and a soul. And by the term soul I understand an immortal though created essence, which is his nobler part"[32], he subscribes to Plato's dualism. In adducing corroborative evidence, he is strictly Scriptural. It must specially be noted that he uses the word *ergastulum* (= a reformatory for slaves) and not *carcer* (= a prison). On the contrary he eulogises the body, "which the heavenly Judge so highly honours *(tam praeclaro honore dignatur)*" and says, "that it were most absurd that the bodies, which God has dedicated to himself as temples (1 Cor. 3:16) should fall into corruption, without hope of resurrection *(sine spe resurrectionis)*".[33] Partee points out that Plato did not teach the resurrection of the body.[34]

Regarding the immortality of the soul, Bavinck emphasises that Plato in his *Phaedo* endeavours to render proof thereof by positing that it, as principle of life, must be immortal.[35] Calvin, however, believes that it was created as such *(supra).*

The remarks of the well-known expositor, Prof. A. de Bondt, and of Abraham Kuyper in this connection are of such importance, that they must be relevated. The former writes that he was deeply impressed when he was first informed about the new theories concerning the soul, and when he heard that the notion that man consists of body and soul must be attributed more to Greek philosophy than to Holy Scripture. After a thorough investigation, he is convinced that Scripture very definitely teaches that man is matter and mind, body and soul.[36] Kuyper says that man's visible and invisible components each has its own being; that mind and matter are not identical. Consequently he rejects the pantheistic view that fails to distinguish

---

[31] *Cf.* Partee, p. 115.

[32] *Inst.* I, 15,2. CR II col. 135s.

[33] *Inst.* III, 25, 7. CR II col. 736s.

[34] Partee, *op. cit.,* p. 56.

[35] Bavinck, *op. cit.,* IV, p. 566.

[36] A. de Bondt, *Dood en opstanding in het Oude Testament,* Kampen. *Vide* pp. 1 and 2.

God from his creation.[37]

Partee calls Calvin "a Christian humanist".[38] However, neither Erasmus nor Jean Sturm influenced him basically.[39] With a trend of thought, which Hepp typifies as "in paganisme ontvangen en geboren"[40], he could in principle have nothing in common. In distinction to Zwingli he banned all "humanistische ideeën" says Bavinck.[41] That he, nevertheless, owed his erudition in a formal sense to a remarkable extent to his humanistic training cannot be denied. Warfield mentions his "acute filological sense and the unerring feeling for language"[42] in this connection.

Although Calvin attached great importance to the Church, as is evidenced by the brilliant exposition in the fourth book of the *Institutes,* his theology could not be described as ecclesiological. Suffice it so say that he declares, "The power of the Church, therefore, is not infinite, but is subject to the word of the Lord *(sed subiecta verbo Domini)"*[43]. He denounces the Papists, who "do not hesitate to subject the Word of God itself" to the hierarchy.[44]

In many passages he is uncompromising in his criticism of scholastic theology. The Romanists appear to be "much nearer to heathen philosophers than to Christ and his Apostles".[45] They, indeed, did not hesitate to give so great authority to Aristotle, that the apostles and prophets were silent in their schools rather than he."[46] In his *Preface*

---

[37] A. Kuyper, *E. Voto Dordraceno,* II, Kampen. *Vide* pp. 217 and 218.

[38] Partee, *op. cit.,* pp. 7 and 13.

[39] For a more detailed discussion *of* F.J.M. Potgieter, *Die Verhouding tussen die Teologie en die Filosofie by Calvyn.* Amsterdam. Pp. 44-9.

[40] V. Hepp. *Gereformeerde Apologetiek.* Kampen, 1922. *Vide* p. 24.

[41] H. Bavinck, *op. cit.,* I, p. 152.

[42] B.B. Warfield, *John Calvin. The man and his work.* Reprinted from *The Methodist Quarterly Review,* Oct. 1909 *Vide* p. 8.

[43] *Inst.* IV, 8, 4. CR II, col. 848.

[44] *Inst.* IV, 7, 30. CR, col. 846.

[45] *Epist. Pauli ad Romanos, cap.* 12, 1. CR XLIX col. 233.

[46] *In Acta Apostolorum,* cap. 17, 28. CR XLVII, col. 417.

to the King of France he writes that the Fathers unanimously "protested against contaminating the word of God with the subtleties of sophists", and condemns their "speculativam theologiam".[47]

Treating of the *Institutes,* Philip Schaff writes, "It is severely logical, but perfectly free from the dryness and pedantry of a scholastic treatise, and flows on like a Swiss river, through green meadows and sublime mountain scenery".[48]

Calvin rates salvation very high, "Nothing is better or more desirable than to save a soul from eternal death",[49] but that does not legitimise soteriological as the correct term to characterise his theology. The famous introductory questions of his *Catechism of the Church of Geneva* settles this question: "Minister: What is the chief end of human life? Child: To know God by whom men were created. Minister: What reason have you for saying so? Child: Because He created us and placed us in this world to be glorified in us".[50]

In connection with epistemology it has already been indicated that Calvin's theology cannot be regarded as being based on the experience of depraved man. He can, therefore, not be regarded as "Erfahrungstheologe", as Bauke maintains.[51]

A more plausible case could be presented that his theology should be termed Christosentric. In his Preface to the *Institutes* he says, "And I undertook this task chiefly for the sake of my countrymen, the French, very many of whom I perceived to be hungering and thirsting after Christ ...[52]" Furthermore, the greater part of the *Institutes* is devoted to Christ and the grace obtained in and through Him. What is more, he is outspoken as to the deity of Christ. Commenting on Col. 1:15, he says, "at the same time we gather from this his ὁμοουσία , for

---

[47] *Inst. Praefactio ad Regem Galliae.* CR II, col. 20s. *Cf.* also his comment on Tit. 1:10, where he rejects "all cold and worthless speculations which contain nothing but empty bombast ..." CR LII, col. 413.

[48] Philip Scaff, *The Creeds of Christendom*[4]. New York and London, 1899. *Vide* I pp. 448-9.

[49] *Epist. Jacobi,* cap. 5,20. CR LV, col. 434.

[50] *Catechismus Genevensis.* CR VI, col. 10.

[51] H. Bauke, *Die Probleme der Theologie Calvins.* Leipzig, 1922. *Vide* pp. 42-3.

[52] CR I, col. 9.

Christ would not truly represent God, if He were not the essential Word of God ..."[53] Christ is "the true and eternal God *(vero et aeterno Deo)* ..."[54]. However, what interests us now is to determine the principle governing his entire theology. With a view to this, the following passage is adduced, "Though Christ is God manifested in the flesh, He is yet made subject to God the Father *(subiicitur Deo patri)*, as our Mediator and the Head of the Church in human nature."[55] From this it is evident that his theology is theocentric and not Christosentric. This agrees with Doumergue's conclusion regarding Calvin's theology: "Elle est théocentrique".[56]

In his *Catechism of the Church of Geneva* the minister asks: "Why do you here mention three, the Father, the Son and the Holy Spirit, since there is no God but one?" The child answers: "Because in the one essense of God we behold the Father, the Son and the Holy Spirit."[57] *Inst. I*, chapter 13 contains the doctrine concerning the Holy Trinity. Besides the deity of the Son *(supra)*, that of the Spirit is proved from Isa. 48:16, 1 Cor. 2:10, Mt. 12:31 etc.[58] prof. Bavinck points out that it was Calvin, who first set out the dóctrine of the *testimonium Spiritus Sancti*, particularly in connection with the contents, form and authority of Scripture.[59] Further, it is of paramount importance that Calvin terms the Trinity, on which the Apostles' Creed[60] as well as the *Institutes* is based, *"fidei nostrae caput"*[61]

But before formulating the final characterisation of his theology it is necessary to consider another approach of the problem. It certainly is true that "Calvin's thought is not based on reason" which is

---

[53] *Epist. Pauli ad Colossenses,* cap. 1, 15. CR LII, col. 85.

[54] *Epist. Iohannis,* cap. 5, 20. CR LV, col. 376.

[55] *In Michaeam,* cap, 5, 4. CR XLIII, col. 371.

[56] E. Doumerque, *Jean Calvin,* Lausanne. *Vide* vol. IV, p. 37. Cf. p. 430.

[57] *Catechismus Genevensis,* CR VI, col. 14.

[58] CR II, col. 101ss.

[59] H. Bavinck, *op. cit.,* I. p. 552. *Cf.* note 5 *(supra)*.

[60] *Catechismus Genevensis.* CR VI, col. 14.

[61] *In Isaiam,* cap. 6, 3. CR XXXVI, col. 129.

perverted by sin.[62] Would this however, vindicate a solution of a formal nature, offered by Bauke, viz., that of a *"complexio oppositorum"*[63] which are dialectically conjoined? This is not only a one-sided view, but it can hardly be said to be explanatory.

Closely related to Bauke's view and equally unsatisfactory is Wendel's suggestion of the juxtaposition of "a whole series of Biblical ideas".[64]

The fact is that one is confronted, on the one hand, by Calvin's aptitude for logic and the cogency of his arguments *(supra)* and, on the other hand, by the contrapolar truths, such as predestination and human responsibility, which he states without any attempt to reconcile them.

Happily, there is elucidative evidence. "Let us, I say, allow the Christian to open his mind and ears to every word of God, which is addressed to him; however, with this proviso, that as soon as the Lord shuts his sacred mouth, he also desists from inquiry ... There is a celebrated saying of Solomon, 'It is the glory of God to conceal a thing' (Prov. 25:2). But since both piety and common sense inform us that this is not to be understood of everything, we must look for a distinction, lest under the pretence of modesty and sobriety we be satisfied by insensible ignorance. This is clearly expressed by Moses in a few words, 'The secret things belong to the Lord our God: but those things which are revealed belong to us, and to our children for ever' (Deut. 29:29)".[65]

By virtue of this "distinction" which Calvin makes between what is revealed and what is kept secret, he opens his mind and ears to the former: he painstakingly analises, differentiates between, e.g., creation and regeneration, grace and meritorius works, and systematically formulates the relevant Scriptural data.

But there also are "the secret things", pertaining to matters relating to the hidden counsel of God; and it is with respect to these that Calvin

---

[62] *Partee,* op cit., pp. 34, 35.

[63] Hermann Bauke, *Die Probleme der Theologie Calvins. Vide* pp. 16 sqq. and p. 32.

[64] Francois Wendel, *Calvin.* London, 1978. *Vide* p. 358.

[65] *Inst.* III, 21, 3 CR II col. 681.

makes the pronouncements, which, according to our criteria, are incompatible. One should always bear in mind that there is an essential difference between the Creator and creation. Hence it follows that the laws of logic, prevalent in the present order of a limited reality, are not applicable to the thoughts of the triune God *(supra)*. And, according to Calvin "we owe to Scripture the same reverence which we offer to God, because it has come from Him alone, and has nothing belonging to man mixed with it" *(supra)*. Furthermore, it "may (not) be subjected to proofs and arguments" *(supra)*. Clearly these latter statements have reference to the *divine revelation* contained in Holy Scripture, which must be accepted in faith and often transcend the standards of human reasoning. This clarifies the position of Calvin, where he simply accepts revealed truths, which do not comply with the laws governing human argumentation.

Accepting the Trinity as the cornerstone of Christian doctrine, the most appropriate term to characterise the theology of Calvin would be: *Trinitarian* – with all that it implies as to revealed truth as well as to the unfathomable counsel of the *living God,* who "so loved the world that He gave his one and only *Son,* that whoever believes in Him shall not perish but have eternal life", and whose *Spirit* lives in the faithful as in his temple. This means that Calvin gave us a theology permeated by the *"unio... mystica",* [66] about which he waxes so eloquent: "what the mind has imbibed (must) be poured into the heart."[67]

---

[66] *Inst.* III, 11, 10. CR II col. 540.

[67] *Inst.* III, 2, 36. CR II, col. 428.

7. CALVIN AND THE THEOLOGICAL TRENDS OF HIS TIME

DR. W. BALKE*

Prefatory remark

The subject at hand does not pose a simple problem. Calvin simply does not allow himself to be categorized, and gave so few references in his work that it is difficult to discern against which trends he set himself and of which he derived something. A great deal of study of detail is necessary. Often what has been done so far is unsatisfactory. Add to that the fact that Calvin had no interest in history, in our historic critical way but that as a man of practical bent he allowed himself to be led through the call for unity, and outside the frontiers of the ecumenical setup he acted as a formidable polemicist. In the scope of this paper one can merely deal with a summary outline of the background against which Calvin should be seen.

Introduction

When Melanchton had to bring the news of Luther's death to the students of Wittenberg, he first made a brief, formal announcement, that "Doctor Martinus Luther has died". But when he went further and said that "He is the man who taught me the gospel", he could hardly control his emotions.

John Calvin made Melanchton's words his own. He too, regarded Luther as the man who had taught him the gospel. When, at the inauguration of the Sorbonne the persecutions raged in Paris, Calvin immersed himself with great passion in the writings of Luther. Throughout his whole life he had the greatest respect for Luther. To Pighius, he described him as an *insignis Christi apostolus,* through whose work and service the purity of the gospel could be restored in his time. In the booklet *De Scandalis* he called Luther the morning star of the Reformation, *primo aurorae exortu.*

In the footsteps of Luther Calvin opposed, with the other Reformers,

* His address is: 3 Grote Street, Den Ham, The Netherlands.

the corruption of the gospel in the Roman tradition. But at the same time he entered into the struggle against the Radicals. More than anybody else he was at home in his era. His universalistic thought, as it were, created an arena in which the most controversial ideas could meet.

He took these ideas, reshaped them and made them serviceable to his own principles. He had the gift to select that which was practically and theologically useful, and to give to these ideas a classically clear and precise form in a beautifully elegant style — to construct all these in a systematic whole and to realize them in practical terms in spite of the greatest obstacles.

The Reformatory camp, as it was established with Rome on the one hand and the Radicals on the other, was richly differentiated. In Calvin's vision there is room for a pluralist vision on the Reformation. No *one* party or individual fully possessed the truth. Truth lay in the dialogue. We think above all of the interesting data of the Genevan "congregations" in which ministers and laymen met in order to investigate the Scriptures together. Solitude would give too much liberty. The last public thing that Calvin had done was attending the Friday "congregation".

It is nothing short of genius to see the way in which Calvin took sides against Rome and the Radicals, which according to a letter to Sadoletus, he lumped together, because to his mind both these sects sought to sever the link between Word and Spirit. Although these two parties would on the surface seem to have little in common, he attacked both because they sought to bury the Word of God in order to make room for their false insights, and to the Duke of Somerset he wrote: "In so far as I understand them, both groups are rabble-rousers who come into revolt against the king and against the conditions in the kingdom. The one group consists of fantastic men who use the gospel as a pretext to bring confusion everywhere. The other consists to men who persevere in the superstition of the anti-Christ of Rome. The libertines, the madmen, would want the world to turn to a libertinist madness, and pretend that the gospel speaks of nothing but the revolt against the authorities and the licentiousness of life. The papists are the open enemies of Christ's mercy and his commandments. The authorities should take action against both of these by the sword. A more important method of going against them, however, would be knowledge of the Word of God. In this the congregation of Christ would have to be the example itself. The congregation would have to let it be seen that temperateness and self-control are the fruits of obedience to the Word of God. The means for revolting against libertinism, then, is the preaching of the Word. Added to that, men should not, as happened in England, out of fear for exorcism, go to other extremes by substituting for the live sermon the reading of pre-prepared sermons". In this context Calvin was thinking of the *Book of Homilies.* From a single passage like the above, Calvin's position with regard to the trends of his time becomes clear. Within the Reformatory camp Calvin above all is intent on unity and cohesion and he reveals the strength of his ecumenical and Catholic attitude. Outside the limits of this attitude he exercised a sharply polemical campaign which was not always strictly fair or which did not leave him always with historical justifiability, but the intentness of this reveals his fear of the dangers emanating from Romanism and Radicalism. Here we also find Calvin's spiritual attitude, and the extent to which he acknowledged the office of government as against both tables of the Law. The kingdom of God can only be promoted through the sword of the Spirit and not through the sword of the government.

Should we ask a question as to the theological trends within and without the reformatory movement, then they reveal themselves in the following fashion:

* *Romanism:* nearer Scholasticism, Mysticism, *devotio moderna* and biblical Humanism;

* *Reformation:* including Luther, Melanchton, Zwingli and Bucer; and

* *Radicalism:* nearer Anabaptism, Libertinism and Anti-Trinitarianism.

Romanism

The Reformation started as an ecclesiastical renewal movement: *Ecclesia reformata semper reformanda.* The reformers did not want a new church. The Reformation became a fact when Luther was excommunicated from his church and when Rome further tried to reveal Luther's insights as heretical to the Scriptures. Rome demanded only blind allegiance to the authority of the church. Rome also seemed not to be willing to justify itself by understanding of the Scriptures, but demanded acknowledgement of the fact that the church had a full grasp on the truth. In principle that should then, according to them, not be seen as a subject for discussion, but should merely be accorded full obedience and allegiance.

Here is to be found the deepest chasm between Rome and the Reformation. The Reformation acknowledges itself only as being bound to the truth of the Scriptures, and also wishes to subject the church to that authority, while Rome wishes to bind man to the truth of the church to which the Scriptures should pay allegiance. In this regard the Reformation says that "I can do no other" — *Sola Scriptura*. When the church is not a creation of the Word, but the Word becomes a creation of the church, then things are radically inverted and the false church becomes a real danger. In principle, Rome could find no answer to the questions that the Reformation posed. In doing that, she would after all have to let go of her pretentions. And the Reformation could not give the obedience that Rome demanded. In doing that, the Reformation would be letting go the truth. All other issues which were raised in the Reformation, such as the doctrine of salvation, the sacraments, the letters of indulgence, should be seen from the viewpoint of this decisive point. The Reformation is above all not in the first place a different vision on mercy or on justice, but is in the first place a different understanding of the church and her authority. From this other viewpoints may be derived. Whoever cannot see this will not be able to see the essential difference between Rome and the Reformation. In its unwillingness to grasp and deal with the issues raised by Luther and Calvin regarding the Scriptures Rome itself tore the fabric of Christianity to pieces. This refusal is the most unecumenical deed ever committed in the history of the church. As opposed to this Calvin says in his letter to Sadoletus that the Reformation is an ecumenical deed of the first magnitude. The Reformation gathered together that which Rome scattered. The Reformation also restored the communion with the Old Church which was destroyed by Rome. And this could only happen because the Word of God was restored to its rightful place. The church is either *ecclesia verbi* or it is no church. But the Bible is not merely a paper Pope. The Scriptures carry their credibility along and have no need of the judgement of the church or of pious men who would prescribe to it. The Scriptures set themselves up as the Word of God, needing no scholasticism or apologetics. These only serve to bury the Word of God under a welter of human systems. Calvin reproached the scholasticists for merely arguing in their schools, so turning God into an object, and concerning themselves endlessly with useless speculation instead of formulating a clear aim and keeping to it. This aim is Christ, because God lives in an inaccessible

51

light, and so Christ is essential for us — He will lead us to God
(Institutes 3.2.1). No speculation is needed but God — no *visio Dei,*
but knowledge of God through Christ is what we need.

In spite of the deformation, a certain "forme d'Église" had remained
in Rome. Calvin wrote that "We deny the papists the name of church
in the sense that we do not deny that some relics of the church
'quasdam religuias ecclesiae' have remained". Calvin pointed out the
baptism. The Roman baptism, while admittedly one corrupted by
many superstitions, has yet retained, in spite of its tainted nature, the
working commanded by Christ, which is that children of believers
should be given this visible sign of being accepted into the church. In
the old covenant circumcision, after all, retained its significance in
spite of all the taint of sin, so that in the times of Josiah and Hiskia no
second circumcision was called for.

The church is the body of Christ, of which the doctrine of the gospel is
the soul. For that reason Calvin fulminated against an official
succession which sought to legitimize itself through ritual instead of
through the doctrine of Christ. As against the *successio apostolica*
Calvin postulat the *successio doctrinae.* The papists strutted in vain
about a chain that they had broken themselves. What could papism
be other than a falling-off from true Christendom? *(CO,* 15, 336).

In the deepest sense the criticism is directed against the evil pretence
that the chair of Rome disposed of the Holy Spirit. It is the mechanical
manner in which the presence and the transmission of the Holy Spirit
in primate and in sacrament was channeled and guaranteed that
Calvin could not accept at all. Rome had broken up the apostolic
succession, the pastoral exhortation about the transmission of the
pura doctrina.

However intense the polemic battle between Rome and Calvin had
been, however, there is no doubt that Calvin had also been deeply
influenced by the same traditions of which Roman Catholicism
aroused.

Thomas Aquinas. It was the lifework of Thomas Aquinas to give
shape to Christendom in a hierarchically structured society. As body
and soul fitted in each other, so the temporal had to be united with the
eternal. Man believed seriously that man could bring all that was
human together in one huge cathedral that man would build to the
honour of God. This universalist ideal demanded a strong intellectual

achievement. In this way Thomas Aquinas appears before us. In his *Summa Theologica* he set the whole ability of the intellect in the service of faith. With the help of Aristotelianism, which he sought to christianize, he came to some harmonizing conclusions. The created world had its continuing source in the uncreated Creator. He had conception of a world which came from God and which would return to Him. He thought synthetically. He knew the *analogia entis,* the *gratia infusa,* the *habitus* of the soul, the grace which nature presupposes, the mutual working of the will with the work of salvation. This realistic theology tended to distinguish clearly, to unite, to bring everything together into a unity, to one enormous synthesis of political power and Christian religion. However, with the deployment of the secular power of the church, the temporal came to rule the eternal and the spiritual and the germ of the dissolution of the synthesis from inside out came to develop.

One can, however, postulate that of this medieval world of cathedrals and thomist systems construction of nature and supernature Calvin definitely retained something. From Thomism Calvin inherited one goodly part of his exquisite sense of unity, universality, order and authority. Through Calvin the awareness of catholicity remained most strongly preserved among the reformers. Exactly because it was in his footsteps that the Reformation was spurred on so comprehensively, his attention remained so strongly fixed on the *una sancta catholica.* More than anybody else Calvin set himself to attain unity in the church. Added to that he had a strong appreciation for the office, and a deep-running mystical awareness of the sacraments, so that he sought, wherever possible, for a linkup with the tradition.

Duns Scotus. This *doctor subtilis* completed the line stretching from Augustine. In contrast to Calvin he subjected the intellect to the will *(voluntarism).* His most significant work is a commentary on the *Sententiae* of Peter Lombardy. Scotus starts from the premise of the limitless love of God and he seeks the foundation of the good in the wil of God. In Scotus already the attention is moved from the general to the individually concrete. In Ethics he taught the primacy of the will. *Deus est diligendus.* The divinely-being-good is the source of all human values. Scotus does not acknowledge an irrational will, because God is He who orders the will in a supremely rational and orderly fashion, *est rationabilissime et ordinatissime volens.* It is only through revelation that the concept of the divine gains concrete shape, which is aimed at the practically necessary as far as man is concerned. Theology is therefore not a *speculatio* but a practical topic.

It has been stated by Locher that Luther is the *Occamist,* Zwingli the *Thomist* and Calvin the *Scotist* among the Reformers. Perhaps there is a traceable influence of Duns Scotus on Calvin through John Major, his teacher in Paris.Torrance has pointed out this in his contribution to the colloquium on Calvin in Strassbourgh in 1964 that Calvin derived some things from Scotus via John Major. In the knowledge of God there is one moment of freedom and one moment of being overwhelmed. As Scotus put it: God is *volens et agens* in his relationship to us, and this results on our side, if we answer to Him, in an *aptitudo obedientiae*. Calvin stresses that all true knowledge of God is the result of obedience. Freedom, being overhwelmed by, personal relation — these are all involved in our knowledge of God.

Occam. In Occam there is once more no harmonious universalism. No Gothic cathedral built from the stones of nature and grace fills the space between God and the world. The relation between God and the world changes. Occam struggles with the problem of freedom. On the one hand there is the *potentia absoluta Dei* which can miss all the *causae secundae.* God's omnipotence does not bind Himself to his creation. The freedom of God borders on the voluntary. When He justifies the sinner He frees him as a gift. On the other hand Occam postulates the freedom of mankind. Man exists as a responsible person. He is free and without coercion in his obedience. This obedience, however, is a virtue in the eyes of God. Both the freedom of God and of man is at issue here.

Via late Nominalism there is a line running from Occam to Luther and Calvin, although this influence had most probably been more profound in the case of Luther.

There is a link between Occam and Calvin in their vision of the freedom of God, which is not bound to any sacramental or human bond, and which disposes in utter freedom of the acceptance or the rejection of sinners. Calvin and Occam also coincide in their openness towards the existential aspect of the reality of religion. When Ganoczy states that Calvin took over from Occam the attitude regarding the *potentia absoluta Dei,* I cannot fully go along with him. Calvin does speak, in his doctrine of predestination and providence or omnipotence, but he was strongly against nominalist formulas, such as *Deus exlex* and *potentia absoluta Dei.*

Mysticism and Devotio moderna. The inspirational force behind late Medieval non-Conformism is the movement of Mysticism. As against Scholasticism, in which reason was so highly regarded, Mysticism taught that the human soul unites itself with God through a strong emotional force. God therefore becomes known through a personal, emotionally loaded experience. Here there is a link with Bernhard von Clairvaux, the reformer of the monasteries and Francis of Assisi, the reformer of the apostolate. Eckhart, Ruysbroeck, Geert Grote, all of them utter a call for turning inward, to asceticism, to a modest inner life, to an immediate meeting between God and the soul in the midst of a secularized Christendom. Thomas à Kempis teaches in the *Imitatio Christi* a mystical lifestyle which is also accessible to the layman as a feasible path through life.

Luther rejects the road of mysticism, for to him it seems like one's own works attained as one sees fit. Calvin points out that all mysticism is rooted in spiritualism. Against these views, therefore, the Reformation puts the Word of God in the centre. Yet the reformers were sensitive to the rejection of mysticists of theological speculation.

Calvin criticised Luther's re-issue of the *Theologia Deutsch,* feeling that it would have been better if it had remained unwritten. Even if it did not contain any heresies, it contained childishnesses thought up by the devil in his cunning to confuse the simplicity of the gospels.

There is a deadly streak of poison in this, and it could well mean the poisoning of the church. Yet there is still, even in Calvin, a streak of mysticism. We think here of mysticism in the circle surrounding Lefévre d'Etaples, and of the influence of the *Imitatio* in the College Montaigu in Paris. Calvin took from that the augustinian and mystical experience of the pettiness of man, and in accordance with Luther he also stressed more strongly the *fides qua* than the *fides quae:* the personal and trusting faith. And the spiritual hunger of the mystics was in Calvin the foundation of the union of *communio mystica cum christo.*

Biblical Humanism. Biblical Humanism was clearly a child of the

Renaissance. *Ad fontes* – this means a new understanding and a new appreciation of the Holy Scriptures. Erasmus, Budé, Lefévre d'Étaples edited critical text editions and supplied these with commentaries. Names such as Valla and Reuchlin should be mentioned in connection with the struggle against the wrong development of the ecclesiastical traditions and obsolescent theological methods. They turned study of the Bible into a true scientific endeavour, a science which should have as its aim to help man experience faith anew and to reform the church. Apart from new investigations into the Scriptures a new interest developed in the Patres. Before his conversion Calvin emerged as the representative of French Humanism. He tied in with the anti-papist and conciliary exposition in which he was joined by Occam, the school of Paris, the mystics and other early humanists. Through his study of Law Calvin had a greater theoretical openness for the realities of social and political life. In his visions which emerge from his commentary on Seneca's *De Clementia,* the various social functions should be directed mutually at each other. In this way Calvin sought in the state too for the true balance between tyranny and anarchy. Calvin also had to account for the spiritual attitude of the Humanists. Bohatec brilliantly accounted for the influence that Budé had on Calvin.

Budé taught a propedeutic function of the classics for his Christian philosophy of life which would have a staurocentric character. Budé effected a curious synthesis of mysticism and biblical thought. It is interesting and has been too little researched, to note that there is already in Budé a theology of the Covenant. He speaks of an eternal, inner divinely *foedus et pactum admirabile,* in which the pre-existing Christ is working as Mediator *(interventor)* and sponsor.

In Calvin the free sciences outside Christ are important gifts of God, but are of no value in the attempt to find true spiritual wisdom. In Calvin one cannot speak of propedeutic value of the classical studies. True knowledge of God is the yardstick by which to measure the value and the true use of the God-given natural wisdom.

The most important difference between Calvin and Humanism lay in the concept of Divinity, and then also in the concept of freedom and the doctrine of immortality. Calvin rejected the rigid, relationless transcendent concept of Divinity of the Classics as well as the formal, naturalist immanent concept of the Renaissance. The philosophically abstract concept of the eternity of God in Calvin becomes a living and dynamic reality of God in his works. Freedom for Calvin is no absolute and unconditioned freedom. It is not in conflict with authority. In fact, freedom truly develops in harmony with respect for authority, an authority not of the Scriptures or of a dogma, but authority emanating from the living God Himself. Scriptures and dogma both only have authority derived from God.

Reformation

Luther. Calvin does not mention Luther explicitly anywhere in the *Institute,* but the first edition of 1536 reveals a thoroughgoing influence of Luther. One notices to what extent Calvin read and absorbed Luther's ideas. Luther's little *Cathechism, De Captivitate Babylonica, De libertate, Christiana* leave their tracks on practically every page. Apart from other sources one finds that it is in Luther particularly that the guideline of the *verbum Dei* emerges most strongly, and which is then seen as a criterion for each tradition. One also finds there the christocentric in the doctrine of revelation and of justice, and a rejection of the concept of free will. There are the concepts of *sola fide* and *sola gratia,* apart from the concept of Christ only and the Word only. Then there is the fundamental criticism in the judgement on the councils, of good works, of false sacraments, and of spiritual service within the papacy. If Calvin did learn his gospel from Luther, then it cannot be denied that he did not hesitate to judge Luther's ideas critically or to correct them, or to formulate them more clearly and to develop them further, extending their depth and scope. He retained great respect for Luther's views but put his own stamp on that which he learnt from Luther. Undoubtedly it is due to the existential doctrine of Luther that the jurist Calvin was prevented from remaining a pure jurist, so that he could understand the church in the sense of an *ecclesia verbi.*

Luther spoke of justice as "my dogma". In the liturgy he made as few changes as possible, and in the church order he remained aloof. Calvin struggled through in all these things. In him the breach with Rome was realized more fully and deeply than in either Luther or the Anglicans. He called the presbyterial synodial form of church government into being. Calvyn also landed in a checkmate position with the pawn of the elder of the Pope of Rome. The elder came to assume world historical significance in Western Europe, in Scotland, America, South Africa. The Atlantic man of today, and modern democratic forms of government, cannot be understood historically without the elder and without the presbyterial institution of the church. Next to Luther it was particularly Bucer whom Calvin had to thank for this. Next to the church order, a new confession and a new liturgy came to be introduced. This meant a complete and idiosyncratic shape for the church. The stability which came to be created in this way in the inner functioning and in the organization is a factor which should not be under-estimated in the maintenance of the Reformation as against the counter-Reformation. One should state clearly that in all this Calvin did not regard himself as reformed in distinction from the Lutherans. Calvin was no calvinist but instead an evangelical Christian who identified fully with the general Protestant cause and who never regarded Wittenberg as a rival of Geneva. He expressed his sense of unity with the Lutherans by signing the Augsburg Confession, although he regarded this as inferior to the French *confession de foy,* as he wrote to Beza and to de Coligny. Calvin's judgement on Luther's personal actions was at times very sharp, although he always retained great respect for him. Calvin was almost childishly pleased about a positive judgement on one of his writings which Luther had expressed — as emerges in a letter he wrote to Farél. In the tractate against Pighius we find a strong defence of Luther — as also in the *supplex exhortatio.* It is noticeable that in all his appreciation of Luther Calvin never called upon his insights as if they were final and fixed. According to Calvin the way of discussing issues is always a good way to find the truth — and the way is always open to improvement. Luther was no oracle to Calvin, but a pathfinder, in whose footsteps we follow and whose track had to continue.

The Reformation did begin with Luther, but it is true that it was not completed in any sense with Luther. Otherwise, according to Calvin, it would be ridiculous to take up the *munus interpretandi,* if it were to be seen as prohibited to deviate from Luther's viewpoint. In contrast to Pighius, Calvin postulated that theological truth is not finally formulated once and for all. The *actus tradendi* is at the same time the *actus formandi.* It is the precious duty entrusted to us that, day and night, we should strive to shape the material we have inherited in such a way that it might best emerge to be used by us. Calvin does not mean by this that the contents of the faith should be changed, but he means in very precise terms that in the theological exhortation *formare* is always equal to *fideliter trader,* although the manner of expression is not unchangeable. The great difficulty with this exhortation is to distinguish between the essential and the accidental. There is full agreement with Luther according to Calvin's insight. The differences between them reside within the boundaries of this fundamental unanimity. To this extent then Calvin saw his labour as falling within a continuing tradition of the reformatory labours of Luther. But continuity does not necessarily imply formal identity — rather legitimate further development. Calvin is the man of *semper reformanda*. He defined the Reformation as a progression *profectus* and a movement *promoveri* (C.O. 8, 59). But this is a movement from a fixed starting-point, in which the extraordinary figure of Luther strikes one, as God's chosen pioneer. Calvin called the ultra-Lutherans epigones or apes, who had no right to call Luther their spiritual father, because the disciple is the one who continues on the course started by the master. The issue is progression *profectus* in the direction of the *reformanda,* while Calvin here evaluates Luther's views on the Eucharist as a regression to the Middle Ages. Calvin does not in the least conserve the Reformation of Luther. He does not develop in opposition to Luther either. He was the greatest and in a sense the only true pupil that Luther had (P. Meinhold). Calvin had the scope of brain and creative talent to create something out of the heritage of Luther which would then reveal his own stamp.

The existing literature on the relationship between Luther and Calvin is to a large extent insufficient. The efforts to sum up their theological differences leave much to be desired. The seeming contrats are indicated much too hastily and often give the impression of being founded on insufficient data. There are often divergences to be observed between them within their own patterns of thought, and this indicates the complexity of the problem. Much more, and more comprehensive historical research is necessary to determine the extent to which Calvin, by his own admission, was a pupil of Luther.

Melanchton. Between Melanchton and Calvin there was a warm and deep friendship which weathered all the storms. They met upon various occasions, and had great respect for each other. The traces of Melanchton's *Loci Communes* are clearly visible here and there in the first edition of the *Institute.* Through Melanchton the meaning of the Law in the new Covenant is intensified. Calvin and Melanchton followed each other in the doctrine of communion. In this most important dogmatic theme of the time both took a mediating role. While both started from Luther in their religious evaluation of the sacraments and their maintenance, both gained from Zwingli the significant interpretation of the initiating words.

Melanchton could not have so much of the doctrine of the predestination. He warned about this as about prideful swearing af a stoic *fatum* in the second edition of the *Loci communes* (1538). Calvin dedicated his tractate against Pighius to Melanchton in 1542. In this insightful treatise Calvin exposed all the arguments directed against the servant's will.

Would Calvin, in doing this, have tried to give Melanchton a gentle hint to remain in the footsteps of Luther? Melanchton wrote back: "As regards the question of predestination, I had a learned friend in Tübingen, Frans von Stade, who used to say that he could accommodate both insights: all things happen according to the providence of God, and yet there are chance events. He did not know how to reconcile these two with each other. Because I hang on to the fact that God is not the source of sin, and yet allows it, so I allow for the feebleness of our knowledge some chance, in the context of the simple fact that David fell through his own free will. I am convinced that because he had the Holy Spirit, he could retain it, and that furthermore, in this struggle the will has a certain latitude. When one should express it with even greater clarity, then it seems that presented in this way it is sufficient to control emotions. Let us therefore accuse our own wills when we fail, but let us not seek the reason in the will of God and let us not rise against Him. Let us keep in mind that God wants to help and that He assists the strugglers: 'Only will to do it,' says Basil, 'and God will meet you'. Let us evoke enthusiasm within ourselves, and praise the limitless goodness of God, who has promised help and who renders this help. But only the praying, says the Lord, come into the promise, because from the Word of God one has to start and his promise should not be opposed but adhered to without our setting the condition first that we should have a glimpse into the mysteries of God ..." (CO, 11, ?). Later Melanchton would say that he preferred not to read the second aim of Calvin's treatise against Pighius dealing with the necessity of all events happening to the fixed ordination of God, for it would be tasteless to say that the scandalous deeds of Nero were essential. "But let us finally cease these questions" (CO, 11, 595). It is an indication of Calvin's greatness that in 1546 he had the *loci communes* translated into French in spite of the doctrinal differences contained therein regarding the doctrines of free will and predestination. Calvin supplied this French edition with a preface written in a warm tone.

Zwingli. Zwingli came to the Reformation via his own way, and so a second centre of the Reformation came into being in Zürich, next to the one in Wittenberg. In his study of the Scriptures Zwingli was

60

initially under the influence of Erasmus. His point of departure is the knowledge of Christ and his forgiving love and mercy. For Zwingli the concern is not in the first place with religious feeling but with knowledge and will. There is also a strong ethical preoccupation which emerges from the attention paid to vocation in both civil and social life. The church to him was at the same time also a social institution aimed at the improvement of the nation. He interspersed the church institution with political power, but with the intention of being better able to counter the corruption of the church in this way.

The influence that Zwingli had is only marginally visible. Calvin used Zwingli's writings very sparingly, although he developed attitudes and ideas very similar to Zwingli's. In accord with Zwingli, for example, he rejected idolatry and the sacrificial character of the Mass. Both these men stressed the omniscience of God, although Calvin, in his doctrine of providence laid greater stress on the *causae secundae* and in his doctrine of providence and of predestination gave more emphasis to the Holy Spirit, as did Bucer. For the rest Calvin did not really want to know anything about Zwingli, and he never regarded the reformer from Zürich very highly. With reference to the doctrine of the sacraments, Calvin wrote that "on these points Zwingli's opinion is false and corrupted. When I saw that these ideas were being adopted by my compatriots with great enthusiasm, I had no compunction about attacking these when I came to France" (CO, 9, 15). He wished that men would not let themselves be drawn too strongly into such matters, and would simply give all glory to God in a clear confession of truth (CO, 10b, 246). Calvin wrote to Viret that "I have not read everything by Zwingli. Perhaps towards the end of his life he repudiated a great deal and improved upon what at first he missed in irresponsible fashion. But I remind myself of how profane the first writings were on the subject of the sacraments" (CO, 11, 241).

The great idolization for Zwingli in which the Swiss and the people of Zürich allowed all traces of his fallible humanity to disappear in the glow of religious and national glory Calvin found incomprehensible. "These good people", he wrote to Farél from Strassbourg, "rebel furiously when somebody dares to regard Luther more highly than Zwingli. It is as if something would be taken away from the gospels if Zwingli should be slighted. And yet this does not achieve all that much for Zwingli, for you know yourself that when these two people are compared, how little Zwingli can really compete with Luther. I am therefore little impressed with the verses by Zebedaus in which he means to have praised Zwingli sufficiently: 'It is not just to think that a greater might be expected'. Of course it is unworthy to say bad things about the shadow and the ash of someone who has died, and not to think with respect of such a one is simply bad. There should, however, be temperateness in the praise, from which the people have deviated here. I am in event so far removed from that, that I can already see some far greater ones, that I expect them and that I wish them to be greater. I ask you, Farél, whether, if people had praised Luther so lavishly, the people of Zürich would not have complained that Zwingli had been slighted. That is stupid, you say. If it could only be that all those who clung to Luther were wise! But these are thoughts whispered into your ear ..." (CO, 11, 24,; see also Calvin to Bullinger, CO, 14, 253).

There was influence of Zwingli on Calvin, but this took place through Bucer. In the comparison of both their theologies Professor G.W. Locher of Berne did pioneering work.

Bucer. The significance of Bucer has only gradually come to be seen. Thanks to the studies of Erichson, Adams, August Lang, Courvoisier and W. van't Spyker the idea developed that Bucer's life and work were important for the full and correct understanding of Calvin. Initially Bucer was under Luther's influence, and later he underwent influence from Zwingli. Towards the end of his life he turned back to the Lutheran sphere. Bucer formed as it were a *trait-d'union* between Zwingli and Calvin. The independence and originality of Bucer lay in his practical orientation. Bucer is above all an exegete and a man of ecclesiastical practice. In his exegesis he is concerned with finding food for the heart. Throughout his commentaries we find edifying remarks. Thus Bucer was rightly called the pietist among the Reformers. In his doctrine of predestination too he was not interested so much in the theory as in the practice. Initially, in line with Zwingli, he denied the sacraments every fundamental salvational meaning. Then again, under Lutheran influence, he acknowledged Word and sacrament as means to salvation. Especially in the commentary on Romans he accords the sacrament significance as a significant, symbolical and at the same time exhibitory sign which imparts mercy. In the *Wittenberger Concordia* he returns almost completely to the Lutheran attitude but he had found the way in which Calvin would later tread on the way to a truly Protestant doctrine of the sacraments without mingling and without the spiritualizing division of the earthy and the spiritual in the sacrament. Calvin would follow in his footsteps and continue the typical conciliatory, ecumenical character of the Strassbourg Reformation in Geneva. We are struck once again by the rich variety possible within the unity of the *doctrina Christi* as perceived through the eyes of Calvin. "It is not necessary that a difference of opinion should necessarily lead to division." Apart from that, Calvin rose far above Bucer as far as method went. Bucer sought to mediate in a way which would not cause annoyance to anyone and so protect the core of the gospel. But Calvin opposes. "Even if you should want a Christ who is acceptable to everyone, then you still cannot fabricate a new gospel." Calvin honoured Bucer's intentions, but in his theological approach he was superior both as an ecumenical and a polemicist.

In the first *Institute* of 1536 we already find traces of Bucer's influence in the outline of the nature of the Christian prayer and in the definition of the church. If Luther could be regarded above all as the preacher of evangelical doctrine, then Bucer could be regarded as the shepherd who, before looking for the preaching of the gospel, sought for the true organization of the church. He is therefore justifiable called the father of the evangelical confirmation.

Calvin would continue Bucer's ideas and praxis critically and with greater consistency, clarity and spiritual strength.

Radicalism

Baptists. The dust has not settled about the Baptists of the sixteenth century in spite of the literature written mostly with apologetic motives by moderns adherents, and mostly made murky by Marxist writers. The movement was of the utmost importance to the spiritual life of the Reformation. Luther revolted against this movement after the gushing fanaticism of Thomas Müntzer and Karlstadt, and Melanchton joined him in this. Zwingli, although he had to do with a different kind of Baptists in the so-called Swiss Brothers, had an equally unsympathetic approach in his attitude to the Baptists. It is once again the conciliatory position assumed by the Genevan Reformers which enabled them, in spite of vicious polemics, to take over the element of truth in the Baptist movement.

Calvin judged the Baptists in rejective fashion, and he rejected their schismatic and revolutionary drive. There is no indication, for example, that he had patience for the pacifist attitude of the Swiss Brothers, or for the concept of the church which rested strongly on personal communion which in turn rested on the personal, conscious choice of faith of the adult. He regarded their *confusio* as dangerious, and with his clear vision he realized that man could easily move from one extreme (pacifism) to the other (revolution, as in Münster). The Baptist realm in Münster instigated Calvin to speed up the publication of the first edition of his *Institute* so that French believers could be released from Anabaptism. Francis I saw in this grounds for persecution.

One could trace this clearly up to the style of the letter to Francis I and the last part of the *Institute*.

His first encounter with the adherents of the idea of adult baptism Calvin had at second hand. In the course of his first sojourn in Geneva, but especially in Strassbourg Calvin would often clash with them. Through the chastisement that Calvin exercised in his congregation in Strassbourg, he also exerted great attraction on the Baptists.

The Baptists were rejected by both the Roman Church and the Reformers. Rome regarded this as an infringement of the ecclesiastical establishment. The reformers saw in the Baptists only rabble-rousers who upset all the order and who rejected all dogma. Their schismatic actions upset the unity of the one catholic church. For Calvin it was not the free choice of man which was a determining factor, but the omnipotence of God. This omnipotence is at work also in the baptism of infants when the elect are incorporated into the body of Christ.

Behind the Baptist movements there remains the essential issue of how to evaluate them, in the sense of the ecclesiastical ideals of the Middle Ages especially mysticism and asceticism came into the picture. The legalism of the Baptists, their shunning of the world, their strict theocratic mode of thinking (in their own circle) and their negative attitude as regards the authorities, their exhortation of the Holy Spirit all rooted in medieval mysticism, while together with the Reformation they acknowledged the authority of the Scriptures. Behind their actions lay their eschatological impatience. The church, the kingdom of heaven should assume visible shape here and now. Their fundamental heresy and confusion lie in the doctrine of *nova creatio*. The old creation had become utterly worthless. Salvation is a completely new-created reality which will replace the old. This leads to their rejection of the Old Testament, their lack of reverence for history, etc. This attitude also had an enormous influence on Christendom.

To counterbalance their confusion and their theological misconceptions, there was their very real seriousness and their enthusiastic radicalism, together with the intensity of their religious response. In them there was a renewal of the old donatistic ideal, viz. the isolation of the holy from the popular church. Their view of the church was of a separate organism as against the state with its independent punishment and church order. One cannot really say that Zwingli conquered the Baptist ideals deep inside. He did save the popular church, in that he determined the rightness of infant baptism as an analogue to Old Testament circumcision, but baptism lost its last vestige of character as a means of grace. Baptism is the sign through which the child is introduced as a member of Christendom, and is then entitled to a Christian upbringing as well as being bound to a Christian way of life. In the Zürich state church no satisfactory answer could be given to the issues raised by the Baptists.

The Strassbourg and Genevan Reformation — in this context one has to mention the names of Bucer, Farél, Calvin with honour next to each other — fulfilled the historical vacation by assimilating the "positive" part of the Baptists (sanctification of life, chastisement and freedom in the church as opposed to the state) into ecclesiastical life. Added to that it is striking to note that sanctification is not regarded in a perfectionist sense by Calvin, because it should never arise out of justification. In matters of discipline too he was ever careful to avoid rigorism. The Baptists either abolished the state, authority, power and violence, or drew these to them in revolutionary fashion. Calvin on the one hand showed great understanding, but on the other hand rejected their *confusio* consistently. The Old Testament had to go on functioning fully alongside the New Testament. This implied an israelization of life, and a new acknowledgement of the fulness of the Bible as a typical symptom of reformatory catholicity.

Libertines. Calvin approached the radical front with much more understanding than Luther and Zwingli. He knew that the Baptists, who wished to be true to the Scriptures had to be sharply distinguished from the Libertines and the Anti-trinitarians. The Libertines enthroned an emotional spiritual character. The Anti-trinitarians were strictly rationalist in character. Calvin did not regard the Baptists as so hopelessly out of line as he did the Libertines. He wrote a separate treatise on the latter group in order to underline the poisonous underlay of the group which under the veneer of spirituality wished to turn people into brute animals.

The first figure of this revolutionary group to be mentioned is the Fleming Quentin Thieffry. Pocque, another adherent, believed in the sleep of souls, against which Calvin militated in the *Psychopannychia.* Calvin reproached them for setting the immediate inspiration of the Holy spirit above the Word of God. They spoke *ex cathedra,* on their own authority, falsifying the Holy Spirit by making the Word of God subservient to their own theological libido. Calvin is unusually sharp in his attack on Libertinism. He wrote to the Queen of Navarre, who had patronised Thieffry and Pocque at her court, and who felt personally affronted by Calvin's attack, that he did not wish to attack her personally, but that he did mean to warn her against this sect which was more dangerous and horrifying than any that had ever existed in the world.

"I see that they do great damage, and they are a fire which will consume away everything, or that they are a disease which will infect the entire world if men did not apply some form of medicine. They are intent on rejecting the pure doctrine, to lead poor souls to perdition and to teach the world to despise God." Calvin knew that he had to issue this warning, because a dog will keep barking if he sees that he is not going to be attacked. "I would be a coward if I saw God's truth so attacked and did not do something, staying instead numbly present."

In his struggle against radicalism Calvin supported the authority of government. They then gladly accepted him as a confederate and even honoured his help materially on one occasion. This happened in Frankfurt, when Calvin, in the course of his visit in 1556 came into contact with a certain Justus Wels.

This man, who had been a professor in Philosophy in Strassbourg, then in Cologne (and there a prisoner for a while because of his reformatory convictions) was, according to Hotman an impudent and talkative man. He maintained that he had received a prophetic revelation which he wanted to discuss in public. His request was acceded to and despite the fact that Calvin's time was very fully occupied, two days were spent in disputation about free will and predestination. Calvin himself wrote little about this but Hotman said that Wels lost all his influence as a result of this dispute, and that Calvin, on the other hand, because of his erudition, sharpness and competence came to be highly regarded by all. The senate of the city expressed their gratitude and instructed three officials to present him with a gift.

Anti-trinitarianism. Calvin's attitude towards anti-trinitarianism is possibly even more violent than his attitude towards Rome. In the doctrine of Rome, after all, Calvin still acknowledged some *vestigae ecclesiae* (baptism). Calvin would postulate that the Christology and the trinitarian doctrine of the Reformation could be seen as similar to that of the Old Church, including Irenaeus and Tertullian. The call to the *Patres* plays an important role in Calvin's thought next to his exhortation to the Holy Spirit. To return to the Scriptures is at the same time to return to the faith of the *Patres* and to confess to the Old Church.

When it comes to the formulation of the mystery of the Trinity, then Calvin refuses to bind himself completely to the inherited words. The dogma itself is for him untouchable.

This emerges above all with regard to Servet. For Servet the issue is the unity and indivisibility of God. He rejects the classical distinction of the three persons of the Divine being. Jesus is as a man the Son of God, that is, He is a form of emanation and manifestation of divinity. For Servet Jesus is a realization of the idea of "God" — incarnation is the result of a natural process. The supposition of the fall of man is unnecessary. The man Jesus Christ is the paradigm of all believers. Servet opposed not only the classical christology and doctrine of the Trinity, but also the concepts of hereditary or original sin, justice and infant baptism.

This heresy is for Calvin a rupturing of the unity of the church and a falsification of the truth.

The struggle against anti-trinitarianism is without compromise. The struggle against Griba'di, Alciati, Blandrata and Stancarus was no less harsh than the one against Servet. They were after all revolutionaries who brought the fabric of society into danger. The later developments in Poland indicated that Calvin did not struggle against the anti-trinitarian heresy in vain.

Conclusion

In Calvin several different trends of tolerant and deeply religious thought came together. There is the reformatory understanding of salvation of Luther, the justification of the godless. Apart from Luther, via Bucer, Zwingli had some influence — Zwingli, the stern theologian who thought from God, and in whom eternal providence and predestination received emphasis next to the mercy of Christ. Then there is the mystical-pietistic idea of Bucer, who also absorbed some Baptist ideas. These different trends all found some echo in the concept of predestination, and were practically realized in the church order of Calvin. In him all these ideas came to find concrete shape in a church order of permanence.

Calvin had the courage to think everything through to the truth of a divine predestination. The deepest root of existence is to be found in the goodwill of God. Modern philosophy is only a slight shadow of this. Here also Calvin's thought reveals catholicity in extreme tension. This ecumenical and catholic pattern of thinking borders on the two frontiers of Rome and of the Radicals. Outside the frontiers of the Reformation man is taught to climb up to God vertically from nature. The Baptist rejection and the Roman division of nature and supernature rest on the same basic premise. Calvin was serious about the entire creation. There can be no mention of a flight from the world. Sin rests not in nature but in the heart of man.

Calvin taught man to live horizontally according to the will and to the glory of God, and so only to attain the true verticality *coram Deo*. Life no longer should be lived in steps, going ever upward in a vertical direction in hierarchic coherence. Grace no longer stands above nature. Justice is narrowly bound to salvation which is all-encompassing. The whole of the earth is involved *sub specia aeternitatis* in *gloria Dei*. Salvation is the lustre of existence. The Law is the guideline of the church and of the nation. Here and now already the kingdom of God has to be erected. This explains the energetic involvement from the point of faith into the historical process and into politics. Calvin never denied his French ancestry. His thought reveals an aristocratic spirit and a refined sense of style. As an untiring ecumenicist Calvin sought to make, not only theologically but also practically, several schools of thought flow together in one riverbed. Each stream which sought to corrupt the *doctrina Christi* was ruthlessly diverted. Romanism and Radicalism fell outside the limits of the ecumene.

As an unrivalled catholic theologian, Calvin encompasses theology and predestination, he encompasses the whole of life. There is nothing that is not holy, because the entire Creation is a *theatron gloria Dei*.

8. CALVIN, AUGUSTINE AND PLATONISM. A FEW ASPECTS OF CALVIN'S PHILOSOPHICAL BACKGROUND

'Augustinus totus noster' (Calvin)
and
'nulli nobis quam isti (i.e. Platonici) propius' (Augustine)

PROF. N.T. VAN DER MERWE*

Introduction: elucidation of the topic

John Calvin is well known as theologian of the sixteenth century Reformation. His leading position is evident from his practical contribution to the religious set-up of those cities where he spent the major part of his life — and also far outside these areas —, as well as from his extensive theological writings on ecclesiastical subjects. His oeuvre include penetrating interchange of thoughts and polemical discussions with numerous authorities, scholars and persons from various walks of life. Even in social, political and educational circles Calvin left his imprint on his times. He had an extraordinary wide ranging interest in a variety of matters which is truly remarkable if one takes into account his schedule of daily commitments.

Of course it is Calvin's literary heritage which is of especial importance to us and which is also more readily accessible than other facets of his life. The budding talent of the young scholar already indicated Calvin's potential as man of letters. As a writer Calvin practised a method which ensured steady intellectual progress, both as an academician who could ply Latin as lingual medium of the learned world as circumstances necessitated and as a clergyman who could voice the intentions of his heart and the message of his mind for his people in their own colloquial speech. All these factors are relevant to the theme of this essay.

Calvin was a scholar with an immense wing-span. But it is important to remember that his thought and writings did not originate in a vacuum. Neither did he merely deduce his views and insights deductively from the Bible. Calvin was undoubtedly a clear-headed

* His address is: Dept. of Philosophy, Potchefstroom University for Christian Higher Education, Potchefstroom 2520 RSA.

scholar, but not such a narrow-minded and rigid intellectualist as he is sometimes portrayed. Characteristic of Calvin — as well as the kernel of his originality — is the way in which he made a distinctive impact on the intellectual climate and within the alternatives of his times. For this reason it is important to know what Calvin's stance in the spiritual milieu of his times was. This fact switches one's attention from Calvin the theologian to the profound thought potential of Calvin's mind.

One can obtain a certain impression of Calvin's thought by investigating for example Calvin's view of philosophy[1]. If, however, one would like to assess the details of the philosophical tradition behind Calvin's intellectual work, one should concentrate not on this facet but rather on the important philosophical trends and authoritative figures of his time and of the past. The interrelationship between Calvin's philosophical background and his total approach — including the influence thereof on his views and insights —, is however a very complex problem with many facets. The fact that certain developments and shifts occurred during Calvin's career as scholar and clergyman, complicates research even more[2]. Concentrating on Calvin as a thinker, as a philosopher, one encounters from a methodological point of view three options. In the first instance one could present a review of the various philosophical ideas which Calvin encountered as well as an account of his reaction to them. Or alternatively one could trace the development in Calvin's attitude towards certain philosophical conceptions and his assimilation or recasting of philosophical ideas. Thus one can ascertain what his final attitude entailed. Or, thirdly, one could identify and elucidate one crucial facet of his philosophical and historical background as a representative example. Or ... — perhaps a combination of these three approaches?

The third approach seems to be the most feasible if one would like to

---

[1] Engrossingly described by J. KLAPWIJK in "Calvijn over de filosofie", *Correspondentiebladen van de Vereniging voor Calvinistische Wijsbegeerte*, March 1972, 26: 13-20; cf. also his "Calvin and Neo-Calvinism on Philosophy", *Philosophia Reformata*, 1973, 38: 43-61, and PARTEE, C., *Calvin and Classical Philosophy*, Leiden, Brill, 1977, especially 13 sqq.

[2] E.g. (decreasing) interest in Stoicism. The problem as such has a bearing on the relationship between view of life, philosophy and academic endeavours (including theological efforts) — aspects which can not be adequately assessed from the literary heritage of Calvin. For an analysis of Calvin's study method cf. J.-D. BENOîT, "The history and development of the *Institutio:* How Calvin worked" in *John Calvin* (Courtenay Studies in Reformation Theology, I), 1965: 102-17.

limit one's research report[3]. By this means one can briefly identify, formulate and illuminate one single hypothesis. It is then also possible to concentrate on one theme. It is thus moreover feasible to elucidate one crucial historical aspect of Calvin's thought — which can indeed be considered to be the decisive core of Calvin's frame of reference —, and limit oneself in this effort to one historical figure. I stress the term 'decisive' to indicate the role of Platonism both during the early Christian period (Augustine) and during the Reformation (Calvin). In this way I think I am in a position to illustrate my findings with reference to but one writing of Augustine, remain on the high way and deliberately avoid detours.

Of course, the first two alternatives present a fascinating challenge, but I feel this endeavour should be reserved for a research project undertaken by a panel of experts and, perhaps, afford subject matter for a future Calvin Congress. The way in which I present the results of my investigation concerning the varied contacts of Calvin with Augustine and Augustine's significance for Calvin, reflect that of a bee carrying off one grain of pollen from a beautiful flower — a valuable and unique, but limited haul.

In short: the *problem* of my essay can be formulated as tracing the main sources, inspiration and ground motif in Calvin's thought. My *hypothesis* is: Plato and Augustine play an important role in Calvin's thought, each in his own way. And finally, the *theme* treated in my essay is: both the problem and the hypothesis mentioned above can be illustrated adequately with reference to the topics of knowledge of God and the significance of revelation. It is interesting to note that a key to this theme is to be found in a certain writing of Augustine. I shall try to elucidate the objective inherent in the above mentioned three facets as briefly as possible to keep the 'golden thread' clearly

---

[3] I had the rare privilege of devoting my undivided attention for a couple of months to one facet of a research project on "the impact of Calvinism". The objective of my research topic was to trace the origins and intellectual links of Calvin's thought with earlier periods, and thus contribute my humble share to the "prehistory" of Calvinism. In the limited time at my disposal I could investigate only a few aspects and describe a fragment — the problem in its entirety merits the attention of an interdisciplinary research team. I have pleasure in conveying my appreciation and gratitude to the University officials who facilitated the research project, to the Human Sciences Research Council for their interest in and assistance with the project, and to Prof. Dr. B.J. van der Walt, Director of the Institute for the Advancement of Calvinism (at present Institute for Reformational Studies) who kindly put the facilities of his Institute at my disposal.

discernible. My first task is accordingly a sketch of the topic: Calvin and Augustine.

A general comparison between Calvin and Augustine in the context of their times

A theme such as 'Augustine and Calvin' requires a comparative study, which is a risky undertaking, for it depends on all sorts of factors, such as point of departure, focal point and objective. The minimum that one should say is that one ought to try to understand Calvin and Augustine as men of their own era, viz. Augustine from the Early Christian period and Calvin from the Late Christian era, a contemporary of the Renaissance and of Humanism. One should therefore try to understand them with the aid of knowledge of *our* era but to judge and evaluate them according to the possibilities and criteria of the era to which *they* belong.

Regarded from this perspective we are today in a very privileged situation. Many learned studies undertaken in the twentieth century have noticeably improved our insight into the intellectual milieu of Calvin's efforts[4]. In the second instance, as far as Augustine is concerned — apart from the enduring merit of several older distinguished works[5] — the intellectual pressure cooker of the

---

[4] E.g. among others BATTLES, F.L., "The sources of Calvin's Seneca Commentary" in *Studies in John Calvin* (Courtenay Studies in Reformation Theology, vol, I), 1965, 38-60; BATTLES, F.L. & HUGO, A.M., *Calvin's Commentary on Seneca's De clementia ...*, Leiden, Brill, 1969; BOHATEC, J., *Budé und Calvin ...*, Graz, Böhlaus, 1950; BREEN, Q., *John Calvin: A study in French Humanism*, Grand Rapids, Eerdmans, 1931; HUGO, A.M., *Calvijn en Seneca ...*, Groningen, Wolters, 1957; KRISTELLER, P.O., *Renaissance Thought ...*, New York, Harper, 1961; NEUSER, W.H. *(ed.)*, *Calvinus ecclesiae doctor; die Referate des internationalen Kongresses für Calvinforschung ...*, Kampen, Kok, 1978; WENDEL, F. *Calvin ...*, London, Collins, 1965; useful bibliography in VAN DER WALT, B.J., *Die denkdekor van die Reformasie*, Potchefstroom, P.U. for C.H.E., 1979; cf. IDEM, *Contemporary Research on the sixteenth century Reformation*, P.U. for C.H.E., 1979. LANE, A.N.S., "Calvin's use of the Fathers and Medievals", *Calvin Theological Journal*, Nov., 1981, 16(2): 149 -205 is an important study which appeared after the completion of my report. For important research literature on Calvin in general consult NIESEL, W., *Calvin-Bibliographie (1900-1959)*, München, Kaiser, 1961; KEMPFF, D., *A Bibliography of Calviniana (1959-1974)*, Potchefstroom, Institute for the Advancement of Calvinism, 1975; DE KLERK, P., "Calvin Bibliography", annually in *Calvin Theological Journal*.

[5] Among others e.g. DINKLER, E., *Die Anthropologie Augustins*, Stuttgart, 1934; GILSON, E., *Introduction à l'étude de saint Augustin*, Paris, Vrin, 1949[3]; HESSEN, J., *Augustins Metaphysik der Erkenntnis*, Berlin & Bonn, 1931; MARROU, H.I., *Saint*

Augustine Festival Year (1954) continued yielding, in the midst of the flood of publications, various studies of exceptional merit[6] which in a certain sense resulted in a new phase in research on Augustine, and which have aided us towards a better understanding of the intellectual struggles of Augustine as a believing Christian in late Antiquity.

Should we keep all this in mind, we are confronted with the following result:

(1)   As individuals both Calvin and Augustine are intellectual giants with a broad cultural base and interest, phenomenal memory and appetite for work, striking personality, attractive style of writing, very talented apologetes, indefatigable in their restless quest for knowledge and their wrestling with topical issues of their times. Both distinguished themselves by an unceasing supplementation of their own insights through study and self-correction, — truly intellectuals who acquired depth and maturity of insight through their childlike faith by close contact with the Word of God. A remarkable fact is that both also had a full life of practical involvement with all the responsibilities of a leadership position in the community of the holy.

(2)   Taking into account the character of their era, one striking trait cannot be overlooked: Augustine lived in a time of cultural decadence — as Marrou described it[7] — in which little collections of "golden thoughts" had their place, simultaneous with the collapse of 'eternal Rome'. As far as the late Medieval period is concerned, it certainly did not rival the creative boiling pot of the golden age of Scholasticism. While the efforts of people like Petrarch and Bradwardine to rise

Augustin et la fin de la culture antique, Paris, De Boccard, 1958[4] (1938). For research literature on Augustine in general consult especially ANDRESEN, C., *(ed.)*, *Bibliographia Augustiniana*, Darmstadt, Wissenschaftliche Buchgesellschaft, 1973[2]; VAN BAVEL, T. & VAN DER ZANDE, F. *(ed.)*, *Répertoire bibliographique de saint Augustin (1950-1960)*, Steenbrugis, In abbatia sancti Petri, 1963 (Instrumenta Patristica, III); annual "Bulletin Augustinien" in *Revue des études Augustiniennes*, Paris, Etudes Augustiniennes.

[6] E.g. to mention rather arbitrarily but a few illustrative examples: BROWN, P., *Augustine of Hippo; a biography*, London, Faber, 1967; COURCELLE, P., *Recherches sur les Confessions de saint Augustin*, Paris, De Boccard, 1950; DU ROY, O., *L'intelligence de la foi en la Trinité selon saint Augustin*, Paris, Etudes Augustiniennes, 1966; KÖRNER, F., *Das Sein und der Mensch ...*, München, Alber, 1959; LORENZ, R., "Der Augustinismus und seine Gegner" in *Die Kirche und ihrer Geschichte. Das vierte bis sechste Jahrhundert (Westen)*, Göttingen, 1970; MAYER, C.P., *Die Zeichen in der geistigen Entwicklung und in der Theologie des jungen Augustinus*, Würzburg, 1969; POLMAN, A.D.R., *Het Woord Gods bij Augustinus*, Kampen, Kok, 1955; SIZOO, A., *Augustinus; leven en werken*, Kampen, Kok, 1957.

[7] *Saint Augustin et la fin de la culture antique*, Paris, De Boccard, 1958[4], 85 sqq.

above Scholasticism and draw inspiration from earlier times, played an important role within the process of trying to create a new spiritual climate, this remained, in the main, a mere trickle. Perhaps this was one of the reasons leading to the tremendous impact, the explosive quality, of the Renaissance, of Humanism and of the Reformation which followed on this. As the Late Medieval Ages offers the major key to the immediate background of Calvin's intellectual milieu, it is of especial significance to the theme of this essay.

But there are at least two important differences: After Augustine's résumé of Christian doctrine and his eminent indication of the course to be followed, a spiritual vacuum emerged with very few substantial contributions. So Augustine became the testator of Antiquity to medieval Christendom. The Renaissance, Humanism and the Reformation on the other hand are three powerful impulses which prepared and launched the so-called 'New Era' and which for this reason also remained more fully absorbed in the whirlpool of ideas. In this way, however, the real intellectual significance as well as influence Calvin and the Reformers had on the Modern Era, is not always clearly visible. Secondly: Augustine had to take into account the dissolution of the culture of Antiquity which carried a *pagan* stamp, as well as the disaster of the fall of Rome. Calvin, on the other hand, had to deal with the spiritual decadence of Christianity and especially of ecclesiastical practice, and come to terms with it.

Should we now look at Calvin's involvement with Augustine, it would seem to have a dual nature, viz. (1) via the writings of Augustine himself, and (2) via the influence of Augustine in the Middle Ages. The Augustinian tradition, for example, can be observed in the role played by the 'Brethren of the common life' with whom Calvin came into contact as a student, but even more extensively in the activities of especially the Augustinian order, which was an important trend next to others such as Thomism. As important centres of new ideas and renewal the monasteries of this order were, in the late Middle Ages, not only opposed to Aristotelian-tinted Scholasticism, but also offered a channel for the Reformation itself, for example for taking note of the thoughts and actions of Luther, who received his schooling within this order[8].

[8] LODS, M., "L'Augustinisme dans les convents Augustins à l'époque de Luther", *Positions Lutheriennes,* 44 (5): 198-206, 1957, cf. especially his conclusions p. 206.

In short: The late Middle Ages evoked much interest in the early Christian period — and particularly in Augustine — by means of a new current, a third synthesis. The Renaissance brought about a new interest in especially Stoicism and Platonism. And early modern Humanism laid solid foundations in Philology for the study of the literary heritage of both early Christendom and Antiquity[9].

Within this atmosphere we see Calvin making his début as a writer with a commentary on Seneca's *De clementia*. Battles and Hugo[10] not only beautifully outlined the intellectual background, educational training and ideals of Calvin in his first publication, but also described the various sources Calvin utilized. Among these sources Augustine also figured. Not long after that, when Calvin completed his so-called *Psychopannychia,* he devoted his attention at the same time to a catechism. This effort would eventually culminate in *the* study for which he gained renown, his 'Essentials of Christian religion'.

L. Smits[11] introduces his authorative and magnificent study on Augustine and Calvin with a remarkable statement: Calvin's significance rests on one book. Soon after his conversion and in spite of his youth, Calvin gave expression to his reformational ideas in his *Institutio christianae religionis,* and throughout his life he kept correcting and enriching this. I hesitate to follow Smits in this generalization, for does this adequately reflect the variety of Calvin's publications? I do think, however, that Smits is substantially correct, for no other work of Calvin seems to illustrate his intellectual development so well. Moreover, his other works also find their historical niche within this context.

---

[9] As a introduction the following general studies can be recommended: KRISTELLER P.O., "Renaissance Philosophies" in FERM, V. *(ed.), A History of philosophical Systems,* Ames (Iowa), Littlefield & Adams, 1958, 227-239; VAN STOCKUM, T.C., "De wijsbegeerte in de tijd van Renaissance, Humanisme en Reformatie" in VAN OYEN, H., *(ed.) Philosophia; Beknopt handboek tot de geschiedenis van het wijsgerig denken,* Utrecht, De Haan, 1967, 223-246; VOLLENHOVEN, D.H.T., *Kort overzicht van de geschiedenis der wijsbegeerte* (voor den cursus MOA), Amsterdam, Theja, 1956, 28 sqq.; WATERINK, J., a.o., *(ed.), Cultuurgeschiedenis van het Christendom,* Amsterdam & Brussel, Elsevier, 1957[2], ch. XXI-XXV (various writers); cf. also my reference no. 4 above: Bohatec, Breen, Kristeller.

[10] BATTLES, F.L. & HUGO, A.M., *Calvin's Commentary on Seneca's De clementia,* Leiden, Brill, 1969; cf. also HUGO, A.M., *Calvijn en Seneca,* Groningen, Wolters, 1957.

[11] SMITS, L., *Saint Augustin dans l'oeuvre de Jean Calvin,* Assen, Van Gorcum, 1957, 1. Cf. also Id., "L'autorité de saint Augustin dans l'Institution chrétienne de Jean Calvin", *Revue d'histoire ecclesiastique,* 1950, 45: 670-687.

It is evident from the careful and penetrating analysis by Smits *that* Augustine kept fascinating Calvin throughout his life. It is also clear *how* this influence exerted itself. Calvin's appreciative description of his relationship with Augustine as "adeo totus noster"[12] seems to be correct and to the point. For Calvin this did however not exclude combining an independent attitude with a loving and respectful criticism of Augustine. This bond of unity with Augustine bears reference to Calvin as an outstanding *thinker* of his times (especially influential as far as Dogmatics is concerned) and not as an exegete — in the latter field Calvin early on in his academic career preferred Chrysostomus[13].

For our subject it is of especial importance, I feel, that in the time when Calvin turned towards the Reformation, and started work on his catechism, it should have been Augustine who "opened his eyes", as he himself testified[14]. Let us try to pinpoint the essentials of how this has happened.

Augustine the Christian

Is it possible to take even a further step and indicate a specific writing of Augustine which smoothed Calvin's way? Smits' feeling is that it is the *De spiritu et littera* of Augustine[15]. Within the philological context in which Smits deals with this matter, it seems an attractive proposition. To the philological evidence I would like to add the following three points to substantiate the argument:

(1) Few writings of Augustine reflect the spirit of the Reformation on the whole and so explicitly and strikingly and concisely, stress so clearly similar truths of faith, as this little publication of Augustine, which gained renown in the sixteenth century. What indeed are the pillars on which the message of this little work rests other, primarily, than 'sola Scriptura', 'sola gratia' and 'sola fide' — to finally conclude

---

[12] Calvin formulated his unanimity with Augustine in various ways, cf. e.g. the examples mentioned by CADIER, J., "Calvin et saint Augustin" in *Augustinus Magister,* II, Paris, Etudes Augustiniennes, 1954, 1038-1056: p. 1040 and SMITS, L., *Saint Augustin dans l'oeuvre de Jean Calvin,* Assen, Van Gorcum, 1957, especially p. 271.

[13] Cf. SMITS, L., *op. cit.,* p. 35.

[14] Excellently elucidated by Smits, cf. *op. cit.,* p. 23.

[15] Ibid.

with 'ipsi gloria in saecula saeculorum'[16]? Should Augustine, seen within this perspective, not rightly be acclaimed a (the?) spiritual father of Christendom and particularly of the Reformation?

(2)   This little treatise of Augustine concentrates on the 'spiritual and litteral' dimension of creation. Did Calvin not in brilliant fashion transform the theme of this work — and as a matter of course also the hermeneutic preferences of Augustine — with the vivifying spirit with which he imbued "dead letters" thanks to his philological care, his fine sense of distinction and his balanced critical awareness in the handling of texts and ideas, linked to a believing and pious obedience to the Word of God? Should one have to search much further than the pious and saintly life style and writing praxis of Augustine to understand why it had been exactly Augustine as Christian who struck and fascinated Calvin?

(3)   Is the important place accorded in this work to the Law not perhaps an additional ground for Calvin's treatment of knowledge of God and the self within the framework of the Law in his first (1536) edition of the *Institutes?* Let us pursue this theme a step further.

An important theme: knowledge of God and the self

In contrast to earlier efforts to determine a fixed core in Calvin's theology, Calvin research of the past few decades by and large seems to shun such efforts because of the rich variety of Calvin's intellectual productivity[17]. Accordingly, when we now state that the theme of knowledge of God and of self strikes every reader of the Institutes as a cardinal pivot of the "Essentials of Christian religion" — increasingly clearly put in succeeding editions —, I am not suggesting that this one facet fully explains the entire intellectual structure of Calvin's

---

[16] The popularity of this work is closely related to the fact that it was included in this era in the last section of the Bible. Accordingly it received extensive interest; cf. e.g. SMITS, *op. cit.,* 23 sq. As far as the ground motif of the Reformation is concerned, cf. the explanation given by B.J. van der Walt in his speech "The relevance to the Black Peoples of Africa of a Calvinistic Cosmoscope" on the occasion of the opening ceremony of the Dimbaza Reformed Bible School, Ciskei, February. 1979 — included in his *Anatomy of Reformation,* Institute for the Advancement of Calvinism, 1981, p. 436-459.

[17] An important and engrossing theory as regards Calvin's method of thinking (especially concerning a basic principle in the structure of Calvin's theology) is F.L. BATTLES' "Calculus fidei — some ruminations on the structure of Calvin's Theology" in NEUSER, W.H. *(ed.), Calvinus ecclesiae doctor,* Kampen, Kok, 1978, 85-110.

thought. It is, however, undoubtedly important.

Is it also characteristic of Calvin? Without closer elucidation, no — because other intellectuals have also used it as a basic framework. In fact, it was in a certain sense, as far as its intention is concerned, a central refrain of the late medieval cult of the inner man. What is then characteristic of Calvin? Let me put it in comparative terms.

Bohatec has clearly indicated how Thomas à Kempis in talking about knowledge of the self stressed the aspect of insignificance and nothingness of man, in other words self-derogation[18], and how Erasmus under his influence also stressed self-knowledge, while Budé mentioned the Stoic definition of wisdom ('rerum divinarum humanarumque cognitio'), but narrowed the definition down to 'cognitio Dei et nostri'[19]. In this way the approach of Antiquity obtained a Christian peak in the "heaven-directed Christian philosophy" ('coelestis Christi philosophia'). This makes one wonder to what extent the theme of nature and grace is still operative. In any case, as regards Calvin, his significance is to be found in the fact that he placed this humanistic interpretation rigorously in the perspective of the Reformation in his *Institutes*, with all the stress on the role of true knowledge of God in relation to the fallen state of man and the function of grace. It is typical of Calvin that he kept on refining this description for years on end. As against the ethical tendency of Erasmus and the philological synthetic vision of Budé, Calvin thus showed himself to have a pronouncedly religious focus.

Should one look at the Christian literary tradition in retrospect for "model examples" of the theme of knowledge of God and man, one cannot help but think of Augustine and Anselm of Canterbury — as far as Anselm is concerned even in an ontological and ontic-epistemological elaboration[20]. Of course this theme is naturally also present in other Christian writers, such as Clement of Alexandria. But let us limit ourselves for the moment to Augustine.

Keeping in mind (1) the sympathetic attitude Calvin adopted towards

[18] BOHATEC, J., *Budé und Calvin*, Graz, Böhlaus, 1950, 31.

[19] Ibid., p. 30 sqq.

[20] Cf. especially his discussion of human knowledge of God in the *Monologion* and *Proslogion* respectively.

Augustine and (2) the familiarity of the formulation Augustine gave in his *Soliloquia*, viz. "Deum et animam scire cupio", one would tend to expect that Calvin would link up readily with Augustine. Yet Smits finds no reference to this work of Augustine in the *Institutes* of Calvin[21]. In fact, Calvin also does not cite other works of Augustine with a strong philosophical flavour[22]. This is remarkable. Calvin after all did not dislike philosophy as such. How should one explain this? In a religious context Calvin is unanimous with Augustine as a Christian scholar and thinker, but selective or hesitative as regards some predilections and philosophical accentuations of Augustine. Would Augustine's emphasis on the soul have been too strong for Calvin? Or would he by remaining silent have tried to express a passive resistance to Neo-platonic traits in Augustine?

Plato and Platonism

Let me present my assessment of the matter in the form of a conjecture. From specific research results[23] it is clear that Calvin's Theory of knowledge and his Anthropology accomodate certain traits going back to Platonism. The question now is: Platonism in what form? The remarkable fact is that Calvin did not, like Budé, show sympathy towards sixteenth century Neo-Platonism, but rather revealed influences of Plato himself. In this way Calvin also moved away from Augustine in so far as Neo-Platonic influences are discernible in him (including among other features an accompanying allegorical exegesis). Of his interest in Neo-Platonism, known then as Platonici, Augustine testified in his first extant writing, the *Contra Academicos*, and he reaffirmed this at the end of his life in his *De civitate Dei*[24]: the school of Plato is the trend which has come nearest to us, to Christian philosophy — "nulli nobis quam isti propius accesserunt".

And now, Calvin? The theologian known for the sacrifice of his heart,

---

[21] SMITS, L., *op. cit.,* p. 146 sqq.

[22] Ibid., p. 146.

[23] Treated e.g. by BABELOTZKY, G., *Platonische Bilder und Gedankengänge in Calvins Lehre vom Menschen,* Wiesbaden, Steiner, 1977; CADIER, J. (reference no. 12 above); WENDEL, F. (reference no. 4 above); cf. also PARTEE, C., *Calvin and Classical philosophy,* Leiden, Brill, 1977.

[24] *Contra Academicos,* III, 20, 43; *De civitate Dei,* VIII, 5. Similar descriptions can be found elsewhere in Augustine's writings.

was, as regards the direction his thoughts took, unanimous with 'the philosopher of the heart'[25]. This was the cardinal and crucial influence of Augustine on Calvin. And yet, for certain structural elements of his philosophy, Calvin falls back on Plato and not one or another trend of Platonism. Plato and not Augustine. Does this seem strange? Perhaps not so strange if one keeps in mind that also in the sixteenth century Platonism counted as the most religious trend. After all, as is well known, the theme of self-knowledge, in its link with a resolute repudiation of overestimation of the self and sham knowledge, has its roots in Socrates. It was indeed the discreet and prudent Socrates who was called the wisest by the Delphic oracle because he had the wisdom to know that he did not really know. But the Socrates who limited himself to verbal communication is known through Plato as writer, his appreciative pupil[26]. Thus a special bond becomes apparent between the humble, religious Augustine of, for example, the *Confessions,* and the modest, unpretentious Socrates from pagan Antiquity, the Socrates who, for all practical purposes figured as the alter ego of Plato in the literary tradition. Philosophy thus is no quibble on words or terms, it touches on profound issues, so basic that one has to acknowledge one's impotence — in actual fact man does not know! With this I may now conclude.

Résumé and prospect

As far as the mandate to focus on self-knowledge is concerned, Socrates' concept of man to a large extent assumed an epistemological apex. This mandate had its origin in the Delphian Apollo. As oracle communicated by Apollo, it entailed a revelation, a divine revelation from the part of the gods in Greek religious experience. It thus made known what man could not produce from within himself, could not discover within himself. The tremendous cultural and historical significance of the theme of self-knowledge was magnificently disclosed by P. Courcelle who offered a marvellous overview of the

---

[25] A. Maxsein deserves credit for his investigation of Augustine's reflection on the role of the heart of man, cf. e.g. his *Philosophia cordis. Das Wesen der Personalität bei Augustinus,* Salzburg, 1966.

[26] In any case more so than Xenophon. An important reason was the fact that Plato used Socrates as his mouth piece in his dialogues — a circumstance which complicates the understanding of the philosophical conception of Plato himself.

development of this motif in the West[27]. In his *Institutes* Calvin made a striking application of the role of revelation to this theme, which echoed widely in its time — a theory of knowledge with great potential and excellent perspectives.

What does the future of Christianity embrace today? I think Christianity is faced with a tremendous challenge. Where Socrates gave the (pagan) religious concept of 'know thyself' a philosophical emphasis which made philosophy the origin and basis of Western science, and where Calvin unfolded the true knowledge of God and self as a perspective for the whole of life, Christianity now has the task to imbue the secularized concept of experience, knowing and data once again with the dimension of revelation — man created by God and subsisting from God's divine Word. In other words, philosophy as such should discover and recognize its roots not merely in science but more important still in religion[28]. And Christianity has the exceptional task of disclosing the real meaning of divine revelation to the modern world.

How would a twentieth century *De spiritu et littera* or *Institutio christianae religionis* appear today? Negatively formulated: I think it would not suffice to repeat the statement of Pascal that God is not the god of the philosophers but the God of Abraham, Isaac and Jacob. No doubt about it, many a philosopher certainly lost his bearings as far as religion is concerned. Perhaps it is even beginning to glimmer through in some regions that a species of liberal theologian is also to be found who has dispensed of the God of Abraham, Isaac and Jacob. This applies equally to scholars in other disciplines as well.

It is also true that religion is an issue of the heart and not merely (or especially) of scientific theories and matters worth knowing. There is, however, a close link. The important thing is a fine balance between (1) walking with God, (2) a dynamic and integral view of life, (3)

---

[27] COURCELLE, P., *Connais-toi toi-même de Socrate à saint Bernard,* Paris, Etudes Augustiniennes, I, 1974; II, 1975; III, 1975. An intensive study of the relationship between this theme and that of revelation would be thoroughly worthwhile. Would it not be rewarding for an historian to trace the history of the theme of self-knowledge and knowledge of God in Protestant circles beyond the limits of the Middle Ages, even as far as the twentieth century?

[28] Cf. POPPER, K.R., "The nature of philosophical problems and their roots in science", *British Journal for the Philosophy of science,* 3, 1952, 124-156, and DOOYEWEERD, H., *A new critique of theoretical thought,* especially vol. I, Amsterdam & Philadelphia, Paris & The Presbyterian and Reformed Publ. Co., 1953.

practical philosophy and (4) academic insight (including disciplines like Philosophy, Theology and the special sciences). The Christian God fits in naturally in the intellectual framework of Augustine, Calvin and other believing scholars on account of their acknowledgement of the relevance of the revelation of God Almighty for the totality of daily life. But God is present in their thought according to the potentialities of *their* times and the interpretation and individuality of *their* minds. Accordingly there is no necessity that as far as a believing scholar — theologian not excluded — is concerned, the God of his heart should be totally different from that of his philosophical predilections. An inherent and integral unity is a real possibility and option! This fact is evident from the writings of Calvin and Augustine — and ... operative also in Plato! The crucial point is: Who is your God and what is the nature of your philosophy? Calvin's scrummage with his 'intellectual friends' is exceptionally enlightening in this respect.

In the second instance the positive side of the coin: A twentieth century "Essentials of Christian conduct in life" should be able to highlight the valuable points and features inherent in the Christian tradition. It should give a practical application to the Good News of salvation in the actual problems and concrete circumstances of the 20th century world. The secularized wisdom of the modern world is in great need of revelation which does not originate in the so-called sophisticated mind of man.

In this context scientific endeavours are not decisive but nonetheless relevant and valuable. Philosophy too draws its source from God and His Word. Contemporary philosophical trends which do not condescend to give a legitimate place in science to God's revelation, show the ever increasing consequences of this choice — an emergency dive into Mysticism or the sterile manipulation of language.

In our final review it is important to stress that philosophical knowledge of the past is essential and bears a factual significance, being relevant also for a twentieth century Calvin Congress.

Intimate acquaintance with Augustine, but also with Plato and Platonism, as well as with other philosophical trends, is necessary and relevant for a thorough understanding of a theologian like Calvin[29].

[29] For the sake of brevity a thorough discussion of more recent insights on Plato,

Perhaps Augustine was very near the target when he described Plato's intellectual concept as most relevant to Christianity. The same applies to Calvin who from a variety of philosophical alternatives accorded a special preference to Plato, retaining nonetheless in the Augustinian tradition of a Christian philosophy his religious independence as a Christian intellectual.

In a nutshell: Calvin was an exceptionally well read and independent and original scholar. Nonetheless, even creative thinkers operate within an intellectual milieu. In the case of Calvin — apart from other influences like Luther —, two sources were exceptionally important: Augustine and Plato. But each in turn had a specific role in the ground motif of Calvin's thought. This is the kernel on which my hypothesis hinges. My conjecture is that Calvin's genius is apparent in the manner in which he transformed and integrated these and other minor influences into the general structure of his mental outlook, remaining at the same time an intellectual giant, independent and with a unique message for modern times. As far as the systematics of Philosophy is concerned, Contemporary Christian philosophy has

Platonism and Neoplatonism in research publications of the past decades — including the new avenues opened up thereby — had to be eliminated. On various grounds the following writings can be strongly recommended as beacons in the literature on this subject: ANDRESEN, C., (ed.), Zum Augustin-Gespräch der Gegenwart. Darmstadt, Wissenschaftliche Buchgesellschaft, 1962. ARMSTRONG, A.H., (ed.), The Cambridge History of later Greek and early Medieval Philosophy. Cambridge, University Press, 1967. ARNOU, R., "Platonisme des Pères" in Dictionnaire de théologie catholique, XIII, 1943. COURCELLE, P., Les lettres grecques en Occident, de Macrobe à Cassiodore. Paris, De Boccard, 1948[2]. Idem, Recherches sur les Confessions de saint Augustin. Paris, De Boccard, 1950. DANIÉLOU, J. Platonisme et théologie mystique. Paris, 1953[2]. DE VOGEL, C.J., Philosohia. Assen, Van Gorcum, 1970. DÖRRIE, H., Platonica minora. München, Fink, 1976. ENTRETIENS SUR L'ANTIQUITÉ CLASSIQUE, III, V, XII, XXI, 1958-1975. Vandoeuvres-Genève, (Fondation Hardt). GAISER, K., Platons ungeschriebene Lehre... Stuttgart, 1968[2]. HOFFMANN, E., Platonismus und christliche Philosophie. Zürich & Stuttgart, Artemis, 1960. KLIBANSKY, R., The continuity of the Platonic tradition during the Middle Ages ... London, 1950[2]. KRÄMER, H.J., Der Ursprung der Geistmetaphysik ..., Amsterdam, Grüner, 1967 (1964). MERLAN, P., From Platonism to Neoplatonism, Den Haag, Nijhoff, 1968[3] (1953). IDEM, Kleine Schriften, Hildesheim, Olms, 1976. MOMIGLIANO, A., (ed.), The Conflict between Paganism and Christianity in the fourth century, Oxford, 1963. SCHUHL, P.M. & HADOT, P., (ed.), Le Néoplatonisme ..., Paris, 1971. THEILER, W., Die Vorbereitung des Neuplatonismus, Berlin & Zürich, Weidmannsche Verlagsbuchhandlung, 1964. IDEM, Forschungen zum Neuplatonismus, Berlin, De Gruyter, 1966. VON IVANKA, E., Übernahme und Umgestaltung des Platonismus durch die Väter, Einsiedeln, 1964. WIPPERN, J., (ed.), Das Problem der ungeschriebene Lehre Platons ..., Darmstadt, Wissenschaftliche Buchgesellschaft, 1972. ZINTZEN, C., (ed.), Die Philosophie des Neuplatonismus, Darmstadt, Wissenschaftliche Buchgesellschaft, 1977. I have just received the important collection of essays by ZINTZEN, C., (ed.) Der Mittelplatonismus, Darmstadt, Wissenschaftliche Buchgesellschaft, 1981, which is a welcome supplement to the volume on Neoplatonism.

advanced far beyond the philosophical problematics of the times of the Reformation. But Calvin's progressive solutions of basic problems in various areas as well as his study method and style of writing are none the less still very instructive and enlightening to contemporary philosophical and theological research.

9.   RENAISSANCE AND REFORMATION: CONTEMPORARIES BUT NOT ALLIES

PROF. B.J. VAN DER WALT*

I do hope that you are going to have the deepest sympathy for my contribution, because it really represents an attempt at the impossible. To force a whale into a sardine tin is no mean feat. And here one is expected to force not less than five whales (Renaissance, Humanism, Stoicism, Platonism and Calvin as representative of the Reformation) into the same tin. The titanic effort assumes even more heroic proportions when one considers that I have exactly fifteen minutes at my disposal in which to commit this academic crime.

*   *   *

I am convinced that Calvin as a reformer (the theme of our congress) can only be fully understood and really appreciated if the background against which he grew up, developed, thought and wrote is also carefully studied.

This sixteenth century décor against which his life and work has to be considered is an extremely complex and many-sided one. There is an unbelievably wide range of factors which we have to keep in mind in the field of the church and religion, in the field of society and politics, and in the field of philosophy and theology.

There is a great deal of variation within each of the trends that we are going to deal with. Apart from that there is a strong degree of reciprocation among the various trends: Renaissance, Humanism and Stoicism can only be dissected neatly afterwards in theory.

In what follows I am merely going to attempt to isolate the deepest religious driving force behind the Renaissance and the Reformation.

The sixteenth century: a spiritual watershed

The turmoil in a number of areas was already noticeable in the late

* Prof. Van der Walt is director of the *Institute for Reformational Studies* (the former *Institute for the Advancement of Calvinism),* Potchefstroom University for Christian Higher Education, Potchefstroom, RSA 2520.

Middle Ages. The sixteenth century became an uneasy period of "Sturm und Drang" with many far-reaching events: repeated epidemics of the plague, agrarian and economic crises and large-scale urbanization with the resultant social upheaval.

A new mercantile middle class was established, and the farmers rebelled against injustices ...

This was also, however, a period of unprecedented broadening of horizons. Apart from the compass and gunpowder, ancient manuscripts and books of great age were discoved and studied. Through the voyages of discovery the world map was extended; the use of paper and of mobile printing, the development of schools and of universities, new ideas (such as those of Copernicus) all heralded the birth of a new world.

And the spiritual leaders were aware of this dawning. Over against the "dark Middle Ages" they began to see their own epoch as a golden epoch, a new epoch of light and enlightenment.

In the dawning of the new era in Western cultural history various intellectual trends came into being, each with the pretension of having *the* light, each secure in the belief that he and he only could offer new certainty and security to European man.

Whoever attunes his seismograph sensitively would see clearly that the ways diverged here. The sixteenth century represents the beginning of the end of the important role that Christendom played in the West for more than a millenium ($\pm$ 500 — $\pm$ 1 500). At this time the secularization of the West started. A new paganism was born. At first it was a little unsteady, and sleepy-eyed, but it would soon conquer the West by storm.

In spite of the mutual dissatisfaction with the Scholastic past the ways slowly but clearly diverged. The Renaissance broke with the mentality of synthesis or compromize because it could not tolerate the Christian and Biblical element contained in Medieval thought. For the Reformation the synthesis between Christendom and ancient pagan thought became unacceptable for exactly the opposite reason, viz. because the Word of God did not come to full justice in it.

As to the question to which source one should turn for light in the new epoch there is no unanimity. The Renaissance looked for new

86

light in a totally different direction than the Reformation.

The Renaissance

We can already discern the difference in Early or so-called Christian Humanism and the thinkers of the pre-Reformation. Both sought to kindle their own flame at the cinders of the patristic age. The motives, however, differed. The precursors of the Reformation returned to Patristic thought, because they were fascinated by the *Scriptural* aspects of it, while early humanist thought was more interested in the question as to how the early Christian thinkers could simultaneously also be *Romans!*

This early form of Humanism was mainly a pedagogical movement, which sought a moral injection (to effect rebirth of church and religion) in the past.

Later Humanism still sought to redream the beautiful ideals of the past. These thinkers, however, delved even further back into the past. The period to which they returned to kindle their light was not so much that of the *Patres* as the Greek and Roman thinkers of Antiquity.

Here we have a still clearer leftish trend. The question now is not so much (as with the Early Humanists) how it is possible to be simultaneously Christian and Roman, but why it is not possible (as in Antiquity) to be purely Roman (that is pagan) in thought. The emancipation from church and religious bonds strengthened. Autonomous, assured, dignified and noble man emerged ever more clearly in spite of the Christian mentality of many individual humanists like, for instance, Erasmus.

Humanism was characterized by a scientific, literary and educational ideal based on a study of Antiquity. (It was confined more to intellectuals in comparison with the Reformation which was a more popular movement.) Humanism was the result of the process of fermentation instigated by the Renaissance in the field of the sciences. It did not, however, consit merely of the grouping of a number of disciplines. A new vision of life was presupposed in it. In his view of life the Humanist dreamt not only of a number of disciplines but also of the end result of schooling therein: a new world in which the new, autonomous man would be dominant.

All too soon the Humanists began to realize, however, that while a glorious past could be recreated in dreams, dreaming within the confines of one's study alone was not adequate to build a new culture. Repristination, after all, did not seem to hold the true answer. The clock of history could not be reset at will. Too much stress on the authority of the writers of Antiquity, for example, checked originality: noble man could not be inhibited thus!

Renaissance man (in this brief survey I do not distinguish sharply between Humanism and the Renaissance) thus took a further step: Man could be reborn of his own power. He did not need the midwife of Christianity any more than that of pagan Antiquity. Man could pull himself up by his own bootstraps and be the source of his own light.

One of the antique trends which beautifully complemented the new spirit of Renaissance man was Stoicism, represented in Antiquity by figures such as Cicero and Seneca. This was a school of thought in which man and his imperturbable moral duties stood in the centre. Renaissance intellectuals liked the doctrine of "back to nature" (in the place of the Scriptural one of grace). The Stoa, however, did not find the laws for moral life *(logoi spermatikoi* of the *Logos)* only in nature. These laws or measuring rods they considered to be implanted in the reasoning faculty of man. Man was thus basically his own lawgiver and autonomous. Rationalism, seminally already present in the Early Stoicism, was eagerly embraced by Renaissance man and would soon assume a leading role in the Western world.

As a result of the initial trend to return to the past, a number of schools of thought dating from Antiquity (such as neo-Platonism, Aristotelianism, Pythagoreism, Epicurism and Scepticism) had revivals in the course of the fifteenth and sixteenth centuries. We cannot go into all these. We have to direct our attention now to a totally different group of men which found their light for a new cultue and society elsewhere.

The Reformation

The reformers also had an eversion from scholastic Medieval synthetic thinking. They broke with it, however, for the exact opposite reason than the Renaissance did, viz. to enable the Word of God to be freed again. Their thought can be regarded as being clearly anti-synthetic, spiritually directed to the right.

The reformers learnt a great deal from Antiquity. Like the precursors of the Reformation they also returned in many respects to the Church Fathers. The motive, however, lay in the fact that the *Patres* could be regarded as representing a purer period in the history of Christendom. Thus Augustine was for Calvin in the first place a guide back to the Word of God.

The Reformation clearly sought its source of light elsewhere. It did not look at pagan Antiquity; it did not look at the enlightened, noble, educated man come of age and reborn through his own devising, following the light of his own intellect. Whether one sought authority from the Pope or from enlightened man was in the eyes of the Reformers equally wrong.

Light for them emanated not from the earth but from Above. The Reformation sought not merely historical change on the horizontal level, but religious change on the vertical level of the relationship of man to God and his Law; not conversion to the past or reaction against the past or conversion from one's own power, but conversion to God and to his Word. Absolute authority belonged to God alone. The Word is the only source of light.

Calvin puts to the test the spirit of the times

It would be wrong — as many are so prone to do — to regard Calvin, out of a sense of piety, as a sort of sixteenth century Melchisedek: a man without beginning or background. He grew up within a certain period and was in many respects a child of his time. From his youth onwards he came into daily contact with all the spiritual trends of his environment. One could even say that his own thinking developed out of a continuing dialogue that he conducted with the various trends of thought current in his lifetime.

It would be wrong to try to explain Calvin's thought merely from extra-Biblical influences. It would be equally wrong, however, to claim that he underwent no influence other than the Bible.

A few remarks regarding Calvin and Humanism, Stoicism, and Platonism should serve to illustrate this.

Humanism

According to experts, Calvin was influenced especially by that type of

Humanism in which Philology, as a result of the literary renaissance, played an important role. This group, in their return to the sources, developed a specific historical philological method which prescribed an attitude of reverence towards the texts of Antiquity. The historical awareness and the effort to be objective towards the sources and to let them speak for themselves was a novelty.

Calvin had a lot to thank Humanism for in this respect. He assumed a similar attitude to the Scriptures. It was an enormous forward step that in his exegesis of the Scriptures he broke with the centuries-old allegorical exegesis, because this had been an important method for reading all sorts of foreign ideas into the Bible and thus effecting a synthesis between Scripture and pagan concepts.

Stoicism

The fact that Calvin's very first writing was a commentary on Seneca's *De Clementia,* would seem to indicate just how intimately he was aware of this school of thought. Some would suggest that Calvin's thought was in fact none other than "baptized Stoicism". The other extreme is represented by those who would plead that there is no evidence whatsoever of Stoic influence on Calvin.

One could, of course, use the concept "influence" in different ways. Personally I think influence of the Stoa can be detected on Calvin's idea of a *lex naturalis* and, concurrently, his idea of a *semen religionis* and *conscientia* (conscience).

Platonism

In research in this field one again has to do with two extreme viewpoints. Where some sin *per defectum* (by omission) by maintaining that Calvin had put aside completely the Platonising tendency (of Augustine, for example), others sin as it were *per exessum* (by commission) by totally over-estimating the influence of Platonism on Calvin.

My own tentative research in this field have convinced me that Calvin's thought underwent influence from Plato (and the neo-Platonists?) not only in the formal sense of word usage but also as regards content. His view of man (especially the way he sees the relationship between body and soul) is perhaps the clearest evidence of this.

I would not, however, go so far as to call Calvin a Platonist. That would presuppose a relationship of master and scholar which in this case definitely did not exist. What Calvin found useful in Plato he used — without becoming a disciple intent on confirming his master's ideas and careful that not one facet of it be changed.

It is a pity that limited time does not permit me to put a few quotations from Calvin's works on the table to illustrate what has thusfar being stated only in very general terms about possible influences of Humanism, Stoicism and Platonism. I do hope it will be possible during discussion of this paper.

Recapitulation

The Renaissance, with all the philosophical schools it revived in the sixteenth century, was at heart a religious movement to the left, away from the Word of God and the God of the Word. Calvin's religious bias was to the right. He was imbued by a different spirit.

Renaissance in essence was a rediscovery of Antiquity, a revival of original *paganism*. The essence of Reformation was the rediscovery of the Word of God, of genuine *Christianity*.

For that reason one has to be very careful not to come to the conclusion that Calvin was influenced by a specific philosophical school merely on the basis of similar word usage and parallel intellectual patterns. A more detailed analysis is necessary in which the relevant systems (e.g. the entire anthropology) can be fully and carefully compared.

One often gets the impression that Calvin did not take the philosophical material of his times too seriously. He normally dealt with it in a remarkably nonchalant manner. He used philosophical ideas as an illustration *of* the truth rather than as a guide *to* the truth. His thought was not carried by these ideas, but these ideas did contribute to the clarification and explication of what he was trying to say. Many times he mentions a certain viewpoint merely to bring out the contrast with his own ideas more clearly.

Calvin's use of Humanism, Stoicism and Platonism can be said to be eclectic rather than systematic. As far as I know, one finds no attempt in his work of a sustained systematic argumentation to deal with a specific philosophy fully and to argue in its favour.

All of this, however, does not take away the fact that Calvin did, as regards some of his ideas (such as his concept of natural law and his anthropology) immersed himself deeply in the philosophies of his time. Whoever reads what Calvin wrote in an unbiased fashion in the light of preceding history would have to acknowledge this.

Calvin's independence, however, is the most striking feature, guaranteed by the fact that the Source of his thought was the Word of God. Perhaps one should not evaluate Calvin negatively by the extent to which he submitted to extra-Biblical influences, but rather positively by inquiring to the extent to which he made a contribution to our renewed better understanding of the Word of God.

* * *

Although it has not happened within the prescribed time limit, the crime has geen committed and the whale is safely ensconced in the tin.

You see, Calvinism does not prevent one from sinning. The only thing is that it takes the enjoyment from the act of sin!

P.S.   For an elaboration in more detail (with bibliographical references) of the material discussed see Chapter 8 ("The intellectual decor of the Reformation with special reference to Calvin") of my book *Anatomy of Reformation*. Potchefstroom, Potchefstroom University for CHE, 1981 (page 164-214).

10.   JACQUES LEFÈVRE D'ETAPLES (c. 1455-1536). CALVIN'S FORERUNNER IN FRANCE

PROF. P.E. HUGHES*

Early in the year 1534 a young man, twenty-five years of age, made the journey to Nérac in the south-west of France in order to meet and confer with an old man, more than three times his age. That young man was John Calvin, and the aged fellow countryman he had sought out was Jacques Lefèvre d'Etaples. We know nothing of what transpired between the two, except that Theodore Beza, Calvin's colleague and successor in Geneva, records that Lefèvre gave Calvin a cordial welcome and, delighted with his visit, "predicted that he would be a distinguished instrument in the restoration of the kingdom of heaven in France" *(Johannis Calvini Vita)*.

This encounter took place at a time when Calvin was very definitely in a state of transition. He was in transition *physically,* uncertain as to what the future might hold for him and as to what might prove to be the right place for him to settle and work in. Not many weeks previously he had fled in disguise from Paris in order to avoid arrest and imprisonment, and perhaps execution. The occasion of this undignified exodus had been the delivery of a public oration in the capital by his friend Nicolas Cop, son of the king's physician, in his capacity as the newly appointed Rector of the University of Paris. The oration was a remarkably bold and clear declaration of evangelical beliefs, affirming the blessedness of those who suffer persecution for the sake of the Gospel and the uniqueness of the grace of God, who through his Word engenders faith and opens our hearts to receive the Gospel. It has been widely held that the real author of this oration was Calvin, not Cop: but this is questionable for a number of reasons. For one thing, the opening section is closely indebted to the exhortation which Erasmus prefixed to the third edition of his New Testament; for another, there seems to be demonstrable dependence on Bucer's Latin translation of a sermon of Luther's on the Beatitudes; and, further, as Wendel has remarked, there is much in the oration that accords

*   His address is: 1565 Cherry Lane, Rydal, PA 19046, USA.

with the evangelical position of Lefèvre — though Wendel is inexcusably misleading when he goes on to make the astonishing assertion that, "after an impartial examination of Lefèvre's writings, whatever has been advanced to show that Levèvre ever really adhered to the Reform or to its theological principles can be cast into the limbo of tendentious legend" *(Calvin: The Origins and Development of his Religious Thought,* 1963, pp. 41, 42). I believe I shall be able to demonstrate that the opposite is the truth. However, whatever the origin of Nicolas Cop's oration, there can be no doubt that Calvin was associated with him in its preparation. Its delivery evoked an immediate response of extreme hostility. Pressed by the Franciscans and the Sorbonne scholastics, the Parliament issued an order for the arrest of Cop and Calvin. Both, going separate ways, managed to make good their escape, the latter, it is said, from an upper window of the collège Fortet by means of a hastily knotted rope of bed-curtains and his identity concealed beneath the garb of a common vineyard labourer (see E. Doumergue, *Jean Calvin: Les hommes et les choses de son temps,* Vol. I, 1899, p. 354).

Calvin was also in transition *spiritually and intellectually.* The Cop incident indicated that his sympathies had been transferred from the unreformed traditions of his upbringing to the doctrines of the evangelical faith, though probably not yet openly so. The meeting with Lefèvre at Nérac may well have decided him to take his stand publicly with the evangelical cause. After the visit to Lefèvre he made the long journey to the town of his birth, Noyon, in the north, and surrendered the benefices which had been procured for him in childhood through his father's influence. He now knew what he had to do. From Noyon he made his way, with stops at Poitiers and Orléans, down to the city of Basel, and there, in the company of congenial spirits, including Nicolas Cop who had found refuge there, he worked diligently at the composition of his famous *Institutes of the Christian Religion (Christianae Religionis Institutio).* It was published in March 1536, a slender handbook of six chapters, which over the next two dozen years would grow into the much more massive work of twenty-eight chapters in four volumes now so familiar to us. The *Institutes* was essentially a contribution to the evangelical cause: addressed by a dedicatory letter to the King of France, the work was an *apologia* designed to win understanding and espousal of the reforming movement by clearly setting forth the biblical principles by which it was animated. The time of the publication of this first edition of the *Institutes* was also the time of the death of Lefèvre (who departed this life in the first months of 1536). The torch that he had lit and carried was now in the hands of John Calvin.

94

Something else of momentous significance to Calvin took place in the year 1536. He had decided to settle in Strassbourg, where the reformed faith had for some time been firmly established under the leadership of Martin Bucer, feeling that there he would find the peace and detachment which would enable him to give himself to study and authorship. The conflict between Francis I and Charles V made it advisable for Calvin to make a détour by way of Geneva, and in the month of July he arrived in that city with the intention of spending no more than one night there. These were perilous times and he was travelling under the assumed name of d'Espeville (in Basel he had used the pseudonym Lucanius); but his identity was made known to William Farel, who, in a manner typical of his fiery zeal, persuaded Calvin to remain in Geneva by pronouncing a curse on the seclusion he was seeking in Strassbourg and demanding that he should devote himself to the promotion of the reformation to which the city was already dedicated. It may be said that Lefèvre, though now dead, had a hand in this crisis of Calvin's career, for Farel had been brought to the evangelical faith in Paris a quarter of a century earlier through the witness of Lefèvre with whom he was then studying.

Who was this man Jacques Lefèvre d'Etaples? And why has the name of this personage, who courageously blazed the trail of evangelical renewal in France and whose reputation was on a level with that of his friend Erasmus (who died in the same year as Lefèvre) at the head of European scholarship in his day, fallen into such neglect? Perhaps the answer to the latter question is to be found in the fact that the reform of the French Church for which he lived and toiled indefatigably was never realized. Today, however, Lefèvre and his worth are being rediscovered and there are encouraging signs that he is at last beginning to gain once more the recognition that is his due.

Lefèvre, a native of Picardy like Calvin, was born in Etaples, a town on the channel coast at the north-east corner of France. The date of his birth is uncertain, but it was probably about the year 1455. As a youth he came to Paris and remained there for many years, first as a student and then as a teacher of philosophy and mathematics at the collège du Cardinal Lemoine, an institution founded for the education of scholars from his home region of Picardy. He was also ordained to the priesthood of the church. If there is one characteristic that gave direction and purpose to the whole of his life, it was his insistence on authenticity; and this authenticity was to be found only at the source, in the genuine and unsullied original or fountainhead of whatever subject one might be studying. In this respect he was a representative of the very best spirit of Renaissance humanism. Together with this went his intense and unremitting dedication as a scholar and a teacher to the work that he had in hand. His prolific output was the harvest of this application. For centuries a polluted stream of Aristotelian philosophy that had wandered far from the source had flowed through the schools and universities of Europe. Lefèvre set himself to remedy this situation by fulfilling the great labour of preparing for the press accurate Latin translations, together with commentaries and annotations, of the many works of the Aristotelian corpus. It is not surprising that his contemporaries praised him as the outstanding Aristotelian scholar of his day.

But the scope of his interest extended far beyond Aristotle. Interspersed with the Aristotelian publications were carefully edited works on mathematics and philosophy, often with his own running commentary, by a variety of authors which issued from Lefèvre's study; editions also of the Hermetic writings, of the works of Dionysius the Areopagite, of the mystical compositions of Ramon Lull, Jan van Ruysbroeck, Nicholas of Cusa, and others; *The Orthodox Faith* by John of Damascus and other works of a theological nature; and then, in the last decades of his life, his immense industry as he concentrated his energies on the task of translating and commenting on the text of Holy Scripture. But this was not all, for his hand was very much in the flow of publications that came from the able younger scholars who were his students and colleagues and who enjoyed the stimulation of his keen intellectual direction and supervision.

Lefèvre was ever a churchman of deep piety and seriousness. But he was none the less searching during the earlier part of his life searching for the pure fountain of truth, first in the philosophers of antiquity, whom he then regarded as theologians close, by reason of their antiquity, to the source of wisdom, and then feeling the attraction of mystical theology with the prospect it held out of the immediate experience of God, and then, finally, his discovery of the Gospel of the grace of God through the mediation of Jesus Christ. His publication, in 1499, of the works of Dionysius is instructive in this respect because it illustrates the transition that was then in process. We now know that these are pseudonymous writings, the composition of an unidentified author probably of the sixth century; indeed, as Lefèvre was aware, Nicholas of Cusa earlier in the fifteenth century had dismissed the author as a Platonist and Nicholas's contemporary Lorenzo Valla had incisively demonstrated the impossibility of the genuineness of these works. Lefèvre, however, was unwilling to abandon the conviction, which had for centuries prevailed in the Church and was still regarded as sacrosanct by the great majority of his contemporaries, that these writings had in fact been composed by St. Paul's Athenian convert, Dionysius the Areopagite (Acts 17:34). Consequently, he saw them as taking us back all but to St Paul himself and held them to be virtually a fount of apostolic and canonical truth.

We should take the publication of the works of the Pseudo-Dionysius, then, as an indication that Lefèvre was moving closer, in intention, even if not in actuality, to the authentic source of Holy Scripture; but it would be another decade before he succeeded in finding the reality for which he was feeling. Moreover, his enthusiasm at this juncture for the compositions of Dionysius was animated by another significant element in the make-up of his personality, namely, his intense spirit of patriotism: he constantly longed and laboured to wean his fellow countrymen away from unworthy preoccupations and to raise them to the highest level of spirituality. Hence his fearless assaults upon the soulless scholasticism and arid sophistries by which the academic world had for so long been dominated, and not least the University of Paris, and his denunciation of the currupt texts retained and used with such complacency and the futile formalities of medieval disputations over piffling points that had not the slightest relevance for serious scholarship or spiritual integrity or, for that matter, for the affairs of everyday life. It was little wonder that Lefèvre had bitter enemies among the self-inflated theologasters of the Sorbonne. The publication of the works of Dionysius fits within the pattern of his compaign for authenticity, and for the improvement not only of his university but of his country; for, according to a tradition which Lefèvre at that time gladly accepted, Dionysius the Areopagite had been the original apostle to France and the first bishop of Paris. Accordingly, he exhorted his fellow citizens: "Applaud your apostle, your first bishop, your parent who first brought you life and light, receive with honour his sacred teachings, and study them to your profit day and night". As always, Lefèvre is completely sincere; there is no suspicion of self-seeking on his part.

A significant milestone in lefèvre's spiritual pilgrimage was reached with the publication, in 1509, of his *Fivefold Psalter (Quincuplex Psalterium)*. Even though he had not yet bidden a final farewell to the ancient philosophers and the medieval mystics, the appearance of this work gave notice that the focus of his attention was now beginning to concentrate on the text of Holy Scripture, in which he had at last discovered the uniquely true source of all knowledge and wisdom.

Lefèvre was now definitely on the way to becoming the man of one book. His heart was now involved as well as his mind. This is made clear in dramatic fashion in the letter of dedication addressed to Cardinal Briçonnet.

While virtually all studies may be expected to bring some degree of pleasure and usefulness [Lefèvre writes], the study of divine truth alone promises not just pleasure and usefulness but the highest happiness: 'Blessed are they who search thy testimonies', the psalmist declares (Psalm 119:2). What study, then, should we pursue more eagerly or embrace more willingly?

Then follows Lefèvre's witness to the crisis of his own personal experience:

> For a long time [he confesses] I pursued human studies and paid little more than lip service to the study of divine things ...; but once I had tased them as it were from a distance, so much light shone forth that human learning seemed to me to be darkness in comparison, and so wonderful was the fragrance they breathed that nothing can be found on earth to compare with its sweetness ... I am accustomed to the cloistered life [he continues], but those who do not know this sweetness in my judgment have never tasted the true food of the soul.

In 1508, the year prior to the publication of the *Fivefold Psalter,* Lefèvre had moved to the Abbey of Saint-Germain-des-Prés at the invitation of his influential friend Guillaume Briçonnet, bishop of Lodève (son of the cardinal of the same name), who was then the abbot and wished with his aid to effect some salutary monastic reforms. Many of the monks, resentful of any change in the *status quo,* took themselves elsewhere, and thus left the way open for serious students to move into the cells they had vacated and to take advantage both of Lefèvre's devout learning and also of the abbey's splended library. Lefèvre told Cardinal Briçonnet that on many occasions he had asked monks who sought nourishment from the Scriptures what sweetness they had derived from their reading, and that for the most part they had replied that they had found nothing but some kind of "literal" sense, especially when they were trying to understand the Psalms (recited in their daily offices), and that this had left them dissatisfied and dejected.

The *Fivefold Psalter* of 1509 was Lefèvre's response to this situation. With its five different Latin versions, the fifth of which was. Lefèvre's own revision of the Vulgate, corrected by comparison with the Hebrew original, this work was, in part, a pioneering essay in textual criticism, and as such it called forth the displeasure of the theological establishment. But more important than this, it was a pioneering work in practical hermeneutics. In the preface Lefèvre propounded his principle of biblical exegesis which was destined to change the course of interpretation in the Church. Though he formulated this principle quite independently, it was a rediscovery rather than an innovation; and the time was undoubtedly ripe for its reappearance. For centuries a fourfold scheme of exposition (comprising four different senses: literal, allegorical, tropological, and anagogical) had been dominant, but in such a way that the literal sense was despised as superficial and of little worth, while the other three senses, which could all be subsumed under the one heading of the allegorical or mystical sense, purported to give the deep "spiritual" significance hidden beneath the rough surface of the scriptural text.

The effect on the Church of the allegorical method was pernicious, because it inevitably fostered an attitude of disdain and disregard for the plain, natural sense of the text and reduced the Bible to a book of intellectual word-puzzles; it led, further, to the spinning out of interpretations of the most elaborate and fantastic character which were as unedifying as they were fanciful; and, worst of all, it had the effect of taking the Bible out of the hands of the common people, who were regarded as ignorant and incapable of delving below the surface, and making it the preserve of inventive academics.

What Lefèvre did was to rescue the *literal* sense of the Scriptures. And by literal he did not mean literalistic; nor did he mean that there could be only one sense for the whole of Scripture. Depending on the context and the *genre* of a passage, the literal sense might be historical, allegorical, ethical, or eschatological, or even two or more of these together. The literal sense, moreover, was the *intended* sense. The psalmist, for example, was not merely writing about his own affairs, but was writing as a prophet through whom the Holy Spirit was speaking. Lefèvre insisted, then, that the proper literal sense was the sense intended by the Holy Spirit. But this sense was missed if the Holy Spirit was not present with regenerative power in the heart and mind of the reader or student of the Bible; and this consideration caused Lefèvre to postulate a *twofold literal sense:* (1) "the improper sense of those who are blind and fail to see, and who therefore understand divine things only in a carnal manner"; and (2) "the proper sense of those who see and are enlightened". "The former sense", he adds, "is fabricated by human reason; the latter is imparted by the divine Spirit". This explains the dejection of the monks with whom he had spoken: they had advanced no further than the improper literal sense of the Psalms. Accordingly, it was with the purpose of displaying the proper literal sense that Lefèvre "attempted to write a short exposition of the Psalms, with Christ as helper, who is the key of David" (of. Rev. 3:7). He showed how, under the inspiration of God's Spirit, the apostolic authors of the New Testament took passages from the Psalms and proclaimed their literal fulfilment in the person and work of Christ, and he arrived at the important conclusion that *"the literal sense and the spiritual sense coincide"*, the true sense being "not what is called allegorical or tropological, but the sense which the Holy Spirit speaking through the prophet intends". This sense was accessible to all persons, whether learned or uneducated, provided they were not strangers to the vital working of the Holy Spirit in their lives.

Lefèvre's hermeneutical principle was adopted and applied by the Continental and British reformers who followed him. Thus it was he who prepared the ground for the restoration of the interpretation of Scripture in accordance with its sane, natural, and christological sense. And one of the first to come under his influence in this respect was an as yet unknown monk named Martin Luther. A little under a hundred years ago (in 1885) a copy of the first (1509) edition of the *Fivefold Psalter* was found in the library of Dresden: its margins were profusely annotated in the handwriting of Luther — an eloquent witness to the great care with which the volume had been studied by the young German scholar. Like Lefèvre, Luther's first endeavours in biblical exegesis were devoted to the Book of Psalms (on which he started lecturing in 1513). It was from Lefèvre that he learnt the primary importance of the literal sense and the twofold distinction within that sense; and in expounding the Psalter he, too, sought to bring out the native sense, that, namely, intended by both divine and human authors, which he described as the "prophetic" literal sense, and which, distinct from the "historic" literal sense, pointed to and was fulfilled in the person and work of Christ. 1509, it may be worth noticing, was not only the year of the publication of Lefèvre's *Fivefold Psalter* but also the year of the birth of John Calvin.

Some three years later, in December 1512, Lefèvre's massive and masterly *Commentary on the Epistles of St Paul,* was published in Paris. This work marks a very considerable advance on the road to reform, for we now find Lefèvre crossing over the boundary into the territory of biblically reformed theology in advance of the Reformers themselves and scaling the heights of theological comprehension which would subsequently be occupied by those whose names were to become famous as leaders of evangelical revival in Europe. In 1512, Luther's nailing of his Ninety-Five Theses to the door of the cathedral in Wittenburg was still five years off, as also was Zwingli's campaign for reform in Zürich, and Calvin was an infant but three years of age. The doctrines which such men would proclaim as belonging to the very heart of the Gospel Lefèvre had already proclaimed with assurance in his commentary on St Paul's Epistles. The work was Lefèvre's own; it was not a rehash of the notions of earlier writers, not a chain of quotations from others, but the result of his own penetration into the mind and spirit of the great apostle. The ground on which he was now taking his stand was that of *sola scriptura.*

It must suffice for me to draw attention to Lefèvre's firm grasp of that doctrine which is central to the Gospel, namely, that the sinner is justified by the grace of God alone *(sola gratia)* through faith in Christ alone *(sola fide),* with the consequence that all the glory must be ascribed to God alone *(soli Deo gloria).* Indeed, these very Latin expressions, which were to become the banner-headlines of Reformation theology, occur and recur in his commentary. Thus he insists that saving righteousness "flows solely from the mercy of God" and that therefore "men ought to give the glory to God alone *(soli Deo gloria),* since it is impossible for them to be saved of themselves and by their own works". He actually calls it "the righteousness of faith and grace".

> Our sins [he writes] are not forgiven except through that propitiation set before God and interceding on our behalf by the blood of redemption, which was shed in the great sacrifice on the wooden altar. All these things are given to us freely; but he alone trod the winepress.

And he applies christologically, and in truly apostolic fashion, the affirmation of Isaiah 53:4f.: "He bore our griefs and he carried our sorrows; the Lord laid on him the iniquity of us all; the chastisement of our peace was upon him; and by his bruising we have been healed"

And who is the sinner [he asks] that, turning to the contemplation and heartfelt invocation of such great goodness of God, does not, with so great a Mediator, find pardon? And when the Apostle speaks of God as justifying him who has faith in Jesus he shows that this righteousness and justification are from God and not from men. Therefore no one should glory in himself and in his own works as though he could be saved by them; for there is no cause for glory save in God alone, in the wounds of Christ, and in his blood (on Rom. 3:21ff.).

All the blessings of the Gospel are effected by God's grace and mercy; and they are most of all necessary for us who have come from the death of sin to life in the Spirit as persons who are in extreme need and poverty. By grace alone *(per solam gratiam)* can we be saved ... For we are saved by his grace through faith - saved not because of ourselves, but by God's grace. For grace is a gift, not a work. And lest we should think that the faith by means of which we are justified is ours, even this is God's gift. Therefore we should attribute everything to God and nothing to ourselves, and so we should glory neither in ourselves nor in works, but in God's grace and mercy alone *(in sola Dei gratia et misericordia)* (on Eph. 2:8ff.).

This is the authentic note of that evangelical faith which is commonly associated with the theologians of the Reformation, but which, as the Commentary on the Pauline Epistles shows, Lefèvre sounded ahead of them. Through diligent study of the Scriptures he had found his own way to the great liberating truths of the Gospel. There were still advances in understanding for him to make and misguided notions for him to discard, but he would never deviate from the straight path along which he was now walking with assurance.

The sincerity of Lefèvre's commitment to the Gospel of grace is strikingly demonstrated in the conversion of William Farel (1489-1565). It was some two or three years before the appearance of the Commentary on Paul's Epistles that Farel, a young aristocrat from Gap (Dauphiné) in south-east France, arrived in Paris to join the company of scholars who were pursuing their studies under the direction of Lefèvre at Saint Germain-des-Prés. In a letter written years later (on 7 September 1527; for the text see A.L. Herminjard, *Correspondance des réformateurs dans les pays de langue française*, 9 vols., 1866-1897, Vol. II, pp. 42ff).

Farel described how he had come as a young man to Paris "burdened with the grossest superstition". "The more I endeavoured to advance and improve myself", he wrote, "the more I slipped backwards". The reading of many religious works left him unsatisfied. "I wished to be a Christian like Aristotle", he explained, "whom virtually all treated as Christian, hoping to eat good fruit from a bad tree". He turned away from the light of the plain teaching of Scripture. But then he went on to describe how the "saintly" Lefèvre was the instrument whose "gentle guidance" God used to bring him to trust in Christ as his sole Saviour and Mediator: "to him, after being driven hither and thither, my soul, once it had reached the haven, clung, and to him alone", he testified. Moreover, "things now took on a new appearance; Scripture began to be full of meaning, the Prophets plain, the Apostles clear, the voice of the Shepherd, Master, and Teacher Christ recognized".

Later, in his autobiographical *Letter to all Lords and Peoples and Pastors* of 1530, Farel narrated how Lefèvre had encouraged him to become a preacher of the Gospel and had "often said to me that God would renew the world and that I would see it"; and he acknowledged that it was Lefèvre who had persuaded him that there was no merit in anyone except Christ alone:

> By his instruction he drew me away from false opinions of merit, teaching me that we have no merits at all, but that all comes from the grace and mercy of God alone, without anyone else possessing any merit. And I believed this as soon as it was said to me.

In 1521 Lefèvre left Paris for Meaux, a city some twenty miles east of the capital, in response to an invitation from William Briçonnet who had been appointed bishop of Meaux at the end of 1515, and who previously had called Lefèvre to his side at Saint-Germain-des-Prés. He now wished Lefèvre to lead the work of reform in his diocese which he had taken over in a deplorable condition of spiritual apathy and disrepair. Lefèvre probably found it a welcome move. His bitter enemies at the Sorbonne had long been demanding his blood. Opponents of his reforming zeal were venomously denouncing him, together with Luther, Erasmus, and Reuchlin, as an antichrist. Lefèvre's impatience with the futile sophistries of academic scholasticism, his insistence on the natural interpretation of Scripture, his defence of Reuchlin in the Pfefferkorn affair, and his challenging, on biblical grounds, of a number of long entrenched traditions and practices were resented by those who could not bear the bubble of their authoritarian self-importance to be pricked.

Convinced as he now was that scriptural ground was the only secure ground, Lefèvre was able to view this hostility with serenity. "Do not take it amiss that many are opposed to my writings", he wrote in 1519 (to Cornelius Agrippa of Nettesheim). "... I believe the day is coming when the truth of these things will be more clearly seen ... Falsehood withers away by itself and at length collapses without an attacker".

Once Lefèvre was at Meaux the prospects for the advance of the Gospel in that diocese and from there to other parts of France looked bright. Briçonnet, the bishop of Meaux, who was himself a member of an influential family and a distinguished ecclesiastical statesman, gave him the full weight of his support and collaborated with him in bringing together a team of outstanding young men to put into effect the programme for the evangelization and spiritual revitalization of the diocese. Briçonnet, moreover, was the close friend and confidant of the king's sister, Marguerite d'Angoulême, who had aligned herself with the evangelicals and was a constant advocate of their cause at the court. The king's attitude seemed to be more vacillating, largely because of vacillating fortunes in the game of international politcs in which he was involved, but he repeatedly came forward as the protector of Lefèvre against the designs of those who wished to do him ill. There was much justification, therefore, for his bright vision of the conquest of France by the Gospel and for his confidence that God would renew the world, even though he might not live to see it. Meanwhile this is the grand objective to which he devoted all of his considerable energy with undeviating singleness of purpose.

In June 1522 his Latin *Commentary on the Four Gospels (Commentarii initiatorii in Quatuor Evangelia)* was published. It confirms the conclusion that the Word of God was now his sole and passionate obsession.

Thus in the preface, addressed to "Christian readers", he affirmed:

The Word of God is sufficient; this alone is enough for the discovery of the life which knows no end; this rule alone is the guide to eternal life; all else on which the Word of God does not shine is as unnecessary as it is superfluous.

It is, indeed, an appeal to the Church to return to the pure source of the living waters of the Gospel:

Would that standard of belief might be sought from the

primitive Church which consecrated so many martyrs to Christ, which knew no rule apart from the Gospel, which had no goal but Christ, and which offered worship to none except the Triune God. Truly, if we lived according to this custom, the eternal Gospel of Christ would flourish now as it flourished then.

But Latin was for scholars, and Lefèvre was well aware that if the populace as a whole were to be reached it would have to be in their own language (this was another basic principle of reform). Accordingly, he set himself to the translation of the Bible into the language of the French people, and in June 1523, just a year after his Latin commentary on the Gospels, his French translation of the Gospels issued from the press. Five months later this French version of the New Testament was completed with the appearance of a volume containing the Pauline Epistles, the Catholic Epistles, the Acts of the Apostles, and the Apocalypse in that order. This work of translation meant, as Lefèvre explained in the preface to the earlier volume, that "the simple members of the body of Christ, having this in their own language, can be as certain of the evangelical truth as those who have it in Latin".

Next to appear, again at an interval of just a few months (in February 1524), was Lefèvre's French translation of the Psalms, and the labour of translating to Old Testament into French was completed in four volumes which were published successively between April and September in 1528; and then, in 1530, Lefèvre's translation of the whole Bible was brought out in a single volume. Thus by tireless application to the task he had set before himself he gave practical expression to his conviction that "the time has now come when our Lord Jesus Christ, our sole salvation, truth, and life, wishes that his Gospel should be purely proclaimed throughout the whole world" (in the preface to the translation of the Gospels). Another work belonging to this period, his *Commentary on the Catholic Epistles,* which was the last of his Latin commentaries, was completed, it seems, late in 1524, though not published until the middle of 1527.

The year 1525 proved to be a year of crisis. During the course of that year — probably in the summer, though the date is uncertain — the publication took place of an anonymous volume in the French language containing the *Epistles and Gospels for the Fifty-Two Weeks of the Year,* each of which was followed by a brief homily or exhortation which was simple, practical, and evangelical in tone. The anonymity may possibly be attributable to an edict of the Sorbonne of

1523 forbidding the publication of any French translations of the Scriptures; but as it was a volume intended in the first place not for the academic world but for use in the parishes of the diocese of Meaux, the mention of authorship probably seemed irrelevant. In any case, Lefèvre's enemies in Paris seized on it and unhesitatingly described it as the work of "Jacques Lefèvre and his disciples". The evidence, in fact, is conclusive that the volume's exhortations were fundamentally the work of Lefèvre, though actually prepared under his close supervision by four of his younger colleagues. The work was essentially an instrument of reform, designed to make an explanation of the teaching of the Bible available to all in simple terms and in the language of the people.

On 6 November 1525 the theologians of the Sorbonne censured 48 propositions extracted from the exhortations, denouncing them variously as heretical, scandalous, odious, false, rash, impious, erroneous, schismatic, Lutheran, etc. A scrutiny of the doctrines condemned by the Sorbonne as "diabolical inventions and heretical fantasies" shows very plainly that they bore what was becoming the hallmark of the teaching of the Reformation, though Lefèvre had learned them from his own independent and prior study of Scripture: such doctrines, for example, as those which affirm that the salvation of the sinner is owed entirely to the grace of God and not at all to any supposed human merit, that justification is not in any degree by works but solely by faith in the perfect atoning work of Jesus Christ, and that therefore it is not to any saint or angel or other creature that we must look for grace and help but only to God, to whom alone belongs all the glory for our redemption.

All the circumstances seemed to be in favour of Lefèvre's adversaries. The king of France (Francis I), who had previously given instructions that Lefèvre was not to be molested, had suffered defeat in battle at Pavia in February of 1525 and been carried off captive to Spain. A few weeks before the Sorbonne's censure of the 48 propositions the Parliament had been persuaded to issue an edict requiring Lefèvre and others to be brought to judgment in Paris. The captive king actually tried to intervene from afar by sending an injunction to stop the persecution of these persons. He reminded the Parliament that the Sorbonnists had previously (in 1523) assailed Lefèvre with accusations and calumnies of which he had been completely cleared, and he demanded that Lefèvre should be free from slander and violence. But the enemies of Levèvre, feeling that the king's message from his Spanish prison could safely be disregarded, were determined to go their own way. Meanwhile however, Lefèvre and some of his friends who had avoided arrest had succeeded in fleeing the country. Lefèvre found refuge and hospitality in the home of Capito in Strassbourg. There he enjoyed the stimulating fellowship of Martin Bucer and other reforming leaders. But the exile did not last long, for the release of the king and his return to France in the spring of 1526 opened the way for Lefèvre and his friends to resume their ministry in the homeland. At the invitation of the king Lefèvre went to Blois, near Orléans, where he was given the double responsibility of organizing the royal library and serving as tutor to Charles, the youngest of the royal princes, then only four years old (his two elder brothers were being held hostage in Spain). Otherwise his energies were concentrated on the task of completing the translation of the Bible into French. The closing years of his life, from 1530 onwards, were spent in the peaceful security of Marguerite's chateau at Nérac, and it was there that Calvin paid him the visit mentioned at the beginning of this paper.

Calvin first came to Paris as a young student in 1523, that is, at a time when Lefèvre was no longer himself in the capital, though not far away in Meaux. It was a time, moreover, when Lefèvre's reputation as a scholar was at its height and his person the centre of controversy, with distinguished friends on the one hand and bitter enemies on the other. It is impossible that Calvin should have been unaware of his fame and unlikely that he would have been unfamiliar with his work and his writings. Was it then that he first felt the influence of this remarkable man? It would be gratifying to have a definite answer to this question, but as things are we must be content to remain in uncertainty.

However much the ways of Lefèvre and Calvin may have differed ecclesiastically, it is not unjust to say that theologically Calvin followed closely the path that had been pioneered by Lefèvre. The provision of the best possible version of the Bible in the language of the people became a matter of the greatest importance for him. His cousin, Pierre Robert Olivétan, was then working on a revision, by careful comparison with the Hebrew and Greek originals, of Lefèvre's translation of the Scriptures which had been published in Antwerp in 1530, and Calvin now joined him in this work. The resulting volume was brought out the following year (1535) in Neuchâtel. Calvin continued to labour at the improvement of the French version of the Scriptures for many years after this. Affinities to the thought of

Lefèvre are evident in the two prefaces (one in Latin and one in French) that Calvin wrote for Olivétan's Bible, not least in the expression of the intense desire to increase in christlikeness, or *christiformitas* as Lefèvre called it, and in the emphasis on the redemptive knowledge of Christ as the supreme purpose of the doctrine of Scripture. The sum of all biblical study and searching, Calvin asserted, is "to know Jesus Christ and the infinite riches comprised in him".

> What more could we demand for the spiritual doctrine of our souls than to know God, to be transformed in him, and to have his glorious image stamped upon us? ... Let all our understanding be concentrated on this point, to learn in Scripture to know Jesus Christ and him only, in order that we may be led by him straight to the Father, who contains in himself all perfection.

In such aspirations the hearts and minds of Lefèvre and Calvin were entirely at one.

11. JOHN KNOX AND THE WORD OF GOD: A COMPARISON WITH JOHN CALVIN

PROF. V.E. D'ASSONVILLE*

Only a few of Knox's works are devoted to certain dogmatic aspects, such as e.g. the sacraments and predestination. What his views were on other important doctrines such as those of the *Holy Scriptures,* the *Covenant of Grace* and the *Church,* cannot be established decisively from any of his writings alone, but must be determined also with reference, inter alia, to the whole variety of letters, controversial documents, discussions and his own record of the Church History of Scotland.[1] This eventually becomes a voyage of discovery through six volumes from which Knox's statements can be gathered in a fragmentary fashion.

And yet, even though Knox, unlike Calvin, did not write any one specific chapter dealing with the Holy Scriptures,[2] we can still soon discover what was his view of the Scripture and what the place of God's Word in his thoughts and that of his fellow Scots Reformers. Fairly recently one of the greatest experts on Knox in our time, Prof W. Croft Dickenson, stated:

"The stress was on the Word of God, and on the rejection of all beliefs and practices for which no warrant could be found in God's plain Scriptures, written and revealed. The call was for a church freed from corruption, and from all man-made ceremony and invention. A church based fair and square on the Word of God, and a church that would preach the Word of God to the people. And reliance upon the

* His address is: Dept. of Ecclesiastical History, Potchefstroom University for Christian Higher Education, Potchefstroom, RSA 2520.

[1] For a full picture of all the works of Knox, see David Laigh, The Works of John Knox, 6 vols. For a few other works, see Peter Lorimer, John Knox and the Church of England.

[2] Cf. Calvin's "De Similitudine ac Differentia veteris et novi Testamenti" in the Institutes of 1539-1554, C.R. 1, p. 801 ff.

Word of God was the very core and essence of the Scottish Confession of Faith."[3]

The extent to which the Reformation cause in Scotland was concentrated around the Word of God from the start, is a subject which is in itself such a wide and exceptionally deep one, that it is impossible for us to examine it thoroughly. Fortunately excellent studies on the subject do exist, though the last word has not yet been said.[4]

However, before we commence with a comparison between Knox and Calvin, a few remarks about the rôle of the Word of God in the 16th century Reformation, will not be out of place here.

The Reformation was a re-discovery of the Word

In essence the Reformation of the 16th century differed wholly from the movements of the *Renaissance* and *Humanism*. Firstly, it was not concerned with a renewal in *science* and *arts* and the improvement of *social* and *political* conditions, but was, in its origin, purely religious in nature.[5] Its principle is briefly and powerfully expressed in the tripartite creed: *Scriptura sola, gratia sola, fides sola,* in other words, the Scriptures alone, grace alone, faith alone!

But this was not a *new* principle; it was the old Gospel of Jesus Christ and which was preached by the apostles in the first century of the Christian era. After the Dark Ages,[6] it was a new *discovery* and

---

[3] The writer of this article personally took this down from an address given by Prof. Dickinson on 11th May 1959, in the St John's Kirk, Perth, in commemoration of a sermon by John Knox in the same church 400 years before. This address by Dickinson was also broadcast by the BBC (Scottish Home Service) and on 11th and 12th May 1959 a report on the address appeared in "The Scotsman".

[4] We refer, inter alia, to the outstanding work of D. Hay Fleming, The Scottish Reformation.

[5] For a more detailed exposition of this, see H. Bavinck, De Hervorming en ons Nationale Leven, Ter Herdenking der Hervorming, p. 7 ff.

[6] With the term "Dark Ages" we do not merely want to repeat a cliche, in which there was no room for "enlightenment" in many spheres, but we use the term in the fullest sense of the word as a description of the religious degeneration caused by the fact that the Scriptures were no longer understood. This in turn caused an atmosphere of pessimism, suitriness and weariness of life to hang over Europe. It can almost be described little better than in the sombre lament of the poet Eustache Deschamps. The decrepitude of the world and the way in which all good things disappeared from it,

re-discovery. As *Columbus* discovered the New World and the Renaissance revived toe old Latium and Hellas, so the Reformation shed new light on the meaning and significance of the Holy Scriptures. The Word of God, as revealed in the Scriptures, began to take over the dominant rôle in the church in a radical way.[7]

We see this, in particular, if we take up, in earnest, the claim of Roman Catholicism that the Pope is the "Vicarius Christi". This is an express attempt to give the church full control over all spheres of life. And with this the church came to rule over the Scriptures as well. The church, according to Roman Catholic theology,[8] precedes the Scriptures temporally and logically. The church was there before the Scriptures and therefore does not owe its origin and authority to the Scriptures, but exists through Christ and the Holy Spirit which inhabits the church. The Holy Schriptures, on the other hand, originated from the church and lends its authority to the church.[9]

Roman Catholic theology correctly saw that the dominion of Christ over all spheres of life is a totalitarian dominion, but the fact that this dominion was further subordinated to the church obviously gave the Scriptures a sub-ordinate rôle. For example, compare the decisive rôle which the church played in regard to the determination of the

becomes the description of the Middle Ages before the break-through of the Reformation:

> "Temps de doleur et de temptacion,
> Aages de plour, d'envie et de tourment,
> Temps de langour et de dampnacion,
> Aages meneur près du definement,
> Temps plains d'orreur qui tout fait faussement,
> Aages menteur, plain d'orgueil et d'envie,
> Temps sanz honeur et sanz vray jugement,
> Aage en tristour qui abrege la vie."

(Uit: J. Huizenga, Herfstij der Middeleeuwen, p. 32.)

[7] This point is not only stressed by protestant theologians, but also the brilliant Roman Catholic scholar, H. Daniel-Rops, conceded it. Roman Church leaders before the sixteenth century were in many aspects no less concerned than the Reformers that much was in need of reform, but one thing remained: "to translate these undeniable excellent intentions into deeds". Cf. Daniel-Rops, *The Protestant Reformation,* pp. 132, 133.

[8] Cf. Bavinck, H. op cit I, p. 480 ff.

[9] Ibid; Berkouwer, G.C. Conflict met Rome, p. 20 ff.

canon at the Council of Trent.[10]

The question is a very simple one: Which is the αὐτοπιστιου *the church* or the *Scriptures?*

This is the facal point of the dispute between Rome and the Reformation. It is the question of *authority.* The *authority of the church* or the *authority of the Scriptures?* In Roman Catholic theology it is the *church* which says: Causa finita est (the matter is decided),[11] but the Reformers demanded: δος μοι που στω (show me where it stands)![12] Irrespective of the differences in their views of the Scriptures on secondary issues,[13] the Reformers did not differ on the "sola Scriptura".

In the stormy times after *Luther* had published his 95 theses there remained to him only one refuge from the authority of the Pope and the Council of the Church, viz the Scriptures alone. It was one of the greatest historical moments in world history when he proclaimed the authority of God's Word over his conscience before the Diet at Worms on 18th April 1521:

"Since then Your Majesty and you lordships desire a simple reply, I will answer without horns and without teeth. Unless I am convicted by Scripture and plain reason — I do not accept the authority of popes and councils, for they have contradicted each other — my conscience is captive to the Word of God. I cannot and I will not recant anything, for to go against conscience is neither right nor sane. Here I stand, I cannot do otherwise. God help me. Amen."[14]

It is impossible to devote more space to Luther and it will suffice to say that throughout his doctrine he clung to the "autoritates Scripturae

[10] Ibid.

[11] Berkouwer, op cit p. 23.

[12] Bavinck, op cit p. 497.

[13] Cf. the views of Calvin and Luther about the canon of the Scriptures.

[14] Bainton, Roland H. Here I stand, A Life of Martin Luther, p. 185; Kooiman W.J. By Faith Alone, p. 64.

divinae."[15]

No less than Luther, *Calvin* also consistently upheld the authority of the Holy Scriptures. It was he who developed a doctrine in this regard in his Institutes in which he stated that nothing "can be more absurd than the fiction, that the power of judging Scripture is in the church, and that on her nod its certainty depends."[16]

Even the letter accompanying the *first edition* of the Institutes, which Calvin addressed to the French king, Francis, was one long plea for the authority of the Scriptures as the "sceptre of God".

"The characteristic of a true sovereign is, to acknowledge that, in the administration of his kingdom, he is a minister of God. He who does not make his reign subservient to the divine glory, acts the part not of a king, but a robber. He, moreover, deceives himself who anticipates long prosperity to any kingdom which is not ruled by the *sceptre of God,* that is, *by his divine Word.*"[17]

The way in which Calvin frequently brings the real secret of the Reformation to the fore, is magnificent. Like a refrain it constantly returns, that the Scriptures do not derive their authority from an ecclesiastical institution or from arguments or proofs, but in themselves alone, through the Holy Spirit:

"Let it therefore be held as fixed, that those who are inwardly taught by the Holy Spirit acquiesce implicitly in Scripture; that Scripture, carrying its own evidence along with it deigns, not to submit to proofs and arguments, but owes the full conviction with which we ought to receive it to the testimony of the Spirit."[18]

---

[15] For a detailed exposition and documentary proof that Luther upheld the "autoritates Scripturae divinae", see J.C.S. Locher, De Leer van Luther over Gods Woord, Amsterdam, 1903.

[16] O.S, III, p. 66: "Vannissimum est igitur commentum, Scripturae iudicandae potestatem esse penes Ecclesiam: ut ab huius nutu illius certitudo pendere intelligatur".

[17] From the "Prefatory address to his most Christian Majesty, the most mighty and illustrious monarch, Francis, King of the French". Beveridge translation, I, p. 5, O.S, III, p. 11; C.R, I, pp. 11, 12.

[18] O.S, III, p. 70: "Maneat ergo hoc fixum, quos Spiritus sanctus intus docuit, solide acquiescere in Scriptura, et hanc quidem esse αὐτοπιστον, etc". Inst (1559), I, vii, 5.

113

These extracts from the Institutes, in which Calvin so unequivocally acknowledges the authority of the Scriptures, can be multiplied tenfold.[19] The "authoritas Scripturae" is prominently in the foreground.[20] The "Scriptures are from God,"[21] they come "from the very mouth of God"[22] and consequently Calvin sees no distinction between the Holy Scriptures and the Word of God, "hence, the highest proof of Scripture is uniformly taken from the character of Him whose word it is."[23]

So central a position does the Word of God occupy in Calvin's plea, that it cannot remain a calm and quiet argument; flushed with his conviction, he utters an urgent appeal: *"Ad verbum, inquam, est veniendum ...!"*

"We must go I say, to the Word, where the character of God, drawn from His works, is described accurately and to the life; these works being estimated, not by our depraved judgement, but by the standard of eternal truth."[24]

And these are precisely the words which *John Knox* must have read in the 1539 Institutes. But he not only *read* them. He suited the deed to the word. The "ad verbum est veniendum" (we must go to the Word) is the one main theme of Knox's reform work. It is precisely in this that he reveals himself as a fiery Calvinist and through this gave the Scottish church its own individual stamp.

And yet, in the *application* of this calvinistic principle of Scriptural authority, Knox often deviated very far from his teacher and showed his own original individuality.

[19] Also Cf O.S, III, pp. 60, 62, 63, 65, 66, 67, 69, 72 ff.

[20] Note how Calvin starts two of the Chapters of the 1559 Institutes: I, vii, 1, taken over from the 1543 edition and I, viii, 1, taken from the 1539 edition; O.S, III, pp. 65 and 71.

[21] O.s, III, p. 70: "a Deo esse Scripturam".

[22] Ibid: "ab ipsissimo Dei ore ad nos fluxisse".

[23] Ibid, p. 68: "Itaque summa Scripturae probatio passim a Dei loquentis persona sumitur".

[24] C.R, 1, p. 293; O.S, III, p. 63.

114

To prove this *similarity* to and *difference* from Calvin in regard to the Word of God further, we shall even have to return to Knox's first public appearance, i.e. when he took refuge with other Protestants in St Andrews in 1547. From the disputes he had with the Roman Catholic leaders and from the summary of his first sermon which still remains, (as Knox expressed it in his own words), we soon gain an indication of the exceptionally important place of the Word of God in all his thoughts. To Dean John Annand, who regarded the authority of the church as supreme, an authority which "damned all Lutherans and heretics", Knox put the typical Reformation principle that the true church must first be defined in accordance with the marks which God's Scripture contains.[25] And in the first sermon which followed on this, Knox stated the mark of the true church to be *"the voice of its own pastor, Jesus Christ"* — in other words, the Gospel.[26]

We say that the definition of the true church in accordance with the mark of the Word is a typical principle of the Reformation, because we find it in most of the confessions of the Reformation.[27]

But what is of great importance to us is the fact that we find the exact thoughts of Knox about the Word as the mark of the true church, *"the voice of its own pastor, Jesus Christ"*, in the first edition of Calvin's *Institutes.* (The possibility exists that he may have used this edition of the Institutes as a catechism in St Andrews.[28])

Calvin also brings the Word as the characteristic of the true church to

---

[25] Dickinson's Knox, I, p. 83.

[26] Ibid.

[27] Cf. The Ten Theses of Berne, Art 1;
   The First Helvetic Confession of 1536 (The Second Confession of Basel), art 14;
   The Lausanne Articles of 1536, art V;
   The Geneva Confession of 1537, art 18;
   The Confession of Faith used in the English Congregation at Geneva, 1556, art IV;
   The French Confession of Faith, 1559, art XXVIII;
   The Augsburg Confession, art VII;
   The Hungarian Confession, MM 428-9;
   Article XIX of the Church of England;
   The Scottish Confession of Faith, 1560, art XVIII;
   The Belgic Confession 1561 ("Nederlandsche Geloofsbelijdenis"), art 29;
   The Second Helvetic Confession, 1566, chapter XVII;
   (Cf further, Philip Schaff, The Creeds of the Evangelical Protestant Churches, London, 1877, Arthur C. Cochrane, Reformed Confessions of the 16th Century, Philadelphia, 1966).
[28] See my "John Knox and the Institutes of Calvin", Durban, 1968, p. 3.

the fore in the image of the Good Shepherd to whose voice the sheep listen:

"Haec enim perpetua est nota, qua signavit suos Dominus noster: qui est ex veritate, inquit audit vocem meam (Ioan 10. 18)."[29]

Calvin was later to expand and develop this principle of the Word as the mark of the true church still further in the later editions of the Institutes[30] but it also consistently remained Knox's belief.[31]

As regards the dominion of the Word over the Church and over all spheres of life, Knox, like Calvin, was in no doubt whatsoever, "as for me, I will be of none other church except of that which hath Christ Jesus to be pastor, which hears his voice, and will not hear a stranger."[32]

The absolute dominion of God's Word over the State, is another of Knox's primary principles. In a sermon which was also heard by Darnley, the husband of Mary Queen of Scots, he stated expressly:

"Kings then have not an absolute power in their regiment what pleaseth them; but their power is limited by God's Word: so that if they strike where God commaundeth not, they are but murderers; and if they spare when God commaundeth to strike, they and their throne are criminal and giltie of the wickednesse that aboundeth upon the face of the earth, for lacke of punishment."[33]

In regard to the *formal principle,* that the Bible is God's Word and that God exercises his authority over church and state and all spheres of life through the Bible, Knox does not differ from Calvin. On the contrary, where the authority of the Scriptures is concerned, he is one of the most fiery exponents of the Reformation. That the final

---

[29] C.R, I, p. 211; Cf. ibid, pp. 75, 77, 212.

[30] O.S, V, pp. 12-16.

[31] "But this Church which is visible and seen by the eye has three tokens or marks whereby it may be known. First, the Word of God ..." etc. (From the Confession of Faith used in the English Congregation at Geneva, 1556, art. IV.)
Cf. further The Scottish Confession of Faith, 1560, art. XVIII.

[32] Dickinson's Knox, i, p. 92.

[33] Laing's Knox, vi, p. 238.

decision is to be found in the Word of God, Knox regarded as a *sine qua non* even to his Queen. When, in the crisis of the conflict between Roman Catholicism and the Protestant faith, she cried out, "Whom shall I believe? And who shall be judge?" his reply is clear and to the point:

"Ye shall believe God that plainly speaketh in his word: and further than the word teaches you, ye neither shall believe the one or the other."[34]

Here all the *subjectivity* of Knox himself, or the individual group or tradition or custom or utility, are simply penetrated by the statement of the one *objective truth* which holds good for everyone: the Word!

But the great *difference between Knox and Calvin* (and Luther as well) relates to Knox's view of the Scriptures. What does he make of the *contents* of the Scriptures?

What, to Knox, is the Word of God?

This Word of God, which, to Knox, occupies such an all-dominating place in theology and church and community, is usually expressed in stereotyped phrases which occur throughout his works, such as:

"The playn Word of God", *"the express Word of God"*, *"God's own express commandment"*, *"express commandement of Jesus Christ"*, *"buke of Godis Law, that is, of all his Ordinances"*, *"the strict Word of God"*, etc.[35]

With these expressions Knox gives us an indication of what he means by "God's Word". If we examine it in the context in which he uses it, we soon realise that he understands the Word of God *literally*, in the strictest sense, precisely as it stands in the Bible.

Luther also regarded the Bible as God's Word,[36] but he did not hesitate to reject the epistle of James as "ein recht strohern

---

[34] Dickinson's Knox, ii, p. 18.

[35] See, inter alia, Dickinson's Knox, i, pp. 89, 91; Laing's Knox, iii, pp. 34, 35, 37, 38; ibid, iv, pp. 437, 468; ibid, v, p. 516; ibid, vi, p. 80.

[36] Locher op cit, pp. 52, 136.

117

Epistel"[37] on the strength of the *content* of the Scriptures in the face of ecclesiastical authority. Thus in Luther we find, in contrast to Knox, the total domination of the substantive *content* of the Bible over the *literal form* of the Scriptures.

In Calvin, however, there is a sound balance between the *letter* and the *sub*-stance of the Scriptures. He is too conservative, on the one hand, to tamper with e.g. the canonicity of the Scriptures, but, on the other hand, he ascribes the primary authority to the substantive content.[38]

However, when we come to Knox, we see that, in comparison with Luther and Calvin, an overemphasis on the literal form of the Scripture above the substantive content. Therefore the Scriptures are, to him, the "express Word of God" or the "playn commandement of God".

In this regard we may then call Knox a *radical* Reformer who knew no middle way even in moderate affairs in which no principles are involved (the so-called "indifferential" of Calvin).

"In religioun thair is no middes: either it is the religioun of God, and than in everie thing that is done it must have the assurance of his awn Worde, and than is his Majestie trewlie honourit, or els it is the religioun of the Devill."[39]

Calvin would have agreed wholeheartedly with this as long as the evangelical character of the Scriptures is not exchanged for a statutory set of regulations. And this is the danger which is constantly present in Knox.

This brings us to the question of the actual *starting-point* in Knox's view of the Scriptures. This he stated even in the castle of St Andrews right at the start of his reform work, viz the Scriptural text of Deut. 12:32 as he himself quotes it:

---

[37] Ibid, p. 200.

[38] For example, Calvin explains the canonicity of the Epistles of James and 2 Peter, not *a priori* but *a posteriori:* "mihi ad epistolam hanc recipiendam satis est, quod nihil continet Christi apostolo indignum". Cf. P.J. Kromsigt, John Knox als Kerkhervormer, p. 325.

[39] Laing's Knox, iv, p. 232.

"'All that the Lord thy God commands thee to do, that do thou to the Lord thy God: add nothing to it; diminish nothing from it.' *By this rule* think I that the Kirk of Christ will measure God's religion, and not by that which seems good in their own eyes."[40]

The same point is made in the "Treatise on Justification by Faith" of Balnaves, with which Knox expresses his complete agreement[41] and after that it is stressed with *much emphasis* in Knox's first work of a theological nature, i.e. his "A Vindication of the doctrine that the Mass is idolatry".[42] In the case of the latter we have already seen how he differs from Calvin on this particular point.[43] Whereas Calvin opposes the Roman Catholic Mass from the point of view of the *content* of the Scripture, viz that it denies salvation by mercy and that the doctrine of transubstantiation makes idols of the elements of bread and wine, Knox opposes the Mass on the strength of the formal fact that it is not commanded by the Scriptures.

The consequence of this view, viz *Deut. 12:32* as "a rule for the Kirk of Christ", cannot but lead to *radicalism* in the spheres of *liturgy* and *ceremony*. When Knox, in England, censured the practice of kneeling as prescribed in the Book of Common Prayer, on the strength of this premise (do nothing which is not expressly commanded), he incurred the opposition of no less a man than *Cramner*. Writing to the Privy Council on 7th October 1552, Cramner rejected Knox's view entirely:

"But, say they, it is not commanded in the Scripture to kneel, and whatsoever is not commanded in the Scripture is against the Scripture, and utterly unlawful and ungodly. But this saying is the chief foundation of the error of the Anabaptists and of divers other sects. This saying is a subversion of all order as well in religion as in common policy. If this saying be true, take away the whole Book of Service. For what should men travail to set an order in the form of service, if no order can be set but that (which) is already prescribed by the Scripture."[44]

---

[40] Dickinson's Knox, i, p. 89.

[41] Laing's Knox, iii, p. 517.

[42] See Supra, p. 24 ff.

[43] Supra, pp. 26 and 27.

[44] Lorimer, op cit, p. 104.

Calvin also saw that Knox's view of the Scriptures as it relates to religious ceremonies goes too far and therefore warned Knox in a letter dated 23rd April 1561:

"In regard to ceremonies, I trust that your strictness, although it may displease many, will be regulated by discretion. We should, indeed, do our endeavour that the Church may be purged of all the defilements which flowed from error and superstition. We should also earnestly strive that the mysteries of God be not polluted by absurd or unmeaning mixtures. With this exception, you know well that certain things, though not positively approved, must be tolerated."[45]

In this regard we have already seen how Calvin makes room in his *Institutes* for the "indifferentia" which is "nihil refert" in the outward ceremonies.[46]

Related to this premise of Knox, we also find that he has an individual view of the Old Testament, which gives his theology and his sermons their own specific stamp. In this respect he differs to such a great extent from Calvin that we must devote some attention to this.

Calvin's view of the Old Testament according to the Institutes

Calvin took so serious a view of the correct approach to the Old and New Testaments and their relationship to each other, that, even in the 1539 edition of the Institutes, he devoted a special chapter to the subject under the heading "De similitudine ac differentia Veteris et Novi Testamenti".[47] He later developed this still further until it occupied two chapters in the final edition (1559).[48]

The similarity and the difference between the two Testaments which Calvin brings to the fore in a long argument, are summarised by Calvin as follows:

"The covenant made with all the fathers in so far from differing from

---

45 Laing's Knox, iv, p. 124.

46 Supra, p. 27.

47 C.R, I, p. 801 ff.

48 Institutes (1559), II, x and xi.

ours in reality and substance, that it is altogether one and the same: still the administration differs."[49]

Elsewhere he states in regard to the *differences* "that they all belong to the mode of administration rather than to the substance" (ad modum administrationis potiusquam ad substantiam).[50]

The unity and substance (substantia) are seen by Calvin to consist mainly in *three* things:

"First, that temporal opulence and felicity was not the goal to which the Jews were invited to aspire, but that they were admitted to the hope of immortality, and that assurance of this adoption was given by immediate communications, by the Law and by the Prophets. *Secondly,* that the covenant by which they were reconciled to the Lord was founded on no merits of their own, but solely on the mercy of God, who called them; and, *thirdly,* that they both had and knew Christ the Mediator, by whom they were united to God, and made capable of receiving his promises."[51]

In these three aspects the Old and the New Covenants or Testaments are the same in essence. The Testaments therefore correspond in regard to their *basis* (God's mercy in Christ); in regard to the *promise* (eternal life) and in regard to the one *Mediator,* viz Christ.

With this it is clear that there are really not *two covenants* but *two administration* of one and the same covenant of Mercy. It may also be called two *phases*.

And if we see this as two administrations or *phases,* it once again points to a difference. But now this difference does not lie in the *substance* (substantia) but in the *manner of administration* (modus administrationis).

Calvin expresses this difference in the mode of exercise in the following points:

1. In the Old Testament God manifested the celestial heritage in

[49] O.S, III, p. 404.

[50] Ibid, p. 423.

[51] Ibid, p. 404.

earthly blessings. This was an inferior mode of exercise which God discarded in the New Testament. The reason: the grace of the life to come was more clearly and plainly revealed in the Gospel. We can now think *directly* about this grace ("recta ad eius meditationem ... mentes nostras dirigit").[52]

2. The Old Testament "exhibiting only the image of truth, while the reality was absent, the shadow instead of the substance, the latter (i.e. the New Testament) exhibiting both the full truth and the entire body".[53]

3. There is a difference between the Law, "calling a doctrine of the letter" and the Gospel "a doctrine of the spirit".[54] However, this is not a difference in *substance* as if the Old Testament was not also an "Evangelium", but is a difference in degree.

4. The Old Testament is a testament of bondage and the New a testament of liberty. Calvin bases this on Rom.8:15 and Gal. 4:22.[55]

5. The Old Testament is a covenant with one people only, viz Israel; the New includes all peoples whom the Gospel of Christ reaches.[56]

We see, therefore, that Calvin upholds the *unity* of *substance* existing between the two testaments, while the difference is one of *degree,* one of "modus administrationis". This is why it was of the utmost importance to Calvin that, in regard to the laws of the Old Testament, we should take into account the circumstances of *time, place* and *nation* ("temporum, loci, gentis conditione").[57] What was initially dark or twilight to the Israelite of the Old Testament is now as clear as day in Christ. It is not *another* light which has come; but the same light which first shone dimly, has now clearly shone through in

---

[52] Ibid, p. 423.

[53] Ibid, p. 426.

[54] Ibid, p. 429: "Ex quibus occasionem accepit Apostolus comparationis huius inter Legem et Evangelium statuendae, ut illam vocaret literalem, hoc, spiritualem doctrinam". Calvin finds the grounds for his statement in 2 Cor. 6.

[55] Ibid, p. 431.

[56] Ibid, p. 433.

[57] Ibid, V, p. 489.

Christmas and Calvary, and the Resurrection and Ascension and Pentecost. In other words, there was a holy evolution in the Revelation of Salvation.[58]

In our view Calvin showed us the way to find a solution based on principle in the important problem in regard to the relationship between the Old and the New Testaments. There is a constant danger, in *theology* and in the *ecclesiastical* sphere, of a mistake in one of two directions: the Old and New Testaments are either stated to be *identical* or stated to differ *substantially*.

Now if we come to Knox, we find that one of the greatest dangers threatening his view of the Scriptures, is the *identification* of the Old and New Testaments. And it is in his interpretation of the Old Testament in particular, that he deviates considerably from the Institutes.

Knox's view of the Old Testament

Right from the outset we must state plainly that Knox's view of the Scriptures is, in general, dominated by his *basic premise,* viz Deut. 12:32, which gives his theology its own peculiar formal character. One remarks immediately that it is a premise based on the *Old Testament*.

The radical way in which it governs Knox's thought has already been pointed out.[59]

But the more we read Knox's works, the more we gain the impression that he not only agrees with Calvin that there is no difference *in substance* between the Old and the New Testaments, but that he overemphasises this. And it is at the expense of the *difference* in the mode of administration (Calvin's "modus administrationis"). This is when *identification* results. To mention a few examples:

The execution of the death penalty on Servetus in Geneva was justified simply by the fact that the Old Testament commands that blasphemers be put to death:

---

[58] Cf. My own work, Kerk en Prediking, Potchefstroom, 1966, p. 20 ff.

[59] Supra, pp. 125-126.

"That God hath appointed death by his law, without mercie, to be executed upon the blasphemers, is evident by that which is written, Leveticus 24."[60]

Knox also speaks of "the Law of God ... which is my last and most assured reason, why, yee ought to remove from honours and to punish with death such as God hath condemned by his owne mouth".[61]

How the application of this view of capital punishment in the Old Testament to the New administration made its mark in the Church of Scotland, can be seen in the "Book of Discipline". It is decreed, in regard to adulterers, that "the offender ought to suffer the death as God hath commanded".[62] Here the process of identification between the Old and New Testaments reaches its peak, and all perspective of Jesus's action in regard to the adultress in John 8 is lost!

In Knox's *method* of interpreting the Scriptures we often find that he transfers things, events and persons from the Old and New Testaments to things, events and persons in his own time so literally that the history of Biblical times and that of the new administration can simply be *equated*. We find this well illustrated in the last sermon which he delivered before King Edward VI and his Court in 1535. His text was John 13:18, "He that eateth bread with Me hath lifted up his heel against Me". With numerous *examples* the conditions in England were construed in accordance with the Biblical pattern. The process of historical equation was repeated over and over again; there was a constant parallel drawn between God's history of the Revelation with the Jewish people and God's constitutional history with the English nation. We then have the following scheme:

The Jewish nation of the Old
Testament   = the English nation;
King David and Hiskia   = Edward VI;
Achitophel   = Dudley, the King's Minister;
Sebna   = the Marquis of Winchester, etc.

[60] Laign's Knox, v, p. 224.

[61] Ibid, iv, p. 498.

[62] Dickinson's Knox, ii, p. 318.

To these examples may be added many more. We are dealing with a particular *method* of interpreting the Scripture which is an inevitable consequence of the over-emphasised identification of the Old Testament with the New. It was the theologian Holwerda who called it the "exemplarische metode" because *one* event from the history of the Bible is broken up into numerous independent fragments of history which are to serve as examples for the present.[63] As a result, the interpretation of the Scriptures takes the form of a *typology, allegory* and *parallel.* One person, event or thing from the Bible is abstracted and coupled horizontally with a person, event or thing from the present. The *stages of development* of the *historical process* in Ecclesiastical history with its *Christocentric* character are no longer noticed. We see, therefore, the importance of Calvin's principle that, for a correct view of the Scriptures, we must take into account *time, place* and *people,* and that we should see the difference between the Old and New Testaments, not as a difference of principle but as a difference in administration ("modus administrationis").

Although Knox never left us an elaborated view about the Word of God, we may nevertheless discover a few general principles from his works:

1. The *great merit* in Knox's work is the fact that he upholds the authority of the Holy Scriptures so unconditionally. In this respect his influence on the Reformation is incalculable and finds magnificent expression in the Scottish "Confession of Faith", Cap XIX:

"... we affirm and avow the authority of the same to be of God, and neither to depend on men nor angels. We affirm therefore that such as allege the Scripture to have no (other) authority, but that which is received from the Kirk, to be blasphemous against God, and injurious to the true Kirk, which always heareth and obeyeth the voice of her own Spouse and Pastor, but taketh not upon her to be mistress over

---

[63] Holwerda, B.: "... Begonnen hebbende van Mozes ...", p. 79 ff. M.B. van't Veer, Christologische Prediking over de Historische stof van het Oude Testament, article in R. Schippers et al, Van den Dienst des Woords, pp. 117-168.

I may perhaps mention my own articles in this regard: "Eksemplariese Prediking — 'n gevaar wat ons kansels bedreig" and "Die gevaarlike -isme", in *Die Kerkblad* of 16 Aug. and 13 Sept. 1961, numbers 1611 and 1618; and the controversy this clicited, numbers 1615 and 1618. Also cf. my article "Die prediking oor die geskiedkundig stof in die Bybel" in *Die Goue Kandelaar,* Potchefstroom, 1963; and also the work "Kerk en Prediking", Potchefstroom, 1966.

the same."[64]

In this important principle there is a wonderful similarity between Knox and Calvin.

2.   However, the differences between Knox's and Calvin's views in the Institutes come to the fore very clearly where the substantive view of the Scriptures is concerned. The principle: The Bible is the Word of God, receives a formal emphasis in Knox because he takes his basic premise from Deut. 12:32.[65] In general, this dominates his application of the Scriptures in religious matters.

3.   Knox's and Calvin's views of the Scriptures also differ radically in their vision of the relationship between the Old and the New Testament. To Calvin there is no essential difference between the two testaments, but in the mode of administration. In Knox these differences are so much in the background that the relationship between the two testaments is one of *identity*.

4.   This, again, relates to the fact that Knox takes little cognisance of the historical development of Ecclesiastical history with its *Christocentric* character. This had a one-sided effect on his preaching.

Knox never could concern himself too deeply with scientific theological issues connected with the Scriptures, about canonicity, etc. He was a practical man who needed action. As Thomas Carlyle said, "This Knox cannot live but by fact".[66] That is why he needed "the playn Word of God".

[64] Dickinson, Ibid, p. 267.

[65] Supra, pp. 125 and 126.

[66] Thomas Carlyle, On Heroes, Hero-worship and the Heroic in History, p. 137.

12. CALVIN AS SCRIPTURAL THEOLOGIAN

DR P.C. POTGIETER*

On 25 April 1564 Calvin summoned his notary and friend, Pierre Chenelat, to take down his last and final will. After two introductory paragraphs, he continued: I furthermore declare, that according to the grace God granted me, I have endeavoured to teach His Word soundly in preaching and writing and always to give true exposition of Holy Scripture.

Calvin's love of God found its deepest expression in his love of God's Word. Holy Scripture was his life's companion more than anything or even anybody else. Above all, he wanted to be a scriptural theologian. I would therefore like to point out three aspects in this regard:

* His thorough knowledge of Holy Scripture;

* His views on Holy Scripture; and

* His application of Holy Scripture

His knowledge of Holy Scripture

One can safely assume that few theologians ever had a better knowledge of Scripture than John Calvin. From his various writings it is quite obvious that he made a particularly thorough study of God's Word. Fruit of this was passed on to us in his published commentaries on nearly all the books of the Bible.

But his thorough knowledge of Scripture is also portrayed in many other writings, for example his letters and his apologies, and, of course, particularly in his *Institutes.* Hence, from the fact that the *Institutes* was published in several editions (4) over a period of more than two decades, we note a remarkable growth in his knowledge of and insight into the Word of God. In every new edition more material was added and applied to substantiate his arguments. His remarkable powers of memory enabled him to compare scripture with scripture

* His address is: University of Pretoria, Hillcrest, Pretoria. RSA 0083.

and to integrate his knowledge into a logical system of Theology.

His views on Holy Scripture

Calvin unconditionally accepted the *divine inspiration* of the Bible. Holy Scripture is nothing but the very voice of the living God, so that, whatever it teaches, should be embraced by mankind. In his commentary on Paul's second epistle to Timothy 3:16, he emphasised the uniqueness of the Bible as the revelation of the one and true God. In no other religion and in no other religious writings could the voice of God be heard.

He was also quite clear on the fact that the authority of Holy Scripture did not depend on the authority of the Church. Its *authority* came from within. It is *autopistos*. The one and only guarantee for the church not to wander off on a way of heresy, was to submit to God's Word.

In this regard, we must pay attention to Calvin's view on the relationship between the *Word of God and the Holy Spirit.* He firmly believed in the *testimonium Spiritus Sancti,* through which we know that the Bible is the Word of God. But then again he points out in his *Institutes* that Holy Scripture is the school of the Spirit of God. In his reply to Cardinal Sadolet he wrote: God knew how very dangerous it would have been for man only to appeal to the guidance of the Holy Spirit in matters of uncertainty. So therefore He linked the guidance of the Spirit, which he promised to his Church, to the written Word of God. In this way there could be no uncertainty and no instability.

In his writings we find a particularly strong relationship between the *sufficientia* and the *perspicuitas* of Holy Scripture. I'd like to quote Benjamin Warfield: Whither the Bible took Calvin, thither he went: where scriptural declarations failed him, he stopped short. In his petition to Charles V, Calvin wrote: Whatever man adds to the Word of God, are lies. When the Bible remains silent, we must remain silent. The teaching of Christ is perfect. That should leave us content.

As far as the *clarity* of Scripture is concerned, God revealed Himself in a way adapted to our understanding. Although it has been suggested that we find something of an accommodation theology with Calvin, there can be no doubt whatsoever that he fully maintains Holy Scripture as the Word of God in the most literal sense.

As to the *necessity* of the Bible, Calvin teaches that God can in no other way be truly known, than through Holy Scripture. The Word of God is the means by which the true church can be distinguished from the false.

His application of Holy Scripture

As far as hermeneutics is concerned, Calvin very strictly maintained the principle of *Sacra Scriptura sui ipsius interpres.* He tolerated no allegorical exegesis. The true meaning of Scripture had to be found in Scripture alone. Berkouwer quite correctly points out that Calvin had the very deepest regard for the text of the Bible, the written Word of God.

His commentaries are characterized by their conciseness and clearness. In 1539 he wrote a letter to Simon Grynaeus in which he stressed the point that a good exegete should never introduce his own thoughts and views.

For Calvin there was no other *basis* for theology than Holy Scripture. The Word of God is the foundation of our faith. Our knowledge of God towards salvation in Jesus Christ is through the Word of God. Holy Scripture leads us to faith in Christ.

But Calvin also emphasized the Bible as foundation for our way of life, for *christian ethics.* Over against the *lex naturalis* of Rome, he kept to Holy Scripture as the only norm and criterion to teach and reprimand man towards a life given to the glory of God. When he had to advise the council of Geneva on the very difficult question of the origin of sin, he wrote that we should not be led by anything than Holy Scripture.

Calvin paid particular attention to the preaching of the Bible. He regarded the preached Word as the true Word of God in so far as it was in agreement with Holy Scripture. But in this the preacher was strongly dependent on the illumination of the Holy Spirit: *Sine Spiritus Sancti illuminatio, verbo nihil agitur.* When the church of Geneva was vexed by many troubles in 1538, Calvin told them in a letter that the origin of their problems arose from the fact that they did not take the Word of God seriously enough. For Calvin the Word of God came first and foremost. He even said that without the Word, the sacraments were no sacraments at all! May I conclude by again referring to the four different editions of the *Institutes.* In spite of the development of his thoughts and the extension of every edition, he never found it necessary to change anything which he put forth as

129

basic truth in the first edition. The reason is obvious. From the very beginning, his sole source was Holy Scripture. Never was his theology built upon philosophy or humanistic ideas. No wonder that there was a constant flow of would be ministers of the word to Geneva.

As biblical theologian Calvin left a theology for posterity — a theology which remains up to date, even though four centuries lie between us and this remarkable man.

13. CALVIN'S VIEW OF MAN IN THE LIGHT OF GENESIS 2:15

OR

MAN: EARTH'S SERVANT OR LORD

PROF. C.J. VOS*

The intent of this essay is not to spell out in any detail the environmental problems which plague our society. It is assumed that the members of this congress are sensitive to them and are committed to the thesis that the earth is the Lord's and that it is our high task to be good stewards of that which God has committed to our care. Moreover, as Calvin has pointed out, "creation is God's vesture"[1], and therefore none of us would wish to be despoilers of that vesture. It is of concern, however, that the Judeo-Christian tradition has been held responsible for the ecological problems we face, and that Calvinism, so it is claimed, has had no small part in aggravating these problems.

A decade ago Paul Ehrlich made the charge that "by destroying pagan animism, Christianity made it possible to exploit nature in a mood of indifference to the feelings of natural objects"[2]. Lynn White, Jr., is probably even more forceful by saying

> Both our present science and our present technology are so tinctured with orthodox Christian arrogance toward nature that no solution for our ecologic crises can be expected from them alone. Since the roots of our trouble are so largely religious, the remedy must also be essentially religious, whether we call it that or not[3].

---

* His address is: Dept. of Religion and Theology, Calvin College, Grand Rapids, Michigan 49506, USA.

[1] *Commentary on the Book of Genesis*, "Argument" p. 60.

[2] Paul R. and Anne H. Ehrlich, *Population, Resources, Environment* (San Francisco: W.H. Freeman 1970), p. 191.

[3] Quoted by the Ehrlichs *op. cit.*, p. 263.

Since it is often claimed that capitalism has been a significant force to exploit natural resources, and it is further claimed that Calvinism has significantly promoted capitalism, it is natural that Calvinism has come under fire[4].

Such charges make it imperative that we review with care the "Judeo-Christian tradition" to see whether the claim is true that this tradition has promoted the wasteful exploitation of resources. Of special interest to this congress is the question of whether or not Calvin and/or Calvinism have encouraged the abuse of the environment as has been alleged. This paper will focus on Scripture as it has been interpreted by Calvin on this and closely related questions.

Review of the Biblical Data

There can be little doubt that the first chapter of Genesis places man in a position of dominion over nature. That man is ruler of the world is apparent from the words of blessing spoken by the Creator:

> Be fruitful and multiply
> and fill the earth and subdue it
> and have dominion
>> over the fish of the sea
>> and over the birds of the air
>> and over everything that moves upon the earth.

(Gen. 1:28 RSV)

The two Hebrew words *radah* and *kabaš* which we commonly translate as "have dominion" and "subdue" respectively are clear and forceful. The word *radah* is commonly used to express rule and dominion, and in Joel 3:13 (Heb. 4:13) it is used for the treading out of

---

[4] John Block, *The Dominion of Man*, (Edinburgh: University Press 1970), pp. 69f., gives an evaluation of the debate triggered by Max Weber's thesis in *The Protestant Ethic and the Spirit of Capitalism,* and the further discussion by R.H. Tawney in his book *Religion and the Rise of Capitalism.* P. Singer in "The Place of Non-Humans" in K.E. Goodpaster and K.M. Sayre, (eds), *Ethics and Problems of the 21st Century* (Notre Dame: University of Notre Dame Press, 1979), p. 193, comments adversely on Calvin's view of animals. In a similar vein of J. Passmore, *Man's Responsibility for Nature* (New York: Charles Scribner's Sons 1974) pp. 13f, 29. Even Francis A. Schaeffer, *Pollution and the Death of Man* (Wheaton: Tyndale House Publ., 1970), p. 124 sees a significant similarity between the "Calvinistic and the deistic concepts of God". Similarly R.M. Chute, *Environmental Insight* (New York: Harper and Row, Publishers, 1971), p. 24.

the grapes. The word *kabas̆*, translated "subdue", is probably even more forceful in that the idea of coercion is evident in its use.

Attempts to dilute the force of *radah* to mean merely that man dominates the scene of creation as a mountain dominates the landscape are not successful[5]. The Old Testament uses the word *radah* more than twenty times and in no case (unless it indeed be Gen. 1:26ff) does it do so to suggest mere prominence. The Hebrew word *kabas̆* is dynamic in expressing the idea of coercoin. It is commonly translated "to tread down," and in Esther 7:8 it suggests rape.

Calvin does not seize upon either of these words for a specific analysis, but it might be well to note that there is no hint in his discussion which might suggest that man has license to deal with creation in an autonomous manner. Instead Calvin is faithful to his cardinal principle that "... true and sound wisdom consists of two parts: the knowledge of God and of ourselves"[6]. In other words, man's right to have dominion and to subdue are not matters which can be dealt with in isolation. It must be recognized that the words in Gen. 1:26 were spoken by a benevolent Father who has put one of his sons in charge; he expects the son to exercise authority in the same way the Father does. "For it is of great importance that we touch nothing of God's bounty but what we know he has permitted us to do; since we cannot enjoy anything with a good conscience, except we receive it as from the hand of God"[7]. Therefore, the force of *radah* and *kabas̆* need in no way embarrass us. Calvin quite candidly points to the "dignity with which he [God] decreed to honor man, namely that he should have authority over all living creatures"[8]. To have dominion and to subdue must not be understood as offering a foundation for tyranny over nature. The force of these words is therapeutic in a world in which animistic views tended to make man a worshipper of nature rather than its wise and benevolent governor. The point of the record is to show "how benificent the Lord had been to them in

---

[5] cf. James Baar, "Man and Nature", *Bulletin of the John Rylands University, Library of Manchester* Vol. 55 (Autumn 1972) 22f.

[6] *Inst.* I, i, 1.

[7] *Commentary* on Gen. 1:28.

[8] *Commentary* on Gen. 1:26.

bestowing on them all things which they could desire ..."[9] Calvin is hardly setting up a "philosophical world and life view" apart from God. Instead he seeks to lead the minds of his readers to piety, that is, to a living and happy relationship between man and God and man and his world.

The second chapter of Genesis provides us with another account of creation, and the verses five and fifteen are of particular interest to us since they indicate another aspect of the relationship between man and the earth. The assumption of this paper is that particularly verse fifteen describes for us the authority that man is to exercise ecologically (and, by extension, sociologically and politically). The fifth verse ends with the statement "there was no man to till the ground". After the description of the garden which the Lord God planted (vv. 8-14) we read, "The Lord God took the man and put him in the garden of Eden to till it and keep it". The word translated "to till" is the Hebrew word 'abad, and it must be observed that most translations avoid the most common meaning of 'abad, i.e., "to serve" by translating it "to till" or "to work" or "to cultivate". There are, however, some notable exceptions. Young's Literal Translation of the Holy Bible (1898) is indeed true to its purpose and in both verses translates 'abad as "to serve". The New American Standard Bible offers the meaning "to serve" in the margin. J. Sperna Weiland, in his commentary Genesis, translates it as "te dienen". But these are the exception, unfortunately, not the rule.

It is easy to see why translators have hesitated to render 'abad in this setting as "serve". It seems unnatural to most of us that man, the superior, should serve the earth, the inferior. Our perspectives influence the manner in which we translate the Bible, but in so doing we often seriously close off the light rays of revelation. Although we must be temperate in our criticism of the translators of the Bible, on this score it might be well to point out that verse fifteen does contain some hint that might have alerted the translators to the fact that "to serve" was not incongruous. Man was to keep (šamar) the garden as well as to serve it. The word šamar is frequently used in Scripture to convey the idea of tenderness and care. Ps. 120, popularly known as the "traveller's psalm", speaks of the Lord as "keeper" six times. It was the Creator's design that man should have that kind of solicitous care for creation.

---

[9] Commentary on Gen. 1:28.

While Calvin does not provide us with an analytic word study of *'abad* and *šamar* it is rewarding to observe how he has caught the intent of these words in his commentary on this passage. He says

> that the custody of the garden was given in charge to Adam, to show that we possess the things which God has committed to our hands, on the condition, that being content with a frugal and moderate use of them, we should take care of what shall remain. Let him who possesses a field, so partake of its yearly fruits, that he may not suffer the ground to be injured by his negligence; but let him endeavor to hand it down to posterity as he received it, or even better cultivated[10].

If we allow the first two chapters of Genesis to function together it is defensible to conclude that for authority to be exercised properly two aspects or dynamics must be operative simultaneously — that of rule (Gen. 1), and that of service (Gen. 2). He who rules but does not serve does not rule well. He who serves but is not permitted to rule does not serve well. Either way the person is deprived of an essential aspect of his humanity. The proper stance of man to the rest of creation is to be its serving lord. In this way he will "image" his Lord.

Man's exercise of authority with respect to nature is in complete harmony with his role in the family, in the church, and in the state. The goal of the believing community is to so influence society's structure that it allows the function of rule and service to come to expression in each person. He who rules and does not serve in his ruling is dehumanized; he who serves and does not rule in his serving is dehumanized.

It is not difficult to document that for Calvin human authority is exercised properly only when it is done in service. In his discussion of man's role as ruler of the earth (Gen. 1), Calvin speaks of man as the "father of the earth"[11]. But it is particularly in Calvin's discussion concerning government in state and church that the "service" dimension of human authority becomes very clear. In his commentary on the words of Jesus, "the kings of the Gentiles exercise lordship over them," Calvin notes that "... if we carefully examine the details,

[10] *Commentary* on Gen. 2:15.

[11] *Commentary* on Gen. 1:28.

135

even kings do not rightly rule unless they serve"[12].

Calvin expounds the same thesis in his discussion of the right relationship between members and classes within society. He clearly sees the import of mutual subjection:

> God has bound us so strongly to each other, that no man ought to endeavour to avoid subjection; and where love reigns, mutual services will be rendered. I do not except even kings and governors, whose very authority is held for the *service* of the community. It is highly proper that all should be exhorted to be subject to each other in their turn[13].

Some of Calvin's statements might leave the impression that he sees a sharp disjunction between the function of rulers in state and the rulers in the church. He maintains that "their being servants does not prevent the kings from bearing sway and indeed, rising above their subjects in magnificent splendor and pomp"[14], but that "the government of the church permits nothing of this sort"[15]. It is doubtful, however, that Calvin means to suggest that such conduct on the part of the rulers of state is ideal or even permissible. Rather it is to be understood as a *modus operandi* everywhere present and well-nigh inevitable in this sinful world. When elevation and power are the only forces which will keep unruly masses under control, then such measures must be employed even though it is regrettable. The church, however, must always proclaim the gospel of Christ in all its fulness by making it clear that such action on the part of civil rulers may be a necessary evil but that it is not the normal procedure of the state.

It must be borne in mind that the masses may be guilty of insubordination which leads to chaos and the dissolution of society. Calvin recognized that problems arise from both the rulers and those ruled. All men find submission repugnant:

---

[12] *Commentary* on Matt. 20:25.

[13] *Commentary* on Eph. 5:21.

[14] *Commentary* on Matt. 20:25.

[15] *Ibid.*

136

But as nothing is more irksome to the mind of man than this mutual subjection, he directs us to the fear of Christ, who alone can subdue our fierceness, that we may not refuse the yoke, and can humble our pride, that we may not be ashamed of serving our neighbours[16].

As Calvin draws our attention the fact that it is Christ alone who can "subdue our fierceness", it becomes evident that he recognizes the tendency of man in sin to want to exercise dominion without service. There is a clear consistency with the portrayal of man in Calvin's comments on Gen. 2:15 with the rest of Calvin's discussion on human authority. Mutual submission is the principle upon which society is to be redeemed and restructured, rather than the enforcement of a well-oiled hierarchy. In marriage it means that husband and wife are submissive to each other (even though that submission may not be identical). The husband wears a crown which the wife does not, but it is the crown of thorns. Calvin does not expound on how wives are to submit, but he points out that

> the community at large is divided, as it were, into so many yokes, out of which arises mutual obligation. There is first the yoke of marriage between husband and wife; — secondly, the yoke which binds parents and children; — and, thirdly, the yoke which connects masters and servants. By this arrangement there are six different classes, for each of whom Paul lays down peculiar duties[17].

Fulfilling the obligations of duty is the dynamic that brings about a blessed society rather than in insistence upon rights. Calvin spares no words to castigate the husband who does not love his wife. "The man who does not love his wife is a monster"[18], for the "strong affection which a husband ought to cherish toward his wife is exemplified by Christ ..."[19]

For children too, the yoke of submission is often repugnant, "for the

---

[16] *Commentary* on Eph. 5:21.

[17] *Ibid.*

[18] *Commentary* on Eph. 5:28.

[19] *Ibid.*

human minds recoils from the idea of subjection"[20], and it is in this area that society experiences a painful malady. Calvin asks, "do we find one in a thousand that is obedient to his parents?"[21] This resistance toward obedience and submission is all the more regrettable when it is observed that obedience is done "in the Lord", and that parents "sit in that place to which they have been advanced by the Lord, who shares with them a part of his honor"[22]. Thus Calvin sees the role of the parent as one who represents God. To disobey the parent is to disobey God; to obey is "a step toward honoring the highest Father"[23]. But "if they spur us to transgress the law, we have a perfect right to regard them not as parents, but as strangers who are trying to lead us away from obedience to our true Father. So should we act toward princes, lords, and every kind of superiors"[24].

On the one hand Calvin advocates that believers recognize the government which has been set over them because it has been instituted by God; but on the other hand, if a government requires action that is contrary to God's law, he does not permit believers to conform. On the one hand Calvin insists that for the government to rule properly and thus represent God worthily it must engage in a benevolent rule which is for the welfare of the subjects; but on the other hand, if the government fails in this, such failure does not *ipso facto* provide grounds for an *en toto* rejection of the authority of that government. On the one hand Calvin expresses in severe terms the erosion of respect and authority rulers suffer when they make unlawful demands; on the other hand Calvin seems not to have a policy of coercive, organized overthrow of the existing government even under such circumstances. No doubt he was influenced by the fact that the New Testament writers advocated submission even to the pagan emperors of their time.

In certain cases, however, Calvin uses language that might incite rebellion. J.T. McNeill points out that

---

[20] *Commentary* on Eph. 6:1.

[21] *Ibid.*

[22] *Inst.* II, vii, 38.

[23] *Ibid.*

[24] *Ibid*

Calvin carefully guards against any endorsement of popular revolutionary action, but in some instances his language is less guarded. See, for example his Comm. Daniel (1561), lecture XXX on Dan. 6:22, where he says: 'For earthly princes lay aside their power when they rise up against God, and are unworthy to be reckoned among the number of mankind. We ought, rather utterly to defy them *(conspuere in ipsorum capita,* lit., "to spit on their heads") than to obey them' (CR XLI. 25)[25].

Calvin's approach to human authority is particularly instructive in that he saw that the cohesiveness of society does not lie in well-defined tables of organization which include the mechanisms of enforcement. The vitality and serenity of society depend on mutual rule and reciprocal submission. In the state of sin it seems to be the unchallenged axiom that submission is for the weak, the unfortunate, the deprived, and the conquered. In God's scheme, however, the strong submit to the weak, the rich serve the poor, the superior (mankind) develops to its fullest potential and beauty the inferior (the earth).

The formula is quite simple. Each person rules; each person serves. Not that all serve and rule in identical ways, but it may be said that he who is called upon to rule the most must be prepared to sacrifice the most. Or to put it conversely: A ruler who profits from his ruling in selfish ways is dehumanizing himself. Or again, a servant who is unwilling to rule by refusing to obey immoral commands is dehumanizing himself. The rulingserving role of man must come to expression in every sphere of life, in ecology, the family, industry, society, and government. But the formula remains the same. All those who rule must serve; all those who serve must rule.

---

[25] McNeill's footnote on *Inst.* IV, xx, 31 *(Library of Christian Classics* Vol. XXI, p. 1518).

SUMMARY

Calvin saw clearly that human authority involved both rule and service to that which was ruled. He anticipated in his comments on Gen. 2:15 that all persons, in one way or another, are privileged to function in this role. Every person has a "rule" over the environment (be the earth or the persons with whom he is in contact in society), and this environment should be benefitted by his presence. For the Christian this involve a mutual and reciprocal submission. Wives are subject to their husbands because wives reflect the submission of the church to Christ. Husbands are in submission to their wives in a simlar manner in which Christ submitted himself for the sake of the Church. Children are to submit to parents in order that they may offer the world a paradigm demonstrating how all mankind should submit to our true Father. Fathers so rule their children that in submitting to the welfare of the children they may reflect the Father who loves the world. Slaves are to submit to masters in such a way that they demonstrate how all mankind will submit to one another when the regenerative work of Christ has repossessed the human heart. Masters are to exercise rule in such a way that they illuminate the benevolent rule of God who is tender over all his works. A mutual, reciprocal submission is the biblical model for the proper exercise of human authority. The first two chapters of Genesis reveal how human authority must be exercised in a sinless world — Gen. 1 emphasizes dominion; Gen. 2 emphasizes service. The work of Christ and his church is the reinstatement of that model.

In this fallen world it is the duty of the church to remind rulers, parents, and masters to follow the biblical pattern of authority if their rule is to be serene and happy. David is offered as a model in that he judged the people in equity. Tyranny carries within it the seeds of decay and destruction. The tendency toward tyranny is well-nigh universal where power is given. In the sinful heart power seeks to absolutize itself for a variety of reasons (greed, egotism, lust for power, etc.). The ruler who has been influenced by the stance of Christ over against his own will no doubt be able to benefit his society in a significant way.

Means must be provided to protect citizens from uninhibited or absolutized power. A plurality of the base of government is desirable. Certain forces in society are charged with protecting the God-given freedom of the people. These forces can be in a variety of forms: parliaments, the church, the witness of the individual either in speech or in writing (Calvin's Prefatory Address to King Francis is an illustrious example). Calvin was a worthy successor of the Old Testament prophets in that while he did not flinch to speak the truth with respect to injustice and tyranny, he did not raise nor support organized rebellion to replace the existing government. Instead he continued to remind rulers and subjects that God is the final arbiter of men's deeds and hearts and will in the course of history destroy tyrannic governments.

Those who found themselves under the rule of tyrannic governments were admonished by Calvin to disobey and command which was clearly against the law of God. In this manner they exercised and preserved their rule over the government. Instead of taking steps to replace the government, believers were urged to pray for the repentance and renewal of the ruler(s). Calvin's stance was that Christianity does not oppose certain groups and support other groups. The message of Christ was for all. Christianity was not simply to give comfort and encouragement to the oppressed, but it was to speak a warning to the oppressor as well. The intent was not a "switching" of roles, the oppressed becoming the oppressor. Rather it was the repentance of the oppressor that was sought in order that true reconciliation might take place and the ruler become a true servant of the people.

14. THE SHADOW AND THE SKETCH

PROF. T.H.L. PARKER*

One of the more striking changes that Calvin made in his new edition of the *Institutio* in 1539 was the insertion of the chapter on the relationship between the Old and the New Covenants. This without doubt reflects his deeper thinking on the weaknesses and needs of theology in his own day. And not in his own day only, we may add; for this is perennially a matter of crucial importance, not only for the health of theology itself, but also for the Church's influence in the world. The way in which the relationship between the Covenants and therefore between the Old and New Testaments is understood will determine (unless inconsistency intervene) a theology, a Church polity, an ethics, a secular politics, a culture. We may perhaps tend think of chapters ix to xi in Book II of the 1559 *Institutio* as a rather irritating parenthesis interrupting the argument on Sin, Law, Mediator. But for Calvin there was a necessary movement within the argument precisely at the point of Law, Mediator.

The purpose of this paper is to draw attention to the question of the relationship between the Covenants as it is understood by Calvin. But it wishes to do this within the sphere of his interpretation of the Old Testament, and therefore we are setting definite limits to our enquiry. Moreover, these limits will be further narrowed by our concentrating on just one image which he is accustomed to use and drawing out its meaning.

In these chapters we meet seven times the word *umbra,* twice the adjective *umbratilis,* and five times the related verb *adumbratio.* There is very much more to these words than the general sense of "shadow", "shadowy", and "shaded" or "outlined" which English translators of the *Institutio* are accustomed to give them. For *umbra* Lewis and Short's Latin dictionary[1] gives eight meanings: "shadow", "the dark part of a painting", "a ghost", "an uninvited guest", "a shady place", "a grayling", "a trace, obscure sign, imperfect copy",

---

* His address is: Dept. of Theology, Abbey House, Palace Green, Durham, England.

[1] Lewis and Short: *A Latin Dictionary* (Oxford, 1966). See also for *adumbrare, Thesaurus Linguae Latinae* (Lipsiae MDCCCC) and, for σκιαγεαφέω, G.W.H. Lampe: *A Patristic Greek Lexicon (Oxford, 1961).*

and "shelter". *Umbratilis* is simpler; it may mean "in retirement" or "at home", or "private". *Adumbratio* is defined as "a sketch in shadow, á là silhouette", "a sketch, outline", or "a false show". *Adumbrare* can, of course, mean "to cast a shadow on something", but it also has a technical sense: "to represent an object with the mingling of light and shade, σκια γεαφέω (therefore not of the sketch in shadow, as the first outline of a figure, but of a picture already fully sketched, and only wanting the last touches for its completion)"; but later the dictionary adds a further sense: "to represent a thing only in outline, and, consequently, imperfectly". When Calvin uses these words of the Old Covenant, which of the many meanings has he in mind?

Let us start with *umbra*.

* John 1.18 'teaches us that the mysteries which were only described obscurely *sub umbris,* have been revealed to us' (II.ix.1. OS III, 399[9]).

* St Paul 'joins the body to the *umbris*' (II.ix.4. OS III, 401[34-5]).

* Calvin quotes Ps. 39.7 (=6 AV): 'he who walks as an *umbra*', and comments, 'By *umbra* he means that there is nothing *solidus* in man, but only an empty appearance, as they say *(inanem apparentiam)*' (II.x.15 OS III,415[35].OC 31,400).

* The patriarchs 'possessed something hidden which does not appear in the *umbra* of the present life' (II.x.17 OS III, 417[16]).

* The Old Testament 'puts forward an *umbram* for the body' (II.xi.4 OS III, 426[12]).

* Heb.10.1 'concludes, therefore, that [the Law] was in itself an *umbra* of good things to come and not the living image of the things *(vivam rerum effigiem)*' (II.xi.4 OS III, 426[31]).

* 'Those who were content with present *umbris*' II.xi.10 OS III, 433[3]).

It is clear enough that *umbra* has no single and constant meaning in these quotations. Sometimes it bears the sense of obscurity and hence, in general, of shadow. But where it is placed in opposition to *body,* it becomes, not precisely emptiness but certainly emptiness shaped like the body over against which it stands. As such it is classed as present in contrast to the future body. Above all, it is opposed to the

143

living image (that is, to the reality).

Umbratilis **is easier to settle in the sense of shadow and obscurity:**

* In Jesus Christ God in a way 'makes himself visible, whereas his appearance had before been *obscura et umbratilis'* II.ix.1 OS III, 399[21]).

* The Old Covenant of the Lord, which he had delivered enwrapped in the *umbratili* and inefficacious observation of ceremonies' (II.xi.4 OS III, 427[24]).

Finally, *adumbrare:*

* 'The Gospel actually points with the finger to what the Law *adumbravit* under types' (II.ix.3 OS III, 401[21]).

* David *'adumbravit* the heavenly mysteries more obscurely than did [later Old Testament writers] (II.x.15 OS III, 415[30]).

* 'The better to commend God's goodness, the Prophets *adumbrasse* it for the people in temporal blessings, as in outlines, so to say; but yet they painted such a portrait *(effigiem)* of it as carried their minds beyond the earth, beyond the elements of this world' (II.x.20 OS III, 424[24]seq.).

* 'He did not give them the spiritual promises naked and open, but as it were *adumbratas* in earthly things' (II.xi.2 OS III, 424[21]).

* The Lord *'adumbrabat* spiritual happiness in types and symbols' (II.xi.3 OS III, 425[31]).

Apart from the fact that the verb is used in connection with 'types', 'temporal blessings', 'earthly things', and 'types and symbols', no clear-cut meaning emerges. But we do have a clue to something more definite in the third quotation, where Calvin speaks of outlines and of painting a portrait. This clue is strengthened when we note that he refers us in the passage to Heb. 10.1. If we then take his commentary in conjunction with the *Institutio,* as he undoubtedly meant us to do, and read his exposition of Heb. 10.1, we find the metaphor fully worked out.

'For the Law having a shadow of good things to come – σκιαν τῶν

μελλόντων ἀγαθῶν   '. His comment runs: 'He borrowed this metaphor from the art of painting. Here *umbra* is applied differently from its use in Col. 2.17, where the ancient ceremonies are called *umbrae* because they do not have within themselves the *solidam substantiam* of the things they figure. But here he says that they were like the rough lines which are the *adumbratio* of the living picture. For painters are accustomed *adumbrare* with charcoal what they intend to express before they lay on the living colours with a brush. This more obscure drawing *(pictura)* the Greeks call σκιαγεαφία   , or, as you would say in Latin, *umbratilem;* whereas their εἰκὼν   is *expressa effigies*. Hence also *eiconicae* are called *imagines* in Latin, representing to the life men or animals or landscapes *(locorum faciem)*. Thus the Apostle makes this distinction between the Law and the Gospel: Under the Law what is today expressed with a masterly hand and in living and varied colours was only *adumbratum* in rough and incomplete lines *(rudibus et inchoatis lineis)'* (OC 55, 121).

But now Calvin has given us a cross reference to Col. 2.17, a verse he mentions also in Inst. II.xi.4, and before we analyse the Hebrews passage we will see what that place and its comment has to say to us.

'Which is a shadow (σκιὰ) of things to come, but the body is of Christ'. Calvin here uses the metaphor in two ways. First he takes *umbra* as opposed to the revealed reality. To adhere to ceremonies, which are *umbrae,* is like contemplating a man's form *ex umbra* when the man himself is present in one's sight. Christ is now before our eyes in the Gospel; we therefore no longer need to look at the *umbrae* of him. Here *umbra* more probably means a man's shadow cast by the light; less probably, his ghost or spectre. He goes on, however, to meet the objection that Christians also do not behold Christ immediately but by means of the Christian sacraments; and now he turns to the other sense of *umbra* in order to distinguish the Old Testament sacraments from the New: 'As painters do not express the image in their first sketch in living colours and εἰκονικῶς   , but first set out rough and obscure lines in charcoal, so under the Law the representation of Christ was unfinished and, as it were, a first draft *(primae manus),* whereas in our sacraments it is seen expressed to the life' (OC 51, 110-11).

The first point to be made is that Calvin seems to reserve the painting metaphor for discussion of the sacraments. We find that it occurs again, together with references to Heb. 10.1 and Col. 2.17, when he comes to the comparison of Old and New Testament sacraments in Inst. IV.xiv.18-25. It is used, therefore, not to distinguish the covenants themselves but the form in which each was given. God did not give the Jews his covenant in the plain and clear portrayal of a finished painting, where the direction and relation of lines and the variety of colours would make the object represented at once recognizable and understandable, but in the obscure indication of a charcoal outline, black lines on plain canvas or wood, which, from its lack of detail and of colour and from its unfilled in body, is recognizable only with difficulty, and can, indeed, present the viewer with problems of ambiguity. What distinguished the finished painting from the sketch for Calvin was its colour, its detail, and its masterly workmanship. It also appears from such quotations as 'David *adumbravit* the heavenly mysteries more obscurely than did [later Old Testament writers]' (II.x.15 OS III,415[30]) that Calvin saw the formation of the painting as a gradual process, with successive writers adding to its creation over the Old Testament centuries. But we must note that his usage differs from the explanation in Lewis and Short: 'not of the sketch in shadow, as the first outline of a figure, but of a picture already fully sketched, and only wanting the last touches for its completion'. For Calvin, on the contrary, the picture is only a rough sketch even at the end of the Old Testament. And when we come to the incarnate Christ and the Gospel the metaphor breaks down; for what takes place is not that Christ gives the final touches to the picture but that he transforms and transfigures it. At this point the other sense of *umbra* is more appropriate; the body appears and renders the earlier shadows of it unnecessary.

Since with *umbra* we are dealing with the concept of light, we must mention a related metaphor which Calvin was very fond of using, in these chapters and also elsewhere. Jesus Christ is the sun of righteousness who at his rising scatters the dark. 'In the beginning, when the first promise of salvation was given to Adam, some weak sparks shone out. Afterwards more was done and a greater fulness of light began to show; this more and more appeared and shed its brightness still further; and then at last all the clouds were scattered and Christ, the Sun of righteousness, fully illuminated the whole terrestrial globe' (II.x.20 OS III,420[7-13]). We may well feel that this metaphor, too, is easily comprehensible in general and certainly helpful, but that it will land us in theological problems if it is pressed too literally. But in general it does convey the contrast between the modes of the two convenants. That Christ did not stand as the last in a line of Old Testament witnesses but was the reality absent from the

146

Old Testament comes out clearly in *Inst.* II.xi.4-6. The Old Covenant, with its figurative ceremonies, 'in the absence of the truth, shows only an image and an *umbra* instead of the body,' but the New Covenant 'exhibits the present truth and the actual body *(corpus solidum)*' (II.xi.4 OS III,426$^{10-13}$). The ceremonies as fugures are *imagines* of the yet absent truth, *umbrae* of the reality. Hence the Old Covenant was temporary and *in suspenso* until the coming of Christ, whose blood-shedding established the new and eternal covenant (OS III, 427$^{26-33}$). Old Testament man, therefore, is characterised by his looking forward into the future: 'mysteries which were descried only obscurely *sub umbris*' (II.xi. 1 OS III,399$^{9-10}$); 'The Lord dispensed the light of his word to them in such a way that they saw it afar off and obscurely' (II.xi.5 OS III,428$^{2-4}$); 'the Law and the Prophets gave the people a taste of the wisdom which would one day be revealed, and they showed it to them beforehand shining afar off' (II.xi.5 OS III, 428$^{12-13}$); the preaching of the prophets was 'obscure, as of things far distant, and it was confined in typesn (II.xi.6OS III, 428$^{25-26}$).

We come to the final part of our paper. I hope it might be thought that our examination of the metaphor, brief as it has been, has thrown a little light on Calvin's view of the difference and similarity of the Covenants. But does it tell us anything about his approach to the Old Testament as an interpreter? Here the first thing we must ask is whether the metaphor is also legitimately to be applied to the set of documents we call the Old Testament. Is the Old Testament the first rough draft in charcoal, with all that that implies of imperfection and ambiguity? Certainly, I am not aware that Calvin ever makes this direct connection. On the other hand, the language he uses about the prophets and other Old Testament writers in the quotations given in our previous paragraph certainly is within the area of our metaphor. It is not easy to escape the conclusion that what is true of the form of the Old Covenant — the priesthood, the sacrifices, the ceremonies, the holy places, the kingdom, the land, and the blessings and punishments determining the history of the people — is also true of the record and interpretation of those institutions and histories. We are, I suggest, justified in saying that Calvin regarded the Old Testament, the record and interpretation of the *adumbrationes,* as itself *adumbratio.* This would therefore be the visual metaphor corresponding to the auditory metaphor of the nurse using baby-talk to her charges.

When we say that in his Old Testament commentaries Calvin was undertaking to expound a set of documents which gave an unfinished and therefore incomplete, and therefore again obscure representation, we must link with it his stated aim as an interpreter — to lay bare the mind of his author. By setting out to lay bare the minds of authors whose writings were *adumbrationes,* first rough drafts, and who could do no more than point to an absent reality of the present *umbrae,* Calvin was accepting a condition and limitation in his exposition. Had he, in the manner of Lefèvre d'Étaples, filled in the picture from the outset, chased away the shadows by making the sun of righteousness arise prematurely, he could not have done justice to his authors. The limitation that he accepts is that he takes the writers as they are, men of the twilight of the Old Covenant, men who lived under and who taught a figurative religion, obscure and incomplete, men who looked forward with unconquerable hope to a mysterious reality. By taking them as they are, his exposition largely partakes of their character. It looks forward with them to him that was to come.

Let me end by giving a good example of this treatment in his exposition of Jacob at the brook Jabbok. The whole account of Jacob's wrestling is interpreted without any reference to Christ at all. The man who wrestles with Jacob is called "God" without more ado and on this level the commentary on the story is one of the most powerful and profound things that Calvin ever wrote. It is when he comes to the verse 'And Jacob asked him, and said, Tell me, I pray thee, they name. And he said, Wherefore is it that thou dost ask after my name?' (Gen. 32.29), that he at last mentions Christ, and then it is as one absent: 'Although Jacob knew God, he was not satisfied with an obscure and lowly knowledge, but desired to rise higher. It is not surprising that the holy man broke out with this prayer. God had revealed himself to him under many coverings *(involucris),* and there was yet no familiar or clear knowledge ... The sum of it therefore is that, although Jacob's prayer was godly, the Lord did not comply with it, because the time of full revelation was not yet come. For in the beginning the fathers had to walk in the twilight of dawn; and the Lord little by little revealed himself to them, until at last Christ the sun of righteousness arose, in whom appeared the perfection of brightness' (OC 23,445-6).

15. CALVIN'S HERMENEUTICS OF HOLY SCRIPTURE

PROF. H.W. ROSSOUW*

Because of its commitment to the Biblical text as its authoritative norm, Christian theology has always been interested in the problems connected with the process of interpretation. If hermeneutics is loosely defined as the theoretical reflection on these problems, one may therefore rightly expect a close relationship between hermeneutics and the theological enterprise. Such a relationship does indeed exist.

For centuries, the difficulties encountered in the theological effort to mediate a correct understanding of the meaning of the Biblical text provided a major impetus in the development of hermeneutics. Conversely, new ideas in the field of hermeneutical reflection often played a distinct role in the reshaping and re-orientation of theological thinking. This was undoubtedly the case in the transition from Medieval theology to that of the Reformers of the sixteenth century.

In his book on the Wittenberg university theology and the beginning of the German Reformation, Karl Bauer has convincingly argued that Luther's new hermeneutics of Holy Scripture was the cornerstone of his entire programme as a Church Reformer.[1] This, of course, does not mean that Luther started off with an a priori and abstract design of new hermeneutical principles which he subsequently applied to the interpretation of the contents of Scripture, thus acquiring a new understanding of the Christian message. Luther's new hermeneutics rather originated and developed in the course of the actual process of scriptural interpretation. It was *in* his theological attempt at understanding the true and central meaning of the Biblical text that Luther made "eine exegetische Entdeckung von hermeneutischer Tragweite"[2] — a discovery which, humanly speaking, launched the Reformation movement.

* His address is: University of Stellenbosch, Stellenbosch, RSA 7600.

[1] Bauer. K. 1928. *Die Wittenberger Universitätstheologie und die Anfänge der deutschen Reformation,* Tübingen, p. 145.

[2] Ebeling, G. 1969. *Evangelische Evangeliumauslegung,* Darmstadt, p. 275.

While there are sufficient historical material for the description of the "Anfänge von Luthers Hermeneutik"[3], the data for doing the same with regard to Calvin's hermeneutics are lacking. From a historical point of view one could at most try to trace the influences at work in the shaping of his hermeneutical conception. In his "Forschungsansatz zur Hermeneutik Calvins" Canoczy points out valuable guidelines for such a study.[4] Canoczy discusses especially four such influences which Calvin incorporated and "fused" in his own "Theologie des Verstehens". These influences are those of the late-Medieval dispute on the relationship between Scripture and church, the movement of Humanism, the fundamental hermeneutical principles of Luther, and the so-called "Paulinism" of the fifteenth and sixteenth centuries.

Canoczy also postulates the hypothesis, amongst others, that Calvin could have been influenced by his intimate knowledge of problematical issues in the juridical sciences of his time. Apart from Canoczy's suggestions, Calvin's acquaintance with classical rhetoric should also be considered — a field which Battles has surveyed with special reference to the function of the concept of *accommodare* in Calvin's theology and commentaries.[5]

Whichever factors contributed to Calvin's hermeneutical views, it seems to me justified to say that both his theological thinking and his ecclesiastical action as a Reformer were, as was the case with Luther, inextricably bound up with his hermeneutics of Holy Scripture. No where did Calvin give a systematic treatise on hermeneutical problems as such. His attention was primarily directed at the practice of Biblical interpretation. Apart from his commentaries and sermons, the *Institutio* itself was offered as an introductory and interpretative aid to the reading and study of Scripture. Calvin's sustained concentration on, as well as his method of scriptural interpretation, rested, however, on hermeneutical presuppositions which he constantly gave account of in the course of his explication of the Biblical text.

[3] Ebeling, G. 1951. Die Anfänge von Luthers Hermeneutik, *Zeitschrift für Theologie und Kirche,* pp. 174 f.

[4] Canoczy, A. 1976. Calvin als paulinischer Theologe. Ein Forschungsansatz zur Hermeneutik Calvins, *Calvinus Theologus* (ed. by W.H. Neuser), Neukirchen-Vluyn, pp. 39f.

[5] Battles, F.L. 1977. God was accommodating Himself to human capacity, *Interpretation,* pp. 19f.

The most basic of these presuppositions, as far as Calvin's hermeneutics *as a Reformer* is concerned, is to be found in his explicit commitment to obey Holy Scripture as the one and only norm for true Christian faith and religion.[6] Usually this commitment is referred to as Calvin's confession of the *sola scriptura;* that is, of the exclusive authority of Holy Scripture — a confession which, properly understood, one can agree with Noltensmeier expresses the underlying "reformatorische Einheit" between Luther and Calvin.[7]

In itself, the emphasis on the *sola scriptura* was not a distinctive feature of the Reformation of the sixteenth century. An appeal to Scripture as the sole and pure *lex divina* was characteristic of various critical viewpoints assumed against papal authority in the course of the Middle Ages.[8] In most of these cases the *sola scriptura* was, however, nothing but a formal juridical thesis in a ecclesio-political dispute, reducing the number of legitimate sources of God's revelation to Scripture alone.[9]

As far as the Reformers are concerned, the *sola scriptura* naturally also implied such a reduction, in the sense of an exclusion, as sources of revelation, of any additional and supplementary traditions beyond that of the scriptural text. The significance which the *sola scriptura* had for the Reformation movement can, however, only be adequately grasped if the hermeneutical relevance of the *sola* is taken into account.[10] Such an understanding of the *sola scriptura* would at the same time reveal that the Reformers' conception of the exclusive authority of Scripture entailed a new view of the nature of this authority and of the way in which it is actually exercised. For the Reformers the confession of the *sola scriptura* originated in the context of a dispute which was primarily of a hermeneutical nature; that is, a dispute in which the real issue at stake was the correct

---

[6] Cf. *CR* 9,473 and 693.

[7] Cf. Noltensmeier, H. 1953. *Reformatorische Einheit. Das Schriftverständnis bei Luther und Calvin,* Graz-Köln.

[8] Cf. Kropatscheck, F. 1904. *Das Schriftprinzip der lutherische Kirche. 1. Band: Die Vorgeschichte. Das Erbe des Mittelalters,* Leipzig pp. 439f.

[9] Cf. Koopmans, J. 1938. *Het Oudkerkelijke Dogma in de Reformatie, bepaaldelijk bij Calvijn,* Wageningen p. 6.

[10] Cf. Ebeling. G. 1964. *Wort Gottes und Tradition,* Gottingen, p. 121: "... das Neue am reformatorischen *sola scriptura* (tritt) darin in Erscheinung dass es auf seine hermeneutischen Relevanz hin verantwortet wird".

interpretation and understanding of the Biblical message.

With regard to this issue, the Reformers had undoubtedly much in common with pre-Reformation theology. In the first place the Reformers shared the fundamental conviction that Holy Scripture was inspired by the Holy Spirit, and that it derived its authority as the medium of God's revelation from this inspiration. Secondly, the Reformers agreed, in accordance with the latter conviction, that the intended meaning of the scriptural text was that of the Holy Spirit. A correct understanding of Scripture is therefore an understanding of its *sensus spiritualis*. Thirdly, the Reformers endorsed the generally accepted rule of *non esse scripturas sanctas proprio sensu interpretandas*. This rule demanded a hermeneutical guarantee against what one might call a subjectivistic interpretation in which the interpreter's own convictions, personal ideas or private preferences determine what is being understood and explicated as the meaning of the text.

The predominant concern of the Reformers was, however, what kind of hermeneutical guarantee the church could have against such a subjectivistic interpretation. How could a true understanding of the *sensus proprius* of the Holy Spirit be secured? It was in response to this question that the Reformers' commitment to the exclusive authority of Holy Scripture had its real polemical significance. Only Scripture itself could safeguard an adequate and reliable understanding of its *sensus spiritualis;* that is, of the meaning intended and communicated by its divine Author. The hermeneutical guarantee against a subjectivistic interpretation was, in other words, not to be sought outside Scripture in a corpus of ecclesiastical authorities, supposedly instituted and ordained by God to lay down the criteria according to which the scriptural text ought to be interpreted. Scripture speaks for itself. It is its own interpreter, the one and only authoritative source and norm for its own understanding and explication.

In this sense, the primary purport of the Reformers' insistence on the *sola scriptura* was the outright rejection of the principle of ecclesiastical tradtition as the authoritative hermeneutical canon for the interpretation of Scripture. This principle rested on the assumption that the scriptural text was in itself obscure, and therefore in need of a supplementary source of "light" to render its true meaning accessible to our understanding. Such a supplementary source of illumination was to be found in the tradition of the church, defined and authenticated by its teaching office.

The hermeneutical doctrine of an extra-scriptural tradition as the touchstone for a correct interpretation of Scripture, amounted for the Reformers to a degradation, if not annulment, of scriptural authority. In order to fully maintain the authority of Scripture — instead of just paying lip-service to it — it had to be conceived of in such a way that the normative function of the scriptural text was not in fact suspended by subordinating its interpretation to cut and dried extra-scriptural standards. For this reason both Calvin and Luther taught the intrinsic clarity of Scripture.[11] In a nutshell, this doctrine meant that the scriptural text contains in itself the source of illumination which guarantees the intelligibility of the message it communicates. Scripture itself takes care, as it were, that its subject-matter is understood in accordance with the *sensus proprius* of its Author.[12]

The new hermeneutics of the Reformers did not, however, consist merely of a proclamation of the clarity, and therefore of the hermeneutical self-sufficiency of Scripture. It also gave an account of what the hermeneutical relevance of Scripture's exclusive authority entailed for the actual interpretation and understanding of the Biblical message. In the rest of this paper I would like to venture some remarks on what seems to me to be the most salient points of this account as far as Calvin's contribution is concerned. I shall attempt this task within the framework of an elementary but basic distinction between two different strands of hermeneutical reflection.

On the one hand, hermeneutical reflection can be focused on the *understanding event* as such. What is the nature of understanding —in general, or with regard to a particular text or type of text? Which conditions must be fulfilled in order to make understanding possible? What objective is being achieved when the intended meaning of a text is properly understood? On the other hand, hermeneutical reflection can be directed, from a methodological point of view, at the *process of interpretation.* In this context, the leading question will be what guidelines or procedural rules should be followed to bring about

---

[11] Cf. Rossouw, H.W. 1963. *Klaarheid en Interpretasie,* Amsterdam, Chapter 2.

[12] Cf. Weber, O. 1955. *Grundlagen der Dogmatik I,* Neukirchen/Moers, p. 354: "Das Kontinuum" des Verstehens-wenn man so will : das "hermeneutische Prinzip" — ist für die Reformatoren keine Instanz *gegenüber* der Schrift oder gar *über* ihr, sondern es erweist sich *in* der Schrift als mächtig".

an adequate understanding of a text.

The first part of my exposition will concentrate on what Calvin had to say on the first set of questions regarding the understanding of Scripture. I shall take as my point of departure Calvin's view of the *scopus* of Scripture. I shall then proceed to his view of the nature of the understanding event corresponding with this *scopus*. Finally, I shall briefly attend to Calvin's view of the conditions for the possibility of such an understanding of Scripture.

The word *scopus* means the end or goal which someone has in view in performing a particular action. In the case of a text, as a medium of communication in a discourse-situation, the word indicates the aim which the author wishes to achieve with regard to his potential readers. In the most general terms, this aim is that of making accessible to the understanding of the reader the subject-matter which is being talked or written about. In asking for the *scopus* of a specific text one has therefore to take into account what the subject-matter of the text is, and how this subject-matter is being communicated.

The *scopus* of Holy Scripture is a central and basic theme in Calvin's hermeneutical reflection. Calvin realised that in order to interpret Scripture correctly, one has to ascertain what the aim is which its divine Author had, and still has, in view, and in view of which the text of Scripture should accordingly be read. In circumscribing the aim which the Holy Spirit, as the Author of Scripture, has in view, Calvin used a variety of expressions which, to my mind, have to be read in conjunction in order to fully grasp his intention.

In its spiritual meaning, Holy Scripture is for Calvin primarily aimed at true religion, as distinct from superstition and idolatry. Calvin described the latter as the product of the vain and prideful human heart, which, through an act of the imagination, creates for itself a god or gods in whom it can lodge its trust.[13] True religion, on the contrary, consists in the relationship of the soul with "the living

[13] Cf. *CR* 25, 81 : "... volunt esse Dei creatores". Calvin referred to a "ad confingendas identidem novas et fictitias religionis libido" *(Inst.* I, 6,3), and to a "irreligiosa religionis affectatio (quia humano ingenio naturaliter insita est)" *(Inst.* II, 8,5).

God", or in the discernment of "who God truly is".[14] In acquainting us with the true and living God, Holy Scripture has true religion as its basic objective.

This indication of the goal of Scripture is, however, in need of a distinct qualification. According to Calvin the goal of Scripture is not to reveal to us the essence or the nature of God as He exists by and in himself *(apud se)*. The essence of God is incomprehensible to us; it surpasses our human capacity for understanding.[15] We should therefore leave to God the knowledge He has of Himself, and not try to apply our human mind to the study of God's essence.[16] Calvin opposed, in other words, any form of speculative theology, bent on fathoming the mysteries of God's essence and rendering these mysteries transparent in a theoretical grasp of the intellect.

Such a speculative theology usually regards the concrete and historical contents of Scripture as nothing but a symbolic or oblique signification of the real *res divinae*. It views its task as that of an intellectual deciphrement of this symbolic signification in order to get a foretaste, as it were, of the eschatological *visio Dei*. Calvin accused the *theologi papales* of being subject to this very misconception about the nature and goal of Scripture when they abandon the humble appearance of the scriptural message, and in their endless disputations *ad incomprehensibile Dei numen evolant*.[17]

The objective of Scripture is not the revelation of the *Deus apud se,* who, in his *nuda majestas,* remains hidden from us. The objective of Scripture is rather the revelation of the *Deus erga nos;* that is, of God as He has turned and directed Himself toward us, accommodating Himself to our human situation of finitude and sin. What Scripture reveals is not the *essentia* of God, but rather his *virtutes*.

Parker has argued that Calvin understood these virtues of God in an

---

[14] *Inst.* II, 8,6 : "... in Deum viventem ..." *CR* 55, 148: "... nisi discernas quisnam verus sit Deus".

[15] *Inst.* I, 5,1: "Essentia ... eius incomprehensibilis est, ut sensus omnes humanos procul effugiat eius numen". *CR* 6, 16: "Neque enim essentiae eius capax est mens nostra".

[16] *Inst.* I, 13, 21.

[17] *CR* 47, 322.

active sense as the ways in which He exercises his glory and majesty (that is, his Godhood) toward mankind.[18] In the revelation of his virtues, God is not showing us *quis sit apud se, sed qualis erga nos*.[19] This, of course, does not mean that when God reveals, in his actions, how He is disposed toward us, He reveals Himself as different from what He is in Himself. He who is revealed is He who reveals Himself. But what God reveals of Himself is not the mystery of his essence. It is rather the mystery of his attitude and activity toward us. This attitude and activity can be summarised in one word, viz. "grace".[20] The purpose of Scripture is to acquaint us with the merciful God.

Since the latter is the purpose of Scripture, it follows that the message of Scripture is not addressed to man in order to satisfy his metaphysical curiosity or his craving for a complete intellectual explanation of the whole of reality. As the message of God's grace, Scripture is addressed to man in the fundamental crisis of his existence, in his need of redemption from a wretched and meaningless life. God's grace is his intention and his enectment of man's salvation. The knowledge of the *Deus erga nos* which Scripture imparts is aimed at man's deliverance from the evil and wretchedness of the sinful human condition, so that man can fulfil his human destiny.

The knowledge of the *Deus erga nos* which Calvin had in mind, is, however, of such a kind that man cannot acquire this knowledge without the recognition and acknowledgement of the fundamental crisis and basic need of his existence. It is in this sense that Calvin defined the *summa sacrae* doctrinae as the *cognitio Dei ac nostri*.[21] While revealing God in his merciful disposition and activity toward us, the goal of Scripture is at the same time to induce in us that self-knowledge which is both the necessary precondition for, and the

---

[18] Cf. Parker, T.H.L. 1952. *The Doctrine of the Knowledge of God. A Study in the Theology of John Calvin*, Edinburgh/London, pp. 53-54.

[19] *Inst.* I, 10, 2.

[20] Cf. *CR* 55, 55: "quod Dei thronus non majestate nuda insignitur quae nos obstupefaciunt: sed ornatur novo titulo, nempe gratia, qui semper nobis in memoriam venire debet quum Dei conspectum refugimus".

[21] *Inst.* I, 1, 1. The 1539 edition reads: "Tota fere sapientiae nostra summa ... duobus partibus constat, Dei cognitione et nostri". On Calvin's view of the nature and meaning of this knowledge, cf. M. Lackmann: Conditio vitae est cognitio Dei, *Evangelische Theologie* 1935, pp. 198f.

concomitant effect of our coming to know the true and living God in the manifestation of his grace toward us. Self-knowledge and the knowledge of God are not two separate "items" of knowledge imparted in isolation from each other. They rather form a unity of reciprocal implication.

Far from being a mere system of intellectual ideas, the self-knowledge which correlates with the knowledge of God, affects our entire self-experience and self-esteem. Calvin described this self-knowledge in various terms, such as the awareness of our *misera calamitas*, the realisation of our extreme spiritual poverty *(egestas)*, or the discovering of the *latens in carne nostra foeditas*. It is the kind of knowledge which exposes the self-confident appraisal of our own virtues as utter self-delusion, which deprives us of our self-righteousness, and which finally plunges us into the utmost desperation.[22] In short, it makes us conscious of our urgent need of salvation.

How is this knowledge of God and of ourselves brought home to us in and through Scripture? Calvin would say by the *doctrina Dei*. In Scripture, God Himself is teaching us. But here again, Calvin's use of the word *doctrina* should be understood correctly. As the means of the *doctrina Dei*, Scripture is not a kind of textbook in the sense of an impersonal deposit of propositional information, to be articulated in and proclaimed as "doctrinal decrees" by a divinely ordained "teaching office". The paradigm for Calvin's use of the word *doctrina* is the pedagogical situation of a teacher having a personal relationship with his pupils, and continuously adapting himself to the level of comprehension of his pupils.[23] According to Calvin, Scripture is "the school of the Holy Spirit"[24], or "the school of God"[25] — a metaphor suggesting an ongoing activity of teaching and learning within the context of a living encounter and fellowship.

That the *doctrina Dei* should be taken in an active sense, is further

---

[22] Cf. Brunner, P. 1925. *Vom Glauben bei Calvin*, Tübingen pp. 7-28 for numerous quotations in this regard.

[23] Cf. Battles: *op cit.*, p. 30.

[24] *Inst. III, 21, 3.*

[25] *CR* 50, 424 and 597.

borne out by Calvin's constant use of the expression *Deus loquens*. It is the speaking God Himself who teaches us.[26] In and through the human words of Scripture God opens his "holy mouth"[27], so that these words may be heard *ac si vivae ipsae Dei voces*.[28] For this very reason, the authority of the scriptural teaching does not need to be vindecated or supported by any other authority outside Scripture. The *doctrina* of Scripture derives the proof of its authority from the person of the speaking God Himself.[29] Because God Himself is actively speaking to us in and through Scripture, Scripture is the *living* Word of God. In this sense the goal of Scripture is not just to inform us about the merciful God, but rather to bring us in the actual presence of the *Deus erga nos*.

According to Calvin, the speaking God teaches us through his living Word in two different forms *(formae docendi)*. These two forms are those of the law and of the gospel. Krusche has argued that Calvin used the words "law" and "gospel" in different senses which should be carefully distinguished.[30] When he dealt with the form or mode of scriptural teaching he applied these words in a rather strict and pointed meaning.

As a *forma docendi* the word *lex* referred for Calvin to the instruction, right through Scripture, of what the righteousness of God demands of mankind. It is precisely by learning through the law the demands of God's righteousness that man can discover his misery, and thus acquire true self-knowledge. The characteristic of the law in this sense is the threats *(minae)* that it implies for man, because of man's utter inability to comply with these demands.

However, as a *forma docendi* the law is not to be viewed in isolation as something standing on its own. The law which is taught by Scripture is always the law of God's covenant of grace. It therefore

---

[26] *Inst.* I. 7, 4: "... manifesta signa loquentis Dei conspici in scriptura, ex quibus pateat coelestem esse eius doctrinam".

[27] *Inst.* I, 6, 1.

[28] *Inst.* 1, 7, 1: Cf. II, 7,5: "... hominum ministerio ab ipsissimo Dei ore ad nos fluxisse".

[29] *Inst.* I, 7, 4: "Deus solus de se idoneus est testis in suo sermo ... summa scripturae probatio passim a Dei loquentis persona sumitur".

[30] Cf. Krusche W. 1957. *Das Wirken des Heiligen Geistes nach Calvin, Göttingen,* pp. 190f.

never functions as a *nuda lex*. On the contrary, the law is "clothed" with the *gratuitae adoptionis foedus*.[31] It is communicated to us within the context of God's gratuitous will for our salvation. The law refers intrinsically to, and functions in conjunction with the *evangelium* as the second mode of scriptural teaching. Once again, the word *evangelium*, in this sense, did not indicate for Calvin a part of Scripture, but rather its continuous assurance of God's saving grace. As a *forma docendi* the gospel is a matter of *promissio;* that is, of a speech act in which God commits Himself to the enactment of our salvation.[32]

Although the *doctrina Dei* of Scripture is communicated to us in two *formae,* it nevertheless has only one *substantia.* The law does not show us a way of salvation in addition, or in opposition, to the way of salvation taught by the gospel. Should the law be misunderstood in such a manner, it becomes a *naked,* but at the same time a *killing* law. In conjunction with the gospel the goal of the law is its *usus elenchticus.* As such it has the purpose of rendering us empty and naked in ourselves, so that we may be filled and clothed by the promise of God's mercy.[33]

Sometimes Calvin used the words "law" and "gospel" more loosely. In such cases they designated not different *formae docendi,* but rather the different manifestations which the one substance of God's teaching had assumed in the course of the historical development of his covenant of grace. It is in this context, as Krusche has pointed out, that Calvin introduced the metaphor of the relation between shadow and reality.[34] In this usage, *lex* (or *tota lex)* referred to the Torah of the Old Testament, the fundamental intention of which became gradually clearer in the course of the scriptural teaching, until it reached full clarity in the gospel of the New Testament. Viewed in this way, the law was already gospel as far as its basic purport was concerned, albeit in shadow form. On the other hand, the gospel, in its full manifestation, encompassed and incorporated the law as a guideline

---

[31] Cf. *Inst.* II, 7, 2.

[32] For Calvin's use of *evangelium* and *promissio,* cf. W.H. Neuser: Theologie des Wortes — Schrift, Verheissung und Evangelium bei Calvin, *Calvinus Theologus,* especially pp. 23f.

[33] Cf. Krusche: *op cit.,* p. 200; Brunner: *op. cit.* pp. 19f. For the view of the law as *praeparatio ad evangelium,* cf. *CR.* 50, 466; 49, 67.

[34] Krusche: *op. cit.,* p. 192.

for the new life in communion with God.[35]

Calvin conceived of the unity of Scripture as that of a series of interpretations in which the *genuinus sensus* of the Torah, as the basic text, was progressively understood and explicated.[36] The latter occurred through the *plenior expositio* of the prophets,[37] and eventually through Jesus Christ, the *fidus* and *optimus interpres legis.*[38] That Christ has to be seen as offering the definitive exegesis of the law, does not primarily bear reference to the Sermon on the Mount. What Calvin had in mind, was rather the conviction that the entire history of Christ's person and work was the final and full manifestation of the spiritual meaning and significance of the Torah. Christ Himself was the *substantia* of the *doctrina Dei,* and therefore of everything that had been taught in shadow form in the Torah and in its subsequent exposition by the prophets. Calvin declared explicitly that in everything it teaches *(doceat),* foreshadows *(praecipiat)* and promises *(promittat),* the law has always Christ as its objective *(pro scopo).* Therefore nobody can understand the law correctly if it is not interpreted with reference to this objective.[39] The law and the prophets have no other goal than Jesus Christ.[40] Christ is the *scopus* and the *summa* of the entire Scripture.[41]

This brings us to the focal point in which all Calvin's ideas on the *scopus* of Scripture are being drawn together. In Christ, and in Him alone, the source and the criterion of true religion has been given to us.[42] Only in Christ could we learn the merciful will of God toward us, and could we find the true life of salvation and, ultimately, the

---

[35] Cf. also Wolf, H.H. 1958. *Die Einheit des Bundes. Das Verhältnis von Alten und Neuen Testament bei Calvin,* Neukirchen, pp. 38f.

[36] Krusche: *op. cit.,* pp. 185f.

[37] *CR* 45, 108; 6, 273 and 36, 19.

[38] *Inst.* II, 8, 7; *CR* 45, 175 and 179; 51, 70.

[39] *CR* 49, 196.

[40] *CR* 45, 486; 47, 125. Cf. *CR* 48, 569; *Inst.* II, 11, 1 and the comment of John H. Leith: "The only real difference between the Testaments is the degree of clarity in the revelation of Christ". (John Calvin-Theologian of the Bible, *Interpretation* 1971, p. 340); W. Niesel: *Die Theologie Calvins,* München 1957[2], pp. 102-107.

[41] *CR* 52, 52.

[42] *CR* 36, 420: "Denique extra Christum et omnis religio fallax est, ac evanida ..."

Kingdom of Heaven. Without Christ as Mediator, we have no access to God.[43] This is so, because the true and living God revealed in Jesus Christ his righteousness, his goodness, his wisdom and his virtue, yes, the whole of Himself *(se totum)*, in order that we could see Him in Christ as in a mirror. Whoever is therefore called God, with a disregard of Christ, is nothing but an idol.[44] All thought about God which somehow ignores the Christ of Scripture, is like a bottomless abyss.[45] It can only result in "vain and airy speculation".[46]

In the final instance, the goal of Scripture is to impart Christ to us. Calvin advised that the word "Christ" should not be taken as merely expressing the *nudum Christi nomen.*[47] As the *scopus* of Scripture, "Christ" refers to God's enactment of our salvation in the drama, as it were, of the incarnation, the life and the deeds, the crucifixion and the resurrection of Jesus Christ. When God speaks to us in and through Scripture as his living Word, it is with the aim of making us participants in this drama, so that we may come to share the blessings of his redeeming grace in the communion with the crucified and risen Christ.[48]

As a cursory survey of Calvin's view of the goal of Scripture these few remarks could have sufficed, were it not for a distinction that Calvin made with regard to the *doctrina* of Scripture which complicates the interpretation of his conception to a certain extent. This is namely the distinction between *doctrina propria* and *doctrina generalis.*[49] For Calvin the first expression indicated the special teaching of Scripture which has our salvation as its objective.[50] The "general teaching" of Scripture, on the other hand, has as its subject-matter the *gloria Dei* revealed in the *opera Dei*. In its "general teaching" Scripture fulfils the function which the signs of God's glory in the works of his

---

[43] Cf. *Inst.* III, 2, 1.

[44] *CR* 52, 85.

[45] *CR* 55, 226.

[46] *CR* 48, 338.

[47] *CR* 55, 214.

[48] Cf. *CR* 48, 388; 49, 313.

[49] For a very helpful dicussion of this distinction, pointing out the lack of clarity in Calvin's account, cf. P. Kertz: *Calvins Verständnis der Heiligen Schrift* (unpublished dissertation), Göttingen 1939.

creation and providence were meant to fulfil, but which we cannot discern, due to our sinful blindness. True religion included for Calvin also the contemplation of the *gloria Dei*, evidenced in his works, and thus the worship of God the Creator.[51] "The burning torch in the building of the world", however, shines in vain, because of our blindness.[52] For that reason, we need Scripture as "spectacles" to restore our sight so that we can perceive the light of God's glory.[53]

The question now arises whether Calvin did not, with the latter views, relax or even contradict his doctrine that Christ is the *scopus* and *summa* of Scripture. Forstman interprets Calvin in this way, and concludes that his theology reveals an inner tension between two different "epistemologies".[54] The issue in this regard is not whether or not Calvin taught the possibility of a natural theology. Both Parker and Krusche, amongst others, have, to my mind, convincingly demonstrated that Calvin did not teach such a possibility.[55] The problem is rather how Calvin's view of Christ as the *scopus* of Scripture could be reconciled with his image of Scripture as "spectacles" which should help us to discover the glory of God *in his works*.

An adequate discussion of this problem would exceed the limits of this paper. In order not to leave it entirely as a loose end, I would like, however, to mention briefly Calvin's introduction to his commentary on Genesis.[56] There he perhaps made the most pertinent remarks on this issue. After touching on the function of Scripture as our guide and teacher in respect of the glory of God in the world, he himself asked whether this is not at variance with Paul's message in 1 Corinthians 1:21.

In his reply, Calvin declared that it would indeed be in vain for anyone

---

[51] Cf. *CR* 6, 459f.

[52] *Inst.* I, 5, 14; *CR* 38, 38.

[53] Cf. *Inst.* I, 6, 1; *CR* 23, 9. Krusche: *op. cit.*, p. 78 has pointed out the discrepancy between Calvin's metaphor of "blindness" and that of Scripture as "spectacles". The latter suggests weak-sightedness, not lack of sight.

[54] Forstman, H.J. 1962. *Word and Spirit. Calvin's Doctrine of Biblical Authority*, Stanford, pp. 38f.

[55] Cf. Parker: *op. cit.*, pp. 25f. and Krusche: *op. cit.*, pp. 67f.

[56] *CR* 23, 9 and 10.

to philosophise on the *mundi opificium,* save for those who, having first been humbles by the preaching of the gospel, have learned to submit the whole of their intellectual wisdom to the foolishness of the Cross. Until Christ has taught us in his own school, we shall find nothing, either below or above, which can elevate us to God. Once we have been taught in the school of Christ, however, we can apply our senses to the consideration of heaven and earth, so that we may thence seek confirmation in the true knowledge of God. For Christ is that image of God in which He presents to our view, not only his heart, but also his hands and his feet. The "heart" of God designated for Calvin the secret love with which He embraces us in Christ. God's "hands" and "feet" referred for Calvin to God's works as they are displayed before our eyes. Calvin concluded with the warning that we are bound to deceive ourselves in our investigation of the works of God, should we ever depart from Christ.

The *scopus* of Scripture is the goal which its divine Author has in view. This goal is accomplished when man actually understands and appropriates the *sensus spiritualis* of Scripture. The next question of hermeneutical significance is what the nature of this understanding event is.

Calvin's answer to this question should be sought in his conception of faith. Understanding the subject-matter of Scripture, communicated by the Holy Spirit, coincides with our having faith. Faith is, as it were, the "sight" through which we can "behold" that which the divine Author has in view.

There can be no doubt about the inter-relationship in Calvin's theology between faith and the understanding of the scriptural message. This inter-relationship is presupposed by Calvin's opposition to the notion of a *fides implicita,* in the sense namely of a "blind" acceptance, of, and assent to the scriptural teaching in obedient subjection to the authority of the church and of its doctrinal decrees. Faith does not consist in ignorance, but in knowledge.[57] We cannot have faith without understanding that which is imparted to us in and through Scripture.

Conversely, understanding the meaning of the Scriptural message was for Calvin a matter of faith. What Scripture conveys to us as the

---

[57] *Inst.* III, 2, 2. Cf. *Inst.* III, 2, 42: "fides ... certa est de veritate Dei persuasio". Cf. also *CR* 42, 331 and 49, 165.

doctrina Dei can only be learned and appropriated in faith. Thus faith is on the one hand the humble recognition of our own spiritual emptiness and helplessness — a recognition ensuing from our being stripped of our self-righteousness through the instruction of the law.[58] On the other hand, faith means to have our refuge in God's benevolence toward us — a state of being brought about by the promise of the gospel that God has committed Himself to the enactment of our salvation.[59] Faith is, in other words, equivalent to the acquisition of that knowledge of ourselves and of God which is being communicated to us by the *doctrina Dei* of Scripture.

It should be clear that the kind of understanding which he regarded characteristic of faith, differed for Calvin from a purely intellectual insight. This does not mean that he had an anti-intellectualistic conception of faith. On the contrary, faith did not for him exclude the exercise of intellectual thinking. But Calvin never viewed faith as a body of ecclesiastical dogmas which need to be made intelligible in a theological system of theoretical explanations and speculative insights. When he spoke of the *intelligentia fidei,* he preferred to call it an understanding of the "soul".[60] And the faculties of the soul consisted for him both in the mind and in the heart. Even though he made this latter distinction, it should be added that Calvin was opposed to any rigid division of the soul into different agencies functioning in isolation from each other.[61]

If one takes this into account, one can interpret Calvin's idea of the soul, "endued with the power of understanding"[62], as referring to the whole inward life of man. Accordingly, the exercise of this power within the context of faith amounts to much more than a mere intellectual apprehension. It involves the whole inward life of man in a kind of total experience — an experience of our minds being persuaded to new convictions, of our attitudes being changed and re-oriented; in short, of our total existence being transformed into a new way of being. Primarily, this experience is what one might call an

---

[58] Cf. *CR* 49, 65: "... quoniam a Deo omnia accipit fides, nihil affert praeter humilem inopiae confessionem".

[59] Cf. *CR* 50, 485: "... et avoir tout nostre refuge à la pure bonté de Dieu". *Inst.* III, 2, 29: "... proprie ... a promissione incipit (sc. fides), in ipsa constat, in ipsam desinit".

[60] Cf. Parker: *Op. cit.,* p. 106.

[61] Cf. Parker: *op. cit.,* p. 107.

[62] Inst. III, 2, 2.

auditive experience, evoking a personal response from us.

According to Calvin there can be no faith *sine auditu*. He explained this by adding *hoc est, sine intelligentia verbi Dei*.[63] Faith is a matter of hearing, and this hearing is equivalent to the understanding of the Word of God. The *objectum* of faith is not the doctrinal decrees of the church. It is the Word of God. Faith and the Word of God together form a "melody".[64] They belong together. On the one hand, faith has no other foundation or support than the living Word of God. Take away the Word, said Calvin, and nothing remains of faith.[65] On the other hand, the Word which has been separated from faith does not in itself confer anything *(nihil conferat)*. The efficacy of the Word, of course, does not depend on us. But the Word cannot reveal its power to us if faith does not provide the access or opportunity *(aditum facit)*.[66]

It is true that Calvin often used metaphors of visual perception to describe the understanding inherent in faith. Thus he referred, for instance, to the "eye" of faith by which we can "behold" God.[67] His insistence on the correlation between faith and the Word of God, however, counteracted the idea of a purely contemplative understanding, so strongly intimated by these metaphors of vision. The correlation between faith and Word rather points in the direction of that kind of understanding which is characteristic of an interpersonal bond, and which is manifested in mutual trust and troth.

Perhaps Calvin's intention can best be expressed in the following way. Taking the initiative, the *Deus loquens* addresses us in and through his Word. Faith is both the experience of hearing God speaking to us, and the act of appropriately responding to Him who speaks. Through his living Word God acquaints us with Himself, revealing to us that He is truly God and that He plights his troth to be God for us. In faith we duly respond to God's "opening Himself up" to us — in reverence and love, in worship and trust, in grateful praise and active obedience. The fact that we respond, and the way in which

---

[63] *CR* 37, 285.

[64] CR 23, 689; Inst. III, 2,6: "... perpetuam esse fidei relationem cum verbo ..."

[65] *Inst.* III, 2, 6. Cf. *CR* 49, 11: "... Dominus per evangelium nos vocat: nos vocati per fidem respondemus".

[66] *CR* 55, 45.

[67] *CR* 49, 326.

we respond, together indicate that we have understood the *Deus loquens*.

Making sense of the scriptural message as God's Word thus amounts to our entering into a personal relationship and communion with God. The kind of understanding involved in such a relationship and communion naturally includes the understanding of what God is saying to us. The Word of God which we may hear and respond to in faith has a distinct content. For Calvin this content was coterminous with the teaching of the scriptural canon in its totality and unity. As religious belief *in* God, faith was therefore also for him logically dependent on our being convinced of, and our believing *that* God is such, and that He acts in such a way, as the teaching of Scripture tells us that He is and acts. Faith is a firm and steadfast *fiducia* in God because it is a certain *cognitio* of God. The response of faith does not only take the form of religious and ethical attitudes and behaviour. It also takes the form of credal statements in which we express and show our understanding of the distinct content of God's Word.

Once again it should be stressed, however, that the credal statements expressing our understanding of the content of the *cognitio Dei ac nostri,* mediated by the teaching of Scripture, were for Calvin all but theoretical judgements of a speculative theology. They were not so much the expression of "insights" which, once achieved, would render us independent of the teaching of the scriptural text itself. They were for Calvin rather the expression of, as it were, "auditives", for the reliability of which we should keep on listening to what God has to say in his Word. One can put it in another way by saying that credal statements were for Calvin confessions in which we recognise and bear witness to the convictions God Himself has persuaded us to (or has convinced us of). Such confessions can never take on an existence independent of the relationship in which they are born. They can never cease, in other words, to be a form of response which is ever anew being evoked by the assurances of our Convictor. That is so, because the God we come to understand in faith is the *Deus loquens.* He never stops speaking to us. Therefore we can only understand Him, and at the same progress in this understanding of faith, if we keep on listening to what God has to say; that is, if we remain faithful students of Holy Scripture.

From what has previously been said about Calvin's distiction between the *Deus apud se* and the *Deus erga nos,* it follows that the understanding expressed in the credal statements of faith bears no reference to the mystery of God's essence. According to Calvin, it is not altogether correct to say, without further qualification, that God is the *objectum* of faith.[68] In faith we have only access to the mystery of God in his merciful disposition and activity toward us. This mystery is the mystery of God in Jesus Christ. Only in and through Christ can we participate in the bond with God.[69] The *scopus* or *obejctum* of faith is therefore Christ,[70] who is Himself the living Word of God. From what has been said so far, it should be clear that Calvin's account of the hermeneutical relevance of the *sola scriptura* was given in terms of the other *particulae exclusivae* of Reformation theology: *sola fide, solo verbo, solus Christus.*

It is hardly necessary to emphasise that the Christ at whom faith is primarily directed, was for Calvin the incarnated, crucified and risen Christ; that is, the Christ of a concrete and unique history. It should be added, however, that Calvin contrasted faith, as the mode of understanding Christ, whith a mere *historica fides,* in the sense of believing the *nuda historia* or the *bruta facta* of events that once happened in the past. Faith is the understanding of these events in their living meaningfulness for us. For the Evangelists, said Calvin, "do not merely relate that Christ was born, and that he died and vanquished death, but also explain for what purpose he was born, and died, and rose again, and what benefit *(fructus)* we derive from those events".[71] Understanding the history of Christ in faith thus means understanding it as *historia salutis,* as the story of God's deeds of salvation and of ourselves as beneficiaries of those deeds.

If making sense of the scriptural message coincides with faith as the response to the *Deus loquens,* the question remains whether there are special conditions for the possibility of Scripture to evoke from us the answer of faith. I think one can distinguish two such conditions in Calvin's hermeneutics of Holy Scripture. These conditions are the preaching of Scripture through the agency of the church, and the inner testimony of the Holy Spirit.

[68] *Inst.* II, 6. 4. Cf. also *Inst.* III, 2, 1.

[69] *Inst.* II, 16, 3.

[70] Cf. *CR* 47, 321; 49, 332; 55, 214.

[71] *CR* 47, 8.

That there can be no faith, according to Calvin, *sine auditu,* should be taken in a literal sense. Scripture exercises its authority as the living Word of God within the context of oral tradition as it takes place in the preaching of the church. As the living Word of God, Scripture is neither a document of metaphysical symbolisation to be deciphred by speculative theologians, nor a legal code for the juridical organisation of an institute. It is a message of salvation addressed to people in religious need. A message requires to be delivered in such a way that the addressee can hear and recognise it as a "word" that concerns him. The deliverance of the scriptural message was for Calvin the true calling of the church, the mandate it received from God.[72] The church is the *fida custos verbi Dei,* said Calvin. But he immediately added that the custody of the church was not meant to be exercised by way of dominion over the Word, but rather through its "propagation" from generation to generation.[73]

This is the reason why Calvin so strongly emphasised the necessity that the *doctrina* of the church should be *pura.* The touchstone for the purity of the church's teaching is its agreement with the *doctrina Dei* of Scripture, and hence the absence of human opinions and traditions. In order to believe, we must be taught correctly *(driotement enseignez).*[74] Such a correct teaching is one that is in accordance with the teaching of God's Word in Scripture.

Calvin's use of the word *doctrina* in connection with the church had, however, the same active sense as was the case with his use of the word in connection with God's teaching in Scripture. Calvin's view of the *doctrina* of the church was not that of a system of doctrinal decrees, or of a body of definitions proclaimed by the teaching office of the church as *credenda.* The *doctrina* of the church coincided for Calvin with the *praedicatio verbi domini;* that is, with the kerygmatic activity of preaching in which the message of Scripture is orally proclaimed in its meaning and significance for an audience of actual listeners.[75] It is in this sense that the *doctrina* of the church is the condition for the possibility of the understanding event in which the

---

[72] *CR* 49, 362.

[73] *CR* 6, 277.

[74] *CR* 53, 361.

[75] Cf. *CR* 47, 12 and 340; Brunner: *op. cit.,* pp. 106f.; Kertz: *op. cit.,* pp. 27f.; Krusche: *op. cit.,* pp. 218f; Wolf: *op. cit.,* p. 72 and Neuser: *op. cit.,* p. 22.

goal of Scripture is achieved. Faith is evoked by the teaching of the church as it is actually heard "with the ears."[76] It is precisely because of this function the *doctrina* of the church has, that it should be kept pure of any unscriptural traditions and human opinions. Gods speaks through the preaching of the church, provided the church takes care that it preaches the pure doctrine of Scripture.

The preached Word is, however, not the only condition for the possibility of understanding Scripture. Calvin added a second condition of decisive importance, namely that of the inner testimony of the Holy Spirit. In the last instance, understanding Scripture in faith is not a human achievement, describable in terms of general epistemological or hermeneutical categories. It is a gift of God, effected by the "secret operation" of the Holy Spirit in us.

By nature we are blind for the treasures of the Kingdom of Heaven. Our hearts resist the gratuitous assurance of God's redeeming mercy. Our ears are closed for the message of Scripture. There can be no understanding of the Word of God unless the Spirit of God "opens our mental eyes",[77] gives us "the heart to understand",[78] or "pierce our ears".[79] Only the Spirit can "form the ears to hear and the mind to understand".[80] "Except the Spirit of wisdom be present, to have God's Word in our hands will avail little or nothing, for its meaning will not appear to us".[81]

Calvin described the secret operation of the Spirit in us, as far as our relation to Scripture is concerned, with concepts like *illuminatio, obsignatio* and *revelatio.*[82] The effect of this inner testimony of the Holy Spirit has two aspects. Firstly, the Spirit persuades us of the divine authority of Scripture so that we can recognise and understand

---

[76] *CR* 25, 109. Cf. *CR* 37, 285.

[77] *Inst.* III, 1, 4.

[78] *Inst.* IV, 14, 10. Cf. *CR* 24, 258.

[79] *CR* 32, 683.

[80] *Inst.* II, 2, 20.

[81] *CR* 55, 347.

[82] Neuser: *op. cit.,* p. 30 has drawn attention to the interesting fact that Calvin used the words *revelare* and *revelatio* only for "die ganz persönliche Offenbarung des Heils in den Glaubenden".

that the teaching of Scripture is indeed the teaching of God Himself. Secondly, the Spirit quides us in the truth of Scripture so that we can discern and understand *what* God is saying to us in the teaching of Scripture.

The conviction of the believer that it is God Himself who speaks to us in Scripture, does not rest on the judgement of the church, nor on rational argument, even though both the testimony of the church and the weight of evidence might be of valuable assistance in assuring the individual in his belief. For Calvin, we are confirmed in this conviction of the divine authority of Scripture by the inner testimony of the Spirit.[83]

While the Spirit is the indispensable and sufficient witness of his own authorship of Scripture, He is at the same the only reliable and authentic interpreter of Himself as Author. Calvin described the Spirit as interpreter of Scripture as such,[84] of the *doctrina evangelii,*[85] and of the prophets.[86] The inner testimony of the Spirit is thus also an act of translation, of making intelligible what whould otherwise remain a sealed book to us. We cannot understand the contents of Scripture as the living Word of God, save for this secret operation of the Spirit.

Although Calvin distinguished between the preached Word and the inner testimony of the Spirit, it had never been his intention to separate these two. On the contrary, he constantly stressed the intimate bond between Word and Spirit. Word and Spirit are joined together. Without the efficacy of the Spirit the *praedicatio verbi* itself effects nothing, but remains fruitless. On the other hand, Calvin warned, in the same context, against the *homines fanatici* who glorify the Spirit while despising the Word. "For it is the spirit of Satan that is separated from the Word."[87] The *verbum praedicatum* is the organ and instrument which the Spirit uses in his work of illumination, sealing and revelation.[88] It is, however, also the organ and the

---

[83] Cf. *Inst.* I, 7, 4.

[84] *CR* 6, 270.

[85] *CR* 49, 344.

[86] *CR* 55, 457.

[87] *CR* 37, 352. Cf. *CR* 47, 354.

[88] Cf. *CR* 7, 176; 49, 439 and Krusche: *op. cit.,* p. 221 for further references.

instrument through which God confers the mercy of his Spirit on us, and through which we may receive this Spirit.[89]

It should be clear that the inner testimony of the Spirit did not represent for Calvin an alternative source of faith, independent of Scripture as it is preached and heard as the Word of God. For the rest, it remains, however, an open question as to how exactly Calvin viewed the bond between Word and Spirit. Krusche has suggested the word "accompaniment" as a solution to the problem.[90] Neuser —to mention only one other commentator — has criticised Krusche's proposal. In his opinion the Spirit does not, according to Calvin, "accompany" the Word, but rather "confirms" it. While faith originates through the efficacy of the preached Word, the inner testimony of the Spirit effects the certainty of faith which is shared by the chosen alone.[91] Neuser's conclusion, based on a careful analysis of the relevant passages in the *Institutio,* is partly supported by a remark which Calvin made elsewhere, stating that Christ promises the Spirit, *qui evangelii doctrinam quasi subscriptor confirmet.*[92] For the purposes of this paper, the exact formulation of Calvin's view in this regard is, however, of lesser importance. The significant point is that both the preaching of God's Word and the inner testimony of the Holy Spirit functioned in Calvin's hermeneutics as conditions for the possibility of understanding Scripture in accordance with its *scopus.*

In the last part of the paper I would like to make a few observations on Calvin's hermeneutical reflection with regard to the process and procedure of interpretation. I shall firstly discuss the implications which Calvin's doctrine of the Spirit as his own interpreter has for this process. This will lead to a consideration of his emphasis on the literal sense of Scripture. I shall then turn to Calvin's hermeneutical guidelines for the exposition of the one *doctrina Dei,* imparted to us in Scripture as a coherent unity. Finally, I shall discuss the sense in which Calvin recognised the hermeneutical relevance of the so-called *analogia fidei.*

Calvin's doctrine that the Spirit is the only true interpreter of Himself

---

[89] Cf. *CR* 40, 457; 50, 466 and 477 and Krusche: *loc. cit.* for further references.

[90] Krusche: *op. cit.,* pp. 228f.

[91] Neuser: *op. cit.,* pp. 30f.

[92] *CR* 47, 335.

could easily be taken to mean that the mediation of a correct understanding of Scripture is a purely mystical event in which the human activity of exegesis has no role to play. Such a spiritualistic interpretation of his view would, however, render inexplicable Calvin's own concern with, and extensive contribution to the exegesis of the scriptural text. It would further be at variance with his conception of the function of preaching as an organ and instrument of the Spirit. Preaching is, after all, not merely a verbal repetition of the scriptural text, but an activity of explication and application. Obedience to the authority of Scripture entailed for Calvin, in theory as well as in practice, the diligent study of Scripture with a view to its oral tradition in the preaching of the church.

What Calvin did mean was that no human procedures of interpretation or exegetical techniques can in itself guarantee the successful communication of the *sensus spiritualis* of Scripture. God uses the ministry of men whom He employs as his delegates to do his work of teaching. But the Spirit is "the only fit corrector and approver of doctrine, who seals it on our hearts, so that we may certainly know that God speaks".[93] The Spirit guides and enlightens those who are given the task of interpretation for others. At the same time the Spirit endues the individual believer "with judgement and discernment, lest we should be deceived by lies".[94] When the church interprets Scripture improperly, God Himself undertakes the office of teacher, and by connecting the external voice with the secret operation of his Spirit, effects renewal.[95]

Calvin had no doubt that the Spirit would govern the human process of interpretation and render his *sensus proprius* intelligible, provided that such a process of interpretation is carried out by faithful men, seriously searching for the pure teaching of God in Scripture. The appropriate attitude of the human exegete should be one, not of prideful confidence in his own opinions, but of humble obedience, and of willingness to let his own findings be questioned and corrected by the text of Scripture.[96] It is only in continuously submitting one's explication to the test of the scriptural text that one can expect the

[93] *CR* 55, 327-328.

[94] *CR* 55, 328.

[95] *CR* 47, 149.

[96] Cf. *CR* 4, 759; 55, 458.

Spirit to purify it of impertinent human opinions.

This means that no product of human interpretation can ever replace the text as a final or infallible exposition of its meaning. The corollary of the doctrine that the Spirit is his own interpreter, is the view that all human exegesis of Scripture is in principle unsettled and incomplete. The latter does not imply that the meaning of Scripture is in itself uncertain, a "labyrinth" or a "nose of wax" that can be twisted at will. In his controversy with Pighius Calvin forcefully opposed such a view.[97] The intended meaning of Scripture is in itself clear. In the last instance, however, only the secret operation of the Spirit, who inspired Scripture, can safeguard an authentic understanding of this meaning. And this work of the Spirit can never be secured by human procedures of interpretation.

Against this background, one can see why Calvin so resolutely rejected the Medieval doctrine of the fourfold sense of Scripture and the hermeneutical rules which were derived from this doctrine. The doctrine of the fourfold sense of Scripture maintained that the scriptural text contains, as it were, different layers of meaning. The first layer, signified by the text in its literal-historical form, is not the real meaning of Scripture. It is in itself only a symbolic representation of a spiritual or mystical sense which is hidden in or behind it. This hidden spiritual sense is the true revelatory content of Scripture, consisting in its turn of three different "senses". In the process of scriptural interpretation we should therefore transcend the literal-historical meaning in an effort to uncover and bring to light its threefold spiritual sense. The methodological clues for the procedure of such a deciphrement were the questions as to what we should believe (allegorical sense), what we should do (moral or tropological sense), and what we may hope (anagogical sense).

Calvin attributed the presupposition of a hidden spiritual sense of Scripture to a misapprehension about the intention of Paul's expression in 2 Corinthians 3:6 that "the letter killeth" — a misapprehension originating with Origen and perpetuated by others.[98] The interpretation scheme developed on the basis of this presupposition gave, in Calvin's view, free play to all sorts of artificial subtleties, far-fetched

[97] Cf. *CR* 6, 268f. For Calvin's criticism of the notion of Scripture as a *nasus cereus,* cf. also *CR* 33, 523; 47, 145.

[98] *CR* 49, 40-41.

fantasies and arbitrary explanations, masquerading as interpretations of Scripture's *sensus spiritualis*. In this way, human opinions became intermingled with the Word of God to such an extent that it could hardly any longer be called an exegesis of Scripture. Consequently the preaching of the church was also deprived of its power and fruitfulness as an organ of the Spirit of God.

According to Calvin, the words *litera* and *spiritus,* as they are used by Paul, bear no reference to different senses of Scripture, but rather to the question whether the one Word of God which comes to us in the words of Scripture, is received with the heart or not. *Spiritus* refers to the *doctrina spiritualis;* that is, to a kind of teaching which is not just spoken by mouth, but which penetrates the soul with a living awareness *(vivo sensu).*[99] The contrast between *litera* and *spiritus* has nothing to do with different modes of explication *(expositio),* but refers to the absence or presence of power *(vis)* and fruit *(fructus).*[100] A "spiritual" interpretation of Scripture is an interpretation in which the Spirit of God is at work, illuminating our minds so that we can discern the pure doctrine of Scripture, and sealing this doctrine on our hearts so that we may enjoy the full benefits thereof. For Calvin the pure doctrine of Scripture is not hidden in a mystical way behind the literal sense of the text. It is, on the contrary, contained in this literal sense. We can only hope to interpret Scripture according to its "spiritual" sense, if in humble obedience to the text we concentrate on its literal sense, thus allowing the divine Author of Scripture to purify our interpretation of any human opinions and unscriptural traditions and prejudices.

In a well-known article Krause has summarised the guidelines which ought to be followed, according to Calvin, if the literal sense of the scriptural text is to be taken seriously as its proper sense.[101] The most important of these is, firstly, to strive after simplicity in a concise and clear exegesis. Lavish and broadly elaborated allegorical interpretations should be avoided. Secondly, one should inquire into the actual intentions of the human authors, paying careful attention to their different historical and geographical circumstances and to their

---

[99] *CR* 49, 39.

[100] *CR* 49, 41.

[101] Krause, H.J. 1968. Calvin's Exegetical Principles, *Interpretation* 1977, pp. 8-18 (originally published in German, *Zeitschrift für Kirchengeschichte* pp. 329-341).

particular institutional positions. Thirdly, the context *(complexus)* of an utterance has to be considered in order to determine its basic purport and its full implications. Fourthly, the exegete should constantly ascertain the justifiability and the limits of a *progressus ultra verba*, a going beyond that which is said by the words themselves. Finally, metaphorical expressions should be identified, and no unjustified conclusions be made because the figurative function of such expressions has not been taken into account.

Calvin therefore advised, in opposition to allegorical methods of interpretation in the widest sense of the word, what could be called a historical-grammatical method of exegesis. In his commentaries Calvin himself applied all the philological and historical knowledge and methods available in his day, and of which he had an excellent command due to his humanistic training. It stands to reason that in such an exegetical approach, the distinctively human qualities of the scriptural text would emerge more clearly. This gave rise to Calvin's occasional critical remarks on certain details in the text. These criticisms, however, had no serious influence on his basic theological assumptions with regard to Scripture. In Calvin's hermeneutical reflection there was no sign yet of the awareness of the theological problems which would later on be raised by the consistent application of the historical-grammatical method of exegesis. What remained for him the dominant hermeneutical point of view, was not the human characteristics of the scriptural text, but the "doctrine of the Spirit of God", given to us in this text "for our use".[102]

Because of the latter, the historical-grammatical and dogmatic-systematic approaches in Calvin's interpretation of Scripture were still indissolubly connected. Indeed, he hardly distinquished between these approaches, which were only later on clearly differentiated in tense rivalry. For Calvin, the historical-grammatical inquiry into the literal sense of the scriptural text was essentially the same as the dogmatic-systematic quest for the one *doctrina Dei* which is communicated to us in the canon of Scripture, and which should be purely preached by the church. That is why his commentaries accompanied the series of re-editions of the *Institutio* since 1539, and that is why he regarded his systematic summary of scriptural

---

[102] Cf. Krause, H.J. 1969[2]. *Geschichte der historisch-kritische Erforschung des Alten Testaments,* Neukirchen, p. 17. Also Leith: *op. cit.,* p. 338: "For this reason it is futile to find answers in Calvin's writings to new questions raised by modern historical consciousness".

teaching as the indispensable frame of reference for the interpretation of the separate books of the Bible. Together, the commentaries and the *Institutio* were intended to facilitate the task of the preacher — a task which Calvin himself performed with persistent zeal and dedication.[103]

Both in theory and in his own practice as an interpreter, the unity and inner harmony of Scripture as the one Word of God functioned for Calvin as a basic hermeneutical guideline in the quest for the pure doctrine of God. God cannot contradict Himself. Therefore the apparent differences and anomalies in Scripture should be attributed to the fact that God accommodated Himself to the different needs and capacities of his chosen people at various times and under various circumstances.[104] For a correct interpretation of Scripture it is essential that these differences and anomalies be explicated in such a way that the coherence of the one *doctrina Dei* is brought to light.

In order to fulfil this requirement, Calvin found another basic hermeneutical guideline in his view of Christ as the *scopus* of Scripture. If Christ is the real objective of Scripture, then He is also the only key which can unlock the door giving us entrance to the truth of God.[105] We should therefore read Scripture in order to find Christ. Whoever deviates from this goal can devote himself for the rest of his life to the study of Scripture, but will never attain the knowledge of the truth which is the wisdom of God.[106] What is valid for the reader, naturally also applies to those who have the task to assist the reader as interpreters. All work of interpretation should point in the direction of this one distination, in order to help the traveller not to lose his way.

This hermeneutical guideline confronts the exegete with the difficult task of showing how the entire Scripture is oriented toward Christ. The crux of this task is, of course, presented by the interpretation of the Old Testament. Through a method of allegorical interpretation, the messáge of Christ can readily be extracted from the text of the Old

---

[103] Cf. Leith: *op. cit.*, pp. 331f. on the interaction between Calvin's systematic and exegetical works and the manifestation of this interaction in his sermons.

[104] Cf. *Inst.* 11, **2**, 13.

[105] Cf. *CR* 52, 87.

[106] *CR* 47, 125. Cf. also *CR* 45, 817; 50, 45; 53, 560 and 24: 75: "Imo quoties in manus sumimus sacros libros debet nobis occurere sanguis Christi, ac si eo scripta esset tota coelestis doctrina".

Testament. However, Calvin's choice of a historical-grammatical method, which demands that the literal sense of the Old Testament should not be abandoned or distorted, excluded the application of allegorical techniques. In various places Calvin himself warned against the practice of "reading into" a text a reference to Christ where the "simple" or "true" meaning contains no such allusion.[107]

How can one stick to the literal-historical sense of the Old Testament, and at the same time interpret it in such a way that its directedness toward Christ is clarified? When one seeks an answer to this question in Calvin's hermeneutical views, it becomes clear to what extent his conception of the literal sense of the text was determined by dogmatic-systematic considerations.

Calvin justified the hermeneutical presupposition that the Old Testament, in its literal-historical sense, teaches Christ, in terms of the dogmatic assumption of the unity in substance of God's covenant of grace.[108] The salvation which the faithful shared *before* the incarnation is the same salvation that the faithful received, and still receive, *after* the incarnation. The difference between Old and New Testament is not the difference between law and gospel in the earlier mentioned strict sense of *formae docendi*. The Old Testament does not function for the Christian church merely as a *praeparatio ad evangelium*. It is in itself already gospel, in the sense of God's *promissio* of his saving grace.

The difference between the two Testaments is to be sought in the fact that the promises of God to the faithful of the Old Testament were given in a vague or shadowy form, while in the incarnated Christ they were manifested clearly. The promises of salvation remain the same, only the modes of "administration" differ. This difference is to be accounted for with reference to the *paedagogia Dei:* the educational strategy of the speaking God who adapts Himself in his teaching to the learning capacity of his pupils.[109] What God teaches in rough outline in the Old Testament, He completes into a full and clear picture in the New Testament, as one would colour a sketch.[110]

---

[107] Cf. Wolf: *op. cit.*, pp. 124f. and Krause: Calvin's Exegetical Principles, *Interpretation* 1977, p. 15.

[108] Cf. Wolf: *op. cit.*, and Niesel: *op. cit.* pp. 102f.

[109] Cf. Krause: *Geschichte,* p. 23.

[110] *CR* 55, 121.

Seen in this way, the New Testament message is the full and clear manifestation of what the literal-historical meaning of the Old Testament conveys. On the basis of these systematic views Calvin justified the Christ-oriented interpretation of the Old Testament. Being a means of communicating the one *doctrina Dei,* the Old Testament could be expected to contain, in its literal historical sense, signs or types *(signa, typi, umbrae, figurae),* pointing to the subject-matter *(res)* which the New Testament presents in full clarity as the person and the work of Christ.[111] To explicate the text of the Old Testament in due consideration of this function of signifying or pointing to Christ, is therefore fully in accord with its literal intention.

That the Old Testament, in its literal-historical sense, preaches Christ, and should be interpreted accordingly, naturally has another side to it. This is namely that the literal-historical sense of the Old Testament also retains its authority and validity for the New Testament church and believer. In its task of preaching the pure doctrine of Scripture the church is therefore also committed to the literal-historical exegesis of the Old Testament. With regard to this commitment, the question can, of course, be asked as to what criteria should be applied to distinguish, within the Old Testament, between that which are relative to the unique historical situation of God's accommodation of his teaching to Israel, and that which pertains to the unchanging substance of God's teaching and as such remains binding for the New Testament church. Perhaps it is the lack of clarity in Calvin's hermeneutics on this point which has earned him the rather unjust accusation that he had subjected the New Testament to the authority of the Old Testament, and that he consequently interpreted Christ "according to Moses".[112]

For Calvin the church has the responsibility to preach the pure doctrine of Scripture. This responsibility can only be fulfilled if the preaching of the church rests on, and is ever anew submitted to and corrected in the ongoing exegesis of Scripture. This view raises the question as to whether Calvin ascribed any hermeneutical relevance to the teaching of the church in the past. Did Calvin, in other words, regard as a hermeneutical guideline what was known, with reference to Romans 12:6, as the *analogia fidei?* Calvin used the term once, but

---

[111] Cf. Wolf: *op. cit.,* p. 128.

[112] Cf. Wernle, P. p. 268. *Der evangelische Glaube. III. Calvin.* (quoted by Niesel: *op. cit.,* p. 102)

without clearly explaining the meaning he attached to it.[113] Yet one could, in the light of the basic tenor of his hermeneutics, and in the light of the methods he displayed in his own practice of interpretation, make some comments in this regard.

A conception of the *analogia fidei* as a doctrinal system, unrevisably and irrevocably defined by an infallible teaching office as the final norm for the exegesis of Scripture, would have been at variance with Calvin's confession of the *sola scriptura*. Calvin rejected, as I have pointed out earlier, the principle of ecclesiastical tradition as an authoritative hermeneutical canon. This does not mean, however, that he denied the doctrinal tradition of the church any hermeneutical significance. Koopmans, for one, has demonstrated to what extent Calvin let himself be guided by the "dogma of the Old Church", not only in the construction of the *Institutio,* but also in his commentaries.[114] This positive attitude toward the confessions of the early ecumenical synods was not motivated, however, by the formal juridical authority they enjoyed in the medieval church as infallible dogmas or doctrinal decrees. Calvin acknowledged the validity of these confessions, only because he judged them to rest on a sound exegesis of Scripture, and, for this reason, to be adequate expressions of the basic articles of the *doctrina Dei.*[115]

Calvin subscribed to the idea that the interpretation of Scripture as the Word of God can never be a private matter.[116] It is the task of the church, because it should always be done with a view to preaching, which is the responsibility of the church. Thus the church, as the historical community of present and past believers, is, as it were, the hermeneutical "continuum" in which scriptural interpretation should be carried out. Exegesis of Scripture as the Word of God does not begin *ab ovo* with the individual interpreter. In undertaking the interpretation of Scripture, one is not only carrying on a common tradition of interpretation, but one is also conditioned, in one's interpretation, by that very tradition. The quest for the pure doctrine

---

[113] Cf. Leith: *op. cit.,* p. 341.

[114] Koopmans: *op. cit.,* chapter 3.

[115] *CR* 6, 277. Cf. Koopmans: *op. cit.,* pp. 28f.; Forstman: *op. cit.,* pp. 25f. and W. Nijenhuis: Calvijns houding ten aanzien van de oudkerkelijke symbolen tijdens het conflict met Caroli, *Nederlandsch Theologische Tijdschrift* 1960, pp. 44 and 46.

[116] Cf. *CR* 7, 32; 55, 458.

of Scripture can therefore only be adequately conducted if it is done in the awareness and the recognition of the established *consensus ecclesiae* with regard to the scriptural message. The agreement in the understanding of Scripture which has already been reached in the historical process of kerygmatic tradition, can only be disregarded at the cost of an untenable biblicism.[117]

But just as much as a biblicistic approach in the exegesis of Scripture is in conflict with the basic motives of Calvin's hermeneutics, the latter is at variance with any form of confessionalism. The established *consensus ecclesiae* did not function for Calvin as an absolute and infallible hermeneutical norm. What the church has already agreed upon to be the doctrine of God, can never replace the scriptural text. Scripture is the living Word of God, not a storehouse of "proff texts" for the demonstration and vindication of the orthodoxy of the church's doctrinal tradition. The established agreement of the church plays a supporting and guiding role in the process of scriptural interpretation. But this role does not imply the status of an once-for-all achievement, to be maintained and guarded against any deviations or changes. On the contrary, every established agreement, handed down in tradition, is always provisional, subject ot the test of, and the possible correction by the self-interpreting Spirit. In this sense the *consensus ecclesiae* remains the goal of scriptural interpretation — a goal that has to be diligently and jointly pursued in the attitude of obedient listeners, tuned in to that which the Spirit of God seeks to impart to the church through the text of Scripture.

The *analogia fidei* was, in other words, indeed the indication of a hermeneutical guideline for Calvin. I hasten, however, to add that Calvin did not view this *analogia fidei* as a foregone conclusion, binding the interpretation of Scripture in a legalistic way. One should rather say that the regulating function of the *analogia fidei* was for Calvin that of an open question, referring us ever anew back to the text of Scripture as the only authoritative source of the communion in faith with God and with our fellow believers.

---

[117] Cf. *CR* 38, 405 where Calvin, in his letter to Simon Grynaeus, emphasised that we should respect the opinions of earlier exegetes and guard against the craving for novelties. He also stressed the necessity that the study of Scripture should be carried out in the community of believers who can mutually help and correct each other in view of a better understanding of the scriptural message.

16. THE HERMENEUTICS OF CALVIN

PROF. L. FLOOR*

Introduction

When we study Calvin, it is not only important to listen to *what* Calvin says, but we also have to note *how* he says things.

In the discipline of Hermeneutics we are wont to talk of a hermeneutic method. There are even those who refer to the *technique of exegesis*.

In his inaugural lecture W.S. Vorster refers to exegetical models *('n Ou Boek in 'n nuwe wêreld,* p. 12). Even in our usage of words in the application of terms and concepts we can learn a great deal from Calvin. The great Reformer does not speak of the method of exegesis or the technique of exegesis. And the term *exegetical models* would have sounded alien issuing from his lips.

Calvin does these things in a different fashion — deeper, more surprising, more spiritually. When he deals with hermeneutics and the question as to the correct interpretation of the Bible, then he uses the beautiful expression *donum interpretationis,* the gift of the exegesis of the Scriptures (CR, 41, 65, Daniel 7:15, 16). This is then a confession of faith. Calvin regards the ability to explicate the Scriptures as a gift, something conferred by our highest and only Teacher, Christ.

Calvin was an exquisite exegete. Apart from his *Institute,* which can be regarded as a monument of exquisite and accurate exegesis, there is the impressive row of his commentaries. It would seem that Calvin was quite pleased with his exegetical labours. In his *Acta Synodi Tridentini cum antidoto* Calvin effects a comparison between the reformatory and the Roman Scriptural exegesis, and then he adds: "We have done more towards an understanding of the Scriptures than all the doctores who have risen in the Roman Church since the inception of Papacy" *(Acta Synodi Tridentini cum antidoto,* ed. Schipper, I, pp. 231, 232).

Calvin, however, had the deep conviction that he could only do his important

* His address is: Dept. of New Testament Studies, Potchefstroom University for Christian Higher Education, Potchefstroom, RSA 2520.

exegetical work because he had received the gift for exegesis from Christ himself. Christ teaches us to understand God's Word through his Spirit.

In the context of understanding the Bible then Calvin often refers to the Holy Spirit.

Calvin did not leave behind a worked-out hermeneutical scheme. Yet we can discern, in his works, clear hermeneutic rules. H.J. Kraus, in his study on "Calvin's exegetische Prinsipien" *(Zeitschrift für Kirchengeshichte,* 79, 1968, pp. 329-341) distinguishes eight special qualities which characterized Calvin's exegesis. In the exegetical principles as found in Calvin there is special stress on the place of the Holy Spirit in the whole process of understanding and interpretation. In his hermeneutics especially Calvin emerges fully as the theologian of the Holy Spirit.

In the context of the understanding of the Bible Calvin often refers to the Holy Spirit. In the new hermeneutics special attention was paid, in the wake of Heidegger, to the analysis of understanding. How does one arrive at understanding? Now it emerges that Calvin already struggled with the problem. This is an indication of how "modern" Calvin really is. For that reason it is very topical today to listen to Calvin, because in contemporary hermeneutics the work of the Holy Spirit is being regarded as unnecessary.

There used to be a fixed conception that hermeneutics was the theory of interpretation or of exegesis. In the twenties and the thirties of this century a whole new style of reflection came to be applied to the problem of hermeneutics. Karl Barth, in his KD (I, 2, 515, 800-830) already foregrounded the problem of understanding ("das Verstehen").

But is was especially R. Bultmann who gave a new content to the concept of "hermeneutics". According to Bultmann language as such is insufficient to the needs of formulating the issue at state beyond misunderstanding. Language has an objectifying function. We have to learn to interpret words and concepts existentially. The hermeneutics of R. Bultmann strives to investigate the ideas or the events which lie behind language and which have been objectified in language. With reference to the Bible the decisive question then is: in what way is human existence understood in the Bible? (Cf. M. de Jonge, Theologie als hermeneutiek, *In: Rondom het Woord,* Theol. Etherleergang der NCRV, 1967, p. 103.)

Then follows the post-Bultmann period, when his two pupils, Ernst Fuchs and Gerard Ebeling, strive to find reality not *behind* but *within* language. They regard language as something which speaks for itself. In the use of language something happens. The speech event creates a relationship. When you call somebody your friend, he becomes your friend.

It would be digressing too far to point out the differences between Fuchs and Eberling. It is also very strenuous to follw the thought processes of these two hermeneutical theologians. It is sufficient for our purpose to know that Fuchs and Eberling mean by hermeneutics to make the speech or the word event take place again. The word which has "set" must become "liquefied" again. In reality this happens by itself, but there are braking influences and obstacles in the word or vocal events and these have to be found and suspended by hermeneutics. At present, however, we are already in the post-Fuchs-Eberling era.

There have been various recent exegetical models which can be applied to help the exegete understand the Bible. There are the models of American "literary criticism", of French structural exegesis, the South African model of argumentative analysis, and the German model of generative poetics. And as if this were not sufficient, there is the newest exegetical model, viz. the communication model of W.S. Vorster, closely linked to that of J. Anderegg.

Without closely analysing all the methods and models, it still has to be stated that in all these methods one gets the impression that understanding can only be effected through the application of hermeneutics.

We find in the newer hermeneutics an over-emphasis on language, the method, the model — and an under-emphasis of the Holy Spirit. If one could only it seems now, learn a competence to handle a method or a model, then we would be able to let the Bible communicate in our time! The hermeneutist is given a prominent, even an indispensable place between the Bible and the listeners. Where this is concerned, we are back in the dark Middle Ages where the priest stands between the Bible and the layman as the only interpreter of the Word of God (cf. J.C. Coetzee: *'n Ou Boek in 'n nuwe wêreld of 'n nuwe Boek in 'n ou wêreld? Nuwer tendense in die Nuwe Testamentiese Wetenskap in Suid-Afrika,* p. 16).

183

Word and Spirit in Calvin

When we start listening to a discourse on Calvin as "the theologian of the Holy Spirit", we must always keep in mind that Calvin had to fight on two fronts: against the Roman Church and against the movement of the Baptists ("Dopers"). The Holy Spirit is essential for the understanding of the Scriptures. He reproached the Roman Church for the fact that the unity between Word and Spirit had been dissolved. The Baptist Movement did the same.

According to Calvin the Pope and the Anabaptists spring from the same root. The Anabaptists separate the Word and the Spirit, and Rome locks the Spirit into the Word and the Sacraments (cf. H. Balke: *Calvijn en de doperse Radikalen,* 1973, pp. 140-143). Against both of these Calvin maintained the *unity* of Word and Spirit. The basis for the authority of the Bible is that God Himself is the One who speaks through and from the Scriptures to us *(Institute,* II, 2, 21).

The mysteries of God can only be understood by men insofar as they have been illuminated through grace by the Holy Spirit.

For that reason the Word can only be rightly understood and accepted in faith through the confirmation of the inner testimony of the Holy Spirit — because God only is both *in* the Scriptures and *in* our hearts — the only adequate Witness for Himself! *(Institute,* I, 7, 4).

Both faith in the Bible and pure interpretation of the Bible are determined through this cohesive factor (God, who speaks through his Spirit in the Word and in the hearts of men).

In 1539 Calvin significantly extends his *locus de Scriptura* (from the *Institute* of 1536). This section then becomes a separate chapter in the 1559 edition. Calvin then states very clearly that the Holy Spirit is linked to the Word inextricably. The Holy Spirit, to which all things are subjected, is itself subjected to the Scriptures. This is not dishonourable or an insult to the Holy Spirit, because the Holy Spirit wishes to be recognised for that which He has put into the Scriptures (CR, 1, 302).

The Holy Spirit, which lived in the apostles and preached through them, continually calls us up to obedience to the Word. The Word is the instrument through which God reveals the illumination of his Word to the faithful (CR, 1, 303). The opinion of the Holy Spirit is revealed in the Scriptures. And the Holy Spirit is not communicated through any means other than the Scriptures.

Calvin carefully stresses that the understanding of the Scriptures is effected through the Holy Spirit, and that the Spirit does it through the Word — therefore wherever the Word is heard. The Word first has to be heard acoustically before the Spirit can transmit it from the ear to the heart (*Institute* IV, 14, 10).

We should not, however, see the Holy Spirit as some sort of accompaniment of the Word, making the Word into an object. It is, according to Calvin, much rather true that the Spirit and the Word together aim at the same object, the heart of man (cf. W. Krusche: *Das Wirken des Heiligen Geistes nach Calvin,* 1957, 228, 229). Calvin never allowed himself to be seduced to the orthodox Lutheran doctrine of the permanent immanence of the Holy Spirit.

In one of his final commentaries, viz. his commentary on Ezekiel, which he wrote shortly before his death, and which should certainly be regarded as one of the most mature fruits of his exegetical labours, Calvin gave special attention to the relation of Word and Spirit in connection with the understanding of the Word of God.

In this commentary Calvin comments on the meaning of language and the Word. We have to keep in mind, Calvin says, that the power, the *efficax,* of the Word is not contained in the sound of the words, because this power comes from the concealed working of the Holy Spirit. This we can learn from the prophet Ezekiel, Calvin says, because on the one hand the prophet assures us that he has heard the voice of God, which ordered him to stand on his feet, but on the other hand the prophet stresses that he was not awakened by the voice until the spirit had set him on his feet (*Commentary on Ezekiel,* 2:1, 2).

Without dividing things, Calvin therefore makes a distinction between the Word of God and the working of the Holy Spirit in order to indicate that the Word in Itself, thus without the Giver (*per se,* as Calvin expresses it) does not have any power.

And then, in the commentary, there is a polemical discussion aimed against the Anabaptists in which Calvin indicates that, although the Spirit imparts power and strength to the Word, it does not mean in the least that the Word, the language, preaching and the explication of the Word have become redundant. This is because it has pleased God to work in this way.

The anthropological background to Calvin's hermeneutics

The theological background to Calvin's very strong emphasis on the Holy Spirit with regard to the understanding of the Bible is undoubtedly his faith in the *corruptio hominis,* the corruption of mankind.

The understanding of the Word is according to Calvin, never a matter of course. This theological background is all too often missing from the newer hermeneutics. And for that reason the Holy Spirit receives so little attention in the contemporary illumination of the speech event. When one is dealing with the causes impeding the understanding of the Scriptures, then Calvin is of the opinion that the greatest impediment towards and understanding of the Scriptures should not be sought in the text or in the language, but in man himself. In his commentary on 1 Corinthians 1:20 he states that man is as little suited to the understanding of the divine mysteries as an ass is for a concert (cf. *Institute,* II, 2, 18; *Harm Evang* Luke 24:25). The Holy Spirit has to make the heart of man susceptible, open his ears and his eyes so that he may understand the Bible (W.F. Krusche, work quoted, p. 225, note 535). L. Goumaz, who has investigated Calvin's commentary on this point, is of the opinion that according to Calvin the Holy Spirit acts as an accompanist to the Word in the process of understanding the Bible: "L'esprit qui accompagne la parole" (L. Goumaz: *La doctrine du solut d'après de Jean Calvin sur le Nouveau Testament,* 1917, p. 321). This does not mean that according to Calvin the Spirit works in separation from the Word in the heart of man in the process of understanding or that the Word only works outwardly and the Spirit only works inwardly. The Spirit works *non ante, nec post sed simul auribus loquitur* (W. Krusche, work quoted, p. 230, note 563).

Because man cannot, from the limitations of his nature, understand the speech of God, the Holy Spirit, who reveals his strength, has to join in the preached Word. Now Calvin becomes very careful. He also knows that this strength of the Spirit of God does not always reveal itself in man. Yet the strength of Spirit is included in the Word in a certain sense, *habet tamen in se quodammodo inclusam* (CR, 55, 50; Hebrews 4:12). With the word *quammodo* Calvin expresses himself very carefully. On the one hand he wishes to do nothing to hamper the free strength of the Spirit, and on the other hand he does not wish to fall into the trap of the Baptists. For that reason he teaches a close link of Word and Spirit without interpreting it mystically, causally or automatically. God has pledged the Spirit to the correct teaching of his Word (W. Balke, quoted work, p. 343).

Calvin has never regarded the understanding of the Word as a matter of course. The Holy Spirit has to be added to it. When Calvin goes on to illuminate the working of the Hoy Spirit in the process of understanding, he states that the Spirit of God does two things: He influences the human spirit (Latin: *mens)* to the extent that the blindness is taken away and he influences the human heart (Latin: *cor)* to subject itself to the yoke of Christ *(Commentary on Luke,* 19:45). Calvin thus accepts a dual working of the Spirit which does not allow division, but which might be distinguished. The one working of the Spirit directs itself at the human spirit and this Calvin calls the *illuminare, illustrare* or *illucere mentes;* the other working of the Spirit is directed at the human heart and this Calvin calls *obsignare* (sealed), *insculpers* (sculpted in) or *infigere* (confirmed), *cordibus* (W. Krusche, quoted work, p. 259, note 727).

And then Calvin adds: the illuminating working of the Spirit is not necessary because of any darkness of the Word itself — the Word is a bright lamp — but the Word shines among the blind and therefore, together with the lighting Word one should also have the illuminating Spirit (W. Krusche, ibid, pp. 259, 260). The Word is like a sun shining on everybody to whom it is preached, but this is fruitless to the blind *(Institute,* III, 2, 34).

The Word cannot penetrate our spirits unless the inner Teacher and the Mentor, the Holy Spirit, has already penetrated (cf. Luke, 24, 45; Psalm 119:18).

In connection with understanding Calvin also often refers to faith. The Word of God is understood when it is believed. Faith, according to Calvin, cannot be separated from understanding, because faith only generates understanding *(Commentary on Acts,* 15:14).

Calvin was deeply convinced of two things: man, in relation to the heavenly message of the gospel could be equated to the relation between an ass and a symphony. And the Holy spirit only teaches us to understand the Word and preaching of the Word.

What was the result of this dichotomous conviction on Calvin's life?

This was once again of a dual nature: Calvin was a man of enthusiastic and sustained study, and Calvin was a man of prayer: *orare et laborare.*

Calvin as philologue and exegete

Calvin's strong stress on the Holy Spirit with regard to the understanding of the Bible did not render him passive. The Spirit gives understanding. He teaches how to do explication, but it is exactly the *donum interpretationis* as a gift of our highest and only Teacher, Christ, which encourages Calvin to aspire to the greatest activity.

As a scientifically schooled philologue and exegete he was precise and competent. And then Calvin left all sorts of exquisite rules for exegesis. These emerged especially in the controversy with the Baptist movement.

* The first principle in exegesis is the principle of clarity and brevity. Calvin called this *perspicua brevitas.* Why? Because the Scriptures are also clear and precise. For that reason our exegesis also has to be like that *(CR, 38, 403).*

* Then follows the second important rule for exegesis. We always have to start looking for the intention of the writer. Calvin calls this the *mens scriptoris* or *concilium auctoris.* What was the original intention of the writer who had been inspired by the Holy Spirit? The prophet Ezekiel, for example, Calvin states, uses — as prophets are wont to do — a *figure extérieure.* When he talks of the soul of man, he uses the word *wind* or *spirit* (37, 9), *(CR 7, 128).*

Do note the words "death" and "grave" in the Psalms, Calvin explains. They who have rejected God and who are then persecuted by his wrath, are called the dead, and their misery is graphically evoked by the image of the grave *(CR, 7, 136).*

* Note also the context in which the text is found. If he looks at the exegesis of the Baptist ministers, Calvin is appalled. In 2 Thessalonians 3:10 Paul states that if somebody does not wish to work, then he should also not be allowed to eat. When one does not note the context, then one has to be cruel enough on the basis of these words to condemn little children to death by starvation *(CR, 7, 59).*

188

* In a text or a passage of Scripture we have to note the real meaning, the *sensus genuinus* or *sensus grammaticus,* and these have to be carefully explicated *(Institute,* IV, 17, 22).

* We have to pay attention to the historical, geographical and cultural circumstances *(circumstantia) (Institute,* IV, 16, 23).

* The exegete also has to ensure whether he may, in his explication, go further than the direct, literal words in the text. Calvin calls this the power of the *progressus ultra verba (Institute* II, 8, 8). In some cases this is an essential demand, such as for example the Ten Commandments. Each concrete commandment, such as those prohibiting adultery, murder and theft covers a much wider field really.

* Imagery in the Bible, such as metaphor, allegory and hyperbole confronts the exegete with real problems. One has to be alert to *etonymicus sermo.* In explication we always have to remain within the bounds set by the Scriptures themselves *(Institute,* IV, 17, 21).

* Calvin then goes on to say that we have to pay note to the *scopus Christus (CR,* 47, 125). We have to read and explicate the Scriptures with the purpose of finding Christ in them. The *scopus Christus* is not regarded by Calvin as an *eclectic* principle, but a principle of revelational history (W. Balke: *Calvijn in de Doperse Radikalen,* 1973, p. 340). (Cf. for these rules Hans Joachim Kraus: Calvins exegetische Prinsipien. *Zeitschrift für Kirchengeshichte,* 79, 1968, S, 329-341.)

In recapitulation, then, one might say that Calvin's exegesis is strongly directed at preaching. The explication of a text has to be directed at the general interest of the church and the practice of the lives of the faithful. (L. Floor: Calvyn se hermeneutiek en sy betekenis vir ons tyd. *In die Skriflig,* 4(14): 12, 1970.)

Calvin is of the opinion that nobody has ever received a full insight into the Scriptures from God. This might well serve to render us humble, and this forces us, according to Calvin, to a brotherly communality of exegetes. In his moving letter to Grynaeus he says that he would like to submit his exegetical results to a brother for adjudication (L. Floor, quoted article, p. 13). We can learn from Calvin that we need each other in our exegetical labours. How stimulating wouldn't it be if we as ministers could not submit our exegeses, done in preparation for sermons, to each other and discuss them!

Not only does Calvin, in his exegetical work, attach great value to the judgement of his spiritual brothers, he also listens with great attention to earlier exegetes, such as the Patriarch Augustine. According to Calvin there is what he terms a *consensus interpretationis,* from which one may devite only in the extremest of cases (H.J. Kraus, quoted word, p. 320).

Calvin's life of prayer and the understanding of the Scriptures

In all his exegetical labours Calvin was deeply convinced that the Holy Spirit worked through the means of the Word, language, the text, preaching and for that reason he was also a man of prayer.

The well-known Calvin expert, E. Doumergue, says in his book *Le Caractère de Calvin* that there is a link between Calvin's praying life and his belief in the Holy Spirit (cf. the Dutch Translation: *Calvijn as mens en hervormer,* 1931, p. 12).

Seeing that the true interpretation of the Bible is a gift from God, this gift may be exhorted from God — indeed, should be asked for.

Only through the beneficence of prayer, Calvin states, do we receive entrance to the wealth put away for us by the heavenly Father *(Institute,* III, 22, 2). Calvin also clearly indicates to us how we should pray. In the first place we should pray with a deep awareness of our poverty and our blindness, with confession of our guilt *(Institute,* 191, 22, 9).

An awareness of our poverty and blindness, our sin and corruption, will lie heavily on our spirits in prayer, but the beneficence of God will raise us up again. Thus, in our prayers, awareness of guilt and faith become true companions, the one frightening us and the other bringing joy. These two have to meet reciprocally in our prayers *(Institute,* III, 22, 11).

Conclusion

In our own day, in which the Holy Spirit has been driven out from the place where the exegete labours, and where we have an over-appreciation of the role of language, of the word, an over-emphasized belief in methods, it has become essential to re-orient ourselves in following Calvin — to re-orient ourselves towards the person and the working of the Holy Spirit in Hermeneutics.

Above all, we have to discipline ourselves to pray daily for the guidance of the Holy Spirit in our exegetical labours.

Behind all our labour and all our struggle to understand the Scriptures, there is the great and the determining Factor of the Holy Spirit. He who laboured in the writers of the Scriptures, also wishes to be present in the exegete of the Scriptures. For that reason the Holy Spirit is the exegete without compare (A.B. du Toit, Die Eksegese van die Sinoptiese Evangelies. *In: Hermeneutica,* Commemorative Volume offered to Professor E.P. Groenewald, 1970, pp. 93, 94).

17. IS CHRIST THE SCOPUS OF THE SCRIPTURES?

The speaker, Professor Hennie Roussouw, again surprised and delighted us with a carefully worded and thoroughly documented paper. This is characteristic of his theological work. Important aspects of what he describes as Calvin's "reformed hermeneutics of the Holy Scriptures" were highlighted and explained. Once again we are filled with gratitude for what we have received via the Church Reformation of the sixteenth century, particularly through the work of Calvin.

Of special importance, to my mind, is the stress the speaker laid on the idea that, although Calvin's "explicit undertaking" to obey only the Scriptures *(sola scriptura)* as a rule for true Christian faith and religion is to be recognised as a fundamental hermeneutic assumption, this *sola* does not, firstly, imply a reduction to a so-called principle of Scripture and, secondly, that it can only be adequately within the context of the other *particulae exclusivae* which gave expression to the Reformers' concept of salvation. This, I should think, is a most accurate and true observation. Everything has not been said with what the speaker calls the "confession formula" of *sola scriptura.* At least two others, a *solus* and a *sola,* viz. *solus Christus* and *sola fide,* are also to be considered.

This also means that the one *solus* does not simply coincide with the others, although they are all very closely related. In any order in which these three concepts might be arranged, it would seem that the one cannot be understood fully without taking into account the context within which it is linked with the other two. Should the speaker agree with this suggestion — and here I should like to introduce a few critical question marks regarding certain points which he stressed in his erudite paper — I am inclined to suggest that the Reformers, particularly Calvin, did not allow their concept of salvation to be assimilated with the formula *solus Christus* to such an extent that it was exhausted by it or disappeared in it.

* His address is: University of the Witwatersrand, Jan Smuts Avenue, Johannesburg, RSA 0002

Undoubtedly for Christian believers "Christ alone" is, and remains, their hymn of praise. Yet, as soon as we distinguish between Christ, on the one hand, and faith which sings His praise, on the other hand, we have already posited a duality, a "twosomeness". Moreover, the hymn of praise is sung not only for Christ but about the nature and works of the trinitarian God. In fact, Calvin himself did so in an almost exuberant way. A Christ, detached from the context of the Trinity, would be inconceivable for true Christian faith. Whenever this may happen — and, indeed, it does happen quite often in theological thinking and in Christian preaching — then He becomes a theoretical abstraction in which faith is actually robbed of its real scope, or He becomes an idol, perhaps a man-god, or god-man. For this reason it is essential that we, elaborating on what we have learnt from Calvin, amongst others, should guard against isolating the *sola scriptura* from the context within which it stands with the *solus Christus* and the *sola fide*. The *solus Christus* in its turn may not, and in reality cannot, be isolated from the totality of God's plan of salvation. This one *solus* is not the sum, the résumé or the scope of the other two. For it is *we* who have to believe in Christ. This twoness, this duality of *we* and *Christ,* should already caution us against simply equating *solus Christus* and *sola fide.* The one is not the other. Furthermore, our faith is not "the end of the matter" (c.f. Ecclesiastes 12:13). Our faith, and that which we believe about Christ, still needs to find expression and shape in our own lives, in the community, in the church and in the world. The world and the lives of men, and the Kingdom of God, in the present and in eternity when God will be "all in all" (I Corinthians 15:28) are *more* than Christ. The Scriptures know about this *more* and testify about it. Of course, the Scriptures also testify of Him, and even (from a New Testament perspective it has to be conceded with Calvin) *centrally* about Him, but definitely not *only* of Him.

The speaker is completely correct when he reminds us that for Calvin, too, the intention of the Spirit is expressed in the true meaning of the Scriptures. In passing, I should like to remark that he could perhaps have given a more lucid account of the question as to how the intention of the Holy Spirit and that of the "human authors" are to be related; firstly, because he states that the real and actual intention of the Scriptures is that of the Spirit and *not* of the human authors. Then, again, he refers to Calvin's "exegetical guideline" according to which a "concise and clear" exegesis should give an account of the true intentions of the human authors themselves. Why was Calvin, "even more than Luther", so concerned to concentrate with such intensity on the "literal sense" of the text of Scripture? Why did he, practising at himself, recommend a "historical-grammatical" method of exegesis, with full recognition of the "human form of the words of the Scriptures", and even in a critical spirit towards certain details in the human text, in order to discover the "doctrine of the Spirit of God"? I ask these questions not out of petty particularity but because I find it necessary to point out that in the reformed context of thought one has to think in a *qualified sense* about the *solus* in the revelation and in the realisation of salvation by *God Himself.* Does God ever (with the exception of the unique divine act of the sacrificial death of Christ) do anything *alone* with His world, on His own, with the elimination of the human role, only for man, and in his place? If even in the *sola scriptura* God preferred not to act *solus,* can salvation then ever be regarded purely as a *gift* of God? Is there not a *realisation* of the purpose, of the intention of the Spirit through God-and-man, comparable to the way in which in the Scriptures an *expression* was given to His intention in human terms? Whereas synergism (the co-operation of man with God) was virtually eliminated in the christological event of the substitution of man by Christ, it never happens pneumatologically. In the *Pneuma* God adopts man as His partner and co-worker.

Thus, the intention of the Spirit may be found in the Scriptures. Human beings have written these down. Human beings also explain these with a view to their appropriation by man. These purely human actions of explanation and appropriation are the means by which the intention of the Spirit is discovered. It is the Spirit Himself who should become the spokesman through the human exegesis of the Scriptures. Is it possible for man, however, to face the enormous challenge of expressing in his own words the true and unambiguous meaning of the Spirit? This would demand human infallibility which is only conceivable in terms of a total eclipse of the fallibility of man by the infallible guidance of the Holy Spirit. The Spirit of truth who guides the church into all the truth (cf. John 16:13) stands in opposition to all arbitrary human interpretations of the Scriptures. According to the speaker, Calvin adopted an absolutely inflexible stand in this respect: "It speaks for itself (I quote) that the *doctrina* or preaching of the church for Calvin may not be the expression of human opinions. It should be the purest doctrine of God Himself as it comes to us through the Scriptures". Yet there is still the element of human activity which Calvin himself did not eliminate. The way in which the infallible guidance of the Spirit and human expression of the pure doctrine of God are interwoven is, however, "a contentious issue in Calvin-literature". The Spirit may "accompany" the preaching of the Word;

He can also "confirm" it. In my opinion it can be said either way.

However, the vital issue at stake is this: did Calvin really hold such an absolutist (by which I mean: perfectionist) opinion about the Word (in Scripture and in preaching, but in this instance particularly about the Word in preaching?). The speaker seems to have sensed the answer to this question. The interpretation of the text of the Scriptures, he states, was not understood by Calvin as a purely "mystical, pneumatic" event in which human exegesis had no role to play. Here I should prefer not to use the words "mystical" and "pneumatic", because both have their place, even an inalienable place (mysticism!) in human exegesis through which the intention of the Spirit as it is apprehended by the human spirit (the pneumatic element!) should be channelled. However, I have grasped the intention of the speaker and, if I did so correctly, I should prefer to use the word "mechanical". Indeed, Calvin did not hold the view that the Spirit utilises man for the interpretation of His intentions in a mechanical way (cf. *Institutes*, III, II, 36).

For this reason I should like to maintain, in opposition to the viewpoint of the speaker, that it is incorrect to state that, according to Calvin, preaching is both the organ *and the instrument* of the Spirit. However intimately Word and Spirit in both the Scriptures and in preaching might be interlaced, such an immediate and mechanically direct link between them, as is implied by the word "instrument", does not exist — and certainly not in Calvin's thoughts. As regards the Scriptures themselves, the link between the Spirit and the human transmitter of the Word is mainly to be understood as an official (ministerial) one *(Institutes* IV, VIII, 2); as regards the way in which preaching is obliged to convey only the intention of the Spirit, the link is a historical and humanly relative one.

Both these qualifications, however, could apply to the Scriptures as well as to the act of preaching. Not only have the servants of God had different ways of teaching at different times but, also, the human dissemination of the Word can never claim to be "the pure doctrine of God Himself". Calvin says it was "the councils" who claimed to have done this. Indeed, Calvin did teach the infallible guidance of the Holy Spirit in the opening and understanding of the Word but this does not happen in such a simple, direct and perfectionistic way. We can learn from the Spirit "unmistakably" what we have been granted in the Word. Yet even the believers, including those who have received more and greater gifts than others, partake, while still in the flesh, only in the first fruits: they only have a foretaste of the Spirit of "indubitable revelation". The deficiencies of the church are still too numerous for it to claim perfection for itself — as did its Roman forebears. Consequently, the believers could be better advised to stay within the confines of the Word of God. This is the reason why, according to Calvin (as the speaker rightly indicates), the Scriptures themselves offer the only guarantee of their correct interpretation and their real intention, i.e. the intention of the Spirit, and the Spirit guides us into all the truth in the manner of the enlightenment of *our* minds, *(Institutes* IV, VIII, 10-13).

Is the authority of the text of Scripture as regards its interpretation an exclusive one, as the speaker states? Is it not an authority which is shared with the human interpreter and is man not co-responsible for its interpretation? To my mind, Calvin was concerned about *this* responsibility which rests upon man. Precisely because "failing man" cannot fulfil this responsibility on the strength of his own intellectual abilities, he should rather stay within the confines of the Word of God. Should he not do this, then he is exposed to the danger (to which he immediately falls prey) of constructing his own doctrines in detachment of the Word, and of claiming divine authority for these.

Here we have to repeat the question: What, in fact, is the intention of the Spirit according to the *sola scriptura?* Is it *solus Christus,* with which it also coincides exactly? Does *solus Christus* provide the guarantee to the interpreter that he will convey the true intention of the Spirit, namely if he interprets all the teachings of both the Old and the New Testament in terms of "Christ alone"? Is "Christ alone" for Calvin the formal and the material principle of the Scriptures? Is Christ for Calvin, as the speaker states emphatically, "that which the Scriptures have to say"? Is He the scope or the ultimate meaning of the Scriptures according to the intention of their Author, the Holy Spirit? I got the impression that the speaker himself is somewhat at a loss when it comes to this reduction of the content of the Scriptures to Christ alone. For this reason he is not satisfied with an understanding of the *virtutes* of God only in terms of what God *is;* these should also be understood in terms of what God *does* in His on-going activity. Would it be appropriate to say that God is *more* than merciful and that He has more in store for the world and for mankind than to extend mercy to them? I am convinced that the speaker himself senses this "more". He states: "Knowledge of the merciful God is essential knowledge for man: knowledge which brings a change in his need but for that reason knowledge without which man cannot fulfil his destiny as man". However, as soon as *the destiny of man* comes into our perspective, we should realise that God is not merciful (concretely speaking: in Christ) *for the sake of being merciful* and *for the sake of Christ.* God is concerned about man and the fulfilment of man's destiny! God has one and the same intention with both the law and the gospel, with both the Torah and the Christ. Both are the perfect gifts of God — so perfect, indeed, that man is exposed by them as a miserable sinner, utterly deprived of the ability himself to be what God had intended.

It is in connection with the destiny of man that the acts of God's mercy and grace are to be contemplated. It was the gift of the law which was incarnated in Christ as our substitute. That which became flesh in Christ was the totality of the law. In Him, it was concentrated into an unambiguous gift of God. That which became flesh in Him was not only the curse and death meted out by the perfect law to fallen mankind but also life as restored and promised by the law. Christ is not the final purpose of God but He has a purpose with the gift of Christ to the world, an objective which encompassed creation in its totality. This was also God's purpose with the law. The knowledge of God which was given to us in the Scriptures, says Calvin, was given with no other purpose than that which is also conspicuous *in creation.* This calls us to the fear of God, then to trust in Him, so that we can learn to serve Him in utter holiness of life, and unfeigned obedience, and also learn that we are wholly dependent on His goodness *(Institutes* I, X, 2).

To this effect Christ was invested with a *ministry.* With reference to I Corinthians 10:4, Calvin says that the eternal Word given to Israel revealed an outline of the office for which Christ was destined *(Institutes* I, XIII, 10). Christ is not the final purpose, neither that of the Scriptures nor that of God. He is the anointed One, the office-bearer of God par excellence but the ultimate intention of God is life completely redeemed. Precisely this gift of redemption is also contained in the law. The law contains an instruction on the perfection of justice, and complete righteousness in the sight of God consists of our absolute obedience to the law. For this very reason the law casts a curse on our imperfection. The very excellence of the law reveals to us our own misery and imperfection.

Calvin asks if this means that God makes a mockery of us by showing us what is true happiness (redeemed life!) and inviting us to participate in it while we are barred from it. In this connection he refers to Romans 10:4: "For Christ is the end of the law, that every one who has faith may be justified". This means, on the one hand,

197

that the law is certainly not in vain. In our defective and faltering obedience to it we *do* give expression to that which we believe about the law, namely that it contains perfect life. For the sake of Christ this is enough for God. For, on the other hand, Christ bore for us the curse of the law which came upon us because we exclude ourselves from its blessings in our inability to live the redeemed life offered by it. Christ *both* realised in our place the true life offered by the law and *He* bore the curse of the law as our substitute. Yet the law is still valid as the model of redeemed life. By ourselves, however, we can only realise it fragmentarily. Yet, in His benificence (in Christ!) God does not reject us because of the imperfections that taint our own works. He forgives us our lack of perfection and allows us to participate in the fruits of the promises of the law, very much as if we ourselves have fulfilled the demands of the law (cf. *Institutes* II, VII, 1-4).

That which became flesh in Christ is the *promise* of beatific, redeemed life which is held out by the law. Both Christ and the law are bearers of the same promise. The difference between the Old and the New Covenant is, therefore, not one of essence but one of ministry. Christ is the very foundation of the promises, contained in both the Old and the New Testament, which are the same promises. Israel's earthly possessions were for them like a mirror in which they could see, as it were, the future heritage of redeemed life. Calvin speaks of the glory of future life when the redeemed will possess the earth as their heritage *(Institutes* II, XI, 1-2). In Christ the *promise* of God became "yea and amen". Thus Christ cannot be the "scope" of the Word, for He Himself is the Word, He is the *promise* of God *in the flesh.* For this reason it would be incorrect to say that the gospel has come to replace the law. It rather came to reinforce and confirm the promises of the law. In Christ, God added a "body", i.e. He gave substance to the "shadows" of the Old Testament *(Institutes* II, IX, 1-4). Thus, in my opinion, the speaker is incorrect if he interprets the thought of Calvin to mean that, for Calvin, the law and the prophets saw Christ as their ultimate object. It is not true that, for Calvin, Christ is the scope of the totality of the Scriptures. What is true, in fact, is that the law, the prohets and the Christ are all bearers of the same promise.

At this point I should like to make a clarifying remark on Calvin's use of the New Testament metaphor of the law as a "shadow" (Colossians 2:17; Hebrews 8:5; 10:1). Christ is, in actual fact, the "image", the "body" of the shadow which can be seen stretching back into the Old Testament. The shadow *can* be cast because the body is not the ultimate reality. There is still something beyond it. The last and ultimate reality is, indeed, "the good things to come" (Hebrews 10:1). Christ stands bodily in the rays of the dawning light and throws the shadow of the promise of God's future in the history of Israel.

The same could be said of Christian existence as such. It is also a mere shadow of the coming Kingdom of God but a shadow which is cast by the body of Christ and which, therefore, is one of substantial truth. For us there are not only the shadows of promises to behold, but also *that* body by which they are rendered "yea and amen". The *promises,* but not that which is promised, were confirmed by the incarnation of the Word: they acquired the truth of the body of Christ. In this way the gospel lays its finger on what was only represented in images in the Old Testament. We indulge in the same favours of God which Israel under the Old Testament had only tasted in measures. Yet we remain in the situation of standing under the *promises* of God: we do not enjoy Christ in any way other than embracing Him, clothed as He is in His promises *(Institutes* II, IX, 1 and 3).

So real is God's promise and so abundant His grace in Christ that, according to Calvin, it would not be wrong to say that through His coming, the heavenly Kingdom of God has been established on earth *(Institutes* II, IX, 4). However, this is the Kingdom *in the modality of promise.* Because — here I quote Calvin almost literally — although Christ offers us the fulness of the spiritual wealth as being present through the medium of the gospel, the promise of this always remains in the safekeeping of hope, until we have thrown off this mortal flesh and assumed the shape of glory of Him who has preceded us. In the meantime, the Holy Spirit commands us to resign ourselves to the promises. Glory in God involves the future as well as the present life *(Institutes* II, IX, 3).

I should like to suggest to the speaker that, if he did not declare Christ so emphatically as the only scope of the Scriptures in the theology of Calvin but could see, as Calvin did, Christ as the means to both the interm end (the sanctification of the world) and the final end of God (eschatological salvation), then he would not be so decidedly opposed to the idea that Calvin also teaches a natural theology. Indeed, Calvin does so explicitly but in a properly reformed manner *(Institutes* I, III-V). However, Calvin has less trouble with natural theology because he does not see Christ as the scope of the entire Scripture. It is not: *creation for the sake of Christ* but: *Christ for the sake of creation* which can be deduced as a fundamental hermeneutic rule from

Calvin's thought. Because the speaker has not elaborated this consistently, he seems to have got stuck in a tangle when the question arose: How, precisely, are we to understand Calvin's vision of Christ as the scope of Scripture in the light of his metaphor of the Scriptures as spectacles which enable us to discover the glory of God in His works of creation? Naturally the question, put in these terms, will rear up like a Medusan head. For if Christ were to be the scope of all the intentions of God; if the *tota scriptura* were to contain only *solus Christus*, then creation would fall away, the sanctification of life would fall away or it would be dissolved so completely in one act of divine salvation that it would be only vertically directed. this would mean a return, finally, to exactly that brand of theology of redemption which the Reformers left behind them.

In conclusion: It is one of the most important priorities of Reformed hermeneutics to keep considering and reconsidering the question carefully: *Cur Deus homo?* So it will be possible for it to abstract from the *sola scriptura*, indeed, the *tota scriptura*, not only *solus Christus* but to see the whole world in its radical depravity and yet destined for radical salvation (un-transsubstantiated) unto the eternal Kingdom of God. The incarnation of the Word was only necessitated by one factor, namely sin, and once sin has been expiated, the world will be *theatrum Dei gloriae*, without spot or blemish. *This* is the scope of the Word — also of the Word who became flesh (cf. *Institutes* II, XI, 16-19; and II, XVII).

18. THE PROBLEM OF THE CONCEPT OF THE "PERSONALITY" OF THE HOLY SPIRIT ACCORDING TO CALVIN

PROF. B.J. ENGELBRECHT*

Remark

Originally this lecture would have dealt with "The Doctrine of the Holy Spirit in Calvin". Whoever has knowledge of the extent of the literature on this subject, however, such as the works of S. van der Linde *(De Leer van de Heiligen Geest bij Calvijn,* 1943) and of Werner Krusche *(Das Wirken des Heiligen Geistes nach Calvin,* 1957), and the earlier works of Warfield, would have to concede that this field is too encompassing for it to be suitable for a single address. For that reason we thought it a good idea to deal with the problems surrounding the "concept of personality" as it emerges e.g. in the doctrine of the Trinity by Karl Barth *(Kirchliche Dogmatik,* Vol. I, 1, 5, Aufl., pp. 375-388), and especially with regard to the Pneumathology of Calvin, as expounded by Krusche (quoted work, pp. 1-13).

The problems surrounding the *concept of personality* in the doctrine of the Trinity as Karl Barth sees it and discusses it in K.D. I, 1, pp. 373-388.

Karl Barth touches upon the concept of person when he speaks of the "trinity in the unity". The unity of God is the unity of that God who revealed Himself and of Whom the revelation has been written down in the Scriptures. This unity of God should not be equated with a singleness or a loneliness of God, and should not be understood, without any further ado, in a numerical fashion. The matter with which it deals should not be subjected to the terms (words) but the terms should be subjected to the issue. The revealed unity of God does not exclude the ordering or the distinction of three persons or better still "the modes of being" of God. Each of these "modes of being" is just as much separately *(and* in mutual conjunction) the one

* His address is: Dept. of Theology, University of Pretoria, Hillcrest, Pretoria, RSA 0002.

true God! The word "person" remains a problematic one, however, because neither the original meaning nor the later (even modern) concept of person has offered a solution of the problem. The word *person* has been used to indicate a distinctiveness in the being of God as against the doctrine of Sabellianism. But because *persona* and *prosōpon* also mean "mask", there is a retreat to Sabellianism. Should one use *hypostasis* instead of *prosōpon,* then the Westerner is prone to think of *substantia* which leads to tritheism. In actual fact no concept can truly and adequately give expression to the issue that we are dealing with here. For that reason one is concerned merely to find a more or less useful concept. Both Augustine and Anselm have stated that the concern is with an *ineffabilis pluralitas, tres nescio quid.* But one has to speak out, not to outline the issue adequately, but not to be silent alltogether *(sed ne tacerere omnino).*

The medieval period took over the definition of Boethius, *persona est naturae rasionabilis individua substantia.* Barth translated this in the following terms: "Person ist das vernünftige Einzelwesen" (which exists independently and which is distinguished from beings having no faculty of thinking). Whoever accepts this definition of "person", however, must inevitably arrive at a tritheism. For that reason Thomas Aquinas, when he applied this definition to God, said that the distinguishing characteristic of a person is that he is a person through an incommunicable attribute and not for the reason that he *is* an "Einzelwesen". He made the concept more precise by saying that *personae (in Trinitate sunt) res subsistentes in divina natura.* They are therefore nothing other than intertheistic *relationes.*

Barth points out that Calvin is fully in line with Augustine and Thomas when saying that when the word person is used with reference to the Trinity it does not have the everyday meaning, and it cannot be equated with a painting in which three little men have been painted and which is then supplied with a caption saying: This is the Trinity! Much rather, the word persons indicates *"les propriétez lequelle sont en 1'essence de Dieu"* (the properties which reside in the being of God).

Melanchton's definition of person *(persona est subsistens vivum, individuum, intelligens, incommunicabile, non sustentatum ab alio)* leads, to Barth's mind, inevitably to a seeming tritheism. The same is true of the nineteenth century concept of person which stresses especially the chacrateristics of *"selfconsciousness"*, and *"individuality"* with regard to the concept of person. When the new

Protestant theology applies this concept of person to the Father, the Son and the Holy Spirit, and then also clings to the idea that God is an "absolute personality", then the question as to whether a Quaternity (and not a Trinity) is being taught, arises prominently.

One could, out of a sense of historical piety, well use the word "person" as a sort of abbreviation (for practical purposes) for the matter that we are dealing with. The concept *Seinsweise* (mode of being) is, however, a better one — not in absolute terms, but relatively better, simpler, and clearer. One could speak of the revelation more accurately in saying that "God is one within three modes of being, Father, Son and Holy Ghost". This means that the one God and Lord, the *one* personal God is what He is, not only in one mode, but in the mode of the Father, ánd in the mode of the Son ánd in the mode of the Holy Spirit.

The concept of *Seinsweise* was repeatedly used in history in the place of "person" and was called, amongst others, *tropos hyparxeos, hypostasis, subsistentia, modus entis.* The God who is revealed in the Scriptures, is the one God who is God three times differently, and who is only the God of revelation in this triple distinctiveness. The God of Sabellianism is not the God of the Scriptures! The concept of "characteristic mode of being" is even better than *Seinsweise* in terms of being a description of the issue intended by the Scriptures. The *one* divine Being is not only one, but according to the revelation "one within three characteristic modes of being". Biblical revelation does, in fact, ascribe to each mode of being a characteristic, proper action, for example in the baptism of Christ, where He stood in the water and the Spirit descended to Him in the form of a dove and the Father called Him his beloved son. And yet this is the work of the one God, the Father, the Son and the Holy Spirit.

We may never ascribe the three "proper" modes of being (eigentümliche Seinsweisen) ontologically to God, because then we divide the divine Being *(essentia)* into three parts, and then we have three gods. The concept "person" is not appropriate to describe this threefoldedness in unity. Should we use the term *modes of being,* however, then we can say that, without ascribing inequality to their Being, Divinity and Dignity, the Father, the Son and the Holy Spirit are three in that their mutual originating relation is inequal, that is: three. In this way then the *formal* qualitativeness of the three modes of being is denoted, that is, that which makes of them modes of being, viz. that they are three in relation to each other. Should we start from the *names* of Father, Son and Holy Spirit, then there is a Generator and a Generated, and *One* which has not been created or conceived, but which came into being through the Generator and the Generated. Should we proceed from the threefold distinction of Revealator, Revelation and Being Revealed, then we can say that just because there is a Veiling of God there can also be an unveiling of God and a Self-communication by God. Calvin, in *Institutes* I, 13, 18 spoke of the *principium agendi,* of the *sapientia in rebus actionis, and* of the *virtus* or *efficacia actionis.* The true modes of being of God are not to be derived from the *content* of each concept, but from their *relation* to each other. The threefoldedness consists in the fact that the being or deeds within which God is God, sometimes springs from a pure Origin and then again from two Emanations, and then in such a way that the first *Emanation* can only be lead back to the Origin and the second *Emanation* can only be lead back to both the Origin *and* the first *Emanation.* These, however, are only analogies to indicate the wholly exceptional divine threefoldedness and the wholly exceptional divine unity. According to the Scriptures, God is only the true God in so far as He stands *in relation* to Himself. This *doctrine of mutual relation* has been maintained throughout history, amongst others by Thomas Aquinas *(persona est relatio ut res subsistens in natura divina),* Calvin*(personam voco subsistentiam in Dei essentia, quae ad alios relata, proprietate incommunicabili distinquitur)* and the Roman Catholic dogmatists such as Pohle, Bartmann, Scheeben, Diekamp and Braun. There is the inclination, more and more, to avoid the term *res subsistentes* and to describe the *modes of being* purely in terms of the reciprocal, mutual *relations of origin* in the being of God Himself. The repetition in God, the *repetitio aeternitatis in aeternitate,* distinguishes the unity of the revealed God Himself from any other thing that we might call unity.

Through using the concepts of *modes of being* and *relations of origin* in the place of the concept of *person,* we have (according to Barth) only a relatively better manner of description of the divine mystery of the Trinity; no terms would ever be able to describe it adequately. The words always have to be subjected to the matter, and not the matter to the words. We have to keep this in mind and strive to avoid both the tritheistic and the modalist errors (heresies). The mystery should always remain mystery. Theology is a rational involvement with the mystery and should see to it that this involvement aids one in making the outlines of the mystery more clearly visible.

The problems surrounding the concept of person in the pneumathology of Calvin as indicated and discussed by Krusche

Krusche points out that K.P. Noesgen is of the opinion that Calvin rather sees the Holy Spirit as "an irresistibly active power emanating from God", and not so much as a person. The question that now arises, is whether a power can also be a person, and then in what way? This question does not yet, however, fully touch upon the problem which Calvin has with the concept of person with regard to the Trinity and specifically with regard to the Pneumathology. What is indicated through this question is apparently a problem of fundamental importance in the theology of Calvin. The fact that Petrus Caroli reproaches Calvin that, in the *Confession de la foy* (1536) he scrupulously avoids the concepts *Trinity* and *Person,* Krusche also takes as an indication that at this stage (1536) Calvin was not too interested in these terms. When Calvin against opponents of the orthodox doctrine of Trinity, does use the full conceptual apparatus of the old Church, then it is remarkable that he uses the concept *Person* in a "careful, guarded, *non-proper* fashion".

Calvin finds the real issue which the doctrine of the Trinity wants to describe, to be present all through the Scriptures, viz. that the Father, the Son and the Holy Spirit are the one, true eternal God and yet in such a way that the Son is not the Father, *and* the Holy Spirit is not the Son or the Father. Krusche rightly points out that Calvin avoids the traditional *dicta probantia* and that he uses only those proofs which will stand up exegetically, in order (for example) to indicate the divinity of the Holy Spirit, as appears from his *Institutes* I, 13, 14 and 15. Calvin would have liked to have regarded this as sufficient, but the heretical doctrine, which wrongly expounds the Scriptures, forces him to use the Trinitarian terminology of the Old Church in order to unfold and exegetize the testimony of the Scriptures as accurately as possible. But this terminology too is not magic formulae, but should in any age and context be tested anew in the light of the Scriptures against any kind of heretical teaching in order to determine whether it is still valid. Calvin in his time and context did not have problems with the encompassing term *Trinitas* and also not with the terms *substantia, essentia* and *ousia* in order to give expression to the divine being; he also did not have so much objection to the Greek term *hypostasis* to express the distinction between Father, Son and Holy Ghost. He says that "le mot de ... *Hypostase* est encore *plus convenable* d'autant qu'il est de l'Ecriture saincte" (in Krusche, quoted work, p. 4). (The word *Hypostase* is even more suitable especially because it appears in the

Holy Scriptures.) The Scriptures are after all "the rule of both thinking and talking correctly". But Calvin did, according to Krusche, have problems with the concept of *persona*. Calvin also did not yet know the modern concept of person "in the sense of an irreducible, spiritually creative individuality with its own 'I-centre', because this would, just like the concept of person of Gentilis, (viz. *substantia intelligens)* imply a plurality of Gods. In order to escape from the dilemma, Calvin chose to reject the word person and to use the word *subsistentia* (Greek *hypostasis,* Hebrews 1) (that is, *mode of being)* in its place. He further adds precision to this concept with the idea of *proprietas (=characteristic idiosyncratic nature). Person* for Calvin therefore is *tres subsistentiae in Dei essentia,* each having its own *proprietas.* It is not true that the word *person* indicates an entity which exists abstractly apart from the *essentia,* because it exists *in the essentia.* Each "person" is a *subsistentia,* a *hypostasis* of the entire *essentia,* but then in such a way that *subsistentia* is not identical to *essentia,* because it belongs to the divine essentia that there are three divine persons *(subsistentiae)* in it. Krusche sums up the entire matter in the following terms: in the relation *essentia-subsistentia,* the *subsistentia* is determined as follows: *subsistentia* is neither a *portio essentiae,* nor *aliquid ab essentiae abstractum,* but is a *hypostasis totius essentiae.* As regards *essentia,* there is therefore no distinction between Father, Son and Holy Ghost, but as regards *subsistentia,* there is a distinction because each has a *proprietas,* a characteristic property with regard to the others. As regards the *essentia,* it holds that the Father, the Son and the Holy Ghost are equal to each other in all respects, also as regards the state of uncreatedness, unbornness, but as regards the person, the *subsistentia,* the Son is of the Father and the Holy Spirit of both of Them. In his *Institutes* 1, 13, 6 we find the well-known definition of person, which is very important in this context. "Under *person,* then, I understand a *subsistentia* in the divine *essentia, a subsistentia* which is related to the other two and which is yet distinguished (from the other two) by an *incommunicable property (proprietate incomunicabili)".* The *proprietates* does not indicate any nominal *distinctiones,* but *real* distinctions regarding the intertrinitarian relations of origin. As regards the relation of Father to Son: "He generated"; as regards the relation of the Son to the Father: "He was generated". But this does not touch upon the *essentia* because then the Father would then be *deificator* or *essentiator;* it concerns only the mode of being, the *subsistentia,* where the Father is *principium, origo et fons deitatis.* We can therefore state (according to Krusche) that each of the three divine persons *(subsistentiae,* modes of being) is the *one* divine being, but we can also say that "the one divine being *is* in three modes of being".

The concept *subsistentia* with its own *proprietas* not only indicates the distinction between the three persons, but the Holy Spirit which, through his *procedere ab utroque* distinguishes Himself from the Father and from the Son, *links,* precisely through that "emanating from both", the Father and the Son with each other. The *unity* of God lies not only in the *essentia,* but is even brought to expression through the *subsistentiae* in so far as the Holy Spirit unites Father and Son with each other.

But the unity in the nature, the essence, of God also comes to expression in the *works* of God. In fact, the economical Trinity which is revealed to us in the Word of God, precedes in practice, but not in fact, the ontological Trinity. While the Scriptures adduce to each of the persons of the Trinity certain idiosyncratic workings, the workings of the Trinity are still those of the three Persons together, because the Father is the *principium agendi,* the Son is the *sapientia agendi* and the Spirit is the *virtus et efficatio actionis.* The special quality of the Father and of the Son in this regard (respectively *principium and sapientia agendi)* is not expounded more fully by Calvin; the fact that the Holy Ghost is the *virtus et efficacia actionis* is in fact worked out more fully, and in that the Holy Ghost is called *virtus, vigor, vis, potentia, energia, effectus, impulsus, instinctus, motus et influxus actionis.* The Holy Spirit is not merely a power, a characteristic or a psychological moment in God or in the divine action. He is fully person (as far as it concerns the "being") *and* subject (as far as it concerns action). There is always the danger that one could stress the *unity* in the trinity too much (modalism) or stress the *threefoldedness* in the unity too much (tritheism). By calling the Son and the Spirit respectively *sapientia* and *virtus* Calvin moves in the direction of a moderate modalism. This happens especially in his statements on creation, where God creates through his wisdom (=Son?) and power (=Holy Spirit?). The distinguishing characteristic of the Spirit *(procedere)* not only links the Father and the Son ontologically but also in his distinctive *action* He fulfils the actions of the Father and of the Son. His distinctive characteristic is exactly that He does not have an action of his own, but that He fulfils the action of the Father and of the Son! Everything that God does, is his doing precisely because it happens through the Holy Ghost. "All divine action is, in its deepest essence, the action of the Holy Spirit! The Holy Spirit is the *manus Dei qua suam potentiam exercet.* Without the work of the Holy Spirit the coming of Christ and his work would have been in vain. One could talk, in dealing with Calvin, of "an all-encompassing working by God through the Holy Spirit". *"Omnes tamen actiones ab eo prodeunt."* Thus far Krusche on the vision of Calvin.

Closer determination of the concept of "Person" by Calvin in the "Institutes" 1, 13, 1-29

The Scriptures teach us of the boundlessness and the spirituality of the one Being of God, and thus all speculation and philosophical statements about God by the small human brain are cut off at the root.

The Scriptures reveal the unity of the being of God as consisting in three persons. Thus God is not merely an empty name fluttering around in our brains, but He is the true God. Calvin wants a simple definition in order to militate against heretic doctrine (such as *tres personae in una essentia),* but now some others (but not Calvin!) have "rejected the term (Person) in vicious fashion as being a human invention". For that reason, Calvin says, we have to look at the concept *person* more closely. When Hebrews 1 verse 3 calls the Son the *charaktēr tes hypostaseōs autou (tou patros)* then it ascribes a certain *subsistentia* to the Father in which He differs from the Son. It cannot be said of the Son that He is the image of the *being* of the Father, because the being of God is simple, indivisible and contained in himself. "The Father, though distinguished by his own peculiar properties ... has expressed his whole person *(hypostasis)* in the Son". The same holds true for the Holy Spirit. It will shortly be indicated that He is not only God, but also that He has a *subsistentia* separately from the Father. This cannot be a distinction in essence, because then we would have three Gods. The distinction touches upon the person. For "person" many words have been used, such as *persona, prosōpon hypostasis,* subsistentia, "but all of them, whether Greeks or Latins even though they differed from each other in word usage, still concurred about the basic issue they were dealing with".

Critical remarks

*   It is therefore untrue to say, as is often done, that Calvin had objections against the concept of person, or that he had problems with it. He cicumscribes it more clearly because "others, in hateful fashion, rejected the concept 'person' on the grounds that it was a human invention".

* In his exegesis of Hebrews 1 verse 3 Calvin purposefully opposes a long exegetical and translation tradition which is still adhered to today. He was aware of the fact that the Vulgate translated *charaktēr tes hypostaseōs autou* with *figura substantiae eius.* (This tradition and view still exist today. *Good News for Modern Man* translates that "... he is the exact likeness of God's own being"; *Die Gute Nachricht* uses "denn er entspricht dem Wesen Gottes vollkommen" and the new Afrikaans translation reads as follows "Hy is die ewebeeld van die wese van God" [He is the image of the being of God].) And yet **Calvin calls the exegesis that would have** *hypostasis* **to mean** "being" in this context, "forced", "anomalous", "inaccurate" and "foolish". The logical exegesis of Hebrews 1 verse 3 would seem to be, however (for us) that the Son (because He is of the same *being* of God) is the image of the *being* of God rather than the image of the *person* of the Father. This exegesis seems even more probable when the first part of Hebrews 1 verse 3 says that the Son is "the effulgence of God's splendour," *and* when the Athanasianum states (Article 6, Schaff, Creeds of Christendom, Vol. II, p. 66) that the glory *(gloria, doxa)* belongs to the *being* of God. James Barr has spoken of the "root fallacy" where one starts from a previously determined fixed meaning of a word and not from the context in order to determine the meaning of a word. It would thus seem as if Calvin proceeded from the meaning that *hypostasis* derived in the context of the Christological struggle in the East and that he then superimposed that meaning on Hebrews 1 verse 3 rather than to let the context of Hebrews itself determine the meaning. For the rest we agree with what Calvin says here in connection with the Trinity, but our opinion is that Calvin cannot use Hebrews 1 verse 3 to substantiate what he wishes to say.

*   *   *

Let us follow Calvin's train of thought further and see what he intends saying: It is especially the heretics, he claims, who "yap about the word 'person' and who strenuously object to it". They demand that all theological terms should come straight from the Scriptures, even as regards every single syllable. This, Calvin feels, places too much of a strain on the theologian. Nothing is to stop us, if we adhere to the rule that "the Scriptures should be the unerring standard for our thinking and talking", to express something that is not so clearly expressed in the Scriptures, in somewhat clearer terms. The terms should, however, always be subjected to the truth of the Scriptures. For the

Church, in its struggle against heretical doctrines it has always been essential to use terms like Trinity and Person, because these terms unambiguously circumscribe what the Scriptures meant and left no opportunity for heretics "for whom the shells of words became corners in which to hide their heresies". As against Arius who claimed that the Son was created, the church declared that the eternal Son was consubstantial *(consubstantialis, homoousios)* with the Father, and against Sabellius who declared that the three persons were merely three characteristics of God without order or real distinction *(distinctio)*, the church delcared that three genuine **subsistentiae** existed within the one God, that there was a Trinity of Persons*(Trinitas personarum)* in the *one* God (or in the unity of God). Calvin would have liked that all the terms be buried as long as one could merely believe that the Father, the Son and the Holy Spirit constituted one God and yet that the Son was not the Father and Holy Spirit was not the Son, but that each had his characteristic mode of being *(subsistentia)*. In the same spirit Hilarius and Augustine apologized for the fact that they had been forced by the heretics to give expression to the unsayable; not that the words could describe the reality adequately, but so that there should not be complete silence. These words are necessary to rip the masks from the heretics and to stop their empty babbling and yet nothing is said that does not appear in the Scriptures. For that reason Calvin leaves aside the struggle surrounding words and defines "person" in the following terms: "Under *person,* then, I understand a *subsistentia* in the divine essence, a *subsistentia* which, although related to the other two, is distinguished from them by incommunicable properties (attributes). By *subsistentia* we would like to understand something other than essence." The three persons "are related through the essence by an indivisible bond which cannot be dissolved, and yet each has a special characteristic through which he is distinguished from the other two ... Here we specifically mention the relation because whenever the name of God is used undefinitely the Son and the Spirit is meant not less, than the Father". Tertullian defined it correctly when he claimed that there is an order or an economy in God which does not suspend the unity of the essence. The Scriptural proof in this respect is to be found in John 1 verses 1-3, Hebrews 1 verse 2, Proverbs 8 verse 22 and John 5 verse 17. In all these verses certain qualities are ascribed to the Son.

Qualities which belong to the divine essence (being), include divinity *(deitas, divinitas)*, eternity*(aeternitas)* glory*(gloria)*, majesty*(majestas) and omnipotence (potestas)*. Both the Son and the Holy Spirit, by virtue of their divinity, are the true Jehovah *(Institutes* I, 13, 9 and I, 13, 15 respectively). From the command to baptism, however, it is clear "that the three persons, in whom alone God can be known, subsists in the divine essence. "The words Father, Son and Holy Spirit point clearly to a *distinctio realis* so that nobody can think they are merely additions through which God can be denoted by his works in various ways." "This *distinctio* is, that to the Father can be attributed the beginning of action, the fountain and the source of all things; to the Son the wisdom, counsel and arrangement of the action; to the Spirit the energy and efficacy of action." There is, however, an order: the Father is first, then the Son from out of Him and then the Spirit emanating from Both of them. These are eternal relations of origin and do not imply a more or a less, an earlier or a later. It also does not endanger the unity of God. As regards divinity, the Son and the Spirit are as one with the Father. "In each hypostasis (person) ... the whole of divine nature is understood, the only difference being that each has its own peculiar subsistence". Christ, relative to Himself, is called God, the *one* eternal God; relative to the Father He is the Son, generated by the Father before all eternity. "When we profess to believe in one eternal God, then by the name God is understood the one simple essence, which comprises three persons or hypostases; and consequently, as often as the name God (or Jehovah) is used without further qualification, it indicates equally well the Son and the Spirit as it indicates the Father. When, however, the Son is joined with the Father, then a *relation* comes into view ... and an *order* is implied, but in such a way that unity of the essence, the Divinity and the eternity of the Son and of the Spirit may not be impaired. "Christ Himself calls the Holy Spirit God in the absolute sense, because nothing prevents us from saying that He (the Spirit) is the whole spiritual essence of God in which the Father, *and* the Son *and* the Holy Spirit are encompassed."

In these matters we have to be very careful "not to let our thoughts or our words go one step further than the limits imposed by the Word of God". When Servet teaches that "Persons are certain external ideas which do not really subsist in the essence of God", when he teaches that "a Person is nothing other then the visible appearance of the glory of God", then it is "a monstrous fiction" existing outside the limits of Scripture. The same is true of his statements "that Christ has no other Divinity than insofar as He has been ordained as the Son of God by the eternal decree of God", or when He declares that "in the essence of God there are parts of God of which each is a part (portio) of God". From this heresy came others such as those who state that

God (the Father) transfused his Divinity on the Son and the Holy Spirit so that He (the Father) could be called the *Essentiator*. When, however, Calvin states we, "sometimes call the Father the source and the principle of divinity *(divinitas)*, we do it in obedience to the Scriptures only to indicate the unity of Being *(essentia)*". If, for example, the Son has been essentiated by God, then "we rob Him of his essence and we make of Him a titular God only". The Bible, however, ascribes each property of God to Christ (except of course his incommunicable properties). As regards *order* and *rank*, the beginning of the Divinity is in the Father (i.e. in *relation* with the Son and the Spirit), but as regards Being, the Divinity belongs not only to the Father. The Son or the Spirit is never subordinated to the Father in the sense of being subjected to Him. Of the Son it may be said, for example, "that his essence is without beginning, but that his person has his beginning in God". Although the Mediator fills the middle position between God and man, his majesty and glory *(majestas et gloria)* are not in the least impaired by this. He has not lost his majesty and glory but He has, on the contrary, merely concealed it. When the Mediator therefore "prays to the Father, he also inludes in that (the divinity of the Father) his own divinity!".

Remark

We will not here go into what Calvin says of the Trinity, and specifically of the concept of "person" in writings other than the 1559 edition of the Institute. The reason for this is that Calvin, by 1559, had thought about the problems surrounding the Trinity very carefully and had expressed himself very clearly and strongly on the problem of heretical doctrines. As would appear from the writings of Van der Linde and Krusche, the study of Calvin's other writings offers no new perspectives or more precise formulations.

Concluding and recapitulating remarks

* As we have already indicated, Calvin himself did not have any problem with the concept of person in the traditional formulation of the doctrine of the Trinity, viz. *una substantia (essentia), tres personae*. He even stated that those who strove to make the concept of Person, a problem, did so in a hateful fashion, through yapping and noisily asserting themselves. This forced, him, however, to give a more precise circumscription of the concept of person, which is nothing but a brief recapitulation of Biblical testimony. How does he do this?

* The answer lies in the fact that he says that the word "person" is a *subsistentia* in the divine *essentia*, which does stand in relation to the other two *subsistentiae*, but which is distinguished from them by at least *one incommunicable characteristic or property (proprietas incommunicabilis)*. The problem, however, remains that Calvin offers no definition of *subsistentia* or of *subsistere*. The only thing that he says in his well-known definition of "person" *(Institutes,* I, 13, 6) (and to which not enough attention is paid) is that: "Under *subsistentia* I prefer to understand something different from *essentia*". It would thus seem as if Calvin, on the basis of the fact that *hypostasis* appears in Hebrews 1 verse 3 (and of which he gives a very questionable exegesis!), and in view of the fact that the final trinitarian formula of the East was *mia ousia, treis hypostaseis, and* in line with Thomas **Aquinas** *(persona est relatio ut res subsistens in divina natura)* taking over the concept (subsistentia (=*hypostasis)* contents himself with these, and does not worry anymore about a more precise definition. The most that becomes clear with regard to the concept *subsistentia* is that

* It is something different from *essentia;*

* the three *subsistentiae,* however, do not exist abstractly away from the *essentia (aliud ab essentia abstractum),* but are hypostases of the whole *essentia (hypostasis totius essentiae);*

* the three *subsistentiae* stand in mutual relation to each other; and

* they are distinguished from each other as real *distinctiones* by means of *proprietates incommunicabiles.*

What these proprietates incommunicabiles are, Calvin describes both in terms of the intertrinitarian relations of origin and of the economical Trinity. Intertrinitarian, for example, it reads that: The Father generated the Son; the Son was generated by the Father and the Holy Spirit emanates from both *(procedere ab utroque).* Economically: The Father is the *principium agendi,* the Son the *sapientia agendi* and the Holy Spirit is the *virtus* or the *efficatio actionis (Dei).*

Karl Barth felt that in using *modes of being* for *subsistentiae,* he used a relatively better word than the traditional "person". We agree with Barth, but then the following has to be understood well:

213

* Purely as a word, the term *mode of being* has a strong tendency in the direction of the modalism;

* in reality *mode of being* is not so much a translation of *subsistentia, but of the well-known concept in trinitarian context, of tropos hyparxeōs, modus entis.*

The statement that Calvin did not know the so-called "modern concept of person", that is, "someone with his own I-centre, from which independent will and action may come", is not quite true. We say this because he definitely knew Melanchton's concept of person (which said, amongst others, *persona est subsistens vivum, individuum, intelligens,* and because we encounter the following statements in Calvin himself: "That He (the Holy Spirit) is the author of regeneration through his own intrinsic power and not through a power derived from elsewhere, is taught in many places in the Scriptures", *and:* "And it is expressed even more clearly elsewhere in the words: 'All these things work one and the self-same Spirit which shares out to everyone separately as He determines' (1 Corinthians 12:11)". Because, had He not been an independent entity subsisting in God, then arbitrary disposal and a will would never have been ascribed to Him" *(Institutes* I, 13, 14). He therefore knew this "modern concept of person" thoroughly, but for the purposes of the formulation of the doctrine of the Trinity, he described it (as emerges clearly from the last quotation) immediately in terms of the concept of *subsistentia (subsistens in Deo).*

Both Calvin and Karl Barth wanted it so that the Holy Scriptures should be "the fixed rule of both our thought and our speech", that the terms would be subordinated to the matter (which emanated from the Scriptures) and not the matter to the terms. The question remains why people (such as Karl Barth) then had so many problems with the concept of "persona" in the comprehensive definition *una substantia (essentia), tres personae?* To my mind the reason should be sought in the fact that theologians such as Barth did not keep account sufficiently of the fact that a definition such as the above, should not stand at the beginning of the doctrine of the Trinity, but at the end. It should never be a definition from which we, *analytically* make deductions from the usual meanings of words, but it should be seen as a definition constructed *synthetically* from all the relevant parts of Scripture regarding the matter under consideration. I regard the *Symbolum Quicunque* as a beautiful example of trinitarian thought which does not draw conclusions analytically from the "usual" meanings of words," but which loads them synthetically with those meanings which are testified to in the Scriptures in regard to the Trinity. They do start, in articles 3 and 4 (cf. P. Schaff, *The Creeds of Christendom,* Vol. II, pp. 66-71) from the comprehensive definition of *una substantia, tres personae,* and then in such a way that the faithful have to believe in *this* fashion: *neque substantiam seperantes, neque personas confudentes.* The following qualities are then ascribed to the *una substantia (Patris, Filii et Spiritus Sancti)* from the Scriptural testimony: *una deitas, aequalis gloria, co aeterna majestas; increatus, immensus, aeternus, omnipotens, deus, dominus,* **non factus, nec creatus, nihil prius aut posterius, nihil majus aut minus,** and then in such a way that there are not three gods, lords, eternals, almighties, etc., but only *One.*

Of the *tres personae* it is said: *alia est enim persona patris; alia Filii et alia spiritus Sancti* and then in such a way that the Father *non genitus est,* the Son *genitus est* and the Holy Spirit *nec genitus, sed procedens.*

A very important aspect of the Calvin's doctrine of the Trinity is that Calvin does not transfer to the *essentia,* the order which the Scriptures ascribe to the Father, the Son and the Holy Spirit, viz. that the Father is the source of divinity *(fons et origo deitatis),* that the Son is *from* the Father, generated by the Father *(genitus)* and that the Spirit is from both by *procedere.* He does not effect this transfer because then the Father would be *deificator* and *essentiator.* He saw the mentioned order rather as being situated in the intertrinitarian **relationships of origin without their eternity or divinity being** affected by these in the least.

A further positive point to be attributed to Calvin's doctrine of the Trinity which also throws light on his concept of person, is that he postulates that each person embodies the entire being of God *(hypostasis totius substantiae).* Whoever does not take full cognizance of this point, giving it due importance in his own thinking, is concerned with a false trinitarian doctrine and has an erroneous concept of person in the trinitarian context.

It is evidence of an exquisite distinctive ability when Calvin (in spite of the rule that the *opera Trinitatis ad extra indivisa sunt)* does not only indicate an "ontological", intertrinitarian distinction of persons, but also an economical distinction of persons, viz. that the Father is the **source of divine action, the Son is the wisdom and the Holy Spirit is** the executive power *(Spiritus Sanctus manus Dei qua suam potentiam exercet).*

In conclusion: It testifies of acute insight in the Scriptural truth when Calvin, right at the beginning of the discussion of the Trinitarian doctrine, states that the God of modalism or the gods of tritheism are inventions of the human brain and speculation, and that the God of Revelation is only the God who reveals Himself as one Being encompassing three Persons.

19. JOHN CALVIN AND THE PROTESTANT HYMNS

DR W.J.B. SERFONTEIN*

Introduction

At first glance the subject of this paper may seem strange to the audience. Calvin and church hymns? How does one reconcile these two diversities?

Was Calvin not, after all, pre-eminantly a theologian and a Reformer? How would he, in the midst of all his great theological work, also find time for something as relatively unimportant as music?

He started his theological work with a doctrinal exposition in His *Institutio religionis christianae,* 1536. This work was continually revised and extended. He was a biblical exegete of repute and in his lifetime he supplied commentaries to almost all the books of the Bible. From the very beginning he was involved in ecclesiastical discussions where a schism had to be prevented in the Christian world. He also kept up an extensive correspondence with colleagues in other cities, he repudiated the heresies of some friends in his letters and he looked after the pastoral needs of others. In addition, he preached three or four times a week and in his later life taught[1].

Because he was known for his organizational talents, he was entrusted, in Geneva and in Strassbourg, with the reorganization of the Protestant congregations. He also wrote new liturgical material and formularies himself[2] for the benefit of the church.

Originally he had not at all intended being a minister so that his training had not prepared him for church music. To add to the problem the customary church music in those days were so bad that one could

---

* His address is: University of Stellenbosch, Stellenbosch RSA 7600.

1 *Francois Wendel. 1976. Calvyn.* Collins, New York.

2 G. van der Leeuw. 1940. *Liturgiek.* Callenbach, Nijkerk.

not reasonably have expected him to take an interest in it[3]. Nor would the view of the music expert and musically well-trained Zwingli[4] that music deserved no place at all in the church service have encouraged him to make a move in this direction.

Although his biographer Doumergue was of the opinion that he harboured a spirit "sensible à la musique"[5], various other historians openly stated that Calvin had no gift for music[6].

The foregoing facts might make one think that Calvin must have been illequipped to dare enter the field of church music, and that he would have had little if any encouragement to move into this specialized field.

And yet, history states that Calvin became a leading figure in church music in spite of his scrappy background. Something must have convinced him to accept the fact that such an important part of public religion could be expressed in hymns that they should under no circumstances be neglected. He made up for his own shortcomings in the training and practical side of music by making a thorough study of the place and possibilities of church music in the Christian congregation. Added to that, he could add the full force of his organizational talent to the promotion of hymns.

Each sensitive member of the audience must agree with me that the subject of this paper is therefore not at all farfetched, but that it would indeed be of the utmost importance to study Calvin's special contribution and merit as regards hymns.

Why did Calvin concern himself with hymns?

The viewpoints that Calvin held regarding the value of church music

---

[3] Exegesis by Calvin of Job 21:12. He points out that the malpractices of some are the result of the malpractice of music itself. *Stemmen uit Geneve,* Volume XXVI, Reformed Library, Goudriaan, 1973, p. 203.

[4] Oscar Söhngen. 1967. *Theologie der Musik,* Stauda Verlag, Kassel. 33f.

[5] Jean Calvin. *Les Hommes et les choses de son temps.* Lausanne, 1899-1917, Volume II, p. 486.

[6] Blankenburg, W. 1975. *In: Protestant Church Music by Friedrich Blume,* Victor Gollancz, London. p. 516 and Winfred Kurzschenkel: *Die Theologische Bestimmung der Musik,* Paulinus-Verlag, Trier, 1971, p. 187.

in the Protestant religious service have never been worked out in detail. These views are widely scattered in his *Institution,* his commentaries on books of the Bible and in his sermons. In the *Epistre au lecteur* of his second hymnal (1542) and in the chapter *Des chants ecclésiastiques* in his *Les ordinances ecclésiastiques* (1561) we find some indication of his viewpoint.

The whole of Calvin's reformatory work can be brought down to *one insight* which would develop into a passion: He wanted the Word of God to have its rightful place in the religious service, and in the private life of the individual — and finally in the State.

In 1524 Martinus Bucer stated that "die claren gotteswort, auf die und nach den wir handelt haben unser neüwerungen oder viel mehr widerbringen auf das recht, alt und ewig ..." and later "so gebrauchen wir uns in der gemein gots kleins gesang noch gepets, das nichts aus gottlicher schrifft gezogen sey"[8]. This was therefore the point of view taken by churchmen of the day who were reformers. Calvin joined them without hesitation.

In the preface to the book *La forme des prières et chants ecclésiastiques* (1542) we find his own viewpoint: "The Psalms were given to King David by the Holy Spirit, so that in singing the Psalms we can be certain that God is giving us the words as if He is singing in us to his greater glory". "We confess that in ordering our faith and religion we wish only to follow the holy Scriptures without the addition of human thoughts"[9].

If he then breaks away from the Roman Church he should see to it that the service does not consist of all sorts of superstitious rituals, but that the Scriptures should proclaim all the glory of the message of salvation, so that the congregation may be so formed by the unadulterated of God that members will be useful citizens, and that the state will also function with the sanction of God.

Being a loyal scriptural theologican and a talented exegete, Calvin

---

[7] Van der Walt, J.J.A. 1962. *Die Afrikaanse Psalmmelodieë.* Pro Rege, Potchefstroom. p. 28.

[8] Quoted by Dankbaar, W.F. 1978. *Hervormers en Humaniste,* Ten Holland, Amsterdam. p. 224.

[9] *Joannis Calvini Opera Selecta,* München, 1926.

was undoubtedly aware of the divine commandment that the glory of God should be proclaimed in song. The many exhortations in the Psalms, to sing to the glory of God, to praise God with all one's energy, were familiar to him and he knew that these exhortations were written in the imperative form.

In the New Testament it was Paul who gave commandments to his congregations: "Speaking to yourselves in psalms and hymns and spiritual songs, singing making melody in your heat to God" (Ephesians 5:19), and "... teaching and admonishing one another in psalms and hymns and spiritual songs, singing with grace in your hearts to the Lord" (Colossians 3:16).

A person like Calvin who meticulously obeyed the exhortations of the Scriptures would not allow any obstacle to hinder him in his determination to put these commandments into practice.

Calvin's interest in hymns stems from his knowledge of liturgy. As Martin Luther before him, Calvin could do nothing else but start his reformatory work with the restitution of the religious service. The Roman Mass simply had to be replaced. In the first place the Mass was conducted in Latin, and a large percentage of the congregation could not understand that academic language from Rome. A young German churchman, Theobald Scwarz, compiled a German Mass in 1524 which was somewhat more Scriptural in nature[10]. Bucer further improved on it and used it in the German-speaking congregations. In Geneva Farél worked in the same direction. Calvin could therefore continue to build on these foundations when he took over the refugee French congregation in Strassbourg. He fulfilled a serious need by writing carefully considered formularies for baptism, communion and marriage ceremonies. Through the translations of Datheen these formularies later became the property of the Dutch-speaking nations.

While the sacrament was heavily emphasized in the Mass, the preached Word now had to come unto its own. Communion would no longer be celebrated as a recurrence of the sacrifice of Christ, but as a communal meal which would commemorate the suffering and death of Jesus Christ.

---

[10] Van der Leeuw, op. cit. p. 147.

The religious service would also become an opportunity to give instruction to the congregation. In the sermon the Scriptures would be expounded but hymns were the means by which he wanted to fix the personal knowledge of the great Scriptural truths in the minds of the members of the congregation. Calvin also distinguished between spoken prayer and sung prayer. If hymns were also used as liturgical prayers, they would become one of the cornerstones of the Protestant religious service. Christ, after all, exhorted mankind to preach the Word, to pray and to celebrate the sacraments[11]. By the time Calvin arrived in Strassbourg (1538), Bucher had already replaced Gregorian chants with psalms[12]. The hymns were sung in German and new melodies were composed by Matthias Greiter, Wolfgang Dachstein, Johan Grüger and others. In this way the prayers and hymns used in the congregations could be comprehensive to everybody.

The reinstated liturgy thus made it essential for Calvin to interest himself in hymns.

It is not a coincidence that the Holy Spirit exhorst us in the Scriptures to rejoice in God. There is after all a strong inclination among men to rejoice in vanities. Instead of allowing us to become swamped by all sorts of vain and corrupt enjoyment, God had granted us the means to become involved in spiritual injoyment. Music is one of the best means of enjoyment. It is essential, however, to understand that it is a gift of God which has been made available to mankind for a special purpose. It may not be used to inculcate licentiousness which could lead to voluptuousness and lechery.

Music has the almost incredible ability to swing man's moods in one direction or another. In the same sense Luther[13] writes that music can change joy into heartbreak, can change despair into courage, can change the proud into the humble and can turn hate and envy into love!

[11] Matthew 6:5-13; 28:19.

[12] Niesel, W. 1938. *Bekenntnisschriften und Kirchenordnungen,* Zolliken, Zürich p. 386.
"Cantus quam Gregorianum unucupant plurma habet absurdia: unde reiectus est merito a nostris et pluribus ecclesiis."
F.W. Dankbaar: *Calvijn zijn weg en werk,* Callenbach, Nijkerk, 1957, p. 68.
The most important objection to the Gregorian chant was the fact that it was recited by priests in a whispered voice — it was therefore inaudible and incomprehensible.

[13] Lob der Musik.

Calvin also realized that hymns could be a bridge. The realization on the part of the reformers that the Scriptures were essential, the place and the function of the Church and the need for the communion of the saints had to be expressed in the congregation in some way or another.

He accepted the correctness of Luther's statement: "Darum haben die Väter und Propheten nich umsonst gewünscht, dass mit dem Worte Gottes nichts enger verbunden sei als die Musik. Daher gab es auch soviele Gesänge und Psalmen, in denen gleichseitig Rede und Stimme an der Seele des Hörers ihr Werk tun, während in den übrigen Lebewesen und Körpern die Musik allein ohne die Rede am Werk ist"[14]. Hymns could be used as a means by which Sriptural truths could be fixed in the minds of the faithful — they could become the funnel through which something could be poured into the minds of men. Calvin realized that the rhymed verse and the musically stressed word would be retained more effectively in the memory than the spoken word. He recognized the possibilities of hymns as religious educational aids. The intention of congregational singing is to create intensive meditation *(méditer)* and a clearer insight *(intelligence)* into the meaning of the words sung[15]. It was not sufficient for Calvin that singing should be done unthinking ore merely emotional — and for this viewpoint he appealed to 1 Corinthians 14:15: "I will pray with the spirit, and I will pray with the understanding also: I will sing with the spirit, and I will sing with the understanding also".

It is not only essential that hymns should be scripturally correct, but the musical style should also be clearly distinguishable from all other kinds of music. Hymns are, after all, part of the public practice of religion when the congregation is in "the presence of God and his angels". For that reason the melodies of hymns should have power and majesty ("poids et majesté"), be modest and temperate (modère et modeste"), and should be in sharp contrast to secular music which is frivolous and changeable ("leger et volage").

Together with Augustine, Calvin points out that listening to the

---

[14] Quoted by Oscar Söhngen, op. cit. p. 92.

[15] Epistre au lecteur.

melody is not as important as understanding the significance of the text.

Nor did it escape the mind of this meticulous researcher that music has the potential to inspire to deeds. As parade music can be used to inspire the soldier to battle, so hymns might be used to call to prayer. Lukewarmness and laziness in the service of god can be changed into enthusiasm by the singing of suitable hymns. He pointed out the great force and energy ("force et vigueur") which can influence the human spirit in hymns. It is able to kindle the soul of man to serve and priase God with great vigour. "Calvyn sei gewissermassen ein Verteidiger der Kirchlichen Musik aus Verstandsgrunden und als Kenner der Labilität der menschlichen Psyche"[16]. The opposite pole of the ability of music used in a call to prayer is one to stimulate to sensuality. For that reason the church often regarded music with suspicion.

Which biblical theologian of today would dare to ignore these obvious advantages that music can have for the congregation? Calvin was clever enough to notice the obvious advantages and to use them in the best possible way. For that reason he devoted himself to collecting all the available written material and studying this carefully. He studied Plato, Ambrosius, Augustine, Luther, Bucer and others in order to find out for himself what possibilities existed for the use of hymns in his services. And even if he was not a practising musician himself, he interpreted the effects of hymns on the human spirit with such acute and clear images that his words had to sink in. In addition he used his organizational ability to create the French Protestant hymns, to give them a fixed place in the religious service and to establish their influence in the religious life of the Calvinist Christian. His personal and close contact with famed musicians and poets of a complete hymnal. It is no wonder then that he is acknowledged as a leading figure in the field of reformed hymns.

An ideal is realized

In this section a portion is taken from Calvin's work, and for the sake of the survey, the material is put in a specific order. Nobody should deduce from this scheme that Calvin worked according to the same scheme.

---

[16] A-E Cherbuliez, quoted by Söhngen, op cit. p. 61.

The first indication that we find of Calvin's involvement with congregational singing in history is in the document compiled chiefly by him but which was submitted on his behalf and on the behalf of Guillaume Farél and Courreault to the Council of Geneva (in 1537) in order to introduce the reforms which they intended to effect in the congregation. This document is known as *Articles concernant l'organisation de l'Eglise*.

In this document they indicate the necessity of ecclesiastical chastisement at the celebration of holy communion and the maintenance of the teaching of the pure doctrine in the congregation. They also refer to the psalter and say that "We prefer that Psalms be sung in the Church, as was the custom in the early Christian Church, and the testimony of Saint Paul who said that it is good to sing with heart and mouth when meeting for prayers. We cannot judge the development and the edification which might result from this before we have put it to the test. Because, truly, in the way we act now, the prayers of the faithful are so cold, that it makes us ashamed. The psalms should kindle in us a fire which would enable us to elevate our hearts to God, and to move us to warmth when calling upon Him and to glorify Him. And above all, everybody would see what gift the Pope and his followers robbed the church of when they relegated the Psalms, which should truly be spiritual hymns, to being muttered among themselves without any true comprehension".

Aulcuns pseaulms et cantiques mys en chant, 1539

One would make a serious error of judgement if one supposed that with the abolition of the Gregorian chants in the religious services of French congregations alternative hymns were available. Those which could most probably be used, were either in Latin or in German and were therefore incomprehensible. In the case of other hymns the melodies were such that they could not be sung in a Protestant congregation[17].

As long as hymns were not available, the religious services had to limit themselves to prayer, reading from the Scriptures, explication or exegesis and communion. What a relief it would have been for Calvin on his arrival in Strassbourg in 1538, having been banned from Geneva together with Farél, to find there congregational singing as

[17] Hasper, H. 1955. *Calvijns beginsel voor de zang in den eredienst*, Volume I, S'Gravenhage. p. 575.

he had vizualized it to himself (in the German congregations, under the guidance of Martin Bucer)! It is true that Zwingli was sceptical about the possibility of orderly mass singing in the religious service, but here it was suddenly proved to be possible[18].

The artistic background of Reformed hymns goes back to the era before 1530. In 1525 Wolf Köpphel published *Treutsch Kirchenampt,* which especially contained new melodies supplementing the Lutheran *Achtliederbuch* (Nurenberg, 1523/249. This was followed in 1526 by *Psalmen, Gebet und Kirchenübung* of which many editions appeared and which had an influence far outside Strassbourg. Between 1537-43 a series of editions of *Psalmen und Geystliche Lieder* and in 1541 the first official *Gesangbuch für Stett und Dorfkirchen* with a preface by Martin Bucer[19] were published.

The trend to use psalms for congregational singing then became established here. In 1538 fully rhymed and musically composed Psalters were published, by Jacob Dachser in Strassbourg, and in 1542 by Hans Gamersfelder in Nurenberg[20]. In 1549 the *Souterliedekens* by Willem van Nuyenveld of Antwerpen appeared, in which the Psalms were rendered in Flemish and provided with secular melodies. With this kind of encouragement and these examples to hand, a young and enterprising theologian could try to find a way out of the *cul de sac* of the French hymn. And where else than in the songs of joy of Israel could the Biblical theologian find his home? In the preface to the commentary on the Psalms he says that "I have the habit of calling this book an anatomy of all the parts of the soul, because there is no affliction of man which is not reflected here as in a mirror. The Holy Spirit Himself here evoked all griefs, sorrows, fears, doubts, expectations, anxieties and despairs — all these confused emotions have been realistically portrayed".

He starts off with a rhymed version of Psalm 46. He wanted to portray the purely Scriptural content for church goers in a comprehensible fashion, and then in such a way that it would remain in the minds of the people. For this purpose *belletrie,* the poetrically beautiful word, was not necessary. The melody which Wolfgang Dachstein, the

---

[18] Blankenburg, op. cit. p. 513.

[19] Ibid., p. 47.

[20] Ibid., p. 133.

organist of the St Thomas Church in Strassbourg composed for Psalm 23 also moved him, and his first hymn read as follows:

> Nostre Dieu nous est ferme appuy,
> vertu, fortresse et seur confort,
> auquel aurons en nostre ennuy
> present refuge et resbon port.
> Douc certaine asseurance aurons
> mesmes quand la terre verrous
> par tremblemant se descrocher,
> et nous en la mer se cacher."

The fact that Calvin never wrote blank verse for which he later had to find melodies, and the choice of really good melodies from the German source is an indication of his artistic judgement. In time Calvin versified Psalms 25, 36, 91, 113 and 138, these having been set to music by Matthias Greiter, choir leader of the St Thomas Church in Strassbourg. His versification of the Song of Simeon and the Ten Commandments most probably also dates from this period. As the hymns became available, they were tested in the congregation of the local French refugees, of which Calvin was the minister. Calvin also sent copies to his friend Farél, who was in Neuchâtel at the time, so that the hymns could also be tried out in that congregation[21].

In one way or another, which cannot be verified any more, the versifications by Clément Marot for Psalms 1, 2, 3, 15, 19, 32, 52, 103, 114, 115, 130, 137 and 143 came into Calvin's possession[22].

The first Reformed Psalter in French probably appeared at the beginning of 1539, containing 18 versified Psalms[23]. These included the five mentioned above, by Calvin, as well as the versified Ten Commandments, the Song of Simeon and the Credo[24]. Thirteen

---

[21] Letter to Farél, included in De Zwart: *Calvijn in het licht zijner brieven,* Kok, Kampen, 1938, p. 38.

[22] It is not impossible, although there is no proof for the fact, that Calvin requested Marot per letter to write the versifications of the Psalms according to his prescriptions.

[23] Of this booklet there is one extant copy, which is kept in the Stadtsbibliothek, München. There are also facsimile prints in the British Museum, London, and in the book of H. Hasper, p. 456ff.
Cf. Ford Lewis Battles. 1978. *The piety of Calvin,* Baker Book House, Grand Rapids. p. 144-165.

[24] Blankenburg, op. cit. p. 517.

versifications by Marot, to music composed by Dachstein and Greiter, were included[25].

La Forme des prières et chantz ecclésiastiques, 1542

From the sources it is not quite clear pricesly what link there had been between Calvin and Marot. The fact that the two men differed in nature and inclination, as well as strongly in religious matters, makes one suspect that any contact between them must have been purely coincidental.

Blankenburg finds that the first meeting between the two men took place as early as 1531[26]. Marot had already started with the versification of texts in 1532. The fact that he was in close contact with the famed expert of Hebrew of the period, Professor Francois Vatable[27] who was a teacher at the Sorbonne University in Paris, provided him with valuable insight into the Psalms. It is also known that he possessed Beza's commentary on the Psalms. The importance of the meeting between Calvin and this poet in Ferrara[28], in 1536, should also not be underestimated.

When Calvin returned to Geneva in 1542, he persuaded Marot to settle in Geneva while he was in danger of his life. There was then a close co-operation between the two men.

In 1542 the second Psalter was published under the direct guidance of Calvin. This was based on the previous book, but the number of Psalm versifications had been increased to 39. Calvin withdrew his own texts for the sake of Marot, except the text of Psalm 113 and the Credo. A striking change is the elimination of the repeated "Hallelujah" at the end of the stanzas of Psalm 138 and the Kyrie Eleison prayer at the end of the stanzas of the Ten Commandments. Calvin had earlier include these incantations in compliance with the customs of the early Christian churches[29].

---

[25] Ibid., p. 519.

[26] Op. cit. p. 518.

[27] Hasper, op. cit. p. 494.

[28] Jedin, H. 1978. *Handbuch der Kirchengeschichte,* Herder, Freiburg. p. 385.

[29] Lietzmann, H. 1953. *Geschichte der alten Kirche,* Volume 2, de Gruyter, Berlin. p. 295.

Prior to Marot's death in 1544 a total of 49 psalms had been versified. Because Calvin could not find anybody to satisfy his high standards, the work of versification was temporarily halted. This was continued only in 1550 by Theodorus Beza[30]. The first part of Beza's versifications was published in 1551 under the title *Pseaumes octante trois de David mis en rime francoise.*

Since 1542 Guillaume Franc had been the leader of singing at the St Peter's Church in Geneva, and he probably acted as musical editor for Calvin. Between 1545 and 1557 Louis Bourgeois filled this post and the texts by Beza were probably set to music by him. After Beza had completed all the texts round about 1560, Pierre Daques, who was probably the mysterious and unidentified "Maître Pierre", completed the musical scores[31].

The final copy of the Genevan Psalter, as it would become known afterwards, was ready for publication in 1562. The publisher arranged that the book should appear simultaneously in various cities. It was an immediate success[32]. In the second half of the sixteenth century no less than 135 editions in French, German and Dutch were published. With the exception of the Bible there are few books which have retained their usefulness so fully in the course of the centuries.

The Biblical Psalm only?

The charge[33] has often been levelled against Calvin's work with regard to hymns that he only worked towards the implementation of Biblical psalms in the religious service. There are, it is true, some statements made by him which might lead one to suspect such an attitude, but the facts tend to remove the "allegation".

In the first place there are many proofs that the word "Psalm-singing" in those days was used with reference to the singing of the congregation, which also included other hymns.

[30] Van Proosdij, C. *Theodorus Beza,* Donner, Leiden, 1895, pp. 8, 16, 29.

[31] Van der Leeuw, G. 1948. *Beknopte Geschiedenis van het kerklied,* Wolters, Groningen. p. 168/9. Blankenburg, op. cit., p. 520.

[32] Henry, Paul. 1849. *The Life and Times of John Calvin,* Whittaker, London. p. 414ff.

[33] Douen, O. 1967. *Clément Marot et le Psautier Huguenot,* Niewkoop, B. de Braaf, Kurszchenkel, op. cit. p. 189.

In the *Articles to the Council* Calvin wrote in 1537 with regard to the "few Psalms" which should be sung in the course of the religious service, that this had the purpose of inspiring the audience to compose similar songs ("pareilles oraysons"), and that in the course of the service similar songs of praise and of gratitude ("pareilles louanges et graces") would be sent up to God with equal fervour.

The heading of the first hymnal is *Aulcuns Pseaulms et Cantiques.* Apart from the 18 versified psalms Calvin also included the versifications of the Song of Simeon, the Ten Commandments, and, nota bene, the Credo, adapted by himself. In the completed Psalter the Our Father and two forms of grace to be said at table were added.

Although the hymns were not included in the official Psalter, there are at least two hymns that Calvin himself wrote: a song of truimph to the glory of Christ called *Epinicion Christo cantatum* (written at Worms in 1541) and an eulogy, *Je te salue mon certain Redempteur,* written at Geneva in 1545[34].

The above-mentioned facts lead me to accept that Calvin devoted himself in the first place to making available the Psalms for the seemingly obvious reason that this was a collection of Biblical hymns. Before he could, however, give any attention to the New Testament hymn for the Reformed Church, he died in 1564. For that reason a statement by H. Hasper would suffice in this respect: "Wij mogen de problematiek, welke tachtig jaar later (he is referring to the Dordt Synod, 1618) in ons Vaderland is opgekomen na de afwijsing der *'Hymni ofte Lof-Zangen op de Christelijke Feestdagen, ende andersinds',* niet overbrengen naar de dagen van Zwick en Calvijn, want het typisch Nederlandsche probleem: 'Psalmen óf Gezangen' bestond voor hen nie. Dit is geen Calvinistisch, maar een nationaal-kerklijk vraagstuk"[35].

An educational task

Because congregational singing meant a totally new beginning for the Reformed congregations, Calvin was realistic enough to realize that fundamental preparatory work had to be done. There were no shortcuts.

---

[34] Quoted by Hasper, op. cit., p. 506.

[35] Ibid., p. 441.

In the Articles to the Council he already states that the children in the schools should devote one hour per day at school to the singing of Psalms[36]. He also arranged that children should help when new hymns had to be learnt by the congregations. Extra time before services was also devoted to learning hymns.

From the beginning Calvin saw to it that there should be a good song leader in the congregations. In Strassbourg he collaborated very closely with the organist, Dachstein, and the leader of singing, Greiter. In Geneva he first appointed Guillaume Franc to this position. He was succeeded by Louis Bourgeois and in 1559 Pierre Daques assumed this position. These men were at the same time responsible for leading the singing in the day school, the Academy and the congregation[37].

Because a strong educational effort had been made with the introduction of the new hymns, the new hymns were quickly accepted and could then begin to fulfil the religious role that Calvin had envisaged.

Conclusion

Although the First Reformed Psalter in French in 1562 was greeted[38] with widespread enthusiasm and hearty acceptance[39], there was also serious criticism. Bovet[40] quotes a critic who judged that the hymns were just good enough to be sung in Protestant Churches!

[36] Coetzee, J.C. 1959. *In:* Hoogstra: *John Calvin, contemporary prophet,* Barker Book House, Michigan. p. 206.

[37] Ibid.

[38] Henry, op. cit., p. 414.

[39] Felix Bovet, quoted by Hasper, op. cit. p. 481, says that "although his versifications do not have the elegance and the ease of the verses by Marot, they are yet not unworthy of the reformer, and the clarity and force can be regained here which characterize his prose". John T. McNeil: *The History and Character of Calvinism,* quoted by Hasper, op. cit., p. 505, says that "His best poem, *Je te salue,* an utterance of warm and personal faith, appeared first in the 1545 Geneva edition of the Psalter".

[40] Emile Doumergue, *In: Calvin and the Reformation,* Fleming H. Revell, New York, 1909, particularly refers to the criticism of G. Ritschl who portrays Calvin as an unbending rigorist, without any human feelings, and therefore not able to create poetry.
Douen, op. cit., says that after the study of the Genevan psalter he came to the conclusion that the melodies of the Psalms can be traced back to folk melodies. Marcus Jenny and Pierre Pidoux, in *Jahrbuch für Liturgik und Hymnologie,* 1956, p. 107ff, reject Douen's view categorically.

Criticism was aimed mostly at the poetic power of the verses and the musical scopes of the settings. Each admirer would have to admit that there are grounds for serious criticism against the literary and the musical aspects of the hymns. But it is not so that artistic considerations should have the most important say in determining the acceptance and the efficacy of the hymn. The spiritual message of the word and the tone is of more importance.

Should a researcher survey the oevre of John Calvin, a superficial judgement about the part he played in the development of the church hymn could well give the impression that it had been merely a sideline. Should his academic, dogmatic and organizational work be seen in a balanced perspective, however, then a totally different conclusion can be arrived at.

Without attempting in the least to denigrate the spiritual value of a work like the *Institutio* for example, I am of the opinion that in the influence exerted by Calvin to establish Biblical truths once again among his people[41] hymns played a greater part than his written testimony. Through the hymn he still addresses the congregation Sunday after Sunday, four centuries after his death, in the course of religious services in Protestant churches all over the world. How many individuals have not been personally affected by that message? Through hymns his influence has extended further than his own school, further even than Reformed Christendom.

I come to this conclusion because I agree with our own Professor J.D. du Toit who has said the following on this issue[43]: "Whoever sings the Psalms, reaches for the heights, because the purpose is the glorification of Jesus Christ, our Lord through the Holy Spirit. Psalm-singing is the ascent of the soul, the outreach of the hand to the concealed treasure of the faithful; it is religious life in its highest form; it is the bridge to the illimitable; it is a courageous deed of faith, the arm stretched out above the stormy waters of life; it portrays descent into the waterfalls of fear, but also the joy on the heights and in the limitless reaches of salvation".

[41] *Histoire du Psautier de Eglises Réformées,* 1872, quoted by Hasper, op. cit., p. 513.

[42] Men like Le Fèvre, Briconnet, Gérard Roussel, Vatable, Olivétan, and others, in this time tried without success to disseminate Biblical teaching.

[43] Message of Totius on the occasion of the inauguration of the first *Afrikaans Psalter and Hymnal,* 29 October, 1944.

20. CALVIN'S CANON LAW AND INFLUENCE ON CHURCHES IN SOUTH AFRICA

PROF. B. SPOELSTRA*

Did Calvin have any direct influence on Canon Law in South African churches?

Traditionally it has been maintained that Calvin was the father of the Presbyterial or even of a Presbyterial-Synodical form of church government. In contemporary times it is being said instead that he was in favour of an Episcopalian form of church government (cf. R. Boon, *Apostolisch ambt en reformatie,* 1965, Nijkerk). R.M. Kinghorn then maintains that the Calvinist synodical ecclesiastical organization and discipline inspired revolution in both England and France. Geneva was the centre of "democratic centralization. Local planning and responsibility devolved in large measure on local consistories and colloquies that were elected at least in part by the faithful of the local church" *(Geneva and Coming of the Wars of Religion in France 1555-1563,* 1965, Geneva, p. 128). J. Bohatec *(Calvins Lehre von Staat und Kirche,* 1961, Breslau, p. 380) feels that A. Kuyper has tied in with Calvin's democratic spirit. Yet one can, with equal justification, argue that Calvin did not advocate a democratic form of government for state or church and that he definitely did not advocate revolution (cf. A. van Ginkel, *De Ouderling,* 1975, Amsterdam, p. 145ff). There is no way in which Calvin can be held responsible for all these contradicting principles.

I could find no work which gives a reasonably ordered view of Calvin's ideas regarding the field of Canon Law. His philosophy was in all probability, rather pretended than interpreted by so called Calvinists. Many church societies would like to claim Calvin as the founder of their form of church government. Few of them, however, would be

* His address is: Hammanskraal Theological School, P.O. Box 59, Hammanskraal. RSA 0400.

able to prove direct influences. Via England and the Netherlands a series of other influences (Roman, Lutheran, Rationalist and Liberalist) were also disseminated to South Africa. It would be a herculean task to single out and compare typically Calvinist ideas within the various English and Afrikaans-speaking church societies in South Africa, within the confines of this paper.

The Power, the Will and the Ordination of God as the foundation of Calvin's philosophy of law

Calvin conceived the concept of *justice* from the basis of the sovereignty of God. Divine power and justice are defined by the Will of God. This Will appears firstly from the Holy Scriptures *(regimen spiritualis)* and secondly from the natural order of things *(regimen naturalis)*. By virtue of his power and authority all men must fear and respect God. The Will of God determines what is right, and is the law of all laws. God calls and uses secular authorities to wield the sword in His Name. Rulers have not only rights but also duties (Jürgen Baur: *Gott und Recht im Werke Calvins,* 1965, Bonn, pp. 5-16; 27-29; 33f). The natural order was not affected so radically by the Fall. In this way too, natural law indicates that it is the Will of God that men should obey their parents and civil authorities.

Calvin stresses both love and justice. Alongside natural law there is the moral law which is nullified by sin (Baur, 54f). The will of God *(regimen spiritualis)* is aimed at reinstatement. The church is primarily the result of the recreating work of the Word and the Spirit of God.Therefore Canon Law is *ius divinum* (Baur, p. 29, cf. *Institutes* and the Roman doctrine of the two swords; B.C. Milner's *Calvin's Doctrine of the Chruch,* 1970, Leiden, p. 58). Calvin's principle for church government is the specific order, "because order is what God wills (ordinatio) and through his Holy Spirit effects ... Wherever the ordinatio and Spiritus Dei are correlated, there is order; where the Spirit works apart from the *ordinatio Dei,* there is the extraordinary". When the Holy Spirit withdraws, "confusion and disorder" follow (Milner, p. 44c. Cf. p. 134, *Institutes* IV, iii, 1; Calvin, Com. Hebrews 5:4, Numbers 17:4).

The Holy Spirit fixes in mankind the *Ordinatio Dei* which is in the Word of God. To a large extent the will or the ordination of God therefore prescribes ecclesiastical ordering. The Law teaches the justice of God, and also reveals our own injustice and controls godlessness (B.C. Milner, p. 75, p. 81f).

233

In civil and church ordination we have to know the will of God and go along with it. God reveals how He desires to be served. For this reason, the Church has to do with the Word of God, the Gospel, as a law of freedom. In Galatians 5:1 God forbids the practice of Roman Canon Law which determined that the faithful could be deprived of the freedom through ordinations which did not appear in the Scriptures (J. Calvin: *Institutes*, IV, x, 8, 10, 11, 12, 13, 14, 15).

Christ the head present in the Holy Spirit in the church

Calvin starts the Fourth Book of the *Institutes of Christian Religion* with: We share in Christ through faith. Do note that he does not say that we achieve a share in the *church*. Because we are weak, means are needed to evoke and to increase faith. For this reason, God has ordained shepherds and ministers to teach us and to serve the sacraments. In the Fourth Book he therefore has to deal with the church, with church government, ordination, power, sacraments and civil order. Thus he begins with the universal invisible church which God has predestined.

In Church government the ordination or will of God excludes basic human stipulations. The essence of the church is unity in faith and not institution or organization (Bohatec, pp. 563-565). Differently phrased: the nature of the church for Calvin is *spiritual*. Faith provides participation in Christ *(Institutes,* IV, i, par. 1). He does not deal primarily with "membership" of the church. The church is merely the means (mother) to gather together the faithful, in order to nourish and govern them. The Holy Spirit gives faith in the Gospel to the chosen. He calls them and settles them into the church together with others in Christ. Therefore the church becomes visible where the Word is preached and where the Holy Spirit works with it. The ordinatio or the will of God allows the covenant of God and the communion with Christ in the visible church, to be there in a unique manner next to the civil ordinations *(Institutes,* IV, i, par. 3). The preaching of the Gospel and the office of the minister "constitute" therefore, practically, the congregation of the faithful as church *(Institutes,* IV, i, 5; cf. Milner, p. 48, p. 53f).

Sohm does Calvin wrong by implying that, like Rome, he departed from the premise of the visible church with its forms of law (Rechtskörper) and then called upon the divine to support his institutional ordination of law (Bohatec, 563-565). It is, in fact, to be wondered at that the excellent jurist, Calvin, did not design a "constitution" and so "found a church". Stated differently: For Calvin the church is essentially an organism and not an institution, although the organism has an institutional pattern.

Calvin regards the church in the absolute sense from the figure of Christ as the only Head out of whom the whole body is constituted and which in conjunction forms a unity (Ephesians 4:16; Institution IV, vi, 9). The church is a pneumatic organism. The elevated Christ works in two ways: directly where the Word and the Spirit act, and in a mediating sense where the elevated Christ, in the Holy Spirit, serves through men so that the church, his Body, the communion with Christ, assumes visible shape. "Darnach Gestaltet Sich das Recht in der Kirche. Es ist das Recht Christi, das sich auf den ganzen kirchenkörper und jeden einzelen erstreckt, und, da Christus durch seinen Geist und sein Word wirkt, als *Wortrecht* und *Geistesrecht* beziechnet werden kann. Weil es in Christus und seinem Wort verwurzelt, so sind alle von ihm geregelten kirchlichen Ordnungen pneumatisch. Darum is die Kirchen Verfassung pneumatisch ... Das Ordnungsrecht der Kirche ist daher kein weltliches Recht, keine juristisch zwingende Gemeinschaftsordnung, sondern ein pneumatisches Ordnungsrecht ... kurz die Regel des Organisch-pneumatischen Wollens in der Kirche ..." (Bohatec, 570f). Milner states that "The unifying principle in Calvin's theology is ... the absolute correlation of the Spirit and the Word: it is the inseparability of the Spirit and the Son ... When the work of the Spirit is correlated with those manifestations of the Word (ordinantiones Dei), order —above all the order which describes the church — appears. Thus the church (order) can only be understood dialectically, as referring simultaneously to the Word and to the Spirit ..."

For Calvin all church government amounts to ministering of the Word of Christ and thereby the edification of the body of Christ. Unity in Christ comes to the fore where the doctrine is kept pure, where a godly life is led and where pure brotherly love is practised. Where this unity of the faithful with their Head, Christ, is maintained and intensified, the church, the body of Christ, is edified. The faithful attain inner renewal (Milner, 172). The kingship of Christ is realized in the church in the spiritual sense in this way *(Institutes* IV, i, p; ii, 4). This is the fruit of the Holy Spirit *(Institutes* IV, i, 6).

Spiritual (Ecclesiastical) and political (Civil) government

On the strength of the will of God Calvin distinguishes unique spheres of secular and ecclesiastical government (cf. *Institutes,* III, xix, 15, IV, xx, 1). The modern concept of "state" is unknown to Calvin. In Calvin's view, God called certain individual(s) to execute his Will *(Institutes* IV, xii, 4, 6). Rulers (governors) are *stadtholders* of God, Dei legati. Consequently, the authorities do not have rights, but duties (cf. Baur, 39f, 117, 120). The authorities themselves therefore have to obey the Ten Commandments and thereby, the Will of God (Baur, 71, 267).

In 1541 Calvin returned to Geneva on the definite condition that the Council acknowledge the right of the servants of Christ to exercise spiritual discipline. He had to deal, however, with the Genevan Little Council, the Council of Twenty and the Council of Two hundred. Due to the efforts of these authorities the Reformation was a fait accomplait by the time Calvin arrived. They were therefore inclined to regard themselves as the guardians of Geneva in both ecclesiastical and civil sense, since they felt that they had inherited the powers previously embodied in and excercised by the bishop, pope or monarch (cf. Boon, 176f; J. Plomp, *De Kerklijke Tucht bij Calvijn,* 1969, Kampen, p. 181).

In the era under discussion authority of "state" or "church" was not an abstract concept as in the sense prevailing at present. Authority was in incorporated in and identified with the person of whoever exercised such authority. He was an individual answerable to God. According to Calvin the will of God sets boundaries for the power of the rulers (Bohatec, 12).

The believers might even be forced to resist the highhandedness of a government by means of passive resistance under the leadership of lesser authorities. Calvin is radically opposed to revolution. A monarchy might easily lead to tyranny while a democracy might, through the will of the masses, lead to unstable government and to anarchy. He therefore prefers government by a responsible aristocrasy.

The civil government must establish freedom so that society might experience order and prosperity according to the will of God. For that reason the authorities must oppose public immorality and even in the civil society, love should prevail *(Institutes* IV, xii, 2.3.8.15; xx 31). Obedience to the authorities, however, is also obedience to God *(Institutes* IV, xii, 22; Baur, 135, 137, 141). Civil and church authorities act like two eyes of the same body. They are linked in God, and have to supplement and acknowledge each other mutually.

Calvin's theocracy is based on the rule of the Word of God. Yet he differs radically from the Roman concept and attitude. He does not acknowledge any priestly dominion over political authority. He rejects both hierocracy and caesaropapism (Baur, 267). Government has to pay homage not to officers of the church but only to the Word. The minister is not the exclusive master of the Word, but does have a calling to elucidate the Word for the authorities. Each believer, is however, also of age, and can judge the ministers by means of the Word. Calvin rejects a state church (Baur, 269), but endeavours, through the co-ordination of the ecclesiastical and political vocation to turn the civil community of Geneva into "city church" and "national church". The Libertines saw this as an infringement of their freedom (Doumergue, *Calvyn in de Strijdtperk*, 203f).

Calvin is opposed to the idea that one and the same person can simultaneously hold civil (secular) and ecclesiastical (spiritual) offices. In his office as spiritual guide and minister he fully advised the civil authorities and co-operated with them, but they themselves carried the responsibility for their decisions. In the same manner the Council could submit confessional and disciplinary issues to the consistory, but the consistory had to decide on ecclesiastical matters and discipline. The government had to exercise authority in the matter of crime. The church council decided on excommunication from holy communion and church society (Plomp, 151, articles of 1537; Baur, 145-147). According to the provisos at the time of the *corpus christianum* in Geneva the church council had to report excommunication to the Little Council. The individual was then usually banished from Geneva on civil grounds as well.

Calvin's unique biblical concept of the church

Calvin's unique concept of church differs in a radical sense from perhaps all contemporary concepts of church. The concept "church" is used nowadays in predominantly clerical, collegial (associative) and institutional sense. For Calvin, however, the church is mostly organism. Should "church" be understood essentially as institution, the South African church societies or associations cannot easily claim Calvinist influence in their church government. As regards doctrine, however, the case may differ somewhat.

By virtue of its nature the church is a unity

By virtue of the Will of God the Holy Spirit brings those whom God has chosen to eternal life, to faith. Through rebirth the Holy Spirit incorporates the faithful into the body of Christ, and builds "eine Einheit in der Vielheit, die erhalten und belebt wird durch das eine Haupt Christus" (Bohatec, 270). Essentially the church is "einen Organismus, dessen Ursprung und Ziel in der Ewigheit liegt ... Dieser mystische Körper ... ist eine Wirklichkeit, kein blosses Schema oder Bild" (Bohatec, 267). These believers consitute the church, the body of Christ.

The spiritual, inner unity which is the church, is revealed in the same confession (even if the similarity is only along the main lines: *Institutes* IV, 1.12), brotherly love and obedience to the Will (the Word and the Law) of God (Institution IV, ii, 5.9.10). For this reason the Reformation broke with the Papacy, but Calvin knew that some true churches still remained under the subjection of the papacy *(Institutes* IV, ii, 12). The seemingly faithful and the unfaithful mingle on earth with the church which knows God *(Institutes* IV, i, 7.13; Baur, 143). The church as a congregation of believers is forced to practise with suitable discipline and in obedience to the Word and the Spirit, the unity of faith and life. In this manner Christ and not essentially the church maintains unity (Bohatec, 419).

Calvin denies that Christ needs an ecclesiastical organization or an institution to maintain unity in the church *(Institutes,* IV, vi, 10). Where Luther proclaimed Christ as the Head of the invisible church, Calvin allows Him to rule in the visible church in so far as the Word rules *(Institutes* IV, ii, 4, viii, 1; Bohatec, 399f). The church is one. Christ, by definition, after all has only one body, and He alone is King of the church. This one church becomes visible reality in that the congregation is a community of faith.

The church is a pneumatic and dynamic organism and not a static institution

For Rome, the church is a priestly institute. Calvin on the other hand postulates that the body of Christ and the kingdom (rule of God) become visible and present in the congregation (church). The congregation is the church of Christ in so far as the Word and the Spirit are obeyed. The church is not visible in bishops and councils, but in the unity of the faithful (Bohatec, 292).

Whoever destroys this unity denies God and Christ *(Institutes,* IV, i, 3.4.5.6.10). The unity of the church is therefore not statically institutional (Bohatec, 346f) but organically dynamic, because it must be continually realised as a unified body in faith and in conduct. Therefore the church is the unity, where the unadulterated Word of God is preached and (NB!) obeyed, and simultaneously where the Sacraments are served and received according to the institution of Christ (Institution, IV, i, 8.9.10; cf. B. Spoelstra, *Calvyn en die grense van die kerk, In die Skriflig,* 1978, no. 45, p. 20f).

"One cannot pursue the study of Calvin's doctrine of the church without being struck by his repeated usage of such metaphors as assimilate the church to an organism, i.e. to a created, living, historically evolving reality ..." (Milner, 7). The relationship of man to Christ, the body to the Head, determines that outside the church there is no salvation (Institution, IV, i, 1.2.3; Bohatec, 351). This unity with Christ cannot be made to equal static outward membership of an institution. By virtue of the essence of faith, the unity with Christ is "something which happens again and again" (Milner, 180, cf. Com. John 11:51, Isaiah 37:26).

The kingship and the body of Christ are Calvin's "deepest and most concrete understanding of the church". The Word of Christ and the Holy Spirit may never be divided, as was done by the Roman Church and by the Anabaptists (Milner, 190f). The ecclesiastical organism therefore lives in "dynamische Mystik, eine Mystik der Tat, eine operative Mystik" (Bohatec, 351). "The church (order) must always be understood, therefore, as existing in the movement from the believer to the Word which occurs in the leading of the Spirit through ordained means. As movement of the Spirit the church cannot be regarded as a static fixed entity, even if it has a certain stability and continuity as a movement of the Spirit through ordained means" (Milner, 192).

The church as a spiritual organism, exists primarily in the faithful because God has chosen and called them to service in all walks of life. The offering of the Word (in preaching, sacraments, teaching, the pastorate and chastisement) promotes this vocation to serve God and does not in itself constitute the essential nature of the church. Yet the church for Calvin, as for Luther, did not have a "offentlichrechtliches Genossenschaft" or "Körperschaft im enger Sinne" (Bohatec, 377-379). Calvin calls the "institutionelle Imperialismus der Kirche" the tyranny which corresponds to the Roman world dominion of antiquity (Bohatec, 442).

The church attains visible shape in the communion service

The church assumes visible shape where communion is celebrated (Bohatec, 276, 280). "God has ordained both the preaching of the Word and the administration of the sacraments, and when coupled with the efficacious working of the Holy Spirit they constitute the order which marks the reality of the church ... According to Calvin, then we cannot think of the church as a legally defined institution ... nor can we conceive it mystically ... Rather, the church must be defined dialectically as union with Christ in, through and together with the means by which the spirit brings us to Him ..." (Milner, 123f). The communion congregation is therefore the ideal image of the unity of the congregation with the Head, Christ (Bohatec, 339). The discipline surrounding communion (cf. *Institutes* IV, XI and XII with the Dordt Rules, 1619, article 16, 23, 61–76, 78) embodies the Calvinean tradition. Excommunication from the communion service is the essence of ecclesiastical discipline.

Calvin therefore consistently defines the church as the body of Christ. (Articles 27–32 of the Conf. Belgicana offer an outline of Calvin's concept of the church.) Milner rightly observes that Calvin's followers described the church in terms of "new construction, membership drives, programmes budgets and the like" because they were indifferent to Calvin's simple and natural concept of the church. Milner states that "in working with Calvin's doctrine of the church I was ... being led straight into the centre of his thought" (Milner, ix).

Formally viewed the church is constituted in the believer's testifying and adherence to the Confessions of Faith. Confession of faith grants entry to communion, and in Geneva it was also regarded as prerequisite for the citizens of the city state. The people had to be "bewuste belijdende volkskerk". The authorities therefore had to support the ecclesiastical officers in this without thereby attaining *ius in sacra* (Plomp, 150). The Reformers had already postulated the indivisible link between confession and communion on 16 January 1837 to the Little Council in Geneva (Plomp, 145f).

"The conception of the church as the restoration of order in the world means that the church cannot be apart from the world, or as a secure corner of redemption in it ... Calvin's political activism, then, may be traced directly to his conception of the church as that movement which stands at the frontier of history, beckoning the world towards its appointed destiny" (Milner, 195). The congregation which is one with Christ in the confession and which comes to the fore in the communion service, stands in the midst of life in a serving capacity. The Gospel (and the church) stands and falls in the dignified celebration of communion and the maintenance of ecclesiastical discipline through excommunication from communion (F.W. Kampschulte, *Johann Calvin. Seine Kirche und sein Staat in Genf.* Reprinted 1972, Geneva, 284-287, Doumergue, 197-199).

The ecclesiastical power of Christ is ministered primarily through the church (the believers)

The church has authority from which nobody may abdicate lightly *(Institutes* IV, i, 10), because the Word and the Sacraments determine the church, and because God Himself is present there in Spirit *(Institutes* IV, i, 9, 11). On the strenght of Matthew 18:15f, Calvin teaches that ecclesiastical discipline and punishment should take place with mutual reprimand from the congregation. The church acts later under the guidance of the elders *(Institutes* IV, i, 22; xii, 1, 2) to attain the goal of the church *(Institutes* IV, xii, 5, 7, 11) (cf. Comm. 1 Corinthians 5, 12 and 14). Although Calvin here distinguishes for practical reasons (and reluctantly) between clerics and believers (Plomp, 250f), his concept of the church (Christ and his body in the visible church) determines that the church (congregation) brings the rule of Christ to fulfilment through the discipline and chastisement of the Word and the Spirit. Independists and Baptists tried to hold on to this unique and unrepeatable place of the congregation (church). Others tried to replace the rule of Christ with the church council or the synod and so lost sight of the unique nature of Calvin's point of departure in connection with his concept of the church.

Each believer is led by the Holy Spirit, and accepts the Word. The believers (the church) must therefore judge whether the preaching of ministers emanates from the Holy spirit, whether it is according to the Scriptures and whether human invention has been added to it. Ministers may not be offended when they are tested against the Scriptures (cf. Commentaries 1 Thessalonians 5:32; 1 Corinthians 14:29, 32; Matthew 18:15f etc.). Calvin taunts the Roman cleric's demand to his flock to be obedient when he himself is not obedient to the Word. Plomp makes the statement that the congregation has the right and the duty to join in dealing with church matters (Postulation XIII). The churchgoing nation must approve and accept every office-bearer of the church but also judge him in faith and in doctrine (Boon, 90, 104). Even if the church officials lead elections, the congregation has to approve the election (Bohatec, 477-488). Without the church, tyranny sneaks in as it did in the Roman Church, and without the guidance of the shepherds the congregation falls into chaos and anarchy as in the case of the Baptists (Bohatec, 493f). As a thorough aristocrat Calvin tempered the "democracy" under the guidance or leadership of the church officials, but he included the congregation in all action, and did not exclude them as so often happens today.

In essence Calvin believed that Christ exercises ecclesiastical power both through the congregation and through the instruments that He uses. Ecclesiastical power is therefore one and the same power of Christ, and not a form of power which springs from the will of the nation or from a mandate of an office or a society. Bohatec talks of the integration motif, the unity of the body, which as ever controls Calvin's philosophy (Bohatec, 421f). Kampschulte (p. 396) says with justification that Calvin uses the congregation as the point of departure and curtails every view which seeks to locate the church in the meeting of pastors. The latter says, unjustily, that Calvin still, also, distinguishes between the spiritual office and the congregation, when both work under the auspices of the same power of Christ.

In each city the church of Christ is present in that one folk or city church. This church may function different in different regions. Calvin, in Strassbourg, served on ethnic grounds, called by a "volunteers' congregation" alongside the "folk church" (Plomp 157).

The four services or offices through which Christ Himself ministers the church

W.D. Jonker *(Om die Regering van Christus in sy Kerk,* 1965, p. 6f) touches upon the core when he indicates that the Reformers, just like Rome, regarded the overseer (the bishop) as the representative of Christ in his church (congregation). Rome accords the bishop governing powers by virtue of the allegation that due to this office the guidance of the Holy Spirit is unfailing (cf. Kampschulte, 404). Calvin on the other hand, links the office to the ministry of the Word. The Lord alone governs his church through His Word. Because He does not live in visible shape among us, He uses the service of men to make this Word known. He teaches us not to look upon the carrier of the Word, but upon the message that he brings (2 Corinthians 4:7).

Service in the church takes place by virtue of the vocation of God and confirmation by the church

Bucer had a significant influence on Calvin's view of ecclesiastical

242

offices (services) (Van Ginkel, 115f; W. van't Spijker, *De ambten bij Martin Bucer,* 1970, Kampen). *The Ordonnances Ecclesiastiques* of 20.11.1941 clearly indicate this. Just like Bucer, Calvin also very definitely had to take cognizance of the wishes of the council of Geneva, (Plomp, 189). The Genevan Church Order 1541, revised 1561, therefore does not give a clear picture of Calvin's ideas.

The servants used by God do not receive their command from a church, a church council or the Council of Geneva. The congregation has to know that God Himself calls servants (elders and deacons), that He determines their tasks, and that He equips them with the Holy Spirit *(Institutes,* IV, iii, 10-16). He confirms in a mediatory sense, through the congregation, the inner calling with an outward one which distinguishes the separate sections of election, approval and the ceremony of installation. The laying on of hands expresses the fact that these servants have to serve under the order of God and in direct relation to Him. Christ and his body, the church, are one. For this reason the servants are simultaneously servants and re-presentatives of Christ and of the church on condition that "das Wort wirkende Christusgeist in ihr herrscht" (Bohatec, 498. Cf. Bohatec 470f; Kampschulte, 398f; Boon, 90, 104f; Doumergue, 336f). In Geneva, however, the Little council appointed the ministers and the elders (Plomp, 189). Calvin calls this a smear on the church *(Institutes,* IV, v, 3).

Calvin therefore takes the called presbyter-overseer, the shepherd or bishop whom he compared with the apostles *(Institutes* IV, iii, 5, 6), and not the church council as the starting point for the church government. He does not know a presbyterial-synodical system of church government (Boon, 221f). Boon says, with justification, that the epigones of Calvin allowed his canon law to become mired in inconsistencies and confusion which led to "voortschrijdende desintegratie" in the reformed churches. Baptists and sects took the congregation under a bishop (overseer) as the point of departure and lived more dynamically than if one had taken the "irreal theory" of the church as a synodal unit as the point of departure (Boon, 193, 204f).

The minister of the Word, shepherd or "bishop".

The ministering of the Gospel by men is the most important nerve end through wich believers are linked with each other in one body, the church. Calvin takes as point of departure in church polity that the church can never be without shepherds (bishops) and teachers

243

(doctores) (Institutes, IV, iii, 1, 2, 4), because the Word they ministered, must keep the church. God calls a shepherd into and to a specific congregation where he represents God in the Word he preaches and the holy sacraments he serves (Kampschulte, 401; Institutes IV, iii, 7). These servants must be "pneumatische persönlichkeiten" so that by means of their service God and Christ Themselves will work in the congregation through the Holy Spirit (Bohatec, 425 ff; Kampschulte, 391). Therefore important actions should then only take place after prayer (Bohatec, 431).

In the first editions of the Institution and in his first church institution in Geneva (1537-1538) Calvin knew practically only the service of the bishop, the minister of the Word, supported by the auxiliary service of deacons (Bohetec, 451). A. van Ginkel (117) indicates that Calvin exercised chastisement in Strassbourg without elders. He himself judged who was to be allowed to partake of communion (cf. *Institutes,* IV, i, 15). His position clearly had a bishop-like character (Plomp, Postulation IV). In Geneva he was the chairman of the meeting of ministers and took decisions. Kampschulte remarks that the co-operation of Calvin and the council made Geneva more of a bishops' city than had previously been the case (412).

Calvin states that the church assumes shape where shepherds and ministers offer the Word and the Sacraments and exercise the chastisement of the Word. The church can and should therefore be identifiable through the mark of the true church *(Institutes,* IV, i, 4-12; iii, 4, 5, 6). Ministers have to be guided by the Holy Spirit (Milner, 142), and should continually be engaged in preaching the Word, in catechism and home visits to the faithful. They should console, strengthen, reprimand, inspire to humility and acknowledgement of guilt, especially in times of despair *(Institutes,* IV, i, 22; xii, 14, 15, 17; Kampschulte, 406f). Each shepherd in Geneva had to take an official oath to that effect (A.D. Pont, 1981 *Die Historiese Agtergronde van ons Kerklike Reg,* p. 25, Genevan Church Order 1561 articles 15-19). Special attention was paid to unity and purity of doctrine (Pont, 1981 p. 25f, GCO 1561. Articles 20-22, by means of proper disciplinary action among the ministers (Ibid, articles 23-34). The noticeable part of it is that only ministers exercised discipline over ministers. The minister (VDM) had to oversee the elders and the deacons *(Institutes,* IV, iii, 12, 13; iv, 1). The minister is the real overseer. Boon says that the VDM "is bij Calvijn een uitgesproken episkopale figuur; hij is bischop van de locale kerk" (Boon, 81).

244

Van Ginkel judges that Boon mistakenly maintains that Calvin separates the overseer of the church from the members (laymen). "Het gaat hem niet om de status, maar om het functionering van een roeping ... het gaat er veel meer om, dat de Heer zelf in dit ambt functioneert in zijn gemeente. Uiteindelijk gaat het veel meer om het werk, dat gedaan moet worden, dan om een preciese afbakening van de ambten" (Van Ginkel, 147).

Boon argues that Calvin's concept that the minister alone must serve the Word and the Sacraments and is the sole carrier of the apostolic, indicates that Calvin did not mean that the elders (presbyters) should rule and that there should be equality between ministers and "governing elders" (Boon, 130f, 136, 201f; Van Ginkel, 145). He calls the minister a "bishop" and he applies the biblical appellations of overseer, elder, shepherd and servant to him *(Institutes* VI, iii, 8). The position of the minister in the church may be compared with that of a constitutional monarch (Boon, 201f). The same pattern was followed in Baptist and Congregationalist churches. Yet it has to be fully understood that Calvin, contrary to bishop-like systems, linked the bishop, (and usually more than one only to the local church (Boon, 204). In contrast to Rome Calvin allocated to each bishop (minister) his own church (congregation). He remains tied to the congregation which called him and for life to the service to which he was called *(Institutes* IV, iii, 7; v, 5, 7, 11; Kampschulte, 401).

Calvin warns against lust for power among ministers who wish to dominate the consciences of believers and who wish to bind them to prescriptions which did not issue from the Word of God directly *(Institutes,* IV, x, 6, 7; xii, 21). Calvin's "bishoply" view of the minister did not involve his "office", person or status, but was tied to the *service* to the Word. For that reason no minister could be overseer over other congregations outside his own parish (Boon, 204).

The teachers or service of doctores

On the strength of the prophetic office in the Old Testament tying in with the central place which the ministerial service to the Word fulfils in the establishment and the maintenance of the church (congregation), Calvin distinguished, next to the shepherds who have to serve the Word and the Sacraments and exercise chastisement, the ministers who have to teach and explicate the Scriptures (doctores) — *(Institutes* IV, iii, 4). They were instructed to deal with the teaching of the young, the training courses at the Gymnasium and the Academy for servants of the Word and for civilian officials. Their services were intimately linked to the School Order of 1559 (Pont, 28, GCO 43-47). These teaching ministers were excluded from church government. They were therefore ministers but not *shepherds.*

It is abundantly clear that according to Calvin's most basic views the Word which was being ministered and not the person in office or authoritive structure should govern, keep and guide the church to be what it should be.

The service of the deacons

Calvin deals often with the deacons of the early church and the deterioration of the deaconry in the Roman Church. The office of caring for the poor is the only other office next to that of governing *(Institutes* IV, iii, 8, 12, 13; iv, 1). He distinguishes two kinds of deacons, viz. one for the care of the poor and one for the care of the sick *(Institutes* IV, iii, 9). The care of the ministry, as in the early church *(Institutes* IV, iv, 5) he does not allocate to the care of the deacons, probably because the Council of Geneva took care of that aspect. Boon judges that Calvin cut through the bond between deacon and sacrament, and therefore broke with the apostolic tradition, limiting the deacon to "social welfare" (136f). The Council of Geneva appointed deacons as its representatives to manage even hospital care and care of the poor at the expense of the Council — under the supervision of the ministers and the elders (cf. Pont, 30f, GCO article 56-67).

Against this background the contemporary embarrassment about the role of the deacon might be explained as arising from past confusion. Today there are conflicting views as to what constitutes service of deacons. In some South African churches he is involved in the church council as an overseer, in the capacity of an "office-bearer", a kind of auxiliary elder, while the elder is merely an assistant to the minister. Perhaps lack of clarity in Calvin's ecclesiastical polity led to this situation.

The governing elders

Calvin proclaimed only two functions or offices, viz. the governing of the church and the care for the poor and the sick. The ministers or bishops should be assisted, with reference to Romans 12:8 by governing elders elected from the ranks of the believers *(Institutes* IV, iii, 8). These governing overseers gather in church council in the same way as the city councillors gather in Council.

Nevertheless Calvin is not clear about the relationship between the minsters or bishops on one hand and the governing elders on the other hand. He refered to the Early Church and acknowledged the presbyter overseer as the primary function and office from whose ranks the ministers were chosen. In the old Church one of them became bishop in the same way as the mayor in the city Council emerged. *(Institutes* IV, iv, 1f). Calvin though named the ministers of Word and sacraments bishops, and restricted the original elders to the task of supervising the congregation *(Institutes* IV, xi, 6). Thereby he denied the original presbyter (elder) or overseer (episcopos) the name of bishop, although he wanted to maintain collegiality of elders and ministers and eliminate the distinction between *clerus* and *laymen*. Idiosyncratic to Calvin, he preferred the aristocratic character of elderhood, even where the elders were elected democratically. Yet the anomaly remained. In Calvin's view the elder was not equal to the minister, and they meant little for the church polity in Geneva in comparison with the ministers (Van Ginkel 149f).

The anomaly with Calvin may be explained. In the first place he adopted the office of elder from Oecolampadius and Bucer between 1538 and 1541, a development which sought to temper the lust for power of the ministers and to involve the congregation according to Matthew 18:17 in an orderly form in the act of excommunication. Secondly they hoped to deminish the inteference of civil authorities in ecclesiastical discipline. In line with the foregoing it can be noted that the Council of Geneva accepted Calvin's Church Order, but reserved the power to appoint only councillors as elders for a year at a time. Those who governed well could be re-elected. Only in 1561 the concession was made that the nomination should be made on an input by the ministers. The mayor of Geneva also presided in the church council. Perhaps the hard reality in Geneva hampered Calvin in clarifying the position of the Scriptural presbyter overseer.

In Geneva the elders therefore served in dual capacity: in civil and in ecclesiastical authority. In theory Calvin viewed them as "Funktionäre Christi" and he did not look upon them as "lay" office-bearers or democratic representatives of the congregation. They represented the congregation in as far they executed the moral task which the law of God lays on the totum ecclesiae corpus (Bohatec, 495f). In reality they represented the Little Council of Geneva at the same time.

247

Because mutual supervision is taught in Scripture and tyranny can be evaded that way, the elders had to govern with the consent and the knowledge of the congregation (Plomp, 88f, 172f, 180). Ganoczy reproaches Calvin, however, that he founds the office of elder on an *ius divinum* and not on the general priesthood of the believers who constituted the church (Van Ginkel, 148).

Calvin basically stated that each elder was called by God *(Institutes IV, iii, 10-15)*. Each elder received an area where he had to supervise the doctrine and conduct of the believers by means of regular home visiting as a means of maintaining ecclessiastical discipline (Plomp, 199). Their oath of office to the Council determined that they would faithfully reprimand transgressors, and report sustained transgressions to the church council (consistory) in an impartial fashion so that the city might be maintained in good order (Pont, 29, GCO, Article 48-55; Van Ginkel, 117f; Plomp, 83, 194). The report to the church council was a secondary phase of his work. The elder in office therefore governed by virtue of his calling and not by virtue of his seat in the church council.

Yet it remains very clear that the elders of Calvin were definitely not the presbyters of the Jews or of the early christian-hellenic communities. They were excluded from the administration and the preaching of the Word and the serving of the Sacraments (Van Ginkel, 83-94, 144-148; cf. Calvin himself, Institutes IV, iv, 2, 3). We can appreciate that Calvin, did, however, give a certain finish to the office of the elder, as he gave relevance again to certain biblical data and laid a basis on which Calvinist churches could further develop the office of elder to suit their own circumstances (Van Ginkel, 142). As such a Calvinist influence is visible in the South African churches with regard to the office of elder.

It was suggested that Calvin had favoured a system of episcopalism in the local church. The *Confession de Foi* (1559) does mention superintendents, but the Chruch Order of 1561 does not. For that reason Van Ginkel tempers Boon's idea that Calvin thinks basically episcopalian. He does warn, however, that one should not absolutize the elder in the philosophy of Calvin and then pretend that Calvin said "wat men zelf denkt" (Van Ginkel, 145f).

Two, three or four offices

It seems at times as if Calvin accepts only *two (Institutes* IV, iii, 8), and

248

then again *three (Institutes* IV, iv, 1) and yet at the same time *four* offices. In some contemporary thinking a distinction is made between office and service and devide the two offices into four services. Calvin speaks of "office" as service *(Institutes* IV, iii, 4). The Scriptures do not separate *office* and *service,* and Calvin also uses the concepts synonymously throughout. In reality the concept *service* qualifies his concept of office, and he does not see office as "dignity" or "position".

Threeway ecclesiatical authority

Christ governs his church. The church is the realm where He governs by means of his Word*(Institutes* IV, ii, 4; vi, 9). The Holy Spirit does not impart the power to men, but through their service the Word that is ministered exercises power and authority *(Institutes,* IV, viii, 2). The ecclesiastical authority, therefore, is spiritual and serving by nature. It should not exceed authoritative pronouncements of the Word of God *(Institutes* IV, viii, 4-9). The believers have been liberated by Christ. They may not be bound in their consciences by one single prescription of man *(Institutes* IV, x, 1).

Through the Word and the Spirit each believer can know the will of God and accordingly serve Him *(Institutes* IV, x, 3, 4, 5). Within this framework of applying the Word of God the church has a threefold authority, i.e. to *teach,* to *govern* and to *legislate (Institutes* IV, viii, 1).

The authority to teach amounts to the authority to determine and to explicate doctrinal content. For this purpose synods are necessary. The authority of the synod, however is exclusively determined by the question of whether its decisions tie in with the Word of God *(Institutes,* IV, viii, 1, 2, 4, 5, 8). Councils do not have any authority, from themselves. Utterances by councils therefore have to be weighed continually on the scale of the Word *(Institutes* IV, ix, 9). Those who teach must only be "Mund Gottes" (Bohatec, 516). The Confession of Faith which constitutes the church is therefore only a reflection of what God teaches in the Word.

The authority to legislate is equally limited on the basis of 1 Corinthians 14:40. The rules laid down by God in his Word have to be observed very strictly. Other rules prescribed by ecclesiastical bodies are of "middle stature" and only necessary when they promote the well-being, religion, unity, order and peace within the church *(Institutes* IV, x, 27, 28, 30; Bohatec, 516, 531). Calvin's *Formalprinzip* lends binding authority to the ecclesiastical determinants when these are derived from the Scriptures. Rieker unjustly calls this a legalistic trait in Calvin to retain, as Zwingli said, only that which God expressly commanded (Bohatec, 383f). Calvin called ecclesiastical rules which bind consciences outside the confines of the Scriptures, a tyrannical force in conflict with the foundational commandment of love (Baur, 64; Bohatec, 386f). Order should not be sought in all sorts of petty concerns, such as, for example, the question as to whether a woman might enter the church with an uncovered head (Institutes IV, x, 29, 30, 31). Ecclesiastical stipulations should remain limited, be useful and should clearly be aimed at the promotion of the church *(Institutes,* IV, x, 32).

The authority to speak of justice emanates from the calling to employ authority in the way that Christ Himself would do it. This is named key authority because it accomplishes the opening up or closing down the intrance to the kingdom of God. (Boon, 52; Calvin, Com. Matthew, 16:19; 18:18). True ecclesiastical government amounts to "disciplines of morals" (Milner, 175). Administration of justice in the church is of a totally different nature to administration of justice in civilian life *(Institutes,* IV, xi, 1). Excommunication is a duty because the person concerned sets himself outside the pale on account of his unworthy conduct or false doctrine.

The muscle or the tendons binding together the church are already present in the mutual reprimand among members of the congregation. When somebody rejects the reprimand of the elder who comes on a home visit, he has to be reported to the consistory (church council) who can then excommunicate him if he does not convert to truth *(Institutes* IV, xii, 1, 2). This means, however, has to be used carefully, mercifully and with distinction between lighter and heavier sins *(Institutes* IV, xii, 3, 4, 6) in order to maintain the honour of God, good morals in the congregation and to bring the sinner to insight and repentance. Disturbed order should be restored *(Institutes,* IV, xii, 5). "Kerkelijke *rechtsplegen* ... ze ist rechtsplegen ... geestelijke *rechtsplegen* ... er wordt niet geoordeelt na menselijke normen, maar uitsluitend 'ex Lege Dei'; de zonden worden bestraft 'ex verbo Domini'" (Plomp, 72). To avoid the danger of hierarchie, abuse of power and tyranny in case one or more bishops should apply excommunication, Calvin then instituted the *consistory* or the church council to handle the key power.

Witherow typified presbyterial church government from the

meaning of the word "presbytary" (The Apostolic Church, 1967, p. 66), meaning then government by the "elders ... in their assembled capacity". The prevailing tendency today is to state that the church council is the basis and determining feature of Calvin's view of church government. This conception denies Calvin his Scriptural understanding of vocation and office as well as his link with the early church. Basic to Calvin's thought was the concept that an individual exercises authority within the confines of the service he has been called to. In that capacity the elder has been called to render a ruling service. It is only consequently and on a secondary level, after the individual efforts had been in vain, that, elders meet in consistory for the radical action of chastisement which might culminate in excommunication.

The church council (consistory)

Calvin justifies the necessity of an ecclesiastical Senate, consistory or church council from the example set by the Council for the civil government of the city. By means of the independent church council the bishops and the elders can lead the church in ecclesiastical judicature *(Institutes* IV, xi, 3, 5, 6; xii, 7, 8, 9, 11). The actions of the church council are actions of the congregation, i.e. church (Plomp, 85). Consequently the co-operation and the consent of the congregation always had to be secured (Bohatec, 422-424).

Calvin, in 1541, imposed to the Council the matter of a church council as a condition for his return to Geneva because he wanted, to ensure independent and unhindered spiritual discipline within the confines of the church. From a letter Calvin wrote to Myconius in 1542 it would appear that the consistory was for Calvin "der Stolz der Genfer Kirche" in the service of the kingship of Christ (Kampschulte, 442). The five ministers with twelve elders, nominated by the Council of Geneva, gathered on a weekly basis usually under the chairmanship of the mayor in order to oversee the spiritual order of Geneva. With the authority of the Council they could subpoena somebody to appear before them. If somebody refused, he could be handed over to the Council (Pont 42f, GCO, Art. 151-153). The principles of this procedure for disciplinary action is included in the Church Order of 1619 in the Netherlands.

The Council of Two hundred decided on 5 February 1560 that the mayor, by virtue of the essential distinction between ecclesiastical and civilian power, would not from then on bring his mace as symbol of authority to the meetings of the consistory in order to lead the church council any more (Ibid., Article 168).

The name "consistory" was derived from the erstwhile bishoply tribunal where ecclesiastical and civilian aspects with regard to marital matters were discussed (Plomp, 182f). Bohatec (546) rejects Sohm's premise that Calvin introduced secular judicature.

Meeting of ministers

Calvin accepts that one church (congregation) may be served by more than one minister. The ministers were compelled to control one an other on a weekly basis. The ministers of the surrounding towns had to attend one of these meetings at least once a month (Pont 25, GCO Articles 20, 21). In order to maintain good order and unity as regards doctrine, preaching, catechism, home visit and the pastorate, two representatives of the Council and of the meeting of ministers, respectively, would visit each church within the Genevan church annually and exercise supervision over the service of the ministers. This visitation was not at all intended in a judiciary sense, but the results were imparted to the meeting of ministers with a view to mutual reprimand (Ibid., Art. 20-38).

The fact that the ministers also met apart from the church council, without the elders having their own meeting, underlines on the one hand the unique position held by the ministers and on the other hand that the ministers did not receive their orders from an ecclesiastical body or a constitution. Every minister was and remained above all a called servant of Christ attached to the congregation.

Definitely different from what Calvin envisaged, but true to the *corpus christianum,* the Council of Geneva had the final authority over the ministers (Ibid., art. 27).

Inter- or synodical church relations

Every local church within a territorial and political unity like Geneva was an independent, complete church, even with its own "constitution" and relationship with the political institutions concerned. In Strassbourg though a separate French congregation came into being and expressed its own identity on ethnic grounds. The concept of a "denomination" or a synodal church unity did not exist in those days.

Each church expressed the body of Christ independently until a crisis with reference to doctrine made a gathering of these churches necessary. Where the ministers of various churches gathered together, they could have better council. Such a gathering can be called synod, although it must be clear that thereby no synodal structure came into being. These synods were ad hoc meetings between supervisors of different churches.

Meetings of the supervisors of Geneva, Basle and other churches were customary *(Institutes* IV, ix, 13). The authority of these "synods", (councils) however, was fallible and had to be judged against the touchstone of the Word *(Institutes* IV, ix, 8, 9: Milner, 149). No synod could claim, of being led infallibly by the Holy Spirit and that it was an image of the church, thereby being empowered to bind consciences *(Institutes,* IV, viii, 10, 13; ix, 1, 2, 3). Calvin rejected the Roman doctrine that the "synod" was an image of the church and that the bishops guaranteed the truth *(Institutes* IV, ix, 3). The synod had no indwelling authority and the meeting of representatives from different local churches constituted no denomination or super "church". We must conclude that meetings of ministers of churches (synods) took place with a view to promote the spiritual unity in faith among the churches and was by no means an organisational structure prescribing denominational conduct.

Some reconnaissance contours regarding influence on South African churches

Calvin's concepts definitely did play a direct and in some cases even a determining role on the Convent of Wezel (1568) and the Dutch ecclesiastic-judiciary development from 1571 to 1619 which crystallized in the Dordt Church Order. This Church Order had no official standing under the curious corpus christianum of the VOC at the Cape. The principles of Calvin played nevertheless a role in the congregations, especially with regard to chastisement.

Although English churches are less well-known to me, I guess this would apply also in the case of the Baptists and the Congregationalists. The Presbiterians experienced perhaps already from Knox a more strongly institutionalized constitutional concept so that the church structure is built on the "presbytary". This latter trend gained dominant influence in South Africa and can even be proofed from the abbreviated institutional formulary for elders in the Gereformeerde Kerk.

253

Calvin's point of departure in the Ordinance of God

The principle to start from the ordinance of God played a decisive role in the various Afrikaans and English church associations until far into the twentieth century, so that conceptions on doctrine, life and viewpoint were tested against the Word of God consciously and directly. Actions of the Dutch Reformed Church and the Anglican Church in the previous century against heretic doctrines were fought out in the Supreme Court. Elsewhere I have indicated the reverence for God and the characteristic of trying in all things to live "naar Gods Woord" among a certain Afrikaner community, wider than the later Reformed (Gereformeerde) Church (cf. *Die Doppers in Suid-Afrika, 1760-1899*, chapters 2 and 3).

Christ the Head of the church by virtue of the Holy Spirit

This concept of Calvin is officially taught and confessed in the Afrikaans churches (cf. the Heidelberg Catechism, Sundays 21, 48; Dutch Confession of Faith, 31, 32). In the simpler, patriarchal and rural communities, actual concern with the guidance of Christ as head of the church previously shaped concepts regarding the church and can be illustrated from the way they understood their responsibility towards liturgy, content of the Word in preaching, upholding Confessions of faith, receipt of the sacraments, etc. Influences during the 19th century, more ministers and more congregations, synodal links and centralized synodal organizations, different denominations and educational development changed this very basic vision of the church. It became custommary to regard church as a mere religious society, a specific institutional unity under synodal control. The concept of the autonomous local church of believers is lost. This might be one reason why sects attack the "denominational" churches. The emphasis in the South African ecclesiastical setup on decisions by church councils and synods, on theology and ministers, might create the impression that man and his relationship to Christ, the justification of actions to Christ and the Holy Spirit have retreated before the institutionalized denominational setup. There is probably an unresolved tension in the South African, churches between the concept that the church is an association determined by "its" leaders and synods and the concept that the church is the one nation of God, the one body of Christ, presented in the many local churches as communities of the faithful. In our time organisation rather than unity in true faith, determines the concept "church".

The distinction between political and ecclesiastical government

Until 1804 the various separate churches (congregations) in South

Africa had local freedom and spiritual independence under the direct care of the VOC and indirect rule of the Klassis Amsterdam. Although they could practise local discipline in Calvin's way, they were institutionally dependent on the idiosyncratic Dutch colonial dispensation. De Mist introduced the revolutionary and rationalistic concept of the church in 1804. After 1806 came the Anglicans with their concept that church and state were intimately connected (caesaropapism). With the aid of the Church Order of De Mist (1804) the political authorities played a dominant role in the Cape Church. The church was even used as an instrument towards anglicising and towards a neutral state educational system. Ministers from the Presbyterian Church of Scotland reacted within the ranks of the Cape Dutch Reformed Church and succeeded in making the church reasonably independent of the governor in Ordinance 7 of 1843. Since 1853 the Dutch Reformed (Hervormde) Church in the ZAR strove to be the church of the state. This boils down to the conclusion that Calvin's influence deminished in the previous century.

The first Reformed (Gereformeerde) churches (congregations) in the Transvaal, the Free State and the Cape Colony introduced themselves in 1859 and 1860 to the various authorities as "Free" churches. They strove, with the English Independists, for the "voluntary principle" so that the dispensation on prvileged churches of the state came to an end. Here Liberalism and the influence of Calvin probably worked in the same direction. South African churches, however, often expected of the "Christian" state in Calvin's way to sanctify society through legislation.

The church as local pneumatic organism

Calvin's unique concept of the church might probably by accident been revealed in the separate churches of the Cape Colony under the reign of the VOC. The cases of chastisement according to the acts of the church council of Geneva (Plomp, 218-232) typify the typical Afrikaans and English puritanical concepts about morals and religious responsibility within the congregation. The experience of the local church as a unified organism in doctrine and in life also led to clashes with church managements and many cases where congregations seceded from specific denominations (viz. e.a. P.B. v. d. Watt: *Gemeentes, nogmaals gemeentes).* It is remarkable that the seceding congregation never doubted that it was a church of Christ, even though it had seceded. Yet church crises were not usually judged with Calvin's seriousness and question as to whether there was unity

255

of doctrine and obedience to the Word of God. Usually a specific ecclesiastical structure was taken as the norm.

The residue of Roman institutionalism, the Dutch formal-juridical slant and especially the rise of eitheenth-century rasionalist ideas about voluntary human associations, largely crowded out Calvin's dynamic view of the church in South Africa. Abraham Kuyper reveals a distinction in his philosophy between the *church as institution* and the *church as organism*. Berkhof joins him in this (Christelijk Geloof, 1973, 413). The church is nowadays seen almost exclusively as *institute,* represented in its professional clerus and meetings. Kuyper's *church as organism* disappears into the sand, or has to be institutionalized in all sorts of Christian institutes (associations, parties, etc.). The loss of the Scriptural (Calvin's *Formalprinzip)* pneumatic organism in exchange for the institutionalized church association (or churches as denomination, church association) probably brings about the crisis besetting so many churches today. It would seem as if the Baptists and the Congregationalists, although they retain the monarchial bishop locally, have held on to something of Calvin's dynamic and organic concept of the church according to the idea of the movement to and from the Word. With his concept that chastisement has the especial virtue of bringing the congregation together around the communion table in a purified sense, Calvin could therefore successfully counter the reproach of the Anabaptists levelled about neglect of the faith among members of the congregation (cf. W. Balke: *Calvijn en de Doperse Radikalen,* 1973). Has this ability not been lost today?

A report to the GES at Nimes in 1980 declares that clericalism and institutionalizing of the church "rob[s] believers of their personal responsibility and treats them as minors who have to listen to the voice of Mother Church ... We admit, however, that as far as the biblical data are concerned, the distinction (institute and organism, BS) seems hardly applicable, for the simple reason that the New Testament writings hardly ever single out the church in its institutional form" (RES, 1980. The Church and its Social Calling, 26).

The influence of Calvin was probably lost with regard to the essential and most fundamental aspect of the concept of church in the post-Calvinist churches worldwide. The congregation as such plays almost no role any more in the present ecclesiastical setup. All attention is directed at the abstract "church unity" of a centralized community with central institutional programmes. The "unity" of the

256

church is seen mostly only in the organizational and institutional sense. The "church" nowadays replaces the Scriptures as Calvin's "Formalprinzip". The decisive question nowadays is not what the Scriptures say, but what the church says. Communion is therefore today rather for the (NB) "members" of the relevant institutional unity than for the faithful who obey the doctrines of God in life and in conviction. Do congregations at all still exercise chastisement mutually? Today the concern seems to be primarily for the structure and not for the quality of the church as the body of Christ.

The four services or offices

Formally the four services of Calvin are recognised in many South African churches. In the liturgical inauguration formulary the influence of Calvin is clearly visible. As in the case of Calvin the minister usually fills the position of the "bishop". Where usually only one minister serve in one congregation, the theory of prebyterial church government amounts in practice to that of a constitutional monarchy within each congregation. The claim that the "offices" are equal nowadays is more a matter of theory than of politics, and questions regarding the aptness of the services of the elders and the deacons respectively, come today often to the fore.

The distictive powers (authority) in the churches

Calvin's distinction between the authority to teach, the authority to govern and the authority to legislate has largely fallen into disuse. In the first place the authority to teach is practically never implemented and the Confessions of the Reformation are seen as adequate. The legislative as well as the judicative powers today are mostly interpreted as secular judiciary principles. The church is viewed as a human social organism and it's powers are deduced from this structure. The structure of the church is no longer a servant of authority, but in itself becomes the authority that legislates and governs. Calvin's distinction between essential and mediocre matters is not sustained anymore.

The will of the Synod replaces the Will of God. The ecclesiastical authority of a synod has become virtually unlimited. It may even take decisions on mediocre matters, prescriptive decisions, moreover, which bind "members".

257

Calvin's influence does not extend any further than the formal being-there of the church council. In a practice where the minister(s) and the elders come together for sensura morum or chastisement before communion, this might still be a reminder of Calvin. In contrast to what the case used to be in the days of Calvin, the synod is today often seen as the image of the church. The Church council and/or the Synod is today quite often accepted, sui generis, as the legislative or the judicative authority. Church Councils have to adapt to Synods for the sake of "unity" and "uniformity" so that an abstract church denomination may come into being. In theory one might take the local church, another the synod and a third both of these in conjunction as the point of departure in determining their concept of canon law.

Epilogue

Formally and traditionally it is easy to presuppose the influence of Calvin on Canon Law in South Africa. The central place that preaching fills in the essential nature of the church is clearly derivative of Calvin. When the canonical-juridical situation is critically and essentially evaluated, however, Calvin's influence is probably less than the influence of Roman Canonical Law, English or Dutch Institutionalism, Roman-Dutch legal principles, Rationalist philosophy, Lutheranism and especially the associative law of the eighteenth century where J.J. Rousseau developed the principles of human autonomy, natural law and social contract. The fact that the *corpus christianum* of the sixteenth to the twentieth centuries has played such a simultaneously interfering and supporting role as regards ecclesiastical institutions may explain why no pure canonical law in the tradition of Calvin could be described in this paper for South Africa.

258

21. THE DOCTRINE OF CALVIN AS TRANSMITTED IN THE SOUTH AFRICAN CONTEXT BY AMONG OTHERS THE *OUDE SCHRIJVERS* — AN INTRODUCTORY SURVEY

DR. J.W. HOFMEYR*

Introduction

The following short survey is very limited in scope. Firstly, it offers a few tentative, orientational and exploratory remarks. Secondly, it is hoped that these few ideas about the possible percolation of Calvin's views via the "oude schrijvers" might serve as a stimulus for those who are interested in exploiting the unworked goldmine of material concerning influences from Europe which have affected the course of South African church history.

That there is a great need for a study of the links between theological trends in the countries of origin, and ecclesiastical and theological developments here, cannot be doubted. Brown, for example, indicates the need for an account of the Dutch Reformed Church and its Reformed history; and he says that the church historian will have to describe the concept of Scripture which members of the Cape church of the eighteenth century held. In so doing he can surely not ignore the scanty literature to which (apart from the Bible) they had access. If the writings of Wilhelmus á Brakel, Bernardus Smytegelt, Coenrad Mel, Aegidius Francken, and the hymns of Willem Sluiter accompanied the preaching of the Word, then we can also expect a "fear of the Lord"[1] Only when we have determined what the beliefs of these members were, can we establish whether particular trends and attitudes were perhaps deviations from the Reformed tradition.

To follow up specific lines and currents from Europe to South Africa

*His address is: University of South Africa, P.O. Box 392, Pretoria, RSA, 0001.

[1] cf. Brown, E. 1974. Die behoefte aan verantwoording van die Kerk en sy Gereformeerde Geskiedenis in ons land, in *NGTT,* Deel XV, No. 1, Januarie. p. 16.

would be a difficult undertaking. A more acceptable approach would seem to be to analyse and then to search for the roots of certain patterns as they developed locally. In essence, then, the question is to discover the theology our forefathers took for granted, by studying the preaching, the pattern of services and the available theological and spiritual literature. This is not, however, an easy undertaking, and it is also not easy to settle the matter.

Defining the concepts

It is desirable here to give a brief definition of some of the terms that will be used. By "oude schrijvers" is meant, broadly, those who, as regards the written and spoken word, followed in the tradition of the Second Reformation. The Second Reformation as an ecclesiastical and theological trend is a concept which is still relatively unknown in our context. One of the greatest experts on the Second Reformation describes it as the radically reformed reformation: "die 'preciesheid' wenst in plaats van vrome (onvrome) algemeenheden, een piëtisme dus, een bewuste wijden van het hele leven aan God"[2]. Although this movement also had other spiritual fathers, it can be contended that the central thrust of the Second Reformation (which involves a personal spiritual piety, an articulated ecclesiology and a theocratic outlook on society) is broadly derived from Calvin. It should therefore be regarded not as a correction but as a development of the Reformation. The classical phase of the Second Reformation shows definite links with Calvin, while the distance between Calvin and the stricter pietism of the later phase of the Second Reformation is much greater. The Second Reformation was, in its nature and essence, not merely a theological, but also and especially an ecclesiastical movement. On the ecclesiastical level the Second Reformation came to grips with the area of tension between involvement in and alienation from the world. In addition, the "praktijk der godzaligheid" (the practice of salvation), is also very important.

The "oude schrijvers" and their writings

We will therefore look at some of the old authors, paying special attention to those writings that were in general circulation at the time.

---

[2] cf. Van der Linde, S. 1957. *Het Gereformeerde Protestantisme,* Nijkerk. p. 9.

Authors such as Bernardus Smytegelt (1665-1739) with his *Gekrookte Riet, Des Christens eenige Troost, Keurstoffen* and *Des Christens Heil en Sieraad* and Wilhelmus à Brakel (1635-1711) with his *Redelijke Godsdienst* were especially well-known in the South African context. Others who also merit mention are Coenraad Mel (1666-1733) *(De Heraut der Eeuwigheid)*, A Hellenbroek (1658-1731) *(Bijbelsche Keurstoffen)* and D.F.W. Krummacher *(Leerredenen)*.

This literature was used not merely as devotional reading matter but was also sometimes presented as sermons. It was through this type of literature that people in the eighteenth and nineteenth centuries developed an understanding of the doctrines of the Reformation. Second only to their Bibles this literature was very precious to our ancestors and also to the Voortrekkers. As these works were practically the only trusted reading matter for the rural pioneer population, their authors were called "auteurs" to distinguish them from other writers.

Apart from the fact that many of these books were privately owned, one finds in the Dessinian collection, which is housed in the South African Library in Cape Town, clear indications that many of them were already in the Cape in the eighteenth century. Joachim Nicolaus von Dessin came to the Cape from Germany in 1727, and remained there until his death in 1761. In the course of his sojourn he built up a collection of almost 4500 volumes. Among these are works by Schortinghuys, Smytegelt, Comrie and W. Teellinck. Another valuable source for determining the number and the distribution of the "oude schrijvers" would be the order lists of books for private and public institutions.

It is sometimes said that these authors were pietistic through and through, and that the devoutness which runs throughout our history like a golden thread, can be ascribed to these elements. However, a clear distinction should be drawn between a positive form of piety and the negative elements of pietism. To this must be added that all devout writers cannot be described without qualification as pietistic. W. à Brakel, for example, strongly warned against certain elements of pietism[3]. The spirit breathed by the works of the "oude schrijvers"

---

[3] cf. Hanekom, T.N. 1952. (red.). *Ons Nederduitse Gereformeerde Kerk*, Kaapstad. p. 210.

also spoke of the fall of man in Adam, his inability to aspire to the good, his salvation through the predestinating grace of God and the absolute sovereignty of God.

The writings of the "oude schrijvers" in particular, exerted a strong influence on religious developments in the eighteenth and nineteenth centuries. Van der Watt sums up their most important views as follows: they revolted against the unspiritual state of the nation, ministers and congregations. They plead also for a personal commitment to Christ. The experienced and tested religion is to them of central importance. Although nothing is done to undermine the church, the office, the sacrament and the Covenant, they regard rebirth as the priority. They also assume a reasonably strong Puritan point of view. They plead for the observance of the Sabbath and the carrying out of the demands of the Lord. The church must be pure and should be cleansed of all that is unholy. Finally, they had a high regard for the Scriptures and for the Heidelberg Catechism[4].

Conclusion

In conclusion, if one looks at the quality of the Calvinism adhered to for example, by the pioneer farmer, there can be little doubt that the spirit of traditional Calvinism did, probably by way of the "oude schrijvers", find a response in the people of the eighteenth and the nineteenth centuries. B. Spoelstra sums it up as follows: In the first place this Calvinism recognised the absolute sovereignty of God. The border farmer was daily aware of his dependence on God in the course of nature, and in the protection and cultivation of his farm. In relation to his neighbour he lived as an independent king, prophet and priest. In relation to God he was deeply dependent, carrying a heavy burden of sin and deeply aware of God's electing grace[5].

The "oude schrijvers" took the truths from Scripture and applied them in daily life, and also gave proof that emphasis was put on life as well as on doctrine. This is an emphasis which in some cases was one-sided, but which nevertheless led to religion becoming a shaping force in daily life.

[4] cf. Van der Watt, B.P. 1976. *Die Nederduitse Gereformeerde Kerk,* vol. 1 1952-1824, Pretoria. p. 83.

[5] cf. Spoelstra, B. 1963. *Die 'Doppers' in Suid-Afrika 1769-1899,* Kaapstad. p. 25.

Alongside the appreciation one has for the Second Reformation and the "oude schrijvers", we should, however, always remain conscious of the extent to which subjective experience is stressed by these authors at the cost of objective truth and the truth of the Holy Spirit. Even in preaching, for example, the Second Reformation with its stress on man and the various personality types among the listeners no longer appealed to God's promises for the facts of salvation and revelation. It was more a case of preaching based on personality traits (division and differentiation of the various listeners) than preaching, which would take God's covenant seriously[6].

What has been discussed in the foregoing is at best a brief reconnaissance of the field. There is still a great need for a contemporary reassessment especially of the Afrikaans churches and their reformed history. In this process the researcher cannot ignore the literature of the "oude schrijvers". On the contrary, an intensive study of the "auteurs" with regard to their influence in the South African context seems to me to be an urgent necessity. The essential question must still be how these authors understood and transmitted Calvin.

W.A. de Klerk once wrote a true word, which to my mind is very relevant to this discussion: "To say that the key to the Afrikaners is Calvinism is not enough. As is the case with all apostles there are as many Calvins as there have been restatements or 'revisions' of the original philosophy"[7].

---

[6] cf. Brienen, T. 1974. *De Prediking van de Nadere Reformatie,* Amsterdam.

[7] cf. De Klerk, W.A. 1975. *The Puritans in Africa : A history of Afrikanerdom.* Manchester, p. 125.

22. CALVIN AND PURITANISM IN ENGLAND AND SCOTLAND — SOME BASIC CONCEPTS IN THE DEVELOPMENT OF "FEDERAL THEOLOGY"

REV. PROF. J.B. TORRANCE*

Covenant or contract?

One of the most significant words of the Bible is the word "covenant". We read about God making a covenant with Abraham, renewing that covenant at Sinai, about David making a covenant with Jonathan, and again with the elders at Hebron when he became king. Jeremiah speaks of a day when God will make a new covenant with the house of Israel, and in the New Testament, Jesus is presented to us as the Mediator of the New Covenant.

"This cup is the new covenant in my blood".

On the one hand God binds Himself to men like Abraham and David with solemn promises. On the other hand He binds Israel to himself under solemn obligations — proleptic of the day when He will bind Himself to mankind and mankind to Himself in Jesus Christ in covenant love. Again we read about men like Joshua, Hezekiah, Josiah binding themselves and the nation in loyalty to God in covenant.

Likewise in Scottish history[1], in the upheavals of the sixteenth, seventeenth and eighteenth centuries, with the break up of feudalism and the emergence of the late post renaissance doctrine of the divine rights of kings and the resultant struggles for liberty, we read about men making "bands", "pacts", "covenants", "contracts", "political

* His address is: Don House, 46 Don Street, Old Aberdeen, 4B2 1UU Scotland.

[1] cf. "Covenant or Contract? A Study of the Theological Background of Worship in Seventeenth-Century Scotland", *Scottish Journal of Theology* Vol. 23, No. 1 (Feb. 1970). Also "The Contribution of McLeod Campbell to Scottish Theology". *SJT* Vol. 26, No. 3 (Aug. 1973).

leagues" to defend their freedom, to preserve the rights of a people vis-a-vis their sovereign and the rights of a sovereign vis-a-vis his subjects. When Charles I sought to change the constitution of the Scottish Church by the Canons of 1636, and sought to impose uniformity of worship by the introduction of Laud's Liturgy in 1637, the response was the National Covenant signed in the Kirk of the Greyfriars in Edinburgh in 1638. Five years later came the Solemn League and Covenant in 1643, with its counter attempt to impose uniformity of presbyterian government and worship in Scotland, England and Ireland. The same year marked the opening of the Westminster Assembly, as a parliamentary commission, to achieve these ends. It is significant for example that the *Westminster Directory for the Public Worship of God* was officially described as "a part of the covenanted uniformity in religion betwixt the Churches of Christ in the kingdoms of Scotland, England and Ireland". The key word throughout was *foedus* – covenant (the word from which our word "federal" comes) — a word which was rich in theological significance as well as a revolutionary symbol in a nation struggling for freedom[2]. It is precisely this period, the late sixteenth and seventeenth centuries, which marks the rise of the so-called "federal theology", or covenant theology, first expounded in England by Dudley Fenner in 1583 and William Perkins in 1590 and in Scotland in 1596 by Robert Rollock, the first Principal of Edinburgh University — the federal Calvinism which was to become the criterion of orthodoxy for the next 250 years. The Westminster Confession of Faith, with the Larger and Shorter Catechisms, was the first Reformed confession to enshrine the scheme of federal theology, though in a mild way.

The background of much of the theological controversy of the day was the emerging socio-political philosophy of "social contract", "contract of government", with its doctrine of the "rights of man" based on "natural law", illumined by the light of reason and given divine sanction by revelation. As Prof. Perry Miller and other American historians have shown, this was the political philosophy of the many

---

[2] During that whole period, from the General Assembly of 1596 right into the eighteenth century, we read about churches and congregations, under the leadership of men like John Davidson of Prestonpans, Richard Cameron, Thomas Boston, Ralph and Ebenezer Erskine, Adam Gibb and others making their covenants with God. Apart from personal covenants we read about some 31 public bands and covenants in Scotland in the years between 1556 and 1683. Innumerable books, politcal pamphlets and sermons were to appear on the subject, by men like David Dickson, James Durham, Samuel Rutherford, Patrick and George Gillespie, Alexander Shields.

puritans who left England to get away from the "tyranny" of British kings and feudal overlords for the "free world" where they would be free to worship God, as they pleased, with whom they pleased, with liberty of conscience, and where no one would "tell them". If on the one hand this word was to prove so influential in the rise of modern democracy (and the so-called "American way of life"), on the other hand it was to have a profound influence on the preaching of the Gospel in England and Scotland.[3]

What then do we mean by the word "covenant" — *foedus?*[4] Clearly there are different meanings of this word, not only in law and politics but also in the Bible, and a flood of light has been thrown on this by recent studies[5].

Let me suggest *one* fundamental meaning. Theologically speaking, *a covenant is a promise binding two people or two parties to love one another unconditionally.* Think, for example, of the marriage service. During the Reformation, the word "covenant" was used in the English Service Book of 1549 and has been retained in our Scottish marriage service. The bride and bridegroom "promise and covenant" to love one another "for better, for worse, for richer, for poorer, in sickness and in health, to love and to cherish, till death you do part". What does all that mean? In a word they promise to love one another

---

[3] Just as people today understand the language of trade unions wage settlements, civil rights, picketing and protest marches, so the people in seventeenth century Scotland understood the language of bands, pacts, covenants, contracts, natural law, the rights of man and the rights of the people. To make a protest in the defence of liberty, people banded together, drew up a covenant, stated the conditions of their allegiance, and fixed their signatures. There was ancient precedent for this in Scotland. Here was a conceptual framework within which Reformed theology was to be recast as "federal Calvinism", and here preachers found a language of communication, a kind of "theology of politics" which could be readily grasped by the man in the street in a land struggling for freedom.

[4] See *Appendix B*, Diagram 1.

[5] For example by scholars like Mendenhall, Hillers, McCarthy and others on Ancient Hittite suzerainty treaties, whose pattern bears a remarkable similarity to the covenants of old Israel.

unconditionally[6]. There is no such thing as conditional love in God or in man, and that fact is enshrined in the theological concept of "a covenant of love". It is precisely this which makes a covenant so different from a *contract*. What is a contract? *A contract, in common parlance, is a legal relationship in which two people or two parties bind themselves together on mutual conditions* to effect some future result. The business world and the political world are full of such contracts. They take the form, "If you do this, then I will do that". "If you build me a house according to such and such specifications, then I shall pay you so much money". Society at large, and the political world in which we live, are built upon a network of such contractual arrangements, whether tacit or explicit. It is significant that in Scots law, which is based on Roman law, a covenant and a contract mean the same thing[7]. The Latin word *foedus* perhaps obscured the difference, for it means both a covenant and a contract. But theologically, it seems to me, they must be carefully distinguished. In the Bible there were many kinds of covenant. For example, there were (a) *bilateral* covenants, as in the classical example of David and Jonathan, covenants between equals. Marriage is a bilateral covenant. Aristotle in the Nicomachean Ethics speaks about *politikai philiai,* political friendships, and like Plato before him, uses the word *suntheke* or *homologia,* a bilateral contract or agreement. On the other hand, in the Bible, there wer (b) *unilateral* covenants, as when in old Israel, at the time of his coronation, a king made a covenant *for* his people, rather in the manner of the suzerainty covenants of the

[6] To use a different illustration, let us suppose here are two people who have a quarrel, and things become so bad that they decide to call in the minister to help them effect a reconciliation. He listens to one side of the unhappy story and then to the other, and no doubt there are faults on both sides. But there comes the point when he says, "Listen, you must forgive and forget!" But so often, back comes the reply, "Well, I'll forgive him IF ..." The moment the minister hears that big word "IF" he knows the person is not going to forgive. Forgiveness is love in action, and *there is no such thing as conditional love.* Only when they are prepared to forgive one another unconditionally, and where there is mutual acceptance of forgiveness, can there be true reconciliation. If someone says, "I'll love you IF ...", that person doesn't know the meaning of love.

[7] Lawyers distinguish different kinds of contract — they are not always bi-laterial. In Scotland you can give your money to the church or a charitable organisation by a "deed of covenant", a contractual arrangement with the fiscal authorities that if you give so much money there will be so much remission of income tax. Traditionally we have talked about the marriage contract. Samuel Rutherford in his Catechism could speak about the covenant of grace as "a contract of marriage" between Christ and the believer, and then go on to speak of the conditions of the contract.

Hittite kings[8].

The important thing is that in the Bible, God's dealings with men in Creation and Redemption — in grace — are those of a covenant and not of a contract, and the word always used is *diatheke* and never *suntheke* in Greek — *berith* in Hebrew. This was the heart of the Pauline theology of grace, expounded in *Romans* and *Galatians,* and this was the central affirmation of the Reformation. *The God of the Bible is a Covenant-God and not a contract-god.* God's covenant dealings with men have their source in the divine initiative, in the loving heart of God, and the form of the covenant is the indicative statement, the promise, "I will be your God and you shall be my people". The God and Father of our Lord Jesus Christ is the God who has made a unilateral covenant *for us* in Christ, binding Himself to man and man to Himself in Christ, and who summons us to respond in faith and love to what He has done so freely for us in Christ[9]. Two things are therefore held together in a biblical understanding of grace, the covenant of love made for man in Christ[10]. (a) On the one hand, it is *unconditioned* by any considerations of worth or merit or prior claim. God's grace is "free grace". (b) On the other hand, it is *unconditional* in the costly claims it makes upon us. God's grace is "costly grace". The one mistake is so to stress free grace that we turn it into "cheap grace" by taking grace for granted — the danger of "antinomianism"[11].

[8] The form of such covenants was "This is the kind of king I am going to be and this is the kind of people you are going to be", as when Solomon's son Rehoboam came to the throne. But the fact that it was a unilateral covenant did not eliminate the need for response on the part of the people. Indeed the people either said "Amen" to it, "God save the king"; or "to your tents O Israel, we shall not have this man to reign over us!" In that instance, Rehoboam's high handed measures split the kingdom in two. The ten northern tribes went off and made Jeroboam the son of Nebat king.

[9] This is fundamental for our understanding of Calvin's repeated emphasis that "Christ has in His flesh completed all parts of our salvation", and that our salvation is not only *per Christum* but *in Christo* (cp. *Institutio* 2.9.2ff; 2.16.19 etc.). Hence for Calvin, the work of the Holy Spirit in evoking faith is to make us cognitively aware *(cognitio)* of *what we already are in Christ*. (Comm. on *John* 10,8ff). This is the basis of his teaching about union with Christ, faith, evangelical repentance, etc., in his critique of Roman theology, and of his insight that assurance is of the essence of true faith (cp. below).

[10] See *Appendix* B Diagram 2.

[11] So characterised by James Hogg, the Ettrick Shepherd in his *The Confessions of a Justified Sinner.*

turn it into conditional grace, in a legalism which loses the meaning of grace — as I think we have seen too often in Scotland in the old Highland practice of fencing the Lord's Table in the exercise of godly discipline.

The fallacy of legalism in all ages — perhaps this is the tendency of the human heart in all ages — is to *turn God's covenant of grace into a contract,* with serious consequences for preaching, worship and pastoral counselling. In the Bible, the form of the covenant is such that the indicatives of grace are always prior to the obligations of law and human obedience. "I am the God of Abraham, Isaac and Jacob, I have loved you and redeemed you and brought you out of the land of Egypt, out of the house of bondage, *therefore* keep my commandments". But legalism puts it the other way round. *"If* you keep the law, God will love you! If you keep the Sabbath day and carry the yoke of the Torah, the Kingdom of God will come!" The imperatives are made prior to the indicatives. The covenant has been turned into a contract, and God's grace made conditional on man's obedience. It was precisely against this inversion of the order of grace that Paul protested in Galatians ch. 3 in his interpretation of the Old Testament and authentic Judaism. You remember this argument. God gave His promises to Abraham, and only 430 years later came the law at Sinai, not to annul the promise, not to impose conditions of grace, but to spell out the obligations of grace, to be the schoolmaster to lead us to Christ. This passage is determinative for Calvin's interpretation of the relation between grace and law[12].

To put it in other words, love, like marriage love, always brings its obligations — its unconditional obligations — but the obligations of love are not conditions of love. To turn a covenant into a contract is to turn categorical imperatives into hypothetical imperatives (to use Kantian language), and hence to weaken the imperatives. Legalism always weakens the character of law. "Do I weaken the law" says the apostle — by seeing it in the context of grace? "No, I strengthen it!" (Rom. III.31). For all that this was heart of the teaching of the Reformation, it seems to me that we find a situation emerging in the

---

[12] *Institutes* 2.7.1; 2.9.4, etc. The Book of the Covenant in *Exodus* — as Martin Buber argued so powerfully in his book on *Moses* — is a covenant, not a contract. Judaism is NOT synonomous with legalism, whatever may have happened at times within Judaism. Far too often Christian theologians have made that fatal equation, as writers like E.P. Sanders have powerfully demonstrated, *Paul and Palestinian Judaism,* S.C.M., 1977.

17th century, not only in Scotland, but also in France, England and New England, where the political struggles for religious and civil liberty (which were the birth pangs of modern democracy) too often led to contractual ways of thinking about God's relation to men, and legalistic interpretations of Calvinism which were to leave an unhappy legacy in much Scottish religion, which was to disturb many of Scotland's ablest theologians in the years to come. I can only indicate in the briefest terms what is a vast subject.

Two important events deeply disturbed Western Europe in the latter half of the 16th century, after the Reformation. The one was the deposition of Mary Queen of Scots in 1567, followed by her execution in 1587, raising in its acutest form the question, "What are the rights of a sovereign vis-a-vis the people?". The other was the massacre of the Huguenots in France on the Eve of St. Bartholomew in 1572, raising the complimentary question, "What are the rights of a people vis-a-vis their sovereign?" These two events gave rise to fierce political controversy. What is the nature and source of human rights? What constitutes lawful government? What is the seat of sovereignty in law? Is it in the monarchy, as defenders of the divine right of kings believed? Is it in the people, as democrats and republicans believed? Is it above both monarch and people in God? How then is it entrusted to men? Is sovereignty limited or unlimited? Is it indivisible, or is it divisible between king and people? What are the source and bounds of kingly power? Is violence ever justified, even if it is in the defence of liberty against a tyrant? John Calvin had taught that only in extreme cases could a representative body in the State —the magistrate —sanction the use of force. Otherwise there should only be passive resistance to a tyrant. The Christian in cases of conscience must resort to prayer, or if need be to flight, or be like Daniel, prepared to go to the den of lions — but never to use the sword. But situations emerged in France and Scotland where the Protestant reformers, even if in a minority, as in France, were prepared to use force in the defence of religious and civil liberty, but they wanted to do it lawfully and constitutionally. It was here they appealed to the concept of covenant between king and people to safeguard both the rights of the king and the rights of the people — a contract of government, based on the law of nature and enshrined in civil law. God only is truly sovereign, but He has given authority to men to govern. Therefore under God all sovereignty is limited and divisible — divisible between king and people, who are answerable to God and one another, and who bind themselves to one another under prescribed conditions[13].

The twin concepts of (a) a people in covenant with God and (b) the universal reign of law had their clear theological counterpart in the rise of "federal theology" in the doctrine of the Covenant of Works. This was the view that God made Adam the child of nature who could discern the laws of nature by the light of reason, and on the basis of nature, law and reason, made a covenant or contract with Adam that if he kept the law of nature, God would be gracious to him and his posterity. But Adam broke the contract of nature, the covenant of works, bringing divine judgement on himself and on all for whom he contracted as the federal head of the race. But God doesn't abandon the human race, having elected some men to eternal salvation, and so makes a covenant of grace for them in Christ — providing in Christ one who would fulfil the conditions of the covenant of works for the elect. This distinction between a covenant of works and a covenant of grace — the covenant of nature and the covenant of the Gospel —was unknown to Calvin and the earlier Reformers, but was expounded in the Westminster Confession of Faith, and became dear to the hearts of many English and Scottish preachers, not least in covenanting days.

As I see it, the federal scheme was built upon a deep-seated *confusion between a covenant and a contract,* a failure to recognise that the God and Father of our Lord Jesus Christ is a covenant-God and not a contract-God. A covenant brings its obligations, its promises and its warnings. But the obligations of grace are not conditions of grace, and it is false in Christian theology to articulate moral obligation in contractual terms. To do so, is to obscure "the unconditional freeness of grace" as later Scottish theologians were to see.

Grace ⟶ Law OR Law ⟶ Grace (the Nature — Grace Model)?

The federal scheme, with its fundamental distinction between a Covenant of Works and the Covenant of Grace, is thus built on the *priority of Law over Grace.* But has this not inverted the biblical order? Calvin in the 1536 edition of the *Institutio* followed the pattern of

---

[13] cp. J.W. Gough *The social contract,* Oxford, second edition ... 1953, chs. 5 and 7 on "Puritanism and the Contract". In J.W. Allen, *History of political thought in the Sixteenth Century,* there is a valuable discussion of Calvin's thought in contrast to his successors. See Appendix A and B (diagram 4 on federal theology).

Luther's Short Catechism of Law — Grace, but subsequently abandoned it as not true to the Bible. His study of the Old Testament and the clear teaching of Paul in Galatians chapter three led him to see the priority of grace over law — that law is the gift of grace, spells out the unconditional obligations of grace and leads to grace — its fulfilment in Christ. He contends for this very eloquently in Book Two of the *Institutio,* expounding law in the context of promise and fulfilment[14].

But the priority of grace over law is true not only in the life of Israel and the story of man's redemption. It is the *grammar of Creation.* Calvin never taught a doctrine of a "covenant of works", nor would have. He is quite explicit "that God has never made any other covenant than that which He made formerly with Abraham, and at length confirmed by the hand of Moses"[15]. But the English Puritan tradition, in the practical concern to use the Law as the schoolmaster to bring men to Christ, universalised from that use of the Law ("law work") and read it back into Creation, into their doctrine of God, and grounded the distinction between the two covenants on it. The two covenants of Works and Grace (Law and Grace) are the two stages by which God executes the eternal decrees, in bringing the elect to salvation. This is precisely how William Perkins expounded it in *The Golden Chain* of 1592, which was so influential on subsequent Puritan teaching. But is this not the Mediaeval *ordo salutis* (of Alexander Hales, etc.) of Man-law-sin-repentace-grace — the order which Calvin sought to reverse?

To often in Western theology (perhaps due to the legacy of Stoicism and Roman concepts of law), in mediaeval Catholicism, in Lutheran thought and in scholastic Calvinism, we see the inversion of the biblical order — the assertion of the priority of law over grace, of nature over grace, with the *resultant* limiting of the Headship of Christ as Mediator to the Church, with all that that means for our interpretation of the relation between Church and State, our preaching, as well as our doctrines of God and of man. The Puritan theologians

---

[14] cf. *Institutio* 2.9.4. "Hence we see the error of those who, in comparing the Law with the Gospel, represent it merely as a comparison between the merit of works and the gratuitous imputation of righteousness ... The Gospel has not succeeded the whole Law in such a sense as to introduce a different method of salvation. It rather confirms the Law, and proves that everything which it promised is fulfilled".

[15] *Comm. on Jeremiah* 31,31ff.

from William Perkins to John Owen embodied the Western *ordo salutis* in their doctrine of effectual calling, of repentance and faith and the Christian life. The same approach gave rise to a powerful "legal strain" in Scottish preaching, against which Thomas Boston, Ralph and Ebenezer Erskine and others were to protest in the so-called "Marrow controversy" in the early eighteenth century, and which led John McLeod Campbell to argue, as Calvin had done, that "the filial is prior to the judicial".

Jonathan Edwards in New England took this to its theological conclusion in teaching that Justice is the essential attribute of God, but the Love of God is arbitrary. God is related to all men as contracting sovereign and judge, but only to some men in grace. This may be the logical corollary of federal Calvinism, but it is not true to the New Testament. God is love in His innermost being, the Father of our Lord Jesus Christ, the Father after whom every family in heaven and earth is named. Love and justice are one in God, as they should be in all our dealings with one another in society.

The federal scheme in these terms made a *radical dichotomy between the sphere of Nature and the sphere of Grace,* of natural law and the Gospel, with the result that the relationship between the Church and the world, Church and State, is no longer understood Christologically as in the Greek Fathers and basically in Calvin and Knox, but in terms of Gospel and natural law. But the separation between Nature and Grace amounts to a reversion to the pre-Reformation mediaeval view that *grace presupposes nature* and *grace perfects nature* — a departure from the emphasis of Calvin that nothing is prior to grace. An illustration of this is the interpretation of the Sabbath in Scotland and Puritan England. The ten commandments are a transcript of the law of nature, and the law of nature (including the law of the Sabbath) is the foundation of society, and for the State consequently to violate the law of nature is to expose the State to divine judgement. Again, such a doctrine of the separation of nature and grace has been the ground of certain doctrines of "the spirituality of the Church" as in the southern United States, where the Church is concerned with "spiritual" matters like the preaching of the Gospel, but civil matters like civil rights and race relations should be left to the State. But are we to interpret the State simply in terms of the orders of creation and preservation, but not also in terms of the orders of Redemption?

273

The Eternal Decress of God and the Practical Syllogism

When we consider the following confessions:[16]

    1553   *Forty-two Articles of Cranmer*
    1562   *Thirty-nine Articles*
    1595   *Lambeth Articles* of Whitgift
    1615   *Irish Articles* of Ussher
    1643-48 *Westminster Confession*
    1658   *Savoy Declaration*

we see two things:

* the growing emphasis on election and the doctrine of the decrees of God — on double predestination, and

* the decided move to a view where *election precedes grace,* so that the interpretation of the Person and Work of Christ is subordinated to the doctrine of the decrees and seen as God's way of executing the decrees for the elect. The result is that grace is limited to the redemption of the elect.

Thus the doctrine of the decrees of God becomes the Major Premiss of the whole scheme of Creation and Redemption. This is clearly a move away from the Scots Confession of 1560, where election is placed after the article on the Mediator in the context of Christology. It is also a move away from Calvin, who expounded election at the end of Book Three of the *Institutio,* as a corollary to grace, after he had expounded all he has to say about the work of Father, Son and Holy Spirit, and *after* his exposition of Incarnation and Atonement.

When the doctrine of the decrees of God becomes the major premiss, what happens? Here again we see the influence of the pragmatic Western legal mind in Puritan thinking with its preoccupation with the How? question and its genius for putting decisions into effect — of applying the "principles" of biblical teaching in the life of the Church (the application of law in concrete situations, in what they called "cases of conscience"). The basic questions therefore become:

* How does God execute the eternal decrees? By creation, providence,

---

[16] Cp. Peter Toon, *Puritans and Calvinism* p. 52ff.

permitting the Fall, Redemption, effectual calling, etc.

* How does God secure the Redemption of the elect? The causes of salvation'', as set out in Perkin's *The Golden Chain,* etc.

* How does God effectively apply the benefits of the Covenant of Grace to the elect, in the life of the believer and in the gift of the means of grace, the Chruch, Word and Sacraments, and how do we structure the Church by Biblical precedent and Biblical principles?

Perhaps the most fundamental practical question which emerges in the pastoral situation under this scheme was the one to which the Puritans devoted so much of their time and writing. *How do I know whether I am one of the elect or not?* How can I find assurance of salvation? Can I ever know whether or not Christ died for me?[17] From the time when Beza, unlike Calvin, taught a thorough-going doctrine of limited atonement, and Beza's thought found powerful mediation in England in the writings of William Perkins, this became a burning issue among English Puritans and Scottish Calvinists.

The answer was "the practical syllogism" *(syllogismus practicus* or *mysticus),* stated in many ways by the English Puritans.

Major Premiss: The truly penitent person is one of the elect.

Minor Premiss: I have truly repented.
(Based on conscience and self-examination).

Conclusion: Therefore I am one of the elect (any may come to the Lord's Supper).

Here as Dr R.T. Kendall has recently argued in his *Calvin and English Calvinism to 1649,* we see a significant departure from Calvin. In terms of a doctrine of universal atonement, Calvin taught that the work of the Holy Spirit, in creating faith as a cognitive act *(cognitio),* is to *direct our minds away from ourselves to what we are in Christ,* so

---

[17] In 1589, Perkins wrote his first major work *A Treatise tending unto a declaration whether a man be in the estate of damnation or in the estate of grace: and if he be in the first, how he may in time come out of it: if in the second, how he may discern it, and persevere to the end.* For a full discussion of this see R.T. Kendall, *Calvin and English Calvinism to 1649* (O.U.P. 1979). Kendall argues that the *ordo salutis* as well as the doctrine of faith and assurance in the Puritans constitutes a radical shift from that of Calvin.

that we may find assurance of election and salvation *in Christ* "in whom all parts of our salvation are complete". But in the supralapsarian tradition of Beza, Gomarus, Perkins, Samuel Rutherford and in the dominant Puritan tradition, faith becomes a "reflex" act where we engage in self-examination, seeking "evidences", "tokens" of election where by "reflection", perhaps after many years, we may infer that we are among the elect and come to some kind of assurance of salvation. Assurance then is *not* of the essence of faith, as in the teaching of Calvin, the "Marrowmen" and John McLeod Campbell in Scotland. A major preoccupation to the Puritans becomes therefore increasingly that of subjective sanctification and self-examination with a self-conscious concern to live according to biblical precedents and principles, with a constant pastoral concern for cases of conscience. Here undoubtedly we see the roots of modern evangelicalism, with the voluntarist stress on repentance, personal decision, acceptance of Christ and commitment to the Gospel to secure salvation. On the other hand it too often gave rise to a kind of "legal preaching" and notions of "legal repentance" with a tragic loss of the Reformation stress on the unconditional freeness of the Gospel and Calvin's doctrine of "evangelical repentance", as a response to the Cross and the gift of union with Christ. But to turn our eyes away from what God has done so freely for us in Christ and to look at ourselves is to lose the joyful assurance of faith which reposes on Christ.

Strengths and Weaknesses of the Puritans

Here I think we see the major strength and yet the weakness of the Puritans — and indeed of the Westminster documents, which are a clear lucid statement of Puritan thought at its best. It lies in their powerful highly motivated *practical concern* to appropriate the blessings of the Gospel and to *apply* the doctrines of grace to the faith and life of the believer. Puritanism arose out of a passionate concern to reform the Church in England and to restructure it by the standards of Holy Scripture[18]. Behind the Westminster documents we see not only the remit of the Long Parliament to secure the ends of the Solemn League and Covenant to find a covenanted uniformity of doctrine, worship and government in the three Kingdoms of Scotland, England and Ireland. We see Puritan biblical preaching, and the

---

[18] See article on "Puritanism: the Problem of Definition" by Basil Hall in *Studies in Church History*, Vol. II Nelson 1965, pp. 283-296.

concern for authentic religious experience, and through it all the Puritan doctrine of the Sovereignty of God and their understanding of the scheme of salvation.

Together with the eternal decress of God, the Bible is the major premiss of every article, written with the conviction that all life and doctrine should be based on biblical precedent and biblical principles[19]. In this way Puritanism was to exert an enormous creative influence on the religion of England and Scotland and (not least on Presbyterianism) throughout the English-speaking world.

The danger however can emerge, that were our paramount concern is the *application* of the benefits of Christ (that believers be "more and more quickened and strengthened in all spiritual graces, to the practice of true holiness") our emphasis can move away from what God has done *for us in Christ* to what *we are to do* to know that we are among the elect and in covenant with Christ. It is not just there that we see the major difference between John Calvin and the Puritans?

---

[19] It is significant that the largest part of the Westminster Confession is given over to the question as to HOW the benefits of the Covenant of Grace are applied to believers (IX-XVIII), followed by chapters on Law and Liberty (XIX-XX), worship and the sabbath day (XXI) and Civil matters (XXIII-XXIV). Only then does the Confession turn to the doctrine of Church and Sacraments (XXXIII-XXXIV), leaving the "last things" to the last chapters (XXXII-XXXIII).

APPENDIX A:

in the wealth of literature which emerged in the form of political pamphlets and sermons, in France, England and Scotland, we can discern three main lines of argument.

There was the historical argument. The concept of a contract of government between king and people was not new, but had a long history in Scotland and in France, as seen from the ancient coronation oaths, as well as the practice of bands and contracts in feudal society. History clearly taught that kings exist by the will of the people, for the good of the people, and may therefore be brought to account for misgovernment. This was the argument of a very influential little work by George Buchanan, the Scottish poet and historian and private tutor of James VI, entitled *De Iure Regni apud Scotos,* which appeared in 1579 (although written ten years earlier in 1569) — a dialogue written to justify the deposition of Mary Queen of Scots and to clear the Scots from the resulting accusation of being a seditious people. The book was not an original one politically — behind it we see the influence of historians like Hector Boece, the first principal of King's College in Aberdeen and John Major, the Scot who taught George Buchanan in St. Andrews and John Calvin in Paris, and who wrote a history of the Scots in 1521. But the book is significant in that it gathers together in systematic form and forceful terms the arguments of earlier radical thinkers. Buchanan's book was condemned by successive acts of Parliament in 1584, 1664 and 1688, not least because of its defence of tyrannicide, but was nevertheless widely read in Scotland. It deeply influenced John Milton in his *Defence of the People of England* after the beheading of Charles I in 1549.

This historical argument was elaborated in a much fuller way by the French Huguenots in terms of French history, particularly in a famous work entitled *Franco-Gallia* by Francois Hotman in 1573, a careful enquiry into the development of French political constitutions from the Romans and the Gauls to his own time.

The Second line of argument was the political one, the explicit appeal to the doctrine of a social contract – or contract of government.

The doctrine of a social contract, though not espoused by political philosophers today, had a long history in European thought, going back to Plato's Republic. It was taught in different forms in the Middle Ages — feudalism itself was a contractarian form of society — and was to be highly influential in the rise of modern democracy. It is generally associated with the names of Thomas Hobbes, writing at a time when the Stewarts were defending their doctrine of the divine right of kings (his *Leviathan* appeared in 1651); John Locke at the time of the Revolution Settlement in England (his two *Treatises on Government* appeared in 1690) and Rousseau, in the France prior to the French Revolution (his *Du Contrat Social* appeared in 1762).

Fundamental to the doctrine of the social contract is the twin view that *liberty* — the human will and not force — is the basis of good government, and that *justice* — that right and not might — is the basis of political order. No-one is above the law.

The doctrine of a social contract is really comprised of two different ideas[20]. (a) Historically, the older notion in European history was that of a *Contract of Government,* the theory that the State (in the sense of government) is based on a contract between ruler and subjects, between king and people. This was the political doctrine of the French Huguenots and the Scottish Covenanters in their opposition to the doctrine of the divine right of kings, and it was in elaborating the concept of contract of government that they used the word *foedus,* covenant, and appealed to Old Testament precedent. This is clearly developed in the writings of John Knox. But *logically,* the notion of a contract of government presupposes a prior condition of society, and so of a "contract of society", for there must be a selfconscious organised society, with some kind of common will, before there can arise the question of how the society is to be governed. (b) Therefore, secondly, beside the contract of government, and logically prior to the notion of a contract of government, there must be a *Contract of Society* — which is normally what we mean by a "social contract". The State is based on society, and hence upon all those contracts which constitute society, which bind members of society together in the family, in the community, in the village, the city, the market place and the church. But if the doctrine of a social contract is logically prior to the doctrine of a contract of government, historically it was developed much later as a full blooded doctrine, after the mid-17th century by Hobbes, Locke and Rousseau. The counterpart of this latter doctrine in Scotland was the concept of a *convenanted nation under God,* and called into existence by God. The Reformation had given to Scotland, or to the Reformed church at least, a common will.

Behind both forms of the doctrine, there was the passionate concern, in the defence of liberty and justice, to base society and constitutional government on the notion of law — and more explicitly the *law of nature* which is the foundation of all true society — the *foedus naturae,* the covenant of nature, which God has made with man. *Fundamental to the rise of democracy and the development of Scottish theology was the belief in the universal reign of law, that all men are under law and hence under the sovereignty of God.* Responsible government presupposes responsibility to God.

There was the biblical argument. Political writers of every persuasion — French Huguenots and Jesuits, defenders of divine right of kings and Scottish Covenanters — ransacked the Bible for biblical warrant and justification for their views. The Huguenot covenant argument was a simple one. In the Old

---

[20] See Appendix A and B (diagram 4 on federal theology).

Testament, Israel was a nation in covenant with the Lord, the covenant made with Abraham and confirmed at Sinai. At first God was their king, but when later, Saul and David and Solomon became kings in Israel, they were kings in a covenanted nation under the Torah, under the law and testimonies of a covenanted nation. They were not absolute monarchs like other oriental despots but were servant kings, and when they became kings, their power was limited by a *twofold* covenant. (a) Firstly, there was the covenant between God, the king and the people, where king and people together made their covenant with God to serve the Lord and to be faithful to the laws and testimonies of Moses. (b) Secondly, a covenant was made between the king and the people, to serve each other, to undergird the first covenant, to preserve true religion in the land, and to acknowledge their limitations of power under God and under law. In this second covenant, French Huguenots and Scottish Covenanters found biblical warrant for the socio-political notion of a contract of government, and just as there was a certain "democratising" of the concept of kingship in old Israel, so the Covenanters attempted to democratise the concept of kingship in Scotland. (Incidentally this is similar to the thesis of Professor Martin Noth against the myth and ritual school of Old Testament scholars).

The most influential book expounding this argument was a pseudonymous Huguenot work which appeared in 1579 called *Vindiciae contra Tyrannos* (a) *Defence of Liberty against Tyrants)* which was translated into English in 1648, the year before Charles I was beheaded, and republished significantly in 1689, and then again in 1924 by the late Professor Harold Laski. Professor Laski regarded it as perhaps the most influential book of the whole period in the story of the rise of modern democracy. It was certainly a work widely read and carefully studied by the Scottish Covenanters. It is beyond the scope of this lecture to say more about this remarkable book, but it is significant for our purpose because it is entirely an exposition of the Old Testament, and yet such an influential exposition of the whole case for popular sovereignty and pupular rights, expounding the biblical concept of covenant in highly contractarian terms.

The significant thing about the Scottish Covenanters is that, in them, we see the gathering together of the three lines of argument I have so briefly outlined, the historical argument from the ancient Scottish precedent of bands and pacts and coronation oaths in the defence of liberty and national sovereignty, the political argument with its appeal to mediaeval notions of contract of government, the biblical argument with its appeal to the Old Testament notion of Israel as a covenanted nation, and of a king in covenant with God and his people in the defence of the true religion.

That threefold argument was the theme of another very influential book written by Samuel Rutherford, entitled *Lex Rex – the Law and the Prince* –written while he was a Scottish commissioner at the Westminster Assembly in 1644, six years after the National Covenant and one year after the Solemn

League and Covenant while he was writing other works expounding the themes of federal theology. This book was really the political manifesto of the Covenanters. The full title of his work is *"Lex Rex, or the Law and the Prince* – a dispute of the just prerogatives of king and people, containing the reasons and causes for the most necessary defensive wars in the kingdom of Scotland, and of the expedition to the aid of their dear brethren in England"*. It was written in reply to a work by John Maxwell, Bishop of Ross, in the defence of absolute monarchy. Rutherford's concern was not merely to expound the *legality* of using force in the defence of religious and civil liberty, but to expound its *rationality* by basing his teaching about society and civil government, not simply on Old Testament precedent, but on *natural law* discerned by the light of reason. It is an extremely erudite work showing that he was highly aware of mediaeval political theory, and familiar with the works of Spanish writers, the works of Mariana, Molina, Suarez, the Catholic Jesuit writers of the League in France, as well as of Grotius and the French Huguenots.

Perhaps there is no more vivid illustration of the confluence of these three lines of argument than the sermon preached by the Rev. Robert Douglas at the Coronation of Charles II at Scone in 1651[21]. His text was the words from 2 Kings XI. 12, 17 — the story of the coronation of Joash, King of Israel, by Jehoiada the High Priest. "And Jehoiada brought forth the king's son and put a crown upon him and gave him the testimony, and made him king and anointed him, and they clapped their hands and said God save the king. And Jehoiada made a covenant between the Lord, the king and the people that they should be the Lord's people; between the king also and the people". No text or passage in the Bible could have been more historically apposite for the occasion, even down to the smallest detail. The young king Joash, like Charles II, was to be crowned; the previous king had been put to death — as had Charles' father two years before; there had been an usurpation of power by Athaliah — as by the Cromwellian party in England; now Jehoiada in the person of Robert Douglas was to present the king to the people; the context of Scotland, like that of old Israel, was a nation in covenant with the Lord; the clear duty was to crown Charles II as king, by effecting a twofold covenant, (a) firstly by bringing him into the existing covenant, so that king and people might make their covenant before God, and (b) secondly by calling him into covenant with the people. So after the sermon, the oath is administered to the king, and he is called to renew the covenants, to sign the National Covenant and the Solemn League and Covenant, to maintain the Reformation in Scotland, and to establish Presbyterian government and doctrine as set forth in the Westminster Confession of Faith and Directory of Public Worship — the law and testimonies of a covenanted nation.

---

[21] See Appendix Diagram 5.

Here we see the whole political philosophy of the covenant movement worked out in practice, and expounded in this sermon, echoing the language of the *Vindiciae Contra Tyrannos* and of Samuel Rutherford's *Lex Rex*, and the Old Testament provides the controlling theme. Listen to Robert Douglas' words: "I come now to the covenant between king and people. When a king is crowned and received by the people, there is a covenant or mutual contract between him and them, containing conditions mutually to be observed ... It is good for our king to learn to be wise in time and know that he receiveth this day a power to govern — a power limited by contract; and these conditions he is bound by oath to stand to, for a king's power is not absolute but is power limited by covenant".

Politically, whatever we make of the philosophy of social contract, whether expounded in biblical terms by the Huguenots, Puritans and Covenanters or interpreted in more philosophical terms in the school of natural law,[22] it embodied two fundamental insights which lie at the heart of democracy, as writers like T.H. Green, Sir Ernest Barker and others have shown, and to which we must be sensitive today, (a) the first is the passionate belief in *Justice,* the conviction that *right and not might* is the basis of all political society and of every system of political order in a true democracy. (b) The second is the passionate belief in *Liberty,* the conviction that *will and human consent, not force* is the basis of government. Our Puritan forefathers contended for this against the "tyranny" of the divine right of kings. We in our day must contend for these convictions against other forms of tyranny, when any individual or group attempts to "hijack" the nation or use force to impose its will irresponsibly on others — be it the tyranny of a minority or the tyranny of a majority. Both of these insights, the belief in the transcendence of Justice over all forms of positive or civil law, and the belief in responsible freedom grew out of belief in the sovereignty of God who as the founders of the American federal constitution were to argue, has created all men equal and mutually responsible, with inalienable rights to life, liberty and the pursuit of happiness. The question for us today is: Can these beliefs survive and thrive *without faith* in the transcendence of God and the transcendence of justice?

[22] See *Appendix* Diagram 5.

APPENDIX B: DIAGRAMS

DIAGRAM 1:   **FOEDUS**   **COVENANT OR CONTRACT?**

COVENANT (FOEDUS)

Indicatives	— prior to	Imperatives (e.g. "10 words")
Promise	⟶	Law (categorical, unconditional)
"I am ___" "I will be ___"	∴	Do this!

CONTRACT (FOEDUS)

IMPERATIVES	— prior to	Indicatives
Law (hypothetical, conditional)	⟶	Promise
Do this!	— IF ___	then ___.

i.e.   (a)   Law not annul promises
"Is law against promises? God forbid!" (Paul in *Gal.* 3:21)

         (b)   Covenant — strengthens law
Contract — weakens law   *(Rom.* 3:31)
(legalism)

DIAGRAM 2:

COVENANT (GRACE)

     (a)   Unconditioned — i.e. "free".

     (b)   Unconditional — i.e. "costly".
in claims and obligations.

DIAGRAM 3:

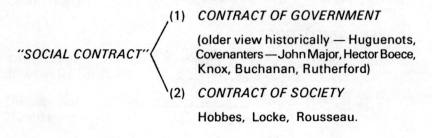

POLITICAL PHILOSOPHY

"SOCIAL CONTRACT"

(1) *CONTRACT OF GOVERNMENT*

(older view historically — Huguenots, Covenanters —John Major, Hector Boece, Knox, Buchanan, Rutherford)

(2) *CONTRACT OF SOCIETY*

Hobbes, Locke, Rousseau.

DIAGRAM 4:

FEDERAL THEOLOGY (Scholastic Calvinism) (e.g. Westminster Confession, and Documents)

N.B. Nature / Grace Model

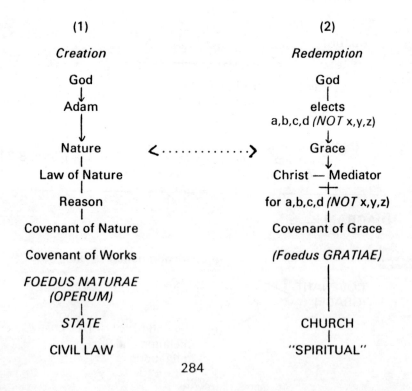

(1)	(2)
Creation	*Redemption*
God	God
↓	│
Adam	elects
│	a,b,c,d *(NOT* x,y,z)
│	↓
Nature <············>	Grace
│	↓
Law of Nature	Christ — Mediator
│	┼
Reason	for a,b,c,d *(NOT* x,y,z)
│	│
Covenant of Nature	Covenant of Grace
Covenant of Works	*(Foedus GRATIAE)*
FOEDUS NATURAE (OPERUM)	│
│	│
STATE	CHURCH
│	│
CIVIL LAW	"SPIRITUAL"

284

DIAGRAM 5:

**Political Theology of the Covenanters
(VINDICIAE CONTRA TYRANNOS, S. RUTHERFORD, ROBERT DOUGLAS)**

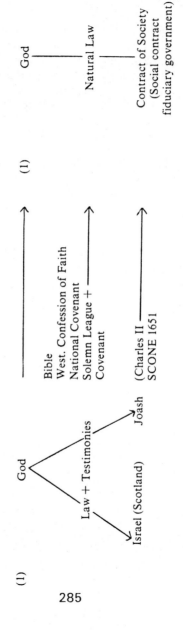

TWO CONVENANTS. 2 King XI. 12, 17.
JEHOIADA (ROBERT DOUGLAS — HIGH PRIEST.

Later development.
One Covenant — Social contract proper.
e.g. J. Locke

(1)

God

Law + Testimonies → Joash

Israel (Scotland)

Bible
West. Confession of Faith
National Covenant
Solemn League +
Covenant

(Charles II —
SCONE 1651

(1)

God

Natural Law

Contract of Society
(Social contract
fiduciary government)

(2)

People ⟷ King (Charles II)

Contract of Government
(coronation oaths)

(2)

No contract of Government
(i.e. no ruling class)

285

BIBLIOGRAPHY

Collinson, P. *The Elizabeth Puritan Movement,* Cape.

Knappen, M.M. *Tudor Puritanism,* Chicago University Press.

Yule, G. 1980 *Puritans in Politics – the Religious Legislation of the Long Parliament in the Light of Puritan Theology and History,* Sutton Courtenay. Library of Reformation Classics (due September 1980).

Porter, H. *Reformation and Reaction in Tudor Cambridge,* C.U.P.

Woodhouse, A.S.P. *Puritanism and Liberty,* Dent.

Haller, W. *The Rise of Puritanism.*

Breward, I. *William Perkins,* Sutton Courtenay Library of Reformation Classics.

Kendall, R.T. *Calvin and English Calvinism to 1649,* O.U.P. 1979.

Gough, J.W. *The Social Contract,* O.U.P.

Allen, J.W. *A history of Political Thought in the Sixteenth Century,* Methuen.

23. CALVIN AND ART

PROF. P.W. BUYS*

Introduction

The aim of this investigation

The purpose of this investigation is firstly to determine what view Calvin had of the arts, and secondly to determine what message his vision of art could have for contemporary art.

Topicality

Contemporary art has become an important exponent of twentieth century secularism. "The arts of today is by and large a storeroom, a museum of our despairs" (Ionesco, quoted without reference to source by Wilson, 1980, p. 25). Wilson (p. 26) underlines the topicality of Calvin's views for contemporary art by the reply that he himself gives to the following questions: "How can we as Christians approach the confusion, chaos and cursing of the arts of our age? How can we bring understanding, and healing of the Gospel, to the bruised and sometimes brutalizing arts of the 20th century? It seems to me that the answer must come from what, to many, will be an unexpected source. It will come from working out, in our age, a Calvinist approach to the arts. The teaching of John Calvin would not only give us understanding but provide purpose and direction to the arts as to how best they can serve God and man".

Thus, in the same way that it was Calvin in particular who helped to liberate art from enslavement by the Roman Catholic Church four centuries ago, so it will be a Calvinist approach which would help to liberate twentieth century man from the humanist, liberal concept of "l'art pour l'art", and existentialism with its credo of "God is dead".

The need for this investigation

Calvin himself did not write an aesthetics or a philosophy of art. But,

---

* His address is: Dept. of Apologetics and Ethics, Potchefstroom University for Christian Higher Education. Potchefstroom, RSA 2520.

as the spiritual leader and man of culture of his day, he had close contact with the flourishing life of art of the Renaissance. At the court of the Duchess of Ferrara, for example, Calvin often came into contact with the famous painter Titian (Goulon, 11 March 1917, p. 75). As a philosopher who wished to bring the whole of life under the dominion of the Word of God, he had, naturally, to gain clarity in his own mind as to the place, the purpose and the nature of the arts. Therefore there are references to beauty and the arts scattered all through his works.

Wencelius (n.d.) fine-combed all Calvin's works in the course of the thirties (of the present century) and collated all Calvin's statements on art and beauty in his *L'esthetique de Calvin*. This is the only standard work on Calvin and the arts. There are of course dangers attached to a compilation such as the one by Wencelius, such as the danger that the schematization of another person's scattered ideas might lead the compiler to make conclusions which the original writer had never intended. If Calvin should have written an esthetics himself, it would most probably have been different from the one compiled ultimately by Wencelius.

The value of this work, however, is that Wencelius brought together is one volume all the statements that Calvin ever made on the arts. It is such a complete work that little opportunity remains for a study of the sources. In this paper, therefore, little that is new will be presented. It is at most an effort to sum up Wencelius' work, in the same way that everybody who has commented on Calvin's views of the arts after Wencelius has done.

Delimiting the investigation

The quoted work by Wencelius covers 428 pages. The limit set for this paper by the organizers of the conference is in the vicinity of 12 typed pages. Therefore one would naturally be able to touch lightly only on the most important aspects of this subject. No attention will be devoted to the significance that Calvin's work and his ideas had for the separate genres in the arts. These will simply be pointed out in passing. Calvin's views on style will similarly have to remain in the background.

Plan of action

In the following order, attention will be given to the various topics: Calvin's statements on beauty and the arts; his message for contemporary art; and finally a résumé of his ideas as they have been developed in the course of the paper.

Calvin's statements on beauty

Calvin's ideas on beauty, which underlie his concept of art, can be expressed in the following main outline: In the first place beauty should never be regarded in isolation from the vision of the Being of God. In the second place, beauty has to be seen in conjunction with God as the Creator. In the third place one has to look at the question about what happens to the beauty of the universe as a result of the Fall. Fourhtly, the deed of liberation of Christ and the sanctifying work of the Holy Spirit will have an effect on the beauty-centred activities of mankind (Wencelius, n.d., p. 15).

God and beauty

Calvin's whole philosophy, including his views on beauty, should always be regarded from one central vision: God and his revelation in the universe.

In any effort to reflect on beauty the Being of God has to be regarded as being foremost. But to want to know God in his essential Being is as hazardous as looking directly into the sun. Mankind is like inhabitants of a valley. High above man the light is encircled by clouds. Only those few who climb the mountan peaks can see the light more clearly. God reveals the luminosity of his Glory when one of these rays penetrates to mankind. He reveals in this way that mankind will see the beauty of his Glory, so that man may learn to worship Him *(Corpus Reformatorum,* indicated in the rest of the paper as CR, XXXVIm 598; cf. Wencelius, n.d., p. 21).

Beauty shines exquisitely from the presence of God. Glorious splendour and presence — these are the two characteristic traits of the beauty of the Being of God (CR, XXXIX, p. 428; cf. Wencelius, n.d., p. 22).

The revelation of beauty by God is trinitarian by nature. The Father is the source of everything — of beauty too. But this beauty would have remained concealed within the Being of the Father, if He had not chosen to reveal it in the glory of the Son. The glory of the Father has been in the process of being revealed in the Son since before Creation. It is like the formal appearance of a king in all his splendour, with his crown, his sceptre, his purple mantle *(CR,* XXIV, p. 428; LV, p. 398; XLVII, p. 388; LV, p. 15; LII, p. 25; cf. Wencelius, n.d., p. 24). As the Father imprinted his Spirit in the Son, who was in the image of God, so the Spirit, which emanates from the Father and the Son, his dynamic, shaping power on Creation, so that God could be glorified through Creation in various ways. The Holy Spirit, therefore, is the divine Artist, who gave his shaping beauty to the universe *(CR* XXXIV, p. 441; cf. Wencelius, n.d., p. 26).

Beauty and Creation

Before Creation (what is meant is probably the *Creatio secunda,* Genesis 1:3ff) there was no beauty visible in the universe, also no order. Darkness covered everything. At a single sign from God the limitless, amorphous and chaotic mass of matter assumed glorious and beautiful shape *(CR,* LI, p. 458; cf. Wencelius, n.d. p. 29).

God is the great Artist and the Architect, who illuminates heaven and earth with his glory. The stars especially are masterpieces in which the wisdom of God is made apparent *(CR,* XXV, p. 368;XLVII, p. 479; VII, p. 14; XXXII, p. 427; cf. Wencelius, n.d. p. 32). The angels, man, plants, flowers, animals, birds, all that God created, all of these are beautiful.

Beauty and the Fall

Creation, which once was the mirror of Divine Beauty, was shattered into splinters by the coming of sin. Man who looks at one of the shards now sees only his own reflection (Wencelius, 1940, p. 251). Everything that Satan touches he deforms. The earth has been cursed because of sin. Everything becomes ugly, rotten and miserable. It is like flowers of which the stems have been cut off — at first they still look beautiful, but gradually they wilt and then wither away *(CR,* L, p. 693; cf. Wencelius, p. 52).

Through the Fall man loses his true insights. He is blinded. Satan attempts to divert him by pseudo-beauty. This pseudo-beauty is a false light, an outward splendour, a false harmony to which man becomes addicted *(CR,* XLVI, p. 277; cf. Wencelius, n.d., p. 53).

Sin has, however, not succeeded in destroying Creation fully. In a universe in which good and evil, heaven and hell, are intermingled, all that is heavenly, pure, beautiful and true serves to eliminate the scum that is floating on the surface (Wencelius, n.d., p. 15).

Beauty and re-creation

God does not leave the fallen Creation to its own devices. He sends his Son to save the world *(CR,* XXIII, p. 554; cf. Wencelius, p. 63). Not only Israel but all the nations share in the mercy which is won by the Son — Israel receives the special mercy and the heathens the general dispensation *(Cr,* XIV, p. 4; cf. Wencelius, p. 63).

The special mercy deploys in Jerusalem, the joy of the whole world for the sake of its beauty (Ps. 48:3). There Jesus Christ, in whom all the fulness — and therefore also the beauty of the Godhead — is embodied is crucified (Colossians 2:9). At the destined moment the glory of Christ will be disseminated to the heathen nations.

Whatever has been deformed by the Fall, is reformed through the redemption, the deliverance of Christ, and restored to beauty. He also opens the eyes of the redeemed so that they can once more see the beauty of God's glory in all his works.

The essence of beauty

Beauty, for Calvin, is not an impersonal principle as it was among the Greeks. It is equally not, as the Thomists would have it, a cathedral which is gazed at from the heights by a sanctified intellectual without an awareness of the tragedy of the Fall.

For Calvin beauty is the emanation, the radiation of the glory of God. Wherever God is to be found, there is beauty to be found. The contitutive elements of beauty are the following: Firstly: clarity, light, reflection of the glory of God. Secondly: harmony, order, as revealed in the Creation of God, his great work of art. Thirdly: fulness, perfection, excellence, ultimateness *(CR,* XXVIII, p. 36; *institutes,* IV, VIII, 12; cf. Wencelius, n.d. p. 46). In one sentence Wencelius sums up all Calvin's statements on beauty: "En résumé, les elements objectifs de la beauté sont la clarté, l'ordre et la perfection" (n.d., p. 47). But then it should be unequivocally clear: beauty is not something that can stand on its own, an independent greatness which has its own existence. "Beauty is an aspect of God, a reflex of his attributes, a reflection of his works" (Wencelius, 1940, p. 52).

For Calvin the beauty of the universe is like a vast fresco which is unrolled throughout the entire course of time. It looks like a gigantic triptych which hinges on the Fall and the Redemption. The first panel is Creation in all its glory. The second is fallen man, who is gradually, in the shape of the chosen, being led to God through Christ. The third is in the process of being painted now: mankind on his march to his eternal destination (Wencelius, n.d., p. 94). With this triptych in mind, one could fruitfully look at Calvin's ideas on art in the light of his ideas on beauty.

Calvin's views on art

God as an Artist

God is the Great Artist, "le grand artisan" (Wencelius, n.d., p. 101), the Divine Architect, the Worker, the "mirus Artifex" *(CR,* VI, p. 258); XLIX, p. 51; Wencelius, 1940, p. 253). The universe is his masterpiece (Wencelius, n.d., p. 101).

Art as a gift of God's general grace

God is "autor et dator omnium artium" *(CR,* XXXIX, p. 694; cf Wencelius, n.d. p. 98). The Author and the Giver gives all this through the working of his Holy Spirit in his general grace without distinction to the faithful and the unfaithful, to the good and the bad. There are, for example, heathen authors in whose works the light of truth shines wonderfully luminously (Calvin, Institutes, II, II, 14, 25,; CR. XXV, p. 58).

The nature, the essence, of art

According to Calvin's concept each activity in which man indulges which assumes a shape of beauty should be regarded as art (Wencelius, 1940, p. 71).

For Calvin art is therefore not a thing apart, something apart from everday life.

The artist can equally well be an artisan as the labourer may be one. As the skilled artisan is a man with specific talent and training for his craft, so the artist is one with regard to art. "Traditionally, and certainly in Calvin's day, the word 'Art' simply meant a high degree of skill or ability and the Artist was essentially a craftsman, someone who could take words, sounds, colours or materials and make something new and wonderful ... He (the Artist — PWB) can be a servant of God in his work, just as Bezaleel and Aholiab were: as Calvin asserts, 'All craftsmen of whatever kind, who serve the needs of men, are ministers of God'" (Wilson, 1980, p. 27).

The purpose of the arts

Art has a dual purpose: to the glory of God and the service of mankind. If man should eat and drink to the glory of God, as Paul exhorts him to do in 1 Corinthians 10:31, then he should definitely also paint, write and compose to the glory of God (Wilson, 1980, p. 27). The service of man can be divided into two sections: teaching, and enjoyment, or to use Wilson's words (he does not mention his sources, unfortunately) "to instruct and amuse" (Wilson, p. 27). Whatever is done for the sake of the glory of God necessarily also has to contribute to the benefit and the edification of man.

Falsification of art

Through sin man's vision has become so warped that he cannot see any further than the immediate phenomena themselves. Instead of perceiving the sign of God's presence in each perceptible manifestation of pure beauty, sinful man accepts the appearance of things as the highest reality and tends to the thing itself into an independent object of prayer (Wencelius, 1940, p. 251). In this way, through the pride and vanity of men, a supernatural meaning is attached to secular things, which in actual fact they do not have (CR, XLIX, p. 53; cf. Wencelius, p. 106).

When the artist forgets that his talent is a gift from God which should be exploited in the service of God, falsification enters into his art. Then it becomes "l'art pour l'art", which endows art with its own independent value, intrinsic to itself and apart from God. This leads to the worship of idols and to blindness and foolishness, as could be found in Athens (CR, XLVIII, p. 403; cf. Wencelius, n.d., p. 119).

Such a falsified art is without limits, and limits constitute the law that artist has to obey. He who gives rein freely to his imagination, transgresses the boundaries of nature. In this way the gift of God is warped and art is corrupted. When man and his art are alienated from God, both become increasingly corrupted (CR, XXXIX, p. 426; cf. Wencelius, n.d., p. 120).

There is even art inspired by Satan. This happens when the artist, like Aaron, forgets his serving, priestly vocation. Aaron himself, when he made the golden calf, was no better than a clown in a theatre, because, when he forsook his priestly vocation, he was spoilt by the taste for the outward splendour of idolatry (CR, XXV, p. 218; cf. Wencelius, n.d., p. 120).

Calvin's contribution to art

Apart from the contribution Calvin made to liberate art from the oppression of the Roman Catholic Church (cf. Wilson, 1980, p. 26; Kuyper, 1898, p. 152) Calvin also did a great deal to promote art.

Calvin, as one of the greatest writers of his era, is generally regarded as the creator of literary French. With his crystal clear, direct and simple style he made an idelible impression on literature written after his period.

The inauguration of the Genevan Psalter with its excellent musical qualities was a direct result of Calvin's labours (Doumergue, 1904A, p. 410 f; Wencelius, 1940, p. 257).

The influence of Calvin in the Netherlands is regarded by Goulon (1917, p. 82) as one of the most important causes behind the flowering of Dutch art in the seventeenth century, the Dutch Golden Age. According to Goulon Rembrandt's art is the ideal typical example of Calvinist influence in the arts.

This will gradually make nonsense of the legend that Calvin should have been hostile to the arts (cf. Doumergue, 1904A, p. 417; 1904B, p. 8 f; Spelman, 1947, p. 25; Pollmann, n.d., p. 5).

Calvin's message for contemporary art

Calvin strove to liberate the arts from the oppression of the Roman Catholic Church and to bring them under the dominion of the Word of God.

The liberalism of the French Revolution strove to free the arts from the sovereignty of God and his Word.

This "liberation" culminated in the cry of "l'art pour l'art".

"The unilateral experience of *l'art pour l'art* of necessity led to an absolutization of art and to an absolutization of certain elements of art. One need only think of Kloos 'deification of art, and Van Deyssel's statement that' the word alone *is'''* (Dekker, 1964, p. 34).

Look in this regard at the statement by Rosenberg (1976, p. 175) on the art of CH Bosman: "If the word was his only religion, poetry was his only God".

In the twentieth century, existentialism with its cry of *God is dead* has made an important contribution to the struggle to liberate art completely from the dominion of God. The revolution of the twentieth century has also been fulfilled in the field of art (Chipp, 1968, p. 501). The post-Christian, post-humanist, neo-paganist, nihilist, anarchist world (cf. Rookmaker, 1970, p. 246) has found its echo in art also. The artist, finely tuned, knows that in a world as dislocated as this one, there is often no other recourse than to seek refuge in the sphere of the absurd. This brings van der Walt (n.d., p. 3) to the conclusion that "more than ever, uncertainty and confusion reign in and around modern literature, as well as regards the plastic arts, such as abstract painting, non-figurative sculpture, leaving aside for the moment atonal music, 'op' and 'pop' art in general ..." Opperman finds it typical of contemporary visions of art that "art is evil ... For art the Fall was essential. The drinking companion of the artist is Satan" (1959, p. 142 f).

Art, according to Dekker (1964, p. 34), is intended in the last analysis to be a norm of life, a valuable spiritual treasure, which has a place in the totality of the cultural heritage of civilized man. But then it has to be a meaningful norm of life. It must have content. It should say something (Boeve, 1959, p. 9). A Christian may make the demand that his artistic heritage be correlated with his life's direction towards God (be it ever so indirectly).

For contemporary art (exceptions left out of consideration for the moment) the following statement by Wilson would seem to be very applicable (1980, p. 25): "The arts have lost their way". He continues: "Today, empty picture frames, or paint-splattered canvases, are presented as works of art and objects without shape or form are exhibited as sculpture. Much poetry is neither poetic nor meaningful; music is oftern merely loud, without harmony or joy, and contemporary literature has little in content or value. Even in the best of drama it now seems necessary to punctuate the dialogue with the gutter language of obscenity or blasphemy. The contemporary arts, having thrown the last shackles of freedom now find, rather than a glorious new freedom, they are descending into anarchy ... So it is no surprise to find a leading American Art Critic confessing that 'today art exists but it lacks a reason for existing'."

If contemporary art should ever want to become a meaningful norm for life, then the artists would be able to listen fruitfully to the message of Calvin which is contained in the following four rules.

Because art is a gift from God, the artist has to conform to the will of the Giver. However beautiful works of art might be, and however much they may be admired by many — they will have no lasting value if they do not conform to the will of God. Art has to be subjected to the Word and the Spirit of God. This is the absolute ground rule in Calvin's vision of art *(CR,* XLVII, P. 7; cf. Wencelius, n.d., p. 109). Art which does not stay in accord with the Word and the Spirit of God is like a flower that has been detached from its stem. It wilts and withers away.

Submission to the Word and the Spirit of God includes obedience to the nature of things. In the nature of the materials that the artist uses, laws of God lie concealed. These have to be discovered. They delimit the arts. The artist has to find his frontiers in the bosom of nature. He has to obey the laws of nature. He sould not try to circumvent the limits set by these laws. Does the rock claim that God is contained within him? No. For that reason, then, the sculptor should make no idols. Deification of art is foolish. Jeremiah rightly taunted King Jehoiakim because he wanted to change the nature of things by means of vain ornaments of his palace *(CR,* XXXVIII, p. 385; cf. Wencelius, n.d., p. 110).

To develop mastery means that the artist has to start humbly. A great deal of hard practice is necessary. The artist has to imitate the servant in the parable of the talents. He owes it to God, the Giver of his talent.

Only the artist who is willing to practise long and hard will attain mastery *(CR,* L, p. 471; cf. Wencelius, p. 111).

Finally, the artist has to be temperate. He has received a special gift from God, but the gift does not deify the artist. For that reason the artist should never presume outside his measure. The gifts of God, after all, are not intended to harm man but have been made available for the wellbeing of mankind. Temperateness has many aspects. It is valid for the artistic vision, for the expression of the vision, and for the use of the gift. Each gift has its own place within the economy of human life. Where art is concerned, balance is essential. One may not ignore art — that would be overdone strictness. One equally should not make art the centre of one's life, because it is not right to make a natural gift the centre of life, of human existence.

Temperateness gives joy. The artist who is conscious of having received his gift from God and who wishes to use it to the greater glory of God brings the art lover into contact with God, and that is joyful. What has to be avoided is joy which is not coherent with the fear of God and the service of man.

This also implies that the artist has to be humble. He should never forget that God is his Example and that, seen next to the Creator, he is nothing. On what could he, a fallen creature, base any grandiose assumptions, anyway? What he does is not from himself, but a gift from God.

Non-observance of these rule usually culminates in an art that is against Christ and an art that believes that art in itself is sufficient unto itself. As regards the first, it is a "noxia pestis", a corrupting pestilence, and as regards the second, "l'art pour l'art", art for the sake of art, is the most dangerous of all obstacles for art.

The credo should therefore not be "l'art", but "l'art pour Dieu". Art should be a gift of God and should be utilized to the glory of God.

Résumé

Calvin is not hostile to art, as has often been suggested. In fact, he has made a real and great contribution towards promoting art.

Calvin worked towards liberating art from the oppression of the church. According to him art should be seen as being in the service of God and not in the service of the church.

Beauty has its origin in God. It is the illuminated vision of his glory. Through the Fall beauty has been corrupted, but through the general grace of God much has nevertheless been retained. Satan is a falsifier of beauty.

God is the Source and the Giver of art. In accordance with his general grace he shares it out to all of mankind and for the service of mankind.

For contemporary art, which has often been the victim of humanism, liberalism and existentialism, Calvin has an important message: Art will only be a meaningful norm of life if it conforms to the glory of God and is practised according to the will of God.

Soli deo gloria

BIBLIOGRAPHY

BOEVE, E.J. 1959. Calvinism and art. *The Banner,* 94:31, 31 July.

CALVIN, J. 1949. Institutes, I-III. Translated from the Latin by A Sizoo. Delft:

CHIPP, H.B. 1968. Theories of modern art. Berkeley : University of California.

CORPUS REFORMATORUM. 1863-1900. Brunswyk, Schwerkse.

DEKKER, G. 1964. Oordeel en besinning. Cape Town, Human & Rousseau.

DOUMERGUE, E. 1904A. Calvijn in het strijdperk. Translated by W.F.A. Winckel. Amsterdam, Kirchner.

DOUMERGUE, E. 1904B. Kunst en gevoel in het werk van Calvijn. Drie lezingen, From the French, by W.F.A. Winckel. Wageningen, Nederbragt.

GOULON. 1917. Der Calvinismus und die Kunst. *Reformierte Kirchenzeitung,* 67:10, 11 March.

OPPERMAN, D.J. 1959. Wiggelstok. Cape Town, Nasionale Boekhandel.

POLLMANN, J. n.d. Calvijns Aesthetica. *(In:* Studiën-reeks no. 4. 's Hertogenbosch, Malmberg.)

ROOKMAKER, H.R. 1970. Modern Art and the death of a culture. S.P. Inter-varsity Press.

ROSENBERG, Valerie. 1976. Sunflower to the sun. Cape Town, Human & Rousseau.

SPELMAN, L.P. 1947. Calvin and the arts. *Buffalo Gallery Notes,* Vol. 12.

VAN DER WALT, P.D. n.d. Die Calvinis en die kuns. Potchefstroom, Institute for the Advancement of Calvinism.

WENCELIUS, L. 1940. Calvyn se kunsfilosofie. (Calvin's philosophy of art. Translated from the French at the responsibility of the editorial board.) *(In:* Federasie van die Calvinistiese Studenteverenigings in Suid-Afrika. Koers in die krisis, II, Stellenbosch, Pro Ecclesia-Drukkery.)

WENCELIUS, L. n.d. L'esthétique de Calvin. Paris, Société d'edition "Les Belles Lettres".

WILSON, J. 1980. For his glory and our good. A Calvinist view of the arts. *Monthly Record.* Free Church of Scotland. February.

24. CALVIN ON ART : CALVIN DEFENDED AGAINST (SOME OF) HIS SUPPORTERS

MR J.J. SNYMAN*

In a discussion of Calvin's concept of art, the following two approaches can be distinguished:

* the significance of Calvin's aesthetics for the contemporary situation; and

* the significance of Calvin's thoughts (in the wider sense) for the contemporary situation in the arts.

Roughly the distinction is intended to deal with both (a) the discontinuity and (b) the continuity between ideas on art in Calvin's time and in our own times, because what Calvin had to say on the arts is not blindly applicable in our times. But with that Calvin is not of course to be disregarded. The position that I would like to defend is that we cannot unqualifiedly go to Calvin's aesthetics (and therefore, according to many of his commentators, his philosophy of art) and take from it material (this is quite apart from those who say we *must)* to help solve the problems of contemporary works of art and practices in the field of art. Calvin's *aesthetics* and *philosophy of art* have become practically completely dated. What does remain a possibility, however, is his view of human culture and man's calling. In this Calvin made real breakthroughs, which are still speaking to us today.

Let me defend my initial statement on the historical relativity of Calvin's view of art:

One should in the first place keep in mind the nature of Calvin's statements on the arts. Art was never one of his major fields of interest. Apart from his Preface to the Genevan Psalter of 1542 Calvin only expressed himself as it were in passing within the framework of other (especially theological) genres on the arts — and then mainly as subsections of other arguments. Even this preface to

* His address is: Dept. of Philosophy, Rand Afrikaans University, P.O. Box 524, Johannesburg, RSA 2000.

the Genevan Psalter is no real aesthetics or philosophy of art. It is rather a short thesis on liturgy, with a focussing on the place and the significance of music in worship. An art-philosophical thesis on music it cannot pretend to be. This does not mean, however, that Calvin did not hold to a view of art (in this treatise also). His thorough schooling in the Humanist rhetorical tradition (of, amongst others, Erasmus and Budé) must testify to such an assumption[1]. But even then it remains valid to assert that Calvin had an implicit concept of art rather than a systematic and articulated aesthetics. And perhaps exactly because it was an implicit view, Calvin stands squarely within the tradition of the late Middle Ages, and therefore he represents not the same significant difference from the prevalent views of his own time in this field — as he did in his view of the church, the calling of man, and even his ideas regarding economics. Even a "systematization" of Calvin's views by Léon Wencelius[2] cannot destroy the impression that in his socalled concept of art and beauty Calvin is nearer to the neo-Platonic philosophic tradition regarding a cosmologic doctrine of beauty. On this front he was not yet able to create a consistent distance from Scholasticism, which borrowed nearly all of its concepts of beauty and art from pagan thought. The neo-Platonic tradition established itself so firmly within the tradition of exegesis[3] of the Scriptures (via *allegoresis,* for which it has such a strong affinity), even after the Middle Ages and the Reformation, that Scriptures are still exegetized within this framework — with a referral always to Calvin, who is quoted as an authority, especially where the focus is on beauty.

In the preceding section Calvin's *so-called* vision of art was discussed. This brings me to a second reason for the statement on the dated quality of Calvin's aesthetics. Calvin, in truth, never did have a doctrine of art in the way Wencelius insists. Calvin refers to music, drama and poetry within the framework of the didascalic literature of the late Middle Ages, that is, within the setup of the so-called free and mechanical arts[4]. Wencelius on his part refers to art in Calvin within

[1] Cf. for example Francois Wendel. 1973. *Calvin. The origins and development of his religious thought.* London, Collins, pp. 27-37.

[2] Léon Wencelius, 1959, *L'esthétique de Calvin,* Les Belles Lettres, Paris, Aubier.

[3] Henri de Lubac, 1959. *Exégese médiévale. Les quatres sens de l'Ectriture.* Paris, Aubier.

[4] Cf. *The Didascalicon of Hugh of St Victor; a medieval guide to the arts.* Translated from the Latin with an introduction and notes by Jerome Taylor. New York, Columbia University press, 1961. Also see John E. Murdoch and Edith D. Sylla (eds.), 1975, *The cultural context of Medieval learning.* Dordrecht, D. Reidel. 1975.

the framework of the Renaissance ideal of art as something elevated which is not incorporated into everyday culture as an object of use[5]. In short, we here have to do with *two different art-historical paradigms* on art, viz. *artes liberales* (the free arts) and *beaux arts* (fine arts). Add to this the fact that nowadays we experience art within a still different paradigm from both Calvin and Wencelius. Not only are our problems regarding contemporary art very real and serious, but we also have problems to bridge the distances between the philosophical frameworks of our own times and those of Calvin, especially with regard to the arts.

The differences in the paradigms (or, as C.A. van Peursen calls it, strategies of culture[6] — a method of explication of which I make grateful use, with some reservations) are, in brief, the following:

In Calvin's view music[7] is one of the seven free or liberal arts[8]. The first three *artes liberales* (called the *trivium*) include grammar, rhetoric and dialectics. The second group (the *quadrivium*) usually includes arithmetic, geometry, astronomy and music. This is a peculiar combination. It could, however, be explained by reference to the Pythagorean doctrine of numbers which plays a role here: the explanation of the relations between the heavenly bodies (in astronomy) makes use of the same proportions as music uses in the composition of the intervals of the various tones. From this one can conclude that these four free arts study different forms of *cosmic* harmony and that astronomy is nothing other than what Boethius (in the fourth century A.D.) already referred to as "the music of the spheres".

The most important aspect of this view of the arts is that it is *no view* of man-made artefacts. Music has to do not with *works* of music but with harmony as such, which, *amongst others,* is manifested in

---

[5] Helmut Kuhn, 1966. "Die romantische Kunstphilosophie." In his *Schriften zur Ästhetik.* München, Kösel, pp. 145-158.

[6] C.A. van Peursen, 1970, *Strategie van die cultuur. Een beeld van de veranderingen in de hedendaagse denk en leefwereld.* Amsterdam, Elsevier.

[7] Cf. Ross James Miller, 1971. *John Calvin and Reformation of church music in the sixteenth century.* Ph.D thesis, Claremont Graduate School and University Center, pp. 300-313. Also see *Ioannis Calvin Opera Quae Supersunt Omnia,* VII, p. 641: "Que nous ayons cette prudence de nous servir des arts tant libéraux que méchanique en passant par le monde pour tendre toujours au Royaume céleste."

[8] Cf. Paul Oskar Kristeller, 1970. "The modern system of the arts." In: Morris Weitz (ed.): *Problems in aesthetics.* London, Collier-Macmillan, pp. 108-163.

sound according to rules corresponding to a cosmological order — thus unchangeable and eternal, and generally comprehensible if the "book of nature" should be read correctly. Seen in this way, art constitutes part of an unreflected orientation as regards the world[9]. What is offered in music happens as a matter of course. It is offered as part of the daily process of living, as one of the many artefacts such as clothing or food. (For this reason the song of the troubadour and of the spiritual hymn differed so little in their key: to love and to pray were for the ordinary people simply different facets of one practice of life which had as its purpose the preparation for a life hereafter.) The conventions which held good for the products of the free and the mechanical arts were determined by the uses that the community had for them. For that reason the conventions governing music, poetry and painting in the Middle Ages were *generally known.* The artist was not respected as an individual creative artist. He was simply a member of a guild, and practised a trade — one among many. It was at most his expertise to create with the limited material and means at his disposal which aroused some curiosity. The Medieval artist was not a creator of wholly new conventions.

A view of the work of art as *artefact* was mostly absent. Yet not completely. God we seen as the Great Artist: an anthropomorphic representation, where analogy to *man and his ability to fabricate* something is said about God (cf. for example Isaiah 45:9). What does happen, is that the one pole of this analogy (human artistic activity as a model for explication of the unknown) is transferred to the second pole, so that human artistic activity in turn is now *derived* from divine artistic activity as *imaging,* the creation of secondary works of art deriving from the primary works of art of the creative deed of God. An *aesthetic* analogy is used to indicate the deed of creation of God and to make it accessible to man. In this way aesthetics becomes a theology (of creation and creativity) and the focus on the problems surrounding the making of things by man is obliterated[10]. In principle everything has already been explained by the indication of an Artist-Creator-God, and what man does is secondary, and therefore, in the face of the mystery of God's creation from nothing everything becomes a matter of course: man, after all, creates from that which as already been created. He only reflects that which God has already

[9] Cf. Wladyslaw Taterkiewicz, 1970. *History of aesthetics II,* Den Haag, Mouton, pp. 178-183, 285-303.

[10] Cf. Wilhelm Perpeet, 1977. *Ästhetik im Mittelalter.* München, Alber, pp. 22-25.

given.

For the individual from the late Middle Ages there is a hierarchical ordering of the arts. Those arts which had to do with the material care of man, such as tailoring, tanning or baking, are relatively low on the scale. They are essential, however, because they serve to uphold life. If man is not fed and clothed, he cannot prepare his soul for the hereafter. The highest art (which has to serve as preparation for man to come to insight as regards the mysteries of the Divine presence) in music, the art form least bound to the material needs of man. Music is the most spiritual of all the art forms. But music is still subservient to theology. Music by itself gives no insight into the Wisdom and the Truth of God. For that one needs a *Divine Theology*.

Wencelius' implicit concept of art with which he approaches Calvin can be circumscribed as that of the *fine arts*. This view of the arts came into its own especially after the Renaissance, and developed under the influence of a non-Christian humanistic culture. Where the Medieval tradition made of aesthetics a creation theology, the Renaissance secularized this theology and made of it a genius aesthetics[11]: the creative man now came to be regarded as something divine. The artist is now regarded as somebody who has received a special kind of grace, who can act as mediator between the higher sphere (of for example the existence of the truth in God) and the lower spheres of the existence of ordinary mortals. The artist is not only a genius — he is also covered with the cloak of the prophet: what he has to say is truth and beautiful beyond any doubt[12]. The artist offers truths which cannot be apprehended in any other way. For that reason he is hailed as an autonomous individual, an ununderstood innovator, a great celebrity, and art becomes something which should have a special status: museums, theatres and concert halls are specifically created for it. This is a phenomenon which has made itself widely known since the middle of the eighteenth century in Western Europe, and which goes hand in hand with the origin of aesthetics as a separate philosophical discipline. Alexander Baumgarten's *Aesthetica* (1750) is the first work to give works of art separate shape (if lesser shapes) of knowledge as truth.

[11] E. Zilsel, 1926. *Die Entstehung des Geniebegriffs*. Tübingen, Mohr.

[12] Rookmaaker, H.R. 1965. *De kunstenaar een profeet?* Kampen, Kok.

This respect for art, which often amounts to a religious reverence for art[13] as a substitute for the contents of the Gospels[14], together with the reverence extended to the artist[15], is something that has been characteristic of the period since the Renaissance. Art in all its ramifications occupies a very lofty place in the scale of cultural values. Art has now become the exclusive *organon* of truth[16], and cannot therefore be dragged down to the mundane and the everyday. It has to be elevated, and often (especially during the Enlightenment) it is entrusted with the task of the moral perfecting of mankind[17], because art could then be said to be less sectarian than (Christian) religion. The use of the term *fine arts* reveals something of this humanistic ideal of the dignity of man and the intrinsic value of his

---

[13] To mention only a few examples: in the first act of Mozart's *Zauberflöte* the three gentlewomen of the Queen of the Night sing the following song of praise to music:

Hiermit kannst du allmachtig handeln
Der Menschen Leidenschaft verwandeln.
Der Traurige wird freudig sein,
Den Hagestolz nimmt Liebe ein.

And the final stanza of Beethoven's *Choral Fantasia* reads like this:

Grosses, das in's Herz gedrungen
Blünt dann neu und schön empor,
Hat ein Geist sich aufgeschwungen,
Hallt ihm stets ein Geisterchor.
Nehmt denn hin, ihr schönen Seelen,
Froh die Gaben schöner Kunst.
Wenn sich Lieb' und Kraft vermählen,
Lohnt dem Menschen Götter-Gunst.

The image evoked by the Dutch poet of the Eighties, Willem Kloos, in his love sonnet "Ik ben een God in't diepste van mijn gedachten" is well-known.

[14] Cf. for example Friedrich Schiller: *Die Schaubühne als eine moralische Anstalt betrachtet:* "Unter so vielen herrlichen Früchten der bessern Bühne will nur zwei auszeichnen. Wie allgemein ist nur seit wenigen Jahren die Duldung der Religionen und Seckten geworden? ... Mit ebenso glücklichem Erfolge würden sich von der Schaubühne Irrtümer der Erziehung bekämpfen lassen ..." Or Richard Wagner on his own musical art (in his *Oper und Drama):* "Das Christentum hat die Einheit der menschlichen Gattung in ahnungsvoller Verzückung verkündet: die Kunst, die dem Christentume ihre eigentümlichste Entwicklung verdankte, die Musik, hat jenes Evangelium in sich aufgenommen und zu schwelgerisch entzückender Kundgebung an das sinnliche Gefühl als moderne Tonsprache gestaltet."

[15] Cf. Friedrich Nietzsche (1966, *Werke III* [Hrsg. Schlechta], München, Hanser, p. 754): "Der Künstler gehört zu einer noch stärkeren Rasse. Was uns schon schädlich, was bei uns krankhaft wäre, ist bei ihm Natur."

[16] Cf. F.W.J. Schelling, 1957. *System des transzendentalen Idealismus.* Hamburg, Felix Meiner, pp. 294, 297. See also his *Philosophie der Kunst,* 1974, Darmstadt, Wissenschaftliche Buchgesellschaft, pp. 1-16.

[17] As for example Schiller and Hegel.

life[18].

In our own age little is left of this reverence for the arts; in fact, the greater part of contempary artistic production is bent upon demythologizing the concept of *fine arts*[19]. Various reasons might be advanced for this, of which the most important would undoubtedly be the disillusionment with the results of the humanistic ideal. Two world wars were necessary to reveal the unstable foundations of this ideal to mankind. For that reason there is a deliberate attempt to break down the concept of art as edifying and elevated. There is a positive side to this protest against the fine arts too: the concern nowadays is rather to integrate that which is aesthetic into life, or to discover in something like the "encountered object" the coincidental nature of beauty as against the deliberately planned beauty of the majestic, created work of art[20]. Amongst others the aesthetic becomes a part of the packaging of the (consumer) world[21]. Elements of form, of colour and of meaning are offered, and the spectator/listener can make of these what he wants to.

When something is presented as art today, it is dependent to a large extent on the public for its effect as a work of art: there has to be a response to that which is offered. In this a great development has taken place in the subjectivization of the aesthetic: during the Middle Ages beauty (according to metrical analogues) was seen as something independent of man. Man would then at most be a *copier* of the *ontic beauty.* After the Renaissance beauty came to be seen as something of the inner experience of man,[22] especially of the artist, in which *expression* is given to something *subjectively attractive.* Since the

---

[18] A very eloquent statement of this is to be found in Beethoven's so-called *Heiligenstadter Testament:* "O Menschen, wenn ihr dieses lieset, so denkt, dass ihr mir Unrecht getan, und der Unglückliche, er tröste sich, eines seinesgleichen zu finden, der trotz allen Hindernissen der natur doch noch alles getan, was in seinem Vermögen stand, um in die Reihe würdige Künstler und Menschen aufgenommen zu werden."

[19] See all the various studies brought together in H.R. Jauss (ed.), 1968, *Die nicht mehr schönen Künste. Grenzphänomene des Äesthetischen.* München, Fink.

[20] Peter Bürger, 1974, *Theorie des Avantgarde.* Frankfurt-am-Main, Suhrkamp, pp. 26-35, 63-81.

[21] For one kind of approach to this problem, see Walter Biemel: "Pop-Art und Lebenswelt." In: Wolfhart Henckmann (ed.), 1979, *Äesthetik.* Darmstadt, Wissenschaftliche Buchgesellschaft, pp. 148-189. As against this phenomenological approach there is the approach of a neo-Marxist like Wolfgang Fritz Haug, 1977 *Kritik der Warenästhetik.* Frankfurt-am- Main, Suhrkamp.

[22] Immanuel Kant: Kritik der Urteilskraft §35.

beginning of the 20th century the reaction of the public has become part of the *event* or the *happening* of the work of art: the description of the response to something now becomes the actual "happening". In this way the boundaries of the aesthetic are often transgressed, exactly in the course of the effort to bring that which was in earlier times revered as a manmade artefact to an "ordinary" human level. Art as a "status symbol" is attacked, and the myth of "beautiful" elevated or great art is demolished (often with great right).

The demythologizing of art shows a similarity with the first cultural strategy: art is nothing special seperated from man's day to day business, but is part of his everyday life and experience. There is nothing mysterious or wonderful about art. The difference with the first cultural strategy (and in fact the similarity with the second one) is the elemination of bonds of convention binding both artist and public.

Should one then desire to state that Calvin's aesthetics and concept of art still have something to say about modern art, then one has to be careful not to step into one or both of two traps. On the one hand a concept (according to Calvin á la Wencelius) of art as beauty is too narrow, while on the other hand such a concept is too wide.

As a result of this view, there is too strong a tendency to see art only as something that is attractive or beautiful, or at any rate only that sort of thing for which one would or should go to a museum. Let me make it clear: there is room in human life for all these things. But this is not the sum total of what is meant by art and the aesthetic. The equate *fine art* with the *classics* and thus also with *Christian* art cannot deal adequately with the idea of the aesthetic in the form of for example advertising or environmental art — which, if one should take seriously Wencelius' prescription that art should reflect the glory of God would deny that these products are art, while the working of advertising rests on a wellknown aesthetic "technique", viz. the offering of a part which has to evoke the whole in the mind of the consumer. If the aesthetic facet of something like a car or a toothbrush cannot be accommodated in a concept of art and the aesthetic as a result of this narrow vision of what constitutes beauty, then a polarization of the aesthetic between the profane and the sacred amongst other things could be the result — and history testifies to the fact that this tension has never been particularly fruitful. This approach is deficient for another reason as well, for it is merely an aesthetics of content, and so misleads the public into

307

thinking that the experience of beauty only has to do with the recognition of beauty. If the work of art is not readily comprehensible, there is always the sanctuary of stating the comfartable *dictum* that taste is a subjective matter. The fact that there is more to a work of art than merely the experience of the beauty of it (although in some works of art this might be the primary ingredient of the enjoyment of the work of art), such as the understanding of suggestion, symbol or motif, the investigation of "clues" and structuring of the whole, will inevitably be negated by this narrow vision.

A concept of art as beauty is too wide — on the other hand. Too often "clean", "pure" art is regarded as being Christian. "Pure" or classical art, such as Mozart's *Zauberflöte* or Beethoven's *Choral Fantasia* or Ninth Symphony, cannot be regarded as Christian, as they stand firmly within the tradition of Enlightenment Humanism. As against this there are the cantatas of Kurt Hessenberg and Penderecki's *Passion of Luke,* or the clown faces of Georges Rouault which are not "pure" or "beautiful" art, and not pleasent to experience, but which are truly Christian in spirit. Let me formulate this dilemma more clearly: If it is postulated that art, in order to be art, has to be beautiful, then very little has been said about art at all. This is *no* guideline in the choice of a style. Style is the paradigmatic (that is, the aspects of lifeview, often in conjunction with aesthetic and philosophical considerations, albeit unconsciously) adaptation of the expressive possibilities of the material. A choice between, for example, a baroque counterpoint and an atonal "harmony" *as such* has nothing to do with any formulable demand of Christian and beautiful art. Because a paradigm unlocks certain aspects of meaning, and covers up others, both these styles can give expression to certain (but then only certain) facets of the Christian experience. But both these styles can also be used for the expression of other kinds of lifeview. Elements such as style, material and genre are ambivalent, even multivalent, when it comes to the manifestation of one or the other "spirit". Can one therefore so clearly and distinctly state what is beautiful and what is Christian?

Ever since Plotinus, goodness and beauty have been identified with God. Within the Christian tradition since Augustine, and especially under the influence of the light metaphysics of high Scholasticism, the following two approaches — also within the intellectual pattern of Calvinism — found fruitful ground:

* God reveals Himself always/only in the form of beauty.

* The beautiful, because it is one of the vestiges of the Divine, is by definition always/only the good.

Both statements are problematic — on Scriptural grounds as well.

In the first place, "Nobody can see God and live". If God then reveals Himself only in beauty, and then as beauty is generally defined in aesthetics after the Renaissance (as in Wencelius too), as the attractive, then these revelations of the beauty of God must of necessity be either partial, veiled revelations, or this *dictum* from Scripture must have a different meaning. Also: can the revelation of God be reduced so to aestheticism? And can one view it so narcisistically that God "would have his glory reflected"? Furthermore: if God reveals Himself in the destruction of the armies of Pharaoh at the Red Sea, or allows his fury to break out at the Crucifixion of Christ or in the final judgement according to the Book of Revelations, can there then be any talk of beauty? All this might well be gripping, but not exactly beautiful. And this then merely undrlines the fact that aesthetics is concerned with more than the merely beautiful.

In the second place, Augustine links the *deformitas* resulting from sin exclusively with the *humilitas passionis Christi.* He has reason for that, amongst others with reference to Isaiah 53. But it becomes very problematical to link sin and grotesqueness with each other within a Christian aesthetics. The God-defiling may also reveal itself within the guise of beauty. In the Book of Revelations the whore of Babylon uses the arts to seduce mankind (which fact underlies the suspicion of many Reformed thinkers regarding the arts). The crux of the matter — which is not clarified in a theology of beauty, not in Augustine, Calvin or Wencelius — is: how should one recognise the grotesqueness underlying the shapes of beauty? Sermons often makes it sound as if this whore will be readily recognizable from the description of the Book of Revelations. This is very much within the naive assumption that one merely has to look out for sex and swear words, and then one would not have to worry anymore, because then one has to do with that which is not beautiful, and therefore not art. Beauty is an ambivalent phenomenon, however, contrary to what Medieval and Renaissance tradition would like to suggest. A philosophy of art which does not take cognizance of this, will too easily revert to a sterile Puritanical canon of proscription or will demand (imperialistically) that *all* products of art should testify to a humanist or Christian vision of reality. Because a hermeneutics of art is lacking

309

one then neglects to cope with the *subtle spirits* of works of art. It is conceded that the (Christian) artists may portray sin, but that he is not allowed to enjoy it or to indulge in the sinful. Should a public, however, be confronted with the tarnishing effect of sin in all its intensity, as in Rouault's prostitutes, or in Etienne Le Roux's *Seven Days at the Silbersteins,* then there is trouble, and a Christian aesthetic which is founded on a theology of beauty is tumped. To counter this "dirty" art, Goethe, or Leipoldt, is advanced as an example of "beautiful" or "pure" art. But even the classical or the folk art of these two artists is not alltogether free from non-Christian elements. The dilemma then seemingly is: rather "beautiful" but humanist art than "dirty" and Christian art. A *Christian* aesthetic of the ugly still remains to be written[23].

If we should desire to ascribe "eternal value" to art, do we not then become victims of the humanist idolatry of art since especially the eighteenth century?

Art is, after all, the contrivance of man, and to reserve eternal value for man, to try to express in that way a sense of the lasting and continuing fascination of the works of a Shakespeare, for example, is in conflict at one point with a basic truth of Calvinism, which is that even the best works contrived by man have been tarnished by sin. The fact that art is manmade is easily lost sight of with another (substantialist) formula which apparently hangs together with the concept of the eternal value of art: art as a gift from God. The motivation for this idea, which is often reiterated, is a Romantic concept[24] (which occurs among both Christians[25] and Neo-

[23] In like Manner Karl Rosenkrantz wrote an *Äesthetik des Hässlichen* following on Hegel's speculative äesthetics (Königsberg, Gebrüder Bornträger, 1853).

[24] E.G. Novalis (1969, *Werke* [Hsrg. Schulz] München, Beck, pp. 384-5): "Die Welt muss romantisiert werden. So findet man der ursprünglichen Sinn wieder. Romantisieren ist nichts, als eine qualitative Potenzierung. Das niedre Selbst wird mit einem bessern Selbst in dieser Operation identifiziert. So wie wir selbst eine solche qualitative Potenzenreihe sind. Diese Operation ist noch ganz unbekannt. Indem ich dem Gemeinen einen hohen Sinn, dem Gewöhnlichen ein geheimnisvolles Ansehn, dem Bekannten die Würde des Unbekannten, dem Endlichen einen unendlichen Schein gebe, so romantisiere ich es ..."

[25] Thus, for example, A. Kuyper (1959, *Het Calvinisme.* Kampen Kok, p. 129): "Staande bij de bouwval van de eens wonderschone schepping, toont dan de kunst ons èn de lijnen van het oorspronkelijk bestek, èn wat de Opperste Kunstenaar en Bouwmeester ons eenmaal nieuw uit de bouwval sal scheppen." See also Dekker, G: (1964, *Oordeel en besinning,* Cape Town, Human & Rousseau, pp. 30-1): "[Die mens] se taak van die voortsetting van die skeppingsproses word 'n poging tot herstel van die verlore skoonheid soos hy dit met sy verduisterde gees droom."

Marxists[26]): art as beauty is born from a longing for a better world. And precisely for that reason then art would be a gift of grace. What is not very clear in this view, especially among Christians, is whether, in talking about art as a gift of grace, one means a special revelation from Divine origin to the artist-seer, or merely the ability of man to create works of art? If it should be the latter, and rightly too, why then does one not hear that the same might be said of for example technology, science or politics? One seldom hears among Calvinists of Economics as a "gift from God". Or might it be that it is still the high esteem in which the Renaissance held art as an instrument of revelation of truth that still influences so many Calvinists? In this the Middle Ages (and Calvin, in as far as he tied in with this) had a much more balanced view: both the free and the mechanical arts (and among the latter economics had a place) were ways, instituted by God, working towards the temporal and eternal benediction of man.

What does Calvin have to say to us about art today?

For the sake of clarity I had perhaps better state it very clearly: direct statements by Calvin about art pose problems, being hardly applicable to the present situation[27]. But by way of a circuitous route he is topical. This circuitous route is his view of the place and the task of man within the Kingdom of God. I feel that one of the most fruitful linking points for a contemporary aesthetics in a Christian Reformed community is to be found in Calvin's vision of the vocation of man, and of human work[28]. It is along this route that one can clearly see

---

[26] Thus, for example, Th. W. Adorno(1972, *Äesthetische Theorie*. Frankfurt-am-Main, Suhrkamp, pp. 21-2): "In ihr [Kunst] ist aber auch der Wunsch am Werk, eine bessere Welt herzustellen." And on p. 204-5: "Die ästhetische Erfahrung ist die von etwas, was der Geist weder von der Welt noch von sich selbst schon hätte, Möglichkeit, verhiessen von ihrer Unmöglichkeit. Kunst ist das Versprechen des Glücks, das gebrochen wird."

[27] A comparison with the so-called aesthetics of Marx and Engels is apposite here. These two philosophers did say a great deal about the arts, but always in passing. A collection of these statements has made it clear that they must have had a sort of nineteenth-century bourgeois view of the arts: a great deal of a certain kind of reverence for amongst others Shakespear could be discerned in both. The development of criticism on the bourgeois stance deduced from Marx's main work, *Das Kapital,* especially by Georg Lukács, indicated that this view of art did not tie in with the foundational principles of Marx's own main interest.

[28] Cf. André Bieler, 1959, *La pensée économique et sociale de Calvin.* Genève, Georg, 1959.

what the radical difference is between Calvin's views and those of the Renaissance and Enlightenment regarding art and culture: man is in the service of Jahweh and cannot be regarded as a substitute of the Creator God. What this implies, however, has still in large parts to be worked out.

If one could embark on a programme, I would like to outline the following as priorities:

A lesson can be taken from criticism on metaphysics expressed in our time. For philosphy of art within the ranks of twentieth century Calvinism this means relinguishing the idea of explaining art from the viewpoint of one or the other theology of beauty. Art has to be seen as a manmade *artefact,* and therefore a *Christian cultural vision* is a condition, rather, for a justifiable Christian vision of art — more than a theology of beauty. If one should be able to "demythologize" the theology of beauty, one could perhaps arrive at the real place of beauty in art, and one could start devoting attention to other, equally fundamental problems regarding art.

Another important task for a philosophy of art within a Christian cultural strategy is the uncovering of the struggle of the spirits[29]: in a certain sense this implies the tarnishing of what has always been cherished as "elevated" art, while these were actually monuments of a non-Christian and even (since the eighteenth century) anti-Christian art[30]. Hermeneutics of art might fulfil a valuable function, and help to stimulate and inspire a discussion of important art of whatever persuasion from the *impasse* of a subjective judgement based on taste. But then one would have to be willing to take a certain tension in one's stride: if one understands something, one has the

---

[29] It would be worthwhile to pay some attention to Hans-Georg Gadamer's (admittedly) humanist reply to the question as to the truth to be found in art (1975, *Wahrheit und Methode,* Tübingen, Mohr, p. 93): "Die Ästhetik wird damit zu einer Geschichte der Weltanschauungen ..." Whether it does then become a history of the coming into being of the truth, as it becomes visible in the mirror of art, according to Gadamer, is to be doubted. This demands a faith in the unhindered and unadulterated working of the truth as something that is historically cumulative — a faith which cannot be defended on Scriptural grounds. The inability of man to revere truth makes it more probable that there will be a history of untruths.

[30] The warning by Wilhelm Perpeet (op. cit. p. 111) is apposite here: "Darum kann eine Geschichte der Ästhetik als Geschichte einer Philosophie des Schönen ... auch nicht als eine des Fortschritts in der Weise geschrieben werden, dass sie mitteilen könnte, ob und wie Bewunderung des Schönen von Epoche zu Epoche zugenommen und ob und wie Begründing dieses staunenswerten Phänomens von Epoche zu Epoche an Unbezweifelbarkeit gewonnen hat."

tendency to appreciate it in one way or another. It could then happen that one understands a great, non-Christian work of art, and simply because the structure of the work is so absorbing, one returns to it again and again. (In the humanities this is not at all strange, for devoted Christians are, for example, experts on Marx or Nietzsche.) From this results a further task, or I should perhaps say that the hermeneutics of art results in one being forced to consider the following issue: What is responsible for the fact that something might become art even in spite of its contents centring on lifeview? In this respect one has to delve deeper than merely considerations of beauty.

Beauty remains one of the major themes of any aesthetics. But then one has to bear in mind the developments in aesthetics in recent times: beauty should not be equated with art without further ado. Kant already proposed an important distinction, which cannot easily be ignored: the naturally beautiful and the beauty of art. With this he has stated that the beauty of art is a humanly *contrived* beauty, as well as the fact that beauty is merely an element of art. A philosophy of art should offer a thorough analysis of the *work character* of art, and here one has to lean heavily on a philosophy of culture.

The liberation that Calvin brought about with his view of the equality and the variety of vocations can be extended to work within a cultural strategy for art. Not only serious and elevated art should be accorded a place in human life — there is also room for such things as decoration, entertainment, etc. Art is not a luxury that one can forego, but constitutes an integral part of the whole life of man. Each individual has his own aesthetic calling, and this should be seen as more compelling than merely making pretty pictures to adorn the walls of houses[31].

---

[31] Cf. Calvin Seerveld, 1974, *A turnabout in aesthetics to understanding.* Toronto, Institute for Christian Studies, pp. 20-21.

25.   CALVIN AND ART. INTRODUCTION TO THE DISCUSSION

PROF. L.F. SCHULZE*

The two previous papers on Calvin's ideas about art are in a certain sense opposites. While Prof Buys follows the exposition of Wencelius, Mr Snyman contends that the views of Wencelius do not really reveal any artistic theory of Calvin.

I sympathize to a large extent with the paper of Prof. Buys, which gives us an overall view of what Calvin actually said in this respect. On the other hand I found the paper of Mr Snyman very well-documented, a fine exposition and very provocative.

Especially because of the thought-provoking statements of Mr Snyman, I will react to certain of his statements by making new ones, which may form the starting point for a discussion.

*   The fundamental point at issue, to be discussed, is the question whether Calvin still essentially belongs to the late Middle Ages. This is the viewpoint of Mr Snyman (cf. his paper, p. 301), and he makes his point, not only by referring to Calvin's views on art, but also by contrasting it to his view of the church and of economy. If it is indeed true, then the Reformers' conception of the relation of Word and Church was indeed totally different from the Medieval view and that Calvin's outright rejection of the Aristotelian doctrine of the unfruitfulness of money ("money cannot beget money"), believed to be founded on natural law, and the consequential admission of the justification of interest, was a fundamental move away from Medieval scholasticism, how can his views on art be essentially Medieval? Mr Snyman's thesis implies a dichotomy in Calvin's world view which, to my mind, is unacceptable.

*   Calvin did not expound a theory of art and Mr Snyman rightly remarks that his ideas about art are casually made. But, Calvin's view of art was part and parcel of his life and world view, which was

* His address is: Dept. of Dogmatics, Potchefstroom University for Christian Higher Education, Potchefstroom, RSA 2520.

something different from the Medieval one, because it was essentially *pneumatological, open* and *dynamic*. About each of these last three words a few remarks:

The world view of Calvin was pneumatological. Perhaps it is better to say the world view was a result of the newly-discovered relation with the living God in faith, which gave the Reformers a new understanding of the nearness, the loving kindness and paternal care of God. It is precisely for this reason that Calvin saw art as part of the ubiquitous working of the Spirit *(Inst.* I, 5, 5). Obviously, Calvin did not transcend his own time in his views on art, but, and this is crucial, he gave a new perspective on the notions of his time *(artes liberales,* etc.); he gave them a stamp of the Spirit; art being His gift for the *wellbeing* and the *pleasure* of man.

In this fundamental relation of the gracious God with man, arts are gifts of God. "Sculpture and painting", says Calvin, "are gifts of God" and ... "both shall be used purely and lawfully — that gift which the Lord has bestowed upon us for his glory and our good, should not be preposterously abused ..." *(Inst.* I, 11, 12).

Calvin's world view was no longer the closed causalistic conception of the Middle Ages. The structure of his thought was open to the ideas of Copernicus, and he saw the world as being led to its "telos". Because of this oppenness the arts and sciences could flourish in Reformed countries.

The world view was dynamic. Mr Snyman still wants to see Calvin's view as a static one. He states that the most important aspect of Calvin's view of the arts as *artes liberales* is, that it is *no* view of artefacts as specifically made by man. Music, he says, has not to do with *works* of music, but with harmony which is, inter alia, manifested in sound organized according to rules of a cosmological order (p. 3-4).

Calvin, however, says in *Inst.* II 2, 4: "Next come manual and liberal arts in learning which, as all have some degree of aptitude, the full force of human acuteness is displayed ... And this capacity extends not only to the learning of the art, but *to* the *devising of something new,* or the improvement of what has been previously learned".

These gifts are "confined to a few individuals". Was his whole engagement in the growth of the Genevan Psalter not a clear proof of what he said in *Inst.* II, 2, 4? The Psalter represents a new type of liturgical music — a simple melodious praise of God, far removed from the polyphonic structure and melismata of the late medieval Church music.

* I hope these remarks can form a basis for our discussion. And by way of a last thought:

● Was Calvin so totally a product of his time that his views are totally obsolete? Or did he, as biblical exegete, discover some biblical principles which are still relevant today?

● Can we honour Calvin's insistence on calling without acknowledging the necessary corollary: that God calls no one without bestowing gifts on him.

● What is the difference between the Renaissance and the Romantic conceptions of art and the artist?

26. CALVINUS REFORMATOR HODIE

PROF. J.A. HEYNS*

Calvin was a man like all other men, sinful and fallible. But in these last few days those of you who prepared and presented lectures, who introduced discussion, and took part in it, have all brought the greatness of this man before our very eyes.

You have helped us to see that Calvin's greatness did not reside primarily in his exceptional intellect, or in the force of his dynamic personality, or even in his unsurpassed dedication to his life's work.

You have shown us very clearly what made him great: all he had in the way of gifts and talents was directed inflexibly to God, offered unreservedly to God's service.

Yet this focus of his life and thought on God did not make of him a mystic who turned his back on earthly things. Far from it! The more the Spirit helped him to offer himself for God's service, the more he served people.

Your valiant efforts to understand Calvin and to share the results of your labours with others are in themselves, then, an imitation of this teacher. And so in conclusion I would most cordially and sincerely thank you one and all.

But now we must go further.

To remain in the past would mean that we had failed grievously to hear the message of the man we have been considering. So if, listening to him, we would move to the future, we have to ask: what has he to say to us.

Let us, then, turn our attention briefly to a few aspects of his message.

Calvin did all he could to bind the men of his day, their doctrine and

---

* His address is: The University of Pretoria, Hillcrest, Pretoria. RSA 0083.

life, unconditionally to the Word of God. And I believe that this is also his basic message to us here and now. Over against superstitious attachment to ecclesiastical pronouncements and tradition, over against the errors of those who would heed the voice of the inner light, Calvin posits the exclusive authority of God's Word over the Church and theology, over government and politics, over science and art. Thereby in principle we escape both the perils of subjectivism and objectivism. But we still have to work out all the implications of the significance of God's Word as the cardinal point towards which all human activities must be orientated.

Scripture has absolute authority, seeing that the God of Scripture is the Creator of heaven and earth, the Centre around whom everything revolves. This sovereignty of God means that he is 'open' to the world, that he has an eye and an ear for the world, that he guides and directs everything. But the world is also 'open' to him: it *allows* him to rule, *allows* him to dictate laws; it knows its need of a relationship with him; in every way it is subject to him. Not only man, but the whole cosmos is subject to God — the organic life of plants and animals, the realms of space and motion, as well as the sphere of numbers. It is this *theocentric* anchoring of reality, which Calvin discerned with such astonishing clarity and defended so indefatigably, that offers an indispensable corrective for our times with its anthropocentric views of reality.

It is precisely his confession of God's sovereignty that enables Calvin to emphasize the doctrine of providence. This is no blind, irrational, impersonal force, determining the destinies of individuals and peoples, for it all rests in God's hands, even though everything does not conform to his will. God knows what he wills, and what he wills he does. Nor is he blind; he perceives the future, and leads his creation towards it. And though we do not know, let alone understand, all he wills for this world, he has imparted to us enough to know that his ultimate purpose is the consummation and perfecting of this world. This is not to imply that Calvin teaches that providence can be deduced from impirical facts, still less that it may be equated with *our* prosperity and *our* success. For Calvin providence is something totally different from a religious sanctification of what happens in history or a desperate preservation of it. It is the *view* faith provides for interpreting facts, the discovery of the *direction* in which God is leading history and creation and humanity. And so, whatever the message of the facts might be, whatever adversity or prosperity we might experience, behind it all there stands the God of love, seeking to lead reality, ruined by sin, back to his original purpose for it. This is why Calvin warns us against localizing God's acts in single events, and then canonizing them so that they become normative.

Calvin also offers us enriching insights into the nature of Scripture itself. In Scripture we encounter the God who speaks; consequently the person who reads the Bible is linked to its text in an attitude of humble obedience and perpetual openness. The Holy Spirit triumphs over the natural resistance of the human heart. He indicates the 'matter' that Scripture wishes to communicate to us, as well as the organ of faith by which we can understand it. This 'matter' is the *scopus* of Scripture, and that *scopus* is Jesus Christ. Here Calvin's thinking is a corrective both to the modern, increasingly speculative ways of dealing with Scripture, and to the equally modern, horizontalistic political and social interpretations of its message. Similarly, his emphasis on the idea that the 'matter' — that is, the key message of the Bible — can be apprehended and understood only by faith is a rejection of any rationalistic approach to Scripture, which attempts to lay bare its message by the penetrating force of human thinking.

But Calvin's stress on *sola Scriptura* is at the same time also a *tota Scriptura*. 'Calvin's theology is not a closed system elaborated around one central idea, but it draws together the whole biblical message. If one searches Calvin's writings for a recurrent emphasis, this is what one finds: Speak where the Scriptures speak, be silent where they are silent.' The modern so-called genitive theologies — for example, the theology of hope, of revolution, of transformation, of development, of liberation, of society — stand condemned before Calvin's principle of *tota Scriptura*. For in them fundamental scriptural truths are often either neglected or constricted into a single theme, on the basis of which the overall message of Scripture is mangled and mutilated.

The principles of *sola Scriptura* and *tota Scriptura*, with Jesus Christ as the *scopus* of the Bible, have far-reaching consequences for Old Testament Science. Because Calvin posits the substantial unity of God's covenant of grace, he deduces that in its literal historical sense the Old Testament proclaims Christ. In fact, as the promise of God's grace, the Old Testament is already the Gospel. Calvin warns expressly against any artificial reading of the witness to Christ into every Old Testament text. We must keep constantly before us the fact that 'God did not give the Jews his covenant in the plain and clear portrayal of a finished painting ... but in the obscure indication of a charcoal outline'. Yet, no matter how vague or shadowy that outline might be, everyone who reads the Old Testament in faith meets Christ there.

For Calvin the exposition of Scripture is not the private domain of a lone theologian or even of a group of theologians. The hermeneutic sphere in which the interpretation of Scripture must take place and from which it is to be proclaimed is the Church, as the fellowship of faith. Here Calvin has a message of indescribably great significance for all Churches the world over, but especially for our South African ecclesiastical situation. In this country we have English-speaking, Afrikaans-speaking, German-speaking, Dutch- and Portuguese-speaking Churches. We also have white and black Churches. Now, says Calvin, the Church — that is, not an individual Church, but all the Chruches together — is called to understand the message of Scripture. In making this assertion, Calvin introduces an amazingly deep dimension, not only into the inter-relationships of our Reformed Churches, but also into our personal relationships with one another. The only authoritative source and bond of a living, vital relationship of faith with God and with one another is nothing less than the text of Scripture. What an overwhelming idea! The understanding of Scripture — that is to say, the voice of God himself — brings us together, and, in the fellowship of brothers in faith, we help one another, correct one another in continuing dialogue, aimed at a better understanding of the message of Scripture and a deeper insight into it. For us in South Africa there is no message more urgent than this!

This understanding of Scripture is a task that is never concluded, never completed, for God never ceases to speak. And as long as God speaks, just so long must man reflect on what God has taught him.

In asserting this, Calvin offers, not only theology, but the Church itself a dynamic dimension: as provisional, defective human labour theology must continually be tested against Scripture, and this also means it must constantly be revised and rewritten. And that in turn implies that the Chruch must never cease to reform, so that it may always remain a reformed Church. So Calvin demands that in the light of Scripture we should be engaged intensively with Church and with theology. Anyone, then, who refuses to accept the task of continued restructuring neglects the very thing to which Calvin summons us all.

In one of his many letters Calvin writes: 'The fact that the Church as the body of Christ is maimed by the disruption of the Churches must be reckoned one of the most serious abuses of our time.' We may assert with every assurance that there was no other reformer so large-hearted, so broad in his outlook concerning the ecumenicity of the Churches of the Reformation, as Calvin. He mourned the divisions among the Protestant Churches, crying brokenly, 'What a spectacle we present to the papists!' He urged that all should pray and strive for agreement on essentials. If in the interests of the Church's unity he was ready as he once said to cross ten seas, we must ask ourselves in all earnestness: How many stumblingblocks are we willing to remove? How far are we prepared to go in begging forgiveness one of another for the wrongs of the past? Which holy cows are we ready to sacrifice for the sake of the unity of the Church?

Though Calvin did not develop a complete theory of the state, he perceived and formulated certain basic principles of the greatest value for consideration. For him the divine origin as well as the dignity of the government are not in question. This he formulated in the sharpest terms, when he declared: whoever reviles the government reviles God; whoever rejects the government rejects God. This demonstration of respect applies, not to the person, but to the office. Moreover, obedience to the government must be willingly given. Not, however, that this implies unconditional, unquestioning obedience! Both the government and its subjects must be obedient to God, and to him alone. And when the government is not obedient to God, its subjects have the right to resist through lesser authorities. In all this Calvin cuts off at their roots the popular notion and the popular platform of the revolutionary spirit that totally disregards the authority of government. On the other hand, he stresses the government's obligation to obey God just as radically.

It was these and many other ideas of Calvin that have inspired his spiritual followers through the centuries, and that summon us anew to pray and to work, and in this way to be what God from eternity has destined us to be: creatures who in art and science, in politics and recreation, know only one passion: *Soli Deo Gloria,* to God alone be the glory!

PUBLICATIONS OF CALVIN AND CALVINISM BY THE *INSTITUTE FOR REFORMATIONAL STUDIES* (c/o Potchefstroom University for Christian Higher Education, Potchefstroom 2520, RSA).

SERIES F2: BROCHURES
5. *Calvijns betekenis in onze tijd* (52 pages) — Prof. K. Runia. 50c
10. *From Noyon to Geneva. A Pilgrimage in the steps of John Calvin (1509-1564).* (70 pages) — Prof. B.J. van der Walt. R3,00.
In preparation
From Darkness to light. A portrait of John Calvin. (About 80 pages) —Miss Jansie van der Walt (About R4,00).

SERIES F3: COLLECTIONS
13. *Anatomy of Reformation. Flashes and fragments of a Reformed Cosmoscope* (542 pages) — Prof. B.J. van der Walt. R10,00.
17. *Calvinus Reformator: His contribution to theology, church and society. (Papers delivered at the First South African Congress for Calvin Research, August 12-14, Pretoria, 1980.)* (323 pages). R7,00.

SERIES F4: CALVINCAUSERIES
1. *Calvyn en die Skrif* (27 pages) — Dr C.F.C. Coetzee. Free.
2. *Bibliografie van Suid-Afrikaanse Calviniana* (53 pages) — Dr D. Kempff. Free.
3. *Calvyn oor die staat en reg* (143 pages) — Prof. L.M. du Plessis. R2,50.
4. *Calvyn en die ekumeniese roeping van die kerk* (21 pages) — Prof. B. Duvenage. R1,50.
5. *Calvyn en die herderlike bediening* (20 pages) — Dr C.J.H. Venter. R1,50.
6. *Soteriologie by Calvyn* (40 pages) — Dr C.J. Malan. R2,00.
7. *Die denkdekor van die Reformasie. Met spesifieke verwysing na Calvyn* (50 pages) — Prof. B.J. van der Walt. R2,25.
8. *Contemporary research on the sixteenth Century Reformation* (31 pages) — Prof. B.J. van der Walt. R2,00.
9. *Calvyn en die Etiek* (93 pages) — Prof. J.H. van Wyk. R3,50.

10. *Calvyn oor kerkregering en kerklike tug* (30 pages) — Prof. G.P.L. van der Linde. R2,00.
11. *Calvyn oor opvoeding en onderwys* (25 pages) — Prof. J.L. van der Walt. R2,50.
12. *Die leer aangaande God by Calvyn* (38 pages) — Dr C.J. Malan. R2,50.

In preparation:
Calvyn en die Musiek — Prof. J.J.A. van der Walt.
Calvyn se beskouinge oor die wetenskap — Prof. M.E. Botha.
Calvyn se beskouing oor sending — Prof. I.J. van der Walt.
Die mensbeskouing van Calvyn — Prof. J.H. van Wyk.
Calvyn en die ekonomie — Prof. W.J. Venter.
Calvyn en die prediking — Prof. V.E. d'Assonville.
Calvyn oor die Homilitiek — Ds. F. Denkema.
Calvyn en die gebed — Dr. H.W. Simpson.

SERIES F5: STUDIES ON THE IMPACT OF CALVINISM IN SOUTH AFRICA

Die inslag van die Calvinisme in Suid-Afrika: 'n Bibliografie van Suid-Afrikaanse tydskrifartikels.

3. *Deel I: Histories en prinsipieel* (270 pages). R5,50.
4. *Deel II: Godsdienstig en teologies* (592 pages). R10,00.
5. *Deel III: Wetenskaplik en opvoedkundig* (404 pages). R7,25.
6. *Deel IV: Maatskaplik en staatkundig* (288 pages). R5,60.
7. *Die Nadere Reformasie* (104 pages) — Dr. C.J. Malan. R4,00.
8. *Gewortel en gegroei. Die inslag van die Calvinisme in Suid-Afrika: 1652-1806* (46 pages) — Dr. D. Kempff. R2,00.
9. *Bestry en bevestig. Die inslag van die Calvinisme in Suid-Afrika: 1806-1900* (54 pages) — Dr. D. Kempff. R3,00.
10. *Christelik-Nasionaal: outentieke, ideologiese of gesekulariseerde Nasionalisme? Die inslag van die Calvinisme in Suid-Afrika: 1877-1910* (60 pages) — Prof. M.E. Botha. R3,50.

A complete catalogue of other IRS-publications is available free of charge at the above-mentioned address.

HIEBERT LIBRARY

3 6877 00047 8973